Terror In America!

Terror In America!

A Muslim Surviving the Federal Prison System

A True Story!

Convict/Author Frank M. Tucci
and
Remy P. Tucci

iUniverse, Inc.
New York Lincoln Shanghai

Terror In America!
A Muslim Surviving the Federal Prison System

iUniverse, Inc.

For information address:
iUniverse, Inc.
2021 Pine Lake Road, Suite 100
Lincoln, NE 68512
www.iuniverse.com

ISBN: 0-595-32496-7 (Pbk)
ISBN: 0-595-66607-8 (Cloth)

Printed in the United States of America

CONTENTS

FOREWORD

The greatest failure in the history of all mankind is our prison system. It is a total flop that both the B.O.P. (Bureau of Prisons) and our society choose to perpetuate.

Yes, punishment is necessary, and it does work. What doesn't work is punishment for punishment's sake—punishment without reason and without improvement to the prisoner.

There are figures to back up that statement—the high recidivism rates, the cost of running prisons, and the proof that crime has increased rather than decreased.

The Federal prison system is designed to create better criminals, your tax dollars at work!

I have written this book in plain and simple words without a lot of prison slang or complicated phrases. It is meant to help anyone facing their first incarceration, and those already "doing time", who want to get things done by using the prison system to their advantage.

Every word in regards to my time in prison is true and I have used the real names of both the Correctional Officers and B.O.P. Staff. Many of them "will sue" me, I sure hope so; the publicity will help Book sales.

Anyone, especially Muslims, facing a first time incarceration needs this book as his or her daily survival guide. By reading it you will learn of the vast differences between County, State, and Federal facilities. If you are reading the book while still "on the street" (not locked-up), when the cell door is locked behind you there will be no panic.

You will already know what is going to happen every step of the way, from arrival at the R&D (Receiving and Discharge) door to the time you are returned to society.

It becomes your choice either to be rehabilitated or return to your old lifestyle, which more than likely will return you to prison.

I believe this book to be a first of its kind, although many inmates have written books about "doing their time" or the "crime" that they committed. But to the best of my knowledge, no one has written what I like to call a daily survival guide for Federal Prison.

You cannot pick and choose where the B.O.P. will send you. So—just relax, swallow hard, and go willingly to where ever they send you. And then use this book and the system to get you moved to where you rather be.

Yes, your fight is just beginning! Sometimes nobody will want to hear or understand what you are going through. You will learn to carry a great burden and most of that learning will be done by you alone. Do not feel frightened when your family or friends leave you. I know you will come through this okay!

In closing, I have written a complete account as possible of something that can never be fully known. It is that unknowable element that made it an interesting book to write, and I hope for you to read. There were some misgivings about the title, "Terror In America" but in the end Remy and I decided that the intent was clear.

PREFACE

"The chances that I am in the right increase geometrically by the vigor with which others are trying to prove me wrong!"

I finished writing the book on June 30, 2001 but the events of a few days later on July 4 changed my life and the book.

It was while locked in Segregation for ninety-eight (98) days that I wrote the Introduction and added it to this book.

The Introduction is the end result of the bias actions of Lieutenant Renkowski and Mr. Barton the S.I.S. Officer at FCI Phoenix. And it also in a big way reflects on Mr. Hy Cohen a book agent in New Jersey.

Now to explain it all to you with the whom, when, and why of it.

My wife Remy mailed Mr. Cohen's agency three chapters of "Doing Time In FCI Phoenix, Arizona" (this book's first title) in its early stages.

Mr. Cohen replied. "The book is good but get us inside the prison quickly and show us the harshness." He went on to add. "It should be truthful and reassuring to the inmate's family that he will survive the experience and return unharmed."

At first I paid no attention to his letter and stored it away as just another rejection notice. But months later, while in Segregation "the harshness" came my way and with Mr. Cohen's thoughts in mind I wrote, "Segregation The Nightmare Begins!"

Lieutenant Renkowski signed my Lock-Up Order and Mr. Barton rubber stamped it by refusing to investigate on my behalf.

At one point I thought I saw the light at the end of the tunnel. I did but it was on a bus taking me to FDC Dublin, California.

Why was I thrown in Segregation? Why did Lieutenant Renkowski sign my Lock-Up Order after day shift Lieutenant Almadover refused to? Why was the S.I.S. not investigating the matter? Even after twenty-six days?

All good questions but each had a bad answer!

INTRODUCTION

"Segregation—The Nightmare Begins."

The first time you are handcuffed and dragged off to the SHU (Special Housing Unit) will scare even the so-called "hard ass inmate". In FCI Phoenix, Arizona, the SHU is a two-story building separated from the rest of the prison.

That meant a walk across the prison compound from my housing unit to "the hole". Make no mistake the guard staff there enjoy parading you in front of the other inmates on your way to punishment.

The SHU (pronounced shoe) is the filthiest part of this prison. Roaches, mice, dirty bare cement floors and peeling paint describe it truthfully. Adding to the punishment there is no air conditioning. Remember where I am? Phoenix, Arizona where the temperatures are at the hundred degree mark at least six months of the year.

My stay in Segregation would last for ninety-eight (98) days and included three "Hunger Strikes", but I am getting a little ahead in my story. So, let's slow down a little and back up a bit.

I guess your first question is why was I thrown in the Segregation? Well, their "Official" reason was—"you have been placed in A.D. (Administrative Detention) for Protective Custody due to threats against your life".

I strongly believe the writing of this book was the true reason for my ninety-eight day nightmare of physical suffering. My wife Remy also endured my ordeal and pain as three times I came within the shadow of death from the Hunger Strikes.

There was a hint at just how badly I would be treated when my wrist watch get "lost". I'll explain that in a few more paragraphs.

10:00 AM July 4, 2001

I was ordered by the unit officer to report to the Lieutenant's office "at once". As is the case whenever Tucci is sent for there are always three or four officers to witness the event.

However, this time there were five. Lieutenants Renkowski and Moreno and three other officers I didn't know at that time. Lieutenant Renkowski, who had signed my Lock Up Order, spoke first, "Tucci, there is a serious threat to fire bomb your cell with you in it". He went on to add. "You are being locked up in P.C. (Protective Custody) while the S.I.S. (Special Investigative Services) looks into the matter".

I was not concerned about the threat but only with how long I would be locked in the SHU.

Who made the threat? How long would I be in there? What about my personal property left in my cell? Could my wife visit while I was in Segregation? Would I still have use of the telephone? I had an endless list of questions but no one was answering! For the

1

ninety-eight days I was in the SHU, Mr. Barton, the chief SIS Officer, never spoke to me nor did he provide me with anything in writing about "the threat".

I hope to get that information via a Freedom Of Information request, when I am released in about twenty months. See you in court, Mr. Barton!

"Tucci take off your watch and empty your pockets", ordered Lieutenant Moreno. That reader was the last time I saw my wristwatch but my prison I.D. and my eyeglasses that were in my pockets did show up later.

If you think I am lying when I say they (the officers) enjoy punishing inmates, read on. I was told to put my hands behind my back so that they could cuff me. The cuffs were put on so tight that two days later I still had rings around my wrists.

I asked "how" can I walk with my cane if my hands are cuffed behind me?" Officer Cane told me "no problem". I thought that they might be getting me a wheel chair. Boy, was I wrong!

Two knuckle dragging officers, yes they looked and acted like gorillas, just lifted me up and half carried half pulled me over to the SHU.

In FCI Phoenix, injustice is an everyday occurrence. What happened to me proved that point? Elsewhere in this book I wrote "The Court gave you a sentence and now the B.O.P. will give you a second one, theirs". My ninety-eight days in Segregation was just that, at second sentence!

Most B.O.P. staff agrees with the above but is forced to go along with the "program". My Unit Manager, Ms. Angus and my Case Manager, Mr. Jbour both (at FCI Sheridan) commented that, "the staff in Phoenix acted in a very unprofessional manner". Gee, what else is new?

Let's not forget all the new sanctions against me where handed out while I was in the SHU, for "Administrative Detention" at the request of Warden B. Ellis and his S.I.S.

Yes, there can be no doubt that I was kept in the SHU for ninety-eight days because of this book! To Ellis and his pet monkey Barton, the book was at first a big joke to them. That was until copies of the $5,000.00 advance check from my publisher somehow got passed around the prison.

If you want to get back at these B.O.P. bastards write a book, short story, or even a newspaper article that gets published. But—be ready to be "kicked to the curb" in retaliation!

Writing this book was no brainer for me. After all I was doing time in FCI Phoenix, Arizona, for the next forty-six months anyway! I have writing skills and there was Remy for the typewriting and researching part.

So, why not make lemonade out of the lemons? Many bad things just happened to me one after the other, once the Warden knew my book would be published.

First, as mentioned earlier, they (the S.I.S.) and Ellis tossed me in Segregation on their trumped-up charge.

Second, while I was in Protective Custody at their request, they proceeded to take my privileges away—visitation, phone and commissary, one at a time.

It keeps getting better folks! But—it was now time for El Viejo (the old one) to take on FCI Phoenix. What did I have left to lose? Nothing. So, the next time a guard went by I banged on the cell door and got him to stop.

"I am going on a Hunger Strike and I am refusing all food and water". The officer didn't know how to react, left quickly and returned with the lieutenant in charge.

Three days later, after missing nine delicious and healthy meals, I was moved to a single man cell, as per B.O.P. policy (PS 5562.04).

That was the good news because now other inmates would not be bothering me coming or going, as was the case in a four-man cell. At last I was alone!

The bad news was, yes this is true, the water coming into the cell was shut off. No drinking water, no water to wash with, before my five daily Muslim prayers, and no water to flush the filthy toilet.

How long could a sixty-two year old man with one kidney and a heart problem last without food or water? I didn't know, but I knew I would find out—one-way or the other!

The first problem was the toilet. With the water shut off I had to ask a guard to turn on the water, which would allow me to flush. It was my lucky day, after about four hours, Ms. Cane, a not so bad officer, turned the water on for quick flush.

The next day I was not so lucky. The officers neither had the time nor knew how to turn the toilet water on. That, pardon the pun, pissed me off.

It's El Viejo time! So, the next time I got them to "flush" was the last time I would ask. What did I do? It was very simple yet effective, I just pissed on the cell door and watched it run out into the hallway.

Hey why should I have to smell an unflushed toilet for hours at a time? It was July in Phoenix, Arizona and the smell would gag a maggot.

After I pissed on the floor a few more times and the officers had to walk through it, someone was always there to "flush" when needed. A small victory but it let them know I wasn't going to take zip from them!

Besides them shutting off the water, there were still more nice things to come my way. Remember that this is a true story as you read on.

Because I was on a Hunger Strike I was not allowed sheets, blankets, a pillow, or even a towel. The mattress was old, dirty and torn in more spots than I wanted to count. Yes, it came with bugs and lice in and on it.

I had no clean clothing, only the same sweaty underwear which I had been wearing for four days at the time.

Clothing is not allowed "strikers", so each day underwear becomes the uniform of the day. Oh, I almost forgot to mention—no shoes or socks. The B.O.P. just wanted me to be as cool as possible in the Arizona heat.

Here's more bad news if you wish to Hunger Strike, no hygiene products, that's right. No soap, shampoo, deodorant, toothpaste, toothbrush, or even a comb. Maybe the B.O.P. thinks you'll eat the soap or toothpaste, or drink the shampoo.

You are not even allowed toilet paper if you are on a Hunger Strike. I'll remind you again, all of this is true.

The B.O.P. has reasoned it all out, if you're not eating, why would you need toilet paper? Their thought is "nothing in, nothing out". Wrong answer, as any medical doctor will tell you.

What's that? A light knock on my cell door, it was Doctor Dana from the Psychology Department. Has he come to help me? Well, I knew he gets paid to listen, so what the hell I'll talk to him?

To his credit the good doctor let me vent for ten minutes or so, when I get started I tend to ramble on. It comes with old age.

Doctor Dana did ask the sixty-four thousand dollar question, "Why are you on a Hunger Strike, Mr. Tucci?" I was having a bad day so I gave him a wise ass one-word answer. "Because".

Then I ended our conversation with a famous quote. "Just because you're paranoid, doesn't mean they're not trying to get you!" The doctor agreed with me and said he'll be back in a few days.

Knock, knock again? Now what? It was Lieutenant Niemayer, one of the best officers at FCI Phoenix. Guess what? He had an "Incident Report" for me from Assistant Warden Mr. John, with two n's Cannon.

The "Report" was for "Lying or providing A False Statement to Staff". That news didn't faze me one bit as the lieutenant quickly added, "I checked the SHU logbook and you weren't lying so I am going to expunge the "shot".

I'll explain. The night before which was the fifth day of my strike, Mr. Cannon stopped at my cell to inquire. "Tucci, did you eat a meal today?" My answer of course was a strong no! Where he got the information that I had eaten a meal I can only guess? Probably from the same person who said my life was in danger?

Readers, here's a little about Mr. "Two n's" Cannon. Physically he looks like a midget on a pogo stick, and like most short men has an attitude that says, "Hey, I am in charge here."

He may have had a hip or leg operation at one time because he walks with a funny sway. It's sort of like a senior citizen with a "Depend" undergarment on, a full one!

The next day was a better one. At 9:30 AM guard informed me, "Tucci you have a visit, what size jump suit do you wear?"

Wonderful, the officer is offering me a clean jump suit (size 2x, orange) but what about some clean underwear, socks, or shoes? "Sorry, no shower or clean undies, but I can get you some slip on sneakers and socks."

The visit could be only one person, my Remy (we were still allowed visits at the time). Because, they just up and hauled me off to Segregation I did not get a chance to warn my wife. She was worried and came to visit, when it was not her week to do so.

Remy knows that I don't like surprise visits but to her this was an emergency! I called her for a few minutes every night (6:30 PM), and with no calls for six days she was very worried.

Leaving the SHU I was handcuffed "in front" and belly chained, and given my cane. The visiting room was far from the SHU and with cuffs and chains it took forever to get there.

Entering, I saw my wife at the very first table, which was piled high with vending machine food. Her eyes lit-up like a pair of beautiful dark almonds. We hugged, she cried.

I told her that I could not eat any of the food she had bought and that I was on a Hunger Strike. More crying and it took a while for me to calm her down that time.

"Remy, I am not eating to protest the false information they used to issue the Lock Up Order". She is from a Third World Nation and in her country, they shoot "protesters", so when I said the word "protest" she started crying again!

She is a strong woman, all a little bit over five feet of her, she calmed down once again and we went on with the visit. We didn't know it then but the following week, Warden Ellis did put a stop to our visits.

We talked about what I needed done from "the outside" and as usual she smiled and said she'd take care of it.

That was our last visit but I still could telephone her, there is <u>one</u> (1) phone call allowed every thirty (30) days from the SHU. Thanks, B.O.P.!

Do you want one more example of how mean spirited the officers and staff at Phoenix can be? On a Friday, late in the day, I received a "letter" from the Warden. After reading the contents I felt like someone had punched me in my <u>one</u> remaining kidney.

"Your visits are suspended due to your on-going Hunger Strike. Staff can not monitor your food intake while in the Visiting Room". That also was a lie!

Every inmate from the SHU that goes to visitation must sit in front of the officer's desk. The officer is no more than six feet away from inmate and visitor. The "staff can not monitor your food intake while in the Visiting Room?"

After that good news I turned-up my "strike" efforts and refused all of my medications, including the Nitroglycerine pills for my heart problems.

It was somewhere around fifteen or sixteen days into my "strike" that Doctor Garcia became an everyday visitor. He is a good man but his hands were often tied as to my welfare, because of Warden Ellis' stupidity.

Everyday the medical department would have me brought to a small room at the beginning of the hall that served as their office. That day's findings were:

a.   I had lost eighteen pounds.
b.   My lips were seriously chapped from no water.
c.   I was now an extreme case of dehydration.
d.   Add to the above that I smelled bad—no shower for sixteen days!
e.   My breath now had the smell of ammonia.

The next day was good as it allowed me to end my eighteen-day Hunger Strike with dignity. However, there were two more "Strikes" yet to come! Thanks, Warden Ellis.

Early in the morning my cell door was unlocked and a new face to me stepped in. He came into the cell alone, no idiot guards with him, and he introduced himself as Assistant Warden Jennings, from the Regional Office.

He went on to mention that he would be in FCI Phoenix for a few months replacing an Assistant Warden who left.

When Ellis took charge of the facility on June 1, 2001 he forced out some of the existing administrative staff. Jennings replaced the only Hispanic staff member at Phoenix FCI.

The new A.W. said that he had read my SHU file, wanted to meet me, and had a few questions for me. Of course, his first question was, "Why does a sixty-two year old man go on a Hunger Strike?" The rest of his questions were more along the B.O.P.'s standard line.

Jennings last question before leaving was. "What would it take to get you to end your Hunger Strike?"

My answer was short and simple—"My visitation restored". He replied, "That's it?" I just nodded my head yes. He said he'd get back to me after lunch, and then left.

Shortly there after the cell door opened again. This time it was Captain Miller, and two officers, one with a wheel chair, and Lieutenant Armondva filming with the prison's video camera.

I was ordered to "get your lazy ass off that bed and get into the chair!" Hey, it was day eighteen without food and I was very weak. So, I yelled back at the Captain, "Fuck you! I'm too weak to get up and walk."

Captain Miller shouted back, and God is my witness, this, "Then crawl your old ass over to that wheel chair!" I just told him a second time to go fuck himself and remained lying in the bunk.

There was nothing else that they could threaten me with, so I could yell, swear, or insult them at will. After all I was in Segregation, on a Hunger Strike, and they had suspended by telephone, visitation, and commissary privileges. They had no weapons left to use on me.

The drama ended when Doctor Garcia and a medical assistant came to the cell and "helped" me into the wheel chair while Lieutenant Armondva kept filming the event.

Once I was in the wheel chair the guard's meanness returned. I was leg chained, belly chained and handcuffed for the short walk over to the hospital unit. The medical staff drew my blood, weighed me, asked for urine; but I could not pee, ran an EKG test, and checked my eyes, ears, and mouth. I could tell by Doctor Garcia's reaction that I was not in the best of shape. A trip to an "outside" hospital for force-feeding?

Quickly I was back in the cell and refusing the noon meal. Yes, even if you are on a Hunger Strike they must offer you a meal at each feeding time. That meant they had to unlock the "trap" in the cell door and leave a try of food thee for about fifteen minutes.

Some of the officers' thought they were slick and asked, "Tucci, are you eating?" If I said no they just passed by my cell without opening the trap or leaving a meal.

When they didn't stop I would yell or swear at them to, "Put a try there I may feel like eating today." If they didn't I reported them to the shift Lieutenant and the medical department. I didn't give them an inch.

My life was now to get better as A. W. Jennings returned at two PM. Sometimes you do get lucky. I did that day.

Warden Ellis was away from the facility on that day and Jennings was "Acting" as warden. He came right to the point. "If I restore your visits will you start eating today?" I sat there thinking, for what seemed like a long time, before answering. My answer was yes, but I had two conditions.

First, before I would eat, I would need a phone call to Remy to tell her that the so-called "war" was over. Second, I wanted a letter mailed to her saying our visits were restored. As you can figure, I had very little trust for B.O.P personnel.

Jennings called officer Johnson over and informed him that I be "allowed one telephone call". That was okay but this old man wasn't born yesterday. I explained to the A.W. that once he left the officers would probably "forget" to let me use the phone. "The phone now or no deal," I ended with.

Well, I thought I lost that round but Jennings turned towards the officer and said only one word, "phone". He stayed there until I dialed the phone and started my conversation with Remy.

My lady was happy to say the least, why she loves me only God knows? Anyway she cried as always and said she be there in two days, a Saturday, early, very early!

With the Hunger Strike over, the SHU officers acted quickly to get back at me with a vengeance, for the "problems" I had caused them. I knew just what to expect but maybe I could stifle them a bit? El Viejo again? Yes!

Before doing battle with the B.O.P. you must have a plan, and an alternative one. Never go up against them without these. But first I must eat and drink water, lots of water.

It was about three PM when the kitchen sent over two trays of the noon meal. Mr. Jennings ordered the food and one of my amigos in Food Service, where my prison job was, doubled the meal.

Try as I may I could not eat! After so many days without food I had no appetite and the sight and smell of it made me nauseous. Sounds like a job for Doctor Dana?

When the supper food came I still had most of the two noon meals left. I knew that I had to eat and drink. So, I started on the soft things that are easiest to digest. Mashed potatoes, jello, oatmeal, and other like foods are a good start after a hunger strike.

With my belly full I went to sleep thinking about Remy's visit and a needed plan against the Warden.

I awoke to a Friday morning, a hot one; the temperature would hit one hundred and ten degrees at noon!

El Viejo and I worked out a plan during the night but it needed to start at once, because it was a Friday. None of the "powers to be" worked on Saturday or Sunday, including most of the medical staff.

When the guard showed up with the breakfast meal I refused it and loudly asked to see Warden Jennings. Not eating would bring him running to my cell, I was sure? If I just told the officer I wanted to see the A.W., chances are he never would pass my request along. Refusing the food would work?

The noon meal came and still no Assistant Warden, I refused the meal. Just in case your keeping track; I ended my eighteen-day hunger strike, and ate two meals in a row.

Where was Jennings? Did the officer tell him I was not eating again? In the SHU the last meal is served between 3:45 and 4:30 PM. What if Jennings doesn't show?

Should I refuse supper? If I did, I would have to go without eating until Monday when Jennings was back, or lose my credibility.

The race was on! Would the food, or the Assistant Warden show up first? He did! Now for my "plan".

"Warden Jennings, Lieutenant Armondra is going to put me back in a three or four man cell. I am very sick and weak and have a bad case of the shits since I started eating again. Can I just have a few days alone to get back on my feet? I said hopefully. "Please?"

"Tucci there is a two man cell empty on the first floor I'll see what I can do," was his short reply. That was good news. The first floor where the two-man cell was had A/C. The bad news was that the cell had a video monitor and every move I made would be on "Candid Camera".

I wouldn't be moved downstairs until Monday, the toilet water was turned on and I was eating again. What else could a man ask for? Maybe a shower? It would be nice to be clean for Remy's visit not like the last time she saw me.

In Segregation I just can't put on my flip-flops and walk to the shower. My cell was on "B" and its day for showers was yesterday.

If you're not on a hunger strike, you get three showers a week, or on every other day. Not so bad you say? Well consider this—its Phoenix, Arizona and one hundred and ten degrees outside and no A/C inside!

There was a small chance I could get to shower. It all depended on who was in charge of the shift. My chance arrived it was Lieutenant Niemayer, a fair and reasonable officer. I banged on my cell door as he was making his rounds.

"Mr. Niemayer my wife is visiting tomorrow could I please get a shower?" He answered, "When was the last time you showered?" "Nineteen days ago," I said with straight face.

Not only did Lieutenant Niemayer allow me to shower he even saw to it that I had clean clothing (underwear). No more nineteen-day smelly underwear!

After my shower I ate the supper meal and looked forward to my visit the next day. The night passed quickly and it was soon time for Remy's visit.

The visiting hours at FCI Phoenix, Arizona are Saturday and Sunday 8:00 AM to 3:00 PM and Monday noon to 8:00 PM, that's it! My wife is always one of the first to arrive at 7:30 or so.

At 8:05 AM, an officer came and told me I had a visit. Usually I didn't get called until 8:45 or later. What's up? Visiting for SHU inmates is not pleasant, even though you look forward to any visit. The officers' routine is meant to break you!

Here's what happens. First you are taken from your cell in only your underwear, no socks, shoes, or a jumpsuit yet. You are then put into a "shower cell", which is just what the name suggests, a shower with bars for a door.

You will next be strip-searched and provided with a clean orange jumpsuit, socks, and blue pull-on sneakers. Don't ask for your sizes, they "don't have any".

Last is the officer's favorite part, the iron. Belly chains and handcuffs for all and sometimes even leg irons.

Normally I would be belly chained and handcuffed, but because I was still weak from my fast, I was wheel-chaired with handcuffs only, to the visiting room.

Hold on, there's one more stop before my visit. You will be brought to the front of the SHU building and left between the enter and outer doors. Here you must wait until an officer comes over to escort you to your visit.

On Saturday and Sunday, as I mentioned before, staff is always in short supply. My escort was Lieutenant Niemayer. I guess he's what could be called a high-priced wheel chair pusher.

"Tucci I had a small problem with your wife this morning", he sighed. Oh shit, what could she have done? I thought. He answered that question in his next sentence. "She got here by taxi (Remy doesn't drive) at about 7:30 AM and was standing out in the heat, so I let her in early. Please tell her I can't let her in early again."

He pushed on to the visiting room, removed my handcuffs upon arrival, and wished me a "good visit." He is a gentleman and a good person. I never had a problem with Mr. Niemayer the sixteen months I was at Phoenix.

Remy was smiling and in the first seat next to the two officers. She had a table piled high with food. Orange juice, coffee, bottled-water, candy and doughnuts for starters. Later she would buy more vending machine food for lunch.

It had been only three weeks since our last visit. Not long as far as times goes, but it just seems that way at age sixty-two. We always hold hands during our visit and that draws stares from some of the inmates.

Why? Maybe because I am not running my hands all over Remy's body, as they do with their "bitches". I bet they think that's all us two old-farts can do. Wouldn't they be surprised!

El Viejo, Remy and I made a plot that day to get me out of Warden Ellis's shit hole, a.k.a. a prison.

After the visits I was strip-searched in the Visiting Room lobby, the whole nine yards including the B.O.P. bend and cough thing. Two officers escorted me back to the SHU with Mr. Ventura pushing the wheelchair.

Here's a little humor for you. Arriving back at the SHU I was put into the "shower cell" and told I would be strip-searched again. That pissed me off and I yelled loudly at the officers.

"Listen you stupid assholes I just was strip searched after my visit and two of you morons brought me directly here. Maybe you think one of the officers passed me dope or something else? Or could it be you are just like Officer Hoffman and like to look at men's cocks?

Officer Johnson, who was in charge that day, said, "fuck it just put the old guy back in his cell".

My next challenge would come in a few days on Monday. Would the A.W. move me downstairs into a two-man cell? Or will I end up back in a three, or maybe even a four-man cell?

Remy and I had a plan, this time she knew what to expect. She is one strong little lady.

On Monday, I was moved downstairs. The A.W. had kept his word and as I expected, the cell was monitored to watch me 24-7! The next day I got a cellmate, Tucker Lewis. He and I had worked in the facility's Food Service prior to the SHU.

Tucker and I would go on to be celled for seventy-five (75) days. He had "checked" himself in for P.C. (Protective Custody) unlike myself; he had real threats against his life.

Tucker Lewis is bisexual and because of a homosexual relationship with his friend "Angel", was threaten by a White Power gang.

Life is now good. I am on the first floor where there is air conditioning and I was getting a shower every other day. Could things be better? It stayed that way for a few weeks.

On 6 August 2001, day thirty-two (32) in "the hole", I got to make a phone call. The staff at FCI Phoenix and I didn't seem to read the B.O.P.'s policy on telephone use the same.

The Policy Statement says, "each inmate in the Special Housing Unit shall be allowed one 15 minutes telephone call for 30 days". To the "staff" that meant I had to be in the SHU for 30 days before I could make a call.

Here's my take on that. Let's look closely at their wording, "shall be allowed <u>one</u> 15 minute telephone call per 30 days". Where does it say after 30 days? It doesn't. Therefore, I argued that I wanted my phone call the first day they locked me up, and the next call would be 30 days later.

No, they didn't see it my way! So if you are in the SHU, for let's say twenty-nine days, you will not get to use the phone. It makes less work for the officers. They need less?

Later that month I received mail from my wife Remy that would change the rest of my time in Segregation. It was entitled Chapter 9, Special Housing Units, and off the B.O.P.'s web site.

The first thing that caught my eye were two headings on Page 1. Disciplinary Segregation Status and Administrative Detention Status. After reading both I found all too many rules "that were disregarded by staff and ignored by Warden Ellis.

Here is the B.O.P.'s own statements on the two. "Disciplinary Segregation <u>Status</u> is, inmates who commit serious violations of Bureau rules. <u>A</u>dministrative Detention Status, may also include inmates who require Protective Custody, a non-punitive status."

Tucker and I were not in there on Disciplinary Segregation Status! We were both there in Administrative Detention Status and should have been treated under those guidelines. I guess the keywords were, "should have been".

Ellis didn't care about Policy Statements, Rules or Guidelines, he treated everyone in Segregation the same, like shit!

With PS 5270.07 in hand Tucker and I went to war. The first battle would be on what I call "the seven-day rule". The next paragraph is a direct quote from Page 10-letter "b" on the subject.

"Inmates who are placed in Administrative Detention for protection but not at their request or beyond the time they feel they need to be detained for their own protection, are entitled to a hearing, no later than seven days from the time of their admission."

I didn't know if having the policy statement sooner would have helped? I doubt it, anyway it is now my thirty-fifth day in the SHU.

Reading their paragraph a second time I got my hopes up. Surely all I had to do was write an "Inmate To Staff Request" and my nightmare in the SHU would be over. Right? Wrong!

If you or someone you know ends up in Warden Ellis's SHU, I feel sorry for you in advance. Remember, the clock is always running in <u>their</u> favor and you must follow their paper-trail rules.

Personally I think Ellis should retire from the B.O.P. and become a football coach. He sure knows how to use the clock to his advantage.

The next attack would be on their "every thirty (30) day rule", also in Chapter 9, on Page 8-A, letter "c". Review Of Inmates Housed in Administrative Detention. I quote directly again.

"Shall hold a hearing and review these cases formally at least every 30 days. The inmate appears before the SRO (Segregation Review Officer) at the hearing unless the inmate waives the right to appear."

My next "review" would be in the first week of October 2001, so I wrote the Warden a Request for Administrative Remedy (A BP 9) to be present at my hearing. Unlike my 30 and 60-day review, I would be there.

The Warden did answer me via Remedy #248308-F1. What was his reply to why I was not at my 30 or 60-day review? I quote him.

"If a threat to the safe and secure running of the unit exists, the Segregation Review Official may elect not to have you removed from your cell for the review". But his last sentence assured I would be at my 90-day review.

It said, "Accordingly you request for Administrative Remedy is granted." Time was flying by quickly from late August to early October of 2001.

Early one morning the guard kicked at the cell door and yelled, "Lewis get ready you're going to medical, I'll be back to get you shortly." Having not requested any medical treatment, it could only mean one thing for Tucker, a transfer.

If you are in the SHU for Protective Custody, it's more than likely you will be moved out of the facility. The question is how long will you be in Segregation?

Tucker returned excited from the hospital unit. "Pops (he always called me that) I am finally leaving this fucked-up place they took chest x-rays!" A chest x-ray was a good clue that he was leaving, as these are done a day or two prior to being moved out.

We were sure he would be "on the bus" early the next morning. In the seventy-five (75) days we were celled together a friendship was formed. He writes to my wife (his Aunt Remy) and has her telephone number on his prison list.

Most of the day was spent going over how Tucker could contact me thru Remy, so that I would know where he ended up. She had his inmate B.O.P. number and could also use the Inmate Locator Line to track him.

Sure enough at 2:30 AM an officer flipped the cell light on and yelled "Lewis, pack your shit I'll be back for you in ten minutes". I have a quick question. Why do the officers refer to an inmate's property as <u>shit?</u>

Tucker was departing after waiting 114 days in the SHU for a transfer. That was a testimonial to the way Warden Ellis ran "his SHU". Let's look back at Tucker's case.

He had signed himself into the SHU for P.C., after threats against his life. He had also names his would-be-attacker to the Warden and the S.I.S. Therefore, he could not be put back into Phoenix prison population. A no-brainer for a transfer and Warden Ellis.

A quick transfer should have been in order for my friend, but 114 days is quick for the way FCI Phoenix did things.

Their main excuse was, "We're looking for a facility that will accept you". That didn't hold water as I later found out by reading PS 5270.07. Here's a direct quote from Chapter 9, Page 11.

"Transfer of a protection case does not require concurrence of the receiving Regional Director". In other words, the Warden could put <u>Tucker</u> on the bus to anywhere, withou<u>t</u> "a facility that will accept you."

Soon the guard was back for <u>Tucker</u>. We shook hands and said all the things inmates say to each other when one is leaving. Then I went back to sleep, it was still only 3:00 AM.

A few days later the shit hit the fan big time! "Tucci I've got a new cellie for you". Said Officer Johnson. I answered with one word "No!" "Are you refusing a direct order to accept cellie?" He asked. This time my answer was two words, "fuck you!"

Early the next morning, at 545 am; Lieutenant Admorva was at my door. Don't these people ever sleep? Maybe it was just part of the punishment?

He said, "I have an Incident Report for Refusing A Direct Order". My reply was only one word. "So!" I was getting good with one-word answers.

Within three days of receiving an Incident Report the UDC (Unit Disciplinary Committee) must meet with and punish you. It was again time for the "El Viejo" side of me to act.

Two days passed and then I was told the UDC wanted to see me. That meant being handcuffed and taken from the cell. Would they bring me a wheel chair? Or could they cuff me in front and allow me to use my cane?

Picture this in your mind's eye. A sixty-two year old man, wearing only his underwear, no socks or shoes, walking lamely with a cane, to a UDC hearing. Not a nice picture?

At FCI Phoenix, they "lived" to degrade you at their every chance. Limp down a long hallway in my underwear and bare feet? No, not El Viejo! I told Officer Brynt I would not go to my UDC hearing.

Hours later the unit counselor, Mr. Hindenberger, brought me their sanction. "No telephone usage for sixty (60) days." This wasn't big deal because I was only allowed one telephone call per month anyway.

There is one thing most of the staff at FCI Phoenix does very well, kick you when you are down! Not just kick you but "kick you to the curb". The very next day after losing my phone privilege, guess what?

It was Déjà vu all over again! Same officer, Mr. Johnson, Same Direct Order, to have a cellmate. Same answers from me. "No and fuck you." Same results, an Incident Report, Same UDC but a different sanction. "No Visits."

That's it, now we do battle, El Viejo said in my mind. I vented my anger at the first guard that came by my cell. "Hey asshole tell the lieutenant I want to see him and that I am starting a hunger strike again."

The lieutenant came almost at once. He informed me that if I was going to hunger strike again he would, "have to search your cell for any commissary food items". He then ordered me over to the cell door to cuff-up. I refused. Did I win that round? No such luck.

September 28, 2001 at noontime.

If you choose not to go along with the prison system you must be ready to suffer the consequences! This day was number eighty-six (86) in the SHU and day six (6) of my third hunger strike. Please get and read B.O.P. policy statement 5562.04—Hunger Strike.

I know you have all heard the old saying—"Smile it could be a lot worst." Well, they were right. I smiled and it did get worst.

I was writing a letter to my wife when I heard my cell door being opened quietly. Within seconds my cell was filled with a gorilla, a jackass, and an ox, and three other officers who didn't fit into any category.

The jackass was the beloved Warden Ellis, the Ox was Mr. Barton of S.I.S. fame, and the gorilla was Officer Gray, who drives the prison's bus. The other three are not worth mentioning by name so let's call them the three blind mice.

"Tucci you're going to a dry cell" (no sink or toilet) said the jackass. That didn't scare me because as the saying goes, "been there done that!" Next the gorilla cuffed me tightly behind my back and with the ox dragged me down the long hallway. Yes, in my underwear, no shoes or socks.

Phoenix's dry cell was on the "hot" second floor, just to the left as you get off the elevator. It doesn't have a solid door but instead bars like the "shower cell" so anyone passing by could look into the cell.

The dry cell was much smaller in size than a standard cell. Sleep was not possible with the cell's location next to the elevator and people coming and going 24-7. Less than ten feet away a chair and desk were put in place for the officers. Yes, I had around the clock friends.

The light in the cell was never turned off. Every thirty minutes the guard would ask if I was all right and then note it in his logbook. Always remember, everything is part of their punishment.

Afternoon and night passed, morning brought the staff visitors. First was Doctor Garcia, who looked annoyed because I was on another Hunger Strike. It meant a lot of paperwork each day for him and the medical department.

Next was the "shrink" Doctor Dana. He wasn't happy either, more paperwork for him also. We talked for a short time and he asked, "what do you want this time?" Once again my reply was one word. "Transfer!"

Doctor Dana informed me that I was on the transfer list. "That's what you say, that's what my Unit Manager says, and that's the SHU Lieutenant's word but its ninety (90) days now and I am still in this shit hole!" I yelled at him! He turned and left.

My last visitor of the day was the new SHU Lieutenant, Mr. Domier. Most staff in Phoenix rotates posts every three months; maybe I would have better luck with the new SHU Officers?

We started talking and he asked me if I would like to move back downstairs and out of the "hot" dry cell. He suggested. "Tucci just relax, I'll send you back downstairs and I'll see you in a day or two for your thirty-day review." That thirty-day review would be on my ninety-second (92) day in "the hole" but who's counting?

I moved back downstairs and later in the day Lieutenant Domier came to my cell. He asked if I needed anything and I told him some juice would be good. He said he would find some and get back right away.

Although I was still on a Hunger Strike juice was allowed. On Page 3 of PS 5562.04 (Hunger Strike) it says this: "Staff shall provide the inmate an adequate supply of drinking water. Other beverages shall also be offered."

I did not have that information for my two prior strikes but I had it now, thanks to Remy.

The lieutenant returned with two, four-ounce boxes of orange juice. He said I could also get one eight-once box of Resource (a meal replacement drink) in place of each meal.

Why the changes? Did he know something? He did! He said, "Tucci, you will be out of here in less than a week you have my word on it".

Well, that sure raised my hopes but I didn't believe Warden Ellis would ever let me out of "his prison". The next day my review was held in Domier office and he again reminded me I would soon be leaving Phoenix. "Your mouth to Allah's ears", was my only reply.

The last few days before my departure were different. At each meal time the medical department sent over juice and a box of Resource. Prior to the juice and drink all I would take was water.

Monday 8 October 2001.

At 8:00 AM two officers came to the cell with a jumpsuit and a wheel chair. I was told to dress quickly (still no socks or shoes) and that they were going to wheel me over to medical.

God I hoped they are bringing me there for chest x-rays. If the case I would at last be leaving Phoenix. It was, and I let off a string of profanities at the guards as they brought me back to the cell.

I knew I was leaving so there wasn't a damn thing the officers could do except swears back at me. They did. That's it, I am out of here I thought to myself.

There was no way I could sleep that night knowing that they would be coming for me in the early morning hours.

The good news was no more of Warden Bernie C. Ellis. The bad news was, no longer would Remy be able to visit. I was sure they would move me far from Phoenix, and they did.

Author's Update:

On 9th October 2001, I was transferred from FCI Phoenix to Dublin, California and then a few weeks later to Sheridan, Oregon. However, I was to spend a total of ninety-eight (98) days in Warden Bernie Ellis's Segregation cells.

To protest those ninety-eight (98) days I went on a "hunger strike" three times! The first time was for eighteen (18) days; the second for fifteen (15) days and the last one was at twelve days and on going when I was thrown on the bus for Dublin.

Arriving at Dublin in a very weak state, and being carried off the bus, the medical staff asked me, "Who was the idiot who signed you off to travel?" I smiled and replied. "Oh, some asshole named Ellis!"

You have now had your Introduction to Surviving The Federal Prison System!

Now back to The Beginning and The Government's Case against me.

PART ONE

The Beginning

CHAPTER 1

The Government's Case

September 1997, Hartford, Connecticut.

Sometimes life can be so damn unfair! At that time I was just coming out of a two-year period of grieving for my late wife. The family home had been sold and many of its furnishings given away. My two children, both in their twenties were out and on their own.

So—I decided to move back to the city, into a small one bedroom, but very comfortable apartment. Now, what do I do? Money was not a problem. There was a good profit from the sale of the house, some of its appliances and my late wife's automobile.

Then one day I took stock of my situation. I was fifty-seven (57) years old and a widower. I needed to do something besides eat and watch the TV!

I started thinking, why not find a job? But—doing what? My whole adult life had been spent in the military.

That Sunday I bought the newspaper, passed over the sport pages and turned to the employment section. One very large ad caught my eye. I can't remember the exact wording but it said something like the following:

"Wanted driver with late model car, valid insurance, and knowledge of the surrounding areas. Pick your own days and hours, flexible schedules for retirees, students, and working moms."

Being a person who doesn't like to waste time, I called the phone number listed in the ad. Yes, they still had some openings I was told, next I was asked to make an appointment for an interview.

Everyone says, "Never go to a job interview on a Monday or Friday." I made my appointment for that Tuesday. With that done I would enjoy the rest of the day and hide from the redheaded divorcee two doors down from me.

A single man at age fifty-seven is a prime target for any woman in the same age bracket. However, there are <u>four</u> women for every man my age. Seeing this is not a love story enough said about that.

Tuesday arrived and I left for the 10:30 AM job interview. The company's office was only a mile and a half from my apartment. That would be a <u>plus</u> if I got the job?

Well, I was surprised; they hired me after checking my driver's license, car insurance, and a visual inspection of my 1996 Lexus. The only job I had on paper was my twenty-one years in the military. I guessed the interviewer was impressed with my retirement rank?

His name was Bob or Rob, I can't remember which, and he asked me to start work the next day.

The job was good for me as I traveled the states of Connecticut, Massachusetts, Rhode Island, or New York. My deliveries were mostly legal papers from one attorney to another in a different city.

Things continued along well for months until one day when I returned to my apartment. The building had an underground parking garage, as usual I swiped the I.D. card in the gate and the overhead door squeaked open. I droved in and parked in my assigned spot.

I started removing some groceries from the car's rear seat, but in less than a minute my life would be changed for the next seven years!

Six (6) men were running towards me from behind some of the parked cars. Three were wearing blue jackets with large letters ATF on them. One had a jacket with FBI lettering on it. The last two were dressed in suits.

All six had guns pointed at me! The two "suits" were carrying shotguns, the other four automatic handguns; I think they were nine millimeter Glocks.

Two of the blue-jacketed agents pushed me into the side of the car, which caused me to drop the groceries to the garage floor. They spread eagled me and patted me down just like you see on TV.

The FBI guy flashed his I.D. and asked. "Are you Frank M. San Tuccio?" Being one to always speak my mind I shouted. "First you guys knock the bag of groceries out of my hand, bang me into the side of the car, pat me down, and then you ask who I am?"

Laughingly one of the "suits" spoke up. "We have a Search Warrant for your car and apartment wise guy!" But before he said that two of the agents were already searching inside the car. The trunk was open and they also had the hood up.

In their zeal they overlooked one little thing, it was not my car they were searching! My Lexus was in the shop for service. They were messing up a "loaner" car.

The car I owned was red, the loaned car was silver. Close enough for Government work, but shouldn't they have checked the license plate's numbers? I never told them it wasn't my car they were tearing apart.

I was handcuffed and taken by four blue jackets to the garage's elevator while the two "suits" continued to search the car. Even if it had been my Lexus they never would have found my well-hidden weapon!

Where in the car was the weapon hidden? You'll never guess. I have crossed both the Canadian and Mexican borders many times and never have they come close to finding my gun.

Try my idea for yourself, it works. Remove the windshield washer bottle from under the hood. Cut it in half at about four inches from it's top. Place your gun of choice in a "Ziploc" bag, then place that "Ziploc" bag into a second bag.

Place the weapon in he bottom half of the washer unit and tape the two half's together using black electrician's tape. Replace the unit back under the hood and refill the reservoir with the darkest blue fluid you can find.

The elevator from the parking garage only went as high as the main lobby floor, which meant changing elevators in the lobby.

Reaching the lobby I was led pass the building manager's office to the main elevators. Some of the other tenants were in the lobby retrieving their mail and looked at me with fear on their faces.

Please remember that I was not "under arrest", all the agents had was a Search Warrant. The handcuffs and display of weapons is just a part of the Government's intimidations!

What do you think my changes of having my apartment's lease renewed are?

It was a short elevator ride to my apartment on the fourth floor. Standing in front of my door I could tell that someone had been in my apartment after I left for work! How did I know?

Easy enough, I used an old "spy" trick. Everyday when leaving the apartment I would carefully place a "match" between the door and the doorframe. The "match" was now on the floor!

The question was, who had been inside the apartment? Could it have been one of the building's maintenance workers? Or, could these agents from hell already have searched the place?

A little fun is next as one of the ATF's finest asked. "Where's your door key Mr. San Tuccio?" Ha, ha, ha, the joke is on him. My answer to (let's call him Mr. Ed, because I considered him a horse's ass) was. "Well, gee I had them when I got out of the car!"

Mr. Ed turned to (I'll call this agent Sloppy) and told him. "Go back down to the garage and look around for his keys!"

I knew exactly where the keys were! When they pushed me into the side of the Lexus I saw my dropped keys and kicked them under the car.

Sloppy returned without the keys but with the office manager in tow. "I couldn't find the fucking keys so I brought this guy to let us in." He reported to Mr. Ed.

I asked the manager. "Ted did anyone show you a Search Warrant?" If you open that door without seeing a warrant I'll sue you and the building's owners!" I didn't have to be polite to Ted because I knew the owners would never renew my lease after this mess.

"May I see the Search Warrant before I unlock the door?" Mr. Ed was starting to lose his cool. "Who's got the damn Warrant?" He asked the other agents. Sloppy answered. "Stevenson does!"

Guess what? Stevenson was one of the two agents still down in the garage searching the car.

I just couldn't pass up a chance to get one more dig in at Ted. "If you open that door I will sue and when you're in Court I want to see you lie under oath that you saw a warrant!" Soon Sloppy was back with the paperwork and the two "suits".

Ted unlocked the door and all eight of us entered my small apartment. I could see with only a quick glance that some one or some bodies, had been in the apartment after I left that morning. My other "spy" tricks didn't lie!

Looking at three things told me what I suspected was true, the apartment had already been searched.

Number one, the middle drawer in the kitchen counter was completely closed. I always left it <u>open</u> about one half inch.

Second, I always left the hall closet door open, with the first two coats close together. The door was still open but the two coats were <u>separated</u>.

Last, the middle kitchen cabinet door (where I kept the dishes) was closed. It was also left open every morning when I left the apartment.

I have a cousin who was an FBI Agent and he once told me. "We sometimes enter a suspect's home or apartment and do our search before we serve the Warrant on them." As Archie Bunker used to say. "God bless America!"

Here are a few clues for you to keep in your mind and to look for if these bastards ever visit you.

1. If they dump-out your dresser drawers on the bed or floor but do not search what they just dumped.
2. If they take your clothing out of a closet, pile it on a chair, couch, or the floor without going thru all the pockets.
3. If they do not look in the bathroom's medicine chest.
4. If they do not search the inside of your refrigerator (my late Uncle Louie use to keep his stub nose 38 caliber Colt in there).

These guys (the agents) were not all that swift with all the "clues" they had left me. Or, had they done that on purpose? But, the telltale clue was the short amount of time the six agents spent searching in my presence.

So—wrapping-up their "search" for my benefit Mr. Ed spoke-up. "Mr. San Tuccio would you please sign here? It's a statement that we have searched your rooms and automobile and have removed nothing."

I gave him the same answer that I use even today dealing with my guards. "No!"

Mr. Ed's next remark told me that he was not as dumb as he looked. "Okay smart-ass, if you don't sign my paperwork we can't prove that we were here. That being the deal we'll have to come back here and do it all over again!"

"Fuck it, I'll sign and don't let the door hit your asses on the way out!" Who in their right mind would want to see these mental midgets a second time?

Jim Beam and I sat down to think things out. Why did they have a Search Warrant? What exactly were they looking for? Maybe my handgun? I knew as a felon I was not allowed to possess a gun. But—I <u>always</u> did, they just never found them.

Nobody at the delivery job knew about my Government visitors so I continued to work there. However, Ted and some of the renters who saw my visitors and me together were now noticeably colder as of late.

Four or five weeks went by and then there were more questions with a phone call I received. The message light on the answering machine was flashing as I entered the apartment.

"Please call Attorney Weinberger's office at (a Hartford phone number) as soon as possible." It was late, about 9:00 PM but I called the number anyway.

Here's what I heard. "You have reached the office of the Federal Public Defender, please call back between 7:00 AM and 5:00 PM."

<u>Now</u> I was worried! Why should the Federal Public Defender call me? At 7:00 AM tomorrow I'll have my answer?

Sleep didn't come easy that night as the phone message kept going around in my head.

My workday started at 7:00 AM, so I would pick-up my deliveries and makes my call while on the route.

Calling in I said. "My name is Frank San Tuccio and I am returning Mr. Weinberger's phone call." Of course I was put on hold and treated to five minutes of "elevator" music. I hate that stuff!

Weinberger came on the phone and said. "Mr. San Tuccio when is a good time for you to come into my office?" I wanted to reply never, but I restrained myself. I did ask. "Why?" But Weinberger said. "Let's not talk about on the phone it would be best if you got in here asap."

At 4:30 PM that same day I was there, cooling my heels in the waiting room. Soon Mr. Weinberger came out to meet me and I followed him back to his office.

I could not hold back my curiosity and spoke even before he offered me a chair. "Why does the Federal Public Defender want to see me?" I knew I would not like his reply.

Composing himself behind the large desk he leaned forward and said. "Well Mr. San Tuccio a few weeks ago the FBI and ATF searched your car and apartment?" I interrupted him before he got to his next sentence.

"So big deal, they didn't find anything, nothing, zero, nada! What's that got to do with me being here?"

"It has everything to do with you being here. You may very well be indicted by a Federal Grand Jury and charged with conspiracy to sell firearms. That, Mr. San Tuccio is serious because of your prior convictions for the same offense."

Weinberger give me some added details. "A weapon was found in Bloomfield, New Jersey on someone the police arrested. That gun was traced to you by the serial numbers. There are many other weapons the Government would like to ask you about."

Okay Frank, now you know what the Search Warrant mess was all about. But what was Weinberger's interest in me? Then the caution light lit-up in my brain. The Government doesn't help ex-convicts; they are offering me a deal!

I wasn't Sunny "the bull", so they probably weren't going to do too much for me. The best thing to do is get-up and walks out of Weinberger's office.

"Sorry Mr. Weinberger but there's nothing that comes to my mind about weapons. You have a good day." I got up and quickly walked back out into the street.

What I needed was a hot shower, a good meal, and a couple of shots of Jim Beam. Not necessarily in that particular order!

CHAPTER 2

The Indictment!

For weeks after my hasty exit from Weinberger's office, when he mentioned "weapons the Government had questions about," it was quite—too quiet!

But then I received a second phone call from him at my job. How did he know where I worked? Were the agents following me?

"Hey, San Tuccio there was a call for you from some attorney while you were out on your route." Said Big Dan. We all called him Big Dan because he was close to 350 pounds!

"Big Dan, did you get a name or phone number for me?" I inquired. He answered. "No, sorry but he said he would call you later at home."

That was a confusing answer. My attorney? Well that could be any one of three of four people.

Was it the attorney who handled the Probate Court case for me? Could it have been the Real Estate lawyer who had been involved in the sale of my home? Or was it the guy I had working on a Social Security Claim for me?

The answering machine's light was flashing three times, which meant that three messages were left. The first and last calls are not important to this story. But—the middle call was Attorney Weinberger!

It was only 4:30 maybe I could still reach him at his office? I dialed the number, got put on hold, and had to listen to that damn awful elevator music again.

Then Weinberger came on and said. "Mr. San Tuccio the Grand Jury has indicted you for conspiracy to buy, sell, and possess firearms. The ATF will be serving an Arrest Warrant on you in a day or two."

To myself I thought. "Oh shit!" I asked the attorney. "But why are you calling me?" Weinberger's reply was almost the same as in our first phone conversation. "Let's not talk about that on the phone. When can you get in here to my office?"

I questioned him. "But why is the Federal Public Defenders office informing me I am about to be arrested?"

"We can help you surrender to the Court instead of being arrested. Also, I'll represent you at a Bail Hearing and that will keep you from being locked-up!"

"Well sir, with all due respect, I can call my own attorney and get that stuff done." I knew Weinberger didn't like that sharp response. His next reply told me exactly what was going on.

"That may be true Mr. San Tuccio but your attorney can't help you with the Federal Prosecutor as we can. The Government is willing to give you little or no prison time for your cooperation."

Simply put, the U.S. Government wanted information as to who, where, when, and what kinds of weapons I had sold.

My family and background did not allow for that kind of behavior. Maybe for Sammy "the bull" it was all right. But—not for a San Tuccio!

A red warning light then came on in my thick head. Slow down Frank, think, go see Weinberger. Find out what the Feds are offering.

"Okay, I'll come in to your office after 4 PM tomorrow." With that done I sat down to think.

Long before 7 AM the next morning I knew just what I was going to do.

Things didn't add up. First, the last "weapons" I had bought or sold was at least five or six years back. Second, none of those were sold in the United States. Third, now they say a gun found in New Jersey has been traced to me? Something is not right!

Four years later I would find out from my cousin, the FBI agent, what the Government's interest in me was? I had no clue that the FBI, CIA, ATF, U.S. Border Patrol, U.S. Customs, and the U.S. Coast Guard all had questions for me.

Inside his office Weinberger was trying to play me like a cheap violin. He offered no new information or even a hint of what the Feds interest in me was, or its case against me.

Weinberger said. "I think the best thing to do is set a time for you to surrender yourself and we'll have a Bail Hearing at the same time. After we get that out of the way we'll discuss your case."

"Why not discuss it now?" I shouted at him. Weinberger didn't answer as he fumbled thru his oversized appointment book.

"Let's see, today is Wednesday, tomorrow and Friday I have a trial. Monday is a holiday, so can you be in my office at 9 AM on the 18th?"

"Do I have a choice?" I yelled back while leaving his office.

What would you do if you had possibly only five (5) days of freedom left, before you had to stand in front of a U.S. District Court Judge?

Back at the apartment Jim Beam and I continued our working relationship!

Was it a good time to run? Living in a one-bedroom apartment made it easy to do so. All I had to do was pack my clothes and throw the TV and VCR in the Lexus's trunk and leave!

But—no, not yet! Why not? Because I haven't heard "what your country can do for you!" If I took off now and there was no prison time in Weinberger's deal, there would be time when they caught-up with me!

Don't panic Frank; what they are charging you with is a billable offense. I knew I could make any amount of Bail. In Connecticut there are San Tuccios' (family) listed in the Yellow Pages under Bail Bonds. So—Bail was no problem.

Those five days before my Court date went by all too fast and then it was that Tuesday.

I arrived at Weinberger's office at 8:50 AM and he was waiting for me in front of the building. To me that seemed strange because the Court was just across the street.

"Mr. San Tuccio we have to hurry because Federal Judges like to start their Court at 9 AM sharp."

During our short walk I asked him if he had anything new to tell me, his reply was. "No!"

At 9 AM on the dot Court was called to order by the Bailiff. There was only one other defendant in the Court, as can be the case with Arraignments.

Mr. Weinberger represented the both of us. She (the other defendant), was called first and Weinberger entered a plea of Not Guilty to possession of drugs for her.

Now it was my turn in front of His Honor. The Bailiff read the charges "Frank M. San Tuccio you are charged with the following. Conspiracy to buy, sell, and possess firearms, how do you plead?"

Attorney Weinberger whispered to me. "Guilty or not guilty Mr. San Tuccio?" Of course I said. "Not guilty!" Never admit guilty even if twenty people saw you committing the crime. Once you say guilty your options become slim to none.

My plea was the easy part of the morning next the judge looked over at the U.S. Attorney and asked. "What amount of Bail is the Government seeking, Mr. Prosecutor?" The reply was like being kicked in the balls. "Fifty thousand dollars cash bond your Honor."

Holy shit! I didn't want to lose $50,000.00! I'll explain what I meant by lose $50,000.00 in chapter 3—The U.S. Court.

To Weinberger I said. "Do something to get that Bond lowered or I'll not cooperate with you or the fucking Government!" I must of said the magic word, because.

"Your Honor, Mr. San Tuccio has surrendered himself here today. Although this is his first court appearance his case has been on-going for almost six months. He is employed and has strong family ties in the community. May Bail please be set at $10,000.00?"

"Mr. Weinberger the Court sets Bail at $20,000/00. Can your client make that Bail?" I nodded my head and Weinberger informed the judge. "Yes, thank you, your Honor."

I made a phone call and within an hour, thanks to my UncleDominic, I was out on Bail.

Many weeks would pass as the attorney and I kept going in and out of Court on his various Motions.

I truly believe the whole thing was set up to wear me down. The U.S. Government was going to charge me with five (5) counts. Each count could get me five (5) years!

Five times five, twenty-five (25) years! At my age (58 then), it was a death sentence. In the next chapter you'll find out why I decided to run!

CHAPTER 3

The U.S. Court.

As the months went by I never asked Attorney Weinberger to enter a guilty plea on my behalf. But, he expected me to do so in return for the Government's deal (plea bargain) he was working on. Yeah, sure!

The term "plea bargain" is mis-named, it should be called forced acceptance. Maybe you agree with me? Whom do you think benefits the most from plea-bargaining? The accused, or the accuser?

Very early in 1998 the U. S. Attorney turned up the heat on my case in two ways.

First, the case was moved from Hartford to the Southern District of Connecticut down in New Haven. Why? No one could answer that question for me.

Second, the Federal Prosecutor was now charging me with twenty-one (21) counts of Possession of a Firearm By A Felon.

So—instead of facing only twenty five years in prison it now became one hundred and five (105) years!

Weinberger told me coldly. "I am very sorry Mr. San Tuccio but it looks like the Government can prove their case against you."

But in reality Attorney Weinberger and Ms. Ogden (the Federal Prosecutor) were both trying to screw me over. They were playing their own version of "good cop, bad cop."

Every court appearance, and there were many (six in eight months) now meant taking a day off from work and a hundred mile round trip. Justice is not swift.

After I finished my route for the day, Big Dan sent me to the main office. Mr. Cook the company's manager was waiting in the doorway.

"We're sorry Frank but we have to let you go. Your work is fine but you have missed too many damn days. Please come back on Tuesday and I'll have your paycheck and the paperwork ready for your unemployment claim."

Well that's just wonderful! I was now out of work, thanks Feds! But it was a Friday, so I started on what would turn out to be a three-year weekend. I'll explain that shortly and in detail in Chapter 4.

Causing you to lose a job is the first step the U.S. Government uses to push you towards their forced acceptance. When you have no money and no job the pressure to plead guilty does increase.

Oh well, there's always Jim Beam and the redhead for now!

There was really no need to panic. I knew that they couldn't prove those twenty-one counts against me. Why was I so sure? Let's just say a "cousin" told me. Never the less the possibility of facing a 105 years sentence would scare the shit out of anyone.

Weinberger didn't have a clue that I also had a real attorney helping me, Mr. John Zocco. He is a trusted family member and that's all I'll say about him in print.

Attorney Zocco obtained copies of all the court documents in the case and his name appears nowhere in the records.

After studying the Feds case Zocco told me. "Frank, their case is weak and more or less bull shit. What they are trying to do is threaten you with the hundred and five years so that you'll tell them something, anything!"

Every time I asked Weinberger a simple question he would go into an erosion mode. It was now easy to see where his loyalties were, with the damn U.S. Attorney's office!

Neither the court records nor the prosecutor's files revealed any witnesses or confidential informants that were to testify against me. How in the hell could they have traced twenty-one guns to me?

All of my gun sales where made outside of the United States. The chances that they found twenty-one guns here in America were almost non-existent!

Attorney Zocco told me a while back. "Even if they gun they found in New Jersey can be traced to you the most time they can give you is five years, maximum." One hundred and five years? I don't think so!

A few more months went by and the case was still on the Pre Trial list. That meant I had to be in the courthouse, but the case was not in front of a judge yet.

After a meeting between Weinberger and the U.S. Attorney, I was told. "They are now willing to drop the sixteen additional counts against you, if you'll plead guilty to the five original counts." Said Weinberger coldly.

Now I was back to the possibility of only twenty-five years in prison. Well, I suppose that was good news compared to a hundred and five years.

I asked Weinberger. "What am I looking at for a sentence if I do plead guilty?"

"Mr. San Tuccio you are a twice convicted felon and both of your priors were selling weapons. You are looking at some heavy time I am afraid. Do you have anything to tell me that I can take to the prosecutor that will help you?"

Weinberger's answer sucked! I told him that I needed to go down to the lobby to make a quick telephone call before I could answer him.

Wasn't it just as Attorney Zocco had said? They wanted information from me, why else would the Government "let" me plead guilty to five counts and only twenty-five years? Cheer up Frank; you'll only be 83 years old when they release you!

As soon as I finished talking with Zocco I knew exactly what I had to do.

The elevator ride back to the seventh floor gave me a little more time to agree with myself.

Meanwhile Weinberger had found an empty conference room and ushered me into it. I spoke first.

"Mr. Weinberger only a fucking moron would plead guilty to a twenty-five year sentence! I am fifty-eight years old, in 25 years I'll be eighty-three! Do you think I'll live to be 83 in a Federal prison? You're asking me to accept a death sentence!" I yelled at him.

My sharp remarks brought him to his feet, almost knocking over his chair as he jumped up. "Now you wait one minute Mr. San Tuccio, you did those other crimes and they convicted you of. And now the Government has caught you for a third time. What the hell did you expect?"

After scolding me he picked up his briefcase and headed back to the lady prosecutor's office.

I left the small room and returned to the lobby placing a second phone call to Mr. Zocco. After our conversation I had a much firmer plan. So, back to the seventh floor and Weinberger.

He was still in the prosecutor's office so I waited in the hallway for what seemed like too long a time.

Coming out of her office Weinberger said. "Okay, the U.S. Attorney will let you plead guilty to one count with a maximum sentence of sixty (60) months. But, you have to agree to cooperate with the FBI and ATF."

Mr. Zocco was indeed right! They just offered to let me plead guilty to only one count and no more than a five-year sentence. All that was good but, to cooperate with the two Federal agencies, never!

Keeping that thought to myself I told the attorney. "Go get something in writing from them before I enter a plea or cooperate with the Feds."

Weinberger was all smiles now as he excused himself and rushed back to Ms. Ogden's office. He yelled over his shoulder. "Mr. San Tuccio you can leave now I'll call you later tonight,"

There was no need to rush back to Hartford so I had supper in downtown New Haven.

Right across from the U.S. Courthouse is a beautiful City park and after a short walk I was at Yale University, Bill and Hillary's old school. It was no big deal to look at!

The fifty-mile trip in rush hour traffic, gave me still more time to work out some of the final details of my scheme. I had it all down in my mind before reaching Hartford.

A good feeling came over me for the first time in many months as I drove into the parking garage. It was the kind of feeling that only happens when a heavy burden is lifted.

Weinberger didn't call that night nor the whole next day. Was that another part of the Government's over all plan? I called his office and was informed. "Mr. Weinberger will be in court for the next few days on a trial."

There were some parts to the plan that I should get started on and I did so the next day.

Attorney Weinberger finally returned my call with his same old bull-shit. "We have what could be our last Pre Trial in two or three weeks. I'll call you as soon as I get the date. See you then."

I really didn't care about the end result of his stupid plea bargain. I would not, as I did twice before, walk meekly off to prison in handcuffs. Screw Mr. Weinberger, Ms. Ogden, and the U.S. Government!

The two or three weeks was good news but now I would have to speed up parts of my plan.

Again I called Mr. Zocco. He explained the Feds system and some of the rules that applied to the case. From that day until the Government hoped to throw me in prison, I had between six and eight weeks.

Nobody suspected, not even the redhead, that on my "sentencing day" I would not be there to surrender myself.

It was eighteen days later when Attorney Weinberger's office called and told me when to be in New Haven. Up until then I had been busier than a kid in a candy store!

Here's some of what I had accomplished while waiting for that call. Anything that I couldn't fit into my travel ready Lexus was to be sold.

Trips to several local pawn-shops dumped these items; the TV, VCR, videotapes, answering machine, a bicycle, cassette music tapes, typewriter, microwave, and a pair of binoculars.

The smaller items were quickly sold by posting a notice on the building's Community Bulletin Board. Things like the coffee maker, toaster, can opener, pots, pans, blender, dishes, table lamps, etcetera, produced $425.00. Added to the pawn-shops money I now had over a thousand dollars.

With all that stuff sold came a downside. I could not cook or watch TV in the apartment! Yes, you may have guessed, the redhead to the rescue! Meals, TV, and more!

The last thing that had to be sold was the furniture. Using the "Yellow Pages" I found and called three used furniture dealers. Each was asked to come up and look at the stuff and to give me their best price.

They were all told that I was waiting for a job transfer but didn't have a firm date yet. Also that I would require a $200.00 deposit if they wished to buy my furniture.

The furniture was almost new, the real heavy oak wood kind and it was not cheap to buy. Asking a $200.00 deposit was not a stretch.

Harry, the last of the three dealers, and I agreed on a price. Then he wrote me out a check on the spot and made out a bill of sale, which I signed.

Next, Harry would be a lucky guy because he would now get to meet Rebecca (she's the redhead). So we walked the two doors down to her apartment and I introduced him.

We agreed that Rebecca would have the key to my place and that she would call Harry, when it was time to pick up <u>his</u> furniture.

For some reason Harry just couldn't stop staring at Rebecca's ample chest! I don't think he heard a word of my instructions to her.

That night I took my bosom friend out to dinner in payment for her future help with Harry and the furniture.

All to soon the time came to report to the U.S. Attorney's office, I remember that day well! It was cold with snow coming down and a very slow drive into New Haven.

At 9:45 AM I was still at least twenty miles from the Courthouse.

In reality being late didn't matter. I was still on the Pre Trial list, which meant the case would not be called in the courtroom.

It was past eleven o'clock when I got off the elevator on the seventh floor and started my search for Mr. Weinberger. The first place to look would be the U.S. Attorney's office.

I asked a secretary if she had seen Mr. Weinberger. She answered coldly. "Mr. Weinberger is in Ms. Ogden's office but I can not disturb them because they are in a conference."

"Excuse me lady, but I was stuck in bumper to bumper traffic for over three hours trying to get here. Could you at least take a note in so that he knows I am here?"

Her answer was very abrupt. "No, but if Ms. Ogden buzzes me I'll let her know you are out here."

This lady had the personality of a wire coat hanger, which of course has none. Your tax dollars pay her so I'll mention her name, Ms. Sanchez.

There was no way of telling how long they would be in "conference", after all I wasn't Weinberger's only client. The hell with waiting—I'll go to lunch.

"When Mr. Weinberger comes out of conference would you please tell him Mr. San Tuccio went to lunch? Thank you." Not waiting for her answer I turned and left the office quickly.

Most U.S. District Courts brake for lunch between 1 and 2 PM, it was only 11:30 AM when I left the building. I would be sure to return no later than 12:30.

When I got back I first looked for Weinberger at the prosecutor's office, but finally found him in his third floor Federal Public Defender's office.

"Where the hell have you been Mr. San Tuccio? I called both your job and apartment! Said my attorney a little too loud.

I answered him. "Didn't the prosecutor's secretary tell you I was there looking for you?"

"No, she did not! Well the main thing is that you are here and we maybe able to put an end to your case today."

I thought to myself, what the bells in hell is he talking about? End the case today?

He continued. "Here's their deal, you plead guilty to one count of Possession of A Firearm By A Felon and the Government will not charge you with any other crimes. But, before you enter a plea in front of the judge you have to talk to the FBI. They're one floor up in this building."

"Why do I have to talk to those assholes?" I asked.

"Because Mrs. San Tuccio they will decide if your cooperation is of value to them and if it warrants your reduced charges."

Now I was angry! "Hey, Weinberger didn't I tell you the last time I was here to get something in writing from them before I plead guilty or cooperate!"

He put on his best lying face and said. "Believe me Mr. San Tuccio I tried but they insisted that they talk to you <u>first</u>.

"Mr. Weinberger do I have a sign on my back that says dunce? What's to prevent the Government from using my information and then still locking me up for more than the sixty months?"

He shouted back at me. "The Government always keeps its word, otherwise there wouldn't be so many snitches or informants would there?" Boy, that sure was comforting to hear, yeah, sure!

My mind was telling me to put an end to the shit right now! Looking straight at him I said. "I'll plead guilty to the one count and take the sixty months time. If they want to charge me with more, no deals, and you can set us down for a jury trial!"

I was already thinking ahead, it didn't matter one count or twenty-one, I was going to run anyway!

Weinberger excused himself, told me not to leave, and went back to the prosecutor's office.

Soon he was back. "Good news, they will let you plead guilty to only the one count with a sixty month recommendation by the U.S. Attorney. But of course the judge could give you more time."

"Fine, let's do that and be done so that I can get things in order before I head to prison." With that said Weinberger told me to go sit in Courtroom Two, and that he would be there in a few minutes.

At the door I read. "Courtroom #2, U.S. District Judge Peter C. Dorsey, Presiding."

My case was called dead last, and there was no one in the courtroom then except Weinberger, the court's personnel and me.

Oh shit! They're going to lock me up as soon as I plead guilty! Now I am really fucked!

The bailiff called out. "The United States versus Frank M. San Tuccio." Weinberger went to the front of the courtroom and motioned for me to follow.

My attorney informed Judge Dorsey that I wished to plead guilty. But before a judge can accept a guilty plea he must canvass the defendant.

Judge Dorsey looked down at me from the bench and asked. "Mr. San Tuccio do you wish to enter a plea of guilty today? Has any offer been made to you in return for your plea of guilty? There were about a half dozen more questions before the judge got to the bottom line.

His last question was. "Mr. San Tuccio do you wish to plead guilty as charged?" I answered weakly. "Yes, your Honor."

Judge Dorsey's last words were. "Very well I accept your plea of guilty and you are to report back to this Court for sentencing on March ___?____ (I forgot the exact date) at 2:00 PM."

To Weinberger the Judge said. "In the mean time you will make an appointment with the U.S. Probation Department in regards to Mr. San Tuccio's P.S.I. (Pre Sentence Interview)."

Here's where things stood at the close of that day. My sentencing day was eight weeks away but I would have to report for the P.S.I. in only two weeks.

It was simple enough to me, get things ready and run! But if I left before seeing the Probation Department I would have only a two-week head start.

So—I'll go see the probation people, keep working on my plan, and then run! That would give me a six-week head start before sentencing day!

That's exactly what I did. Weinberger and I reported to Ms. Sullivan at the U.S. Probation office in Hartford. She rattled off, and I answered about a hundred questions before she told Weinberger.

"In about two weeks I'll send my report over to you and Judge Dorsey." I thanked Weinberger for his help and enjoyed the short drive to my apartment. Everything had to move faster now!

Rebecca and I went out to dinner again and I told her I would be leaving in a few days, she cried.

I spent the night in her apartment and in the morning we started packing the clothing and other stuff for the Lexus. I was almost ready for my three year, fugitive from justice, trip!

Trust me, the Government is not smart enough to find anyone. Without their snitches they couldn't find shit in a toilet bowl!

You must outsmart them Frank, I kept thinking to myself. What can be done to throw them off the track? A false trail was needed; here are some of the things I did.

First, it was now the middle of the winter in Connecticut, so I left all of my winter boots, coats, and clothing hanging in the closets!

Second, I made a trip across the street to a travel agent. There I picked up airline flight schedules, travel brochures, and tourist flyers for Florida. These were left around the apartment. Also, they knew I had a sister and daughter living there.

Third, five local banks provide me with certified checks of $4,000.00 each. Remember; always get checks for less than $5,000.00, and only one large check per bank. Larger checks are reported to several Government agencies.

The only bank trail I left was made many months before by withdrawing twenty thousand dollars from the bank that held the proceeds from the sale of my home.

The food in the refrigerator and on my shelves was moved to Rebecca's place. Anything else she wanted was her's for the taking. She was as busy as a true Wal-mart shopper as she gathered up the drapes, sheets, blankets, pillows, bath towels, small rugs, and even the spare light bulbs!

I spent the last night at Rebecca's apartment and in the early dawn light we said our good bye. She made me promise to write when, "You get where you are going." Yes, I did write her!

As I was driving out of the garage, Eddie, the security guard said. "Good morning, Mr. San Tuccio. Going on a vacation trip?"

Eddie had a big mouth and was always gossiping about other people in the building. Anything I told him would get back to the office and hopefully the Feds.

"Yes, Eddie, I am headed down to Florida for a little sunshine." I joked.

The basis for my false trail had just been perfectly laid! So, now let's start "On The Run!"

CHAPTER 4

"On The Run!"

Within minutes of leaving the parking garage I was at the downtown Hartford traffic connector. Interstate 91 went North and South, Interstate 84 ran East and West. Which direction Frank?

There was no need to rush; it would be at least six weeks before the Feds start looking for me. So, I decided to visit Cape Cod in Massachusetts, for a last vacation in the Northeast.

For you readers who don't know, Cape Cod is a seaside resort area. It was now winter and its off-season but the Cape is beautiful anytime of the year.

I knew that my bail would be called (forfeited) for not showing-up in court. Oh well, there goes twenty thousand dollars! I'll call my Uncle Dominic (the Bondsman) and let him know I had skipped out. He's family, no problem! Remember if you are going to run you need two things, money and a strong will!

A week later I returned from the Cape and found a motel room near Bradley Airport in Windsor Locks, Connecticut.

Now it was time to finish the last things up and get "On The Run!" Las Vegas was my planned destination, now to get there from here!

The tricks that work for an old man with a white beard, who walks with the aid of a cane, may not work for you. What follows is all true. Please take notes for your "next time."

I had to get out of Connecticut fast, that meant no trains, buses, or driving my car. Fly only! To drive on the interstates is the dumbest thing you can do. If you get stopped for a traffic violation and they "run you", you're a dead duck.

I needed a plane ticket but how do I get one (this was long before 9/11 happened) without showing an ID?

Think now, do you give up? The answer is K.I.S.S. (Keep It Simple Stupid). In fact it was so simple that I still think about how things could have gone wrong.

This is what I did. Telephoning a travel agent I asked the price of a one-way ticket to Las Vegas. She quoted me a price and we played "Let's Make A Deal" until I got a better price.

I asked. "Could the ticket be picked up tomorrow? Is it alright if I send someone to get it for me?" She answered yes, to both questions.

The next day at the travel agency I asked for Mr. Garofolo's ticket and paid cash. No ID needed. One problem solved. Next was a fast trip to Wal-Mart to buy the largest suitcase I could find.

Now my last and biggest problem was what do I do with the Lexus? The idea light came on in my thick head. Ship the car to Vegas!

Back to the Yellow Pages, I lucked out on the first company I called. "Yes we can ship your automobile to Las Vegas, in fact we have a new terminal there."

I hurried over to the company's loading site, paid cash for the Lexus's ride, and used my Master Charge to leave there with a rented Buick.

I used the credit card so that the Feds would know I had rented a car but would not know the Lexus was being trucked west. A pretty smart move, right?

Now comes the trickiest part of the whole plan. How do I get on the plane <u>without</u> showing an ID? There is an old saying—"Timing is everything", I sure hoped so!

I had only two days to zero hour! I drove over to the airport and went to the U.S. Air terminal section and checked out their daily flight to Vegas, the flight I had a ticket for.

My whole afternoon was spent watching and checking on certain details for "the plan". Leaving there, I was now ready for operation Run!

After a good night's sleep, and early that morning, I drove the rented car into the airport's long-term lot. That would get me weeks or maybe months before the airport police got around to checking on it.

Inside the U.S. Air terminal I took a seat as far away from the ticket counter as I could find. I had only the one large suitcase. In time they called the boarding for my flight. Remember, "Timing is everything".

I had gone over my plan many times in my head and I was sure it would work, well I hoped it would. K.I.S.S. I kept saying to myself. K.I.S.S! Just then the loudspeaker came on, "U.S. Air to Las Vegas last call"!

That was my clue to get moving, my heart was pounding a hundred miles an hour. From a long distance away from the ticket counter I yelled. "Please hold the plane I have a ticket!"

Picture this in your mind's eye. A very old man pulling a large heavy suitcase and hobbling along on a cane.

I even stopped a few times to appear to be catching my breath. The ticket clerk called to one of the plane's stewards who came towards me pushing a wheelchair. She then motioned for a skycap to take my bag.

I was now at the counter and my bag was headed into the plane. The clerk asked for my ticket and I handed it to the stewardess (remember I was in a wheelchair), who handed it to her. After hitting a few keys on the computer and checking the ticket she said. "Have a nice trip Mr. Garofolo!"

If I had been asked for ID my story was, "that it's in my suitcase" which was already headed into the plane. She didn't ask! So on to Las Vegas.

Arriving in Vegas is always wonderful, many, many, happy memories danced in my head. Oh Frank, this isn't a "Soap Opera", okay back to the story.

By George I did it, left Connecticut without leaving any sort of paper trail! Now what's next?

First, I needed a place to stay and second, something to drive until my car caught up with me.

Hotel/Casino rates in the center of Las Vegas are always cheap. My favorite casino is called Circus-Circus it is located right on what is called "the strip."

Tourists (suckers) are big business here so almost every hotel or casino sends a shuttle bus out to the airport. The one for Circus-Circus is always easy to spot and it was a free ride to their casino/hotel.

Why try to rent a car at a busy airport counter? A rent a car's airport agencies are always checked first by the Feds. At "C.C." (as the natives call Circus-Circus) I called an in town rent a car company from the room. They would send a limousine over for me and bring me back to their agency for the paperwork.

Did I use a credit card for the car rental or hotel room? Hell no, in Vegas they are use to CASH! Sorry Feds, no paper trial from Las Vegas.

So, with those two things done I went out to enjoy Las Vegas, or as some folks still call it, "Loss Wages."

Meanwhile, back in Connecticut. By the day I was scheduled to be in court there, I had been in Las Vegas for weeks! Sorry Judge Dorsey but a man has to do what a man has to do!

I was a no show but did the Feds start looking for me? No, not yet but the Court Clerk did send me a certified letter!

Weinberger did a little bit better. He sent an investigator to my ex apartment, which of course he found empty! Yes, Harry got his furniture. I know all that because I had called Rebecca several times from Vegas. She knew better than to ask where I was.

Rebecca told me about hearing Ted (the apartment manager) letting the Feds in. She was never one to miss much! She also told me about the Certified letter from the Court.

She said. "The mailman was putting mail in the boxes when I went downstairs to get mine. He asked me if you were home because he had a Certified letter for you. I could see the envelope and it was from the U.S. Court."

Three years later I would get to read that letter in Attorney Weinberger's file.

I forgot to mention it but my "family" has many business contacts in Vegas and I could have hid out there for a long time. But, it's not a good idea to stand still when the Government is on your ass!

The Lexus arrived, packed with my clothing and two handguns. The plan was to take Interstate 15 North to Utah but first the car needed new license plates, and I needed a Nevada driver's license.

Next stop Kinko's. Three forms were needed for the Lexus, a title application, bill of sale and a registration application for new license plates.

A nice young lady pulled up the DMV's website and printed out the forms for me, for which I tipped her twenty dollars. She now would remember me on my return trip.

Back at Circus Circus I made out the paperwork selling the car to our friend Mr. Garofolo (me). Want to take a guess at what address I wrote on the forms? Why Circus Circus of course!

The Feds would soon be looking for a 1996 Red Lexus, with Connecticut license plates in the name of San Tuccio. But now, just like a Las Vegas magic act, the Lexus was Rose, had Nevada plates, and was owned by a Mr. Garofolo!

Here's how that was done, please feel free to take notes, as it did work for this convict/author.

At Kinko's again. "Hello Nancy, is there anyone here who is a Public Notary? Nancy was the lady I had tipped twenty dollars the day before.

She answered. "Yes, as a matter of fact I am the Notary for the store." She smiled no doubt thinking about another twenty-dollar tip.

"Would you please notarize my signature on the bill of sale you helped me with yesterday?" I handed her the form, my Connecticut driver's license, and a second twenty-dollar bill.

Nancy read over the bill of sale, then checked the driver's license, and finally said. "Please sigh here, and here Mr. San Tuccio." Then she also signed it and stamped it with her Notary's Seal. She didn't ask about Mr. Garofolo's signature that was already on the form as the "buyer".

Early the next morning I was at the DMV dressed in a suit and tie. Everyone knows how busy these places are, so use that to your advantage. Just to let you know, State workers are not hired for their intelligence!

It was a Friday, a busy day, and every clerk looked worn-out at only 8:30 in the morning. Looking around the large noisy room I found what I was looking for, the Auto Dealers Only window. I'm not an Auto Dealer? Again take notes.

Here's where careful planning comes in to play. The day before, I had called the DMV and asked the manager's name of he Auto Dealer's section. I have since forgotten her name but it was a Ms. Somebody.

the Dealers window I handed the forms into the clerk. "Excuse me sir but this window is for Auto Dealers." He replied like a jerk.

"I am an Auto Dealer, Ray's Auto Service, we sold Mr. San Tuccio's car on consignment and I'm just doing Mr. Garofolo a favor by bringing in the paperwork." I said with authority.

You'll remember that I am wearing a suit and tie? Now for the name-drop. "If there's a problem please call Ms. Somebody, she knows me."

The clerk was not about to call over the "boss" who knew me. He took back the papers, banged this, stapled that, hit the computer a few times and said. "Two hundred sixty dollars please."

Just like that Mr. Garofolo (me) became the owner of a rose colored Lexus with Nevada tags. "Here's your license plates sir." I almost started to laugh, but caught myself, took the plates and hurried out the door! Viva Las Vegas!

I would stay at Circus Circus, until I received the new paperwork from the DMV in the mail. That's fine, this place is wonderful! But—I still had one more trip to make to the DMV.

What for? Why a clean Nevada driver's license, what else? How is that possible? Here's how!

Again, timing is everything. I arrived there just thirty minutes before closing time. No suit and tie this time, jeans, tee shirt and sneakers. First stop was the Information Window.

"I have an out of State driver's license what form do I need to get a Nevada license?" I smiled at the clerk.

She handed me the paperwork, instructed me to fill it out, and then go to the Cashier's Window. Here again timing and a crowd help.

While filling in the form I made a few slight changes. First, Frank M. San Tuccio now became Frank M. Tucci. Second, my date of birth was changed from 1940 to 1950.

Remember these clerks are basically lazy! They will <u>not</u> look all that closely at the license you hand over to them. But, they will check to see if you have a <u>valid</u> one, via their computer.

While waiting for the computer's answer she picked up my form and typed that into her computer. Beep, beep, the computer said my license was good. Next she said. "Six dollars please, now report to the photo unit for your new license."

Walking out the door I couldn't help but whistle a happy tune!

Next stop Wal-Mart to buy a twenty-dollar pre-paid phone card. This is the best and safest way to make calls if you are "On The Run." I have more to say about phone cards in a later chapter.

With the card bought I headed uptown to the Rio Casino, which is one of the older gambling places in Las Vegas. A friend of the "family" worked there and I needed a favor.

But first a little food and fun! If you have never been to Las Vegas you have a treat waiting for you, especially the food.

Food in <u>all</u> the casinos is very inexpensive, good, and large portions are served. They don't worry about losing money on the meals; they'll make it up double and then some, on the gaming side of the casino!

And for the non-gourmet eaters there is a Burger King located almost in the middle of "the Strip".

You can eat free at most any casino if you know the ropes. I did because Vegas and I are very old friends.

My late Uncle Louie started taking me there when I was only a teenager. I went along to help him pick up "new suitcases." Sorry Feds, no details!

Once inside the Rio I headed straight for the cashier's cage for a two dollar roll of nickels and to cash one of my bank's checks.

In Las Vegas cashing a large "certified check" is never a problem, mine was for $4,000.00. The lady cashier handed a pen and asked. "Do you have a photo ID?" I sure did, and a Nevada one, thanks to their DMV.

The two-dollar roll of nickels would get me at least ten dollars worth of free drinks as I played the slots. Yes, free drinks; just find one of the pretty and young cocktail waitresses that circulate the gaming floor 24-7.

At least a dollar tip to the waitress each time she brings you a free drink is recommended. Or, you can try the following. Find one of the ladies that caught your eye, call her over and say something like this:

"Hi Sweetie, I'll be playing the slots in this area and I hate to wait for drink refills." Now hand her a ten-dollar bill and finish up by saying. "Please bring me two shots of Jim Beam (or your drink of choice)."

Most of the casinos have a rule of serving only one drink at a time. But—because of your ten-dollar tip you can bet the farm that she'll return with your two drinks! When she does, tip her five dollars more and watch the service you'll get until you leave the casino!

Now it was time for the real reason I was in the Rio. When Dawn (as her name tag said) brought my fourth or fifth round of drinks I asked. "Do you know a tall skinny guy who works here in the maintenance department? He's my cousin."

Dawn answered yes, but didn't know if Tony was working that day. So, she directed me to the maintenance office in the back of the Rio.

No help needed. Outside of the office, next to the time clock was a posted work schedule. Tony would be in at 4:00 PM.

With a few hours to kill I headed for a pay phone to call Rebecca. It's not what you're thinking! I needed to know what was going on with the Feds back in Connecticut.

To say the redhead was happy to hear from me would be a gross understatement. Knowing I could trust her I told her. "Guess where I am? Las Vegas!" Her quick reply surprised the hell out of me!

"Wow Frank you are really in Las Vegas! I've never been there, I'll fly out and you can show me all the sights!" Believe me, there was no way I could talk her out of it.

After the shock of Rebecca's phone call I met with my cousin Tony. He said that the "favor" was as good as done and to check back with him in a few days.

Two days later I was at the Las Vegas Airport. Rebecca looked pale getting out the airplane, her bright red hair made her look even paler. Oh, I forgot it was still winter back east.

Standing in front of the car she saw the Nevada license plate and said. "It looks like you're not coming back to Connecticut any too soon!"

Entering the lobby at Circus Circus was an adventure. Rebecca always was a second look girl! She caught the desk clerk's eye, who saw I was with her "Oh, Mr. Garofolo I have a message for you!"

The note said. "Everything is set." Tony.

On the way to the room she asked. "Frank, who's Mr. Garofolo?" Smiling, I said. "Me!"

That night we made the rounds of some of the casinos. The Tropicana, MGM, New York, Caesar's Palace, and the last stop was the Rio.

Cousin Tony was very interested in knowing more about "that sassy redhead." But—we had to talk some serious business first. Rebecca excused herself and headed off to play the slots.

The paperwork came from the DMV on the Lexus. Rebecca had left that Sunday, and it was now time to get "On The Road Again." So, on to the Rio, Cousin Tony, and to firm up the favor I had asked.

Tony had contacted a "family" member in Mesquite, Nevada, which is about a hundred miles North on I 15. He had set up a job for me at the Oasis Casino, no questions asked, no ID needed. Thanks Cousin Tony!

I bid farewell to Vegas and headed towards a soon to be great place to work. Elvis's old song was in my head, "Viva Las Vegas!"

Two hours later the highway billboard sign said. "Mesquite, Nevada the Fastest Growing Town In Nevada!" Although it was a small place it boasted of having four casinos.

Just off the Mesquite Exit and to the left, was the beautiful Oasis Hotel/Casino. It was the town's oldest one and connected to the "family" in New Jersey. Sorry again Feds, but no details!

At their maintenance department I asked for Sal my new boss. I was warmly greeted with. "So you're Tony's cousin from Jersey!" His second remark was right to the point. "How long do you need to stay here?"

After informing me of my job duties Sal got on the phone and found me a free room at the River Queen Casino. It was owned by the Oasis and about a mile up the road.

Things couldn't be better for about six months, until I had a chance reunion with an old service friend, Johnny.

But first let me explain a little about Mesquite, Nevada to you. Mesquite and the four casinos are about two miles from the Arizona border on its North. If you keep on going North on I 15 thirty-eight miles later you're in Saint George, Utah.

Are you getting the picture yet? Utah, the Mormon Church, no gambling, and no drinking of alcoholic beverages for the Mormons who live there. But—there, just South of Saint George was four casinos!

On any give day most of the cars in the Oasis's parking lot had Utah tags on them. I am not saying that most of the cars from Utah were Mormons drinking or gambling, but my friend Johnny <u>was</u> all of the above!

Now back to the "reunion."

Part of my job was watering the large and beautiful plants in the casino's foyer, which I was doing at the time. Then, from the direction of the registration desk, I heard. "Frank, Frank San Tuccio!"

Shock jumped thru my body, I was scared to turn around! Was it a Federal Agent about to arrest me? Looking over at the desk, my heart raced as the face the voice came from started towards me.

Well I'll be damned, it looked like Johnny-D! It was Johnny—D! The last time I saw him was twenty-five years ago when we were both mustered out.

We exchanged handshakes, hugs, pats on the back, and had a few rounds of Scotch Whiskey. Johnny—D was a Mormon but he loved his booze.

His questions ran the gambit but the last one would again bring a change to my life.

"Sir (I was his C.O.) Why are you working in a place like this?" I told Johnny—D that I was "On The Run" from the Government and facing a long time in prison. To which he replied.

"Well sir, you'll have less of a chance of getting caught if you come back to Utah with me. If I can run into you at a casino so can the Feds!"

We kept talking for a while and he filled me in on his last twenty-five years. I did the same for him

Johnny—D was the owner of several automobile dealerships in and around Saint George. He also had a high standing in his Ward (the Mormon Church).

Later, as I walked him to his car I knew he was right and that I would be "On the Road Again" to Utah.

The next day Sal and I said good-bye and I pointed the Lexus towards Utah.

CHAPTER 5

"Utah, Arizona, and Remy!"

This was the hardest chapter in Part One for me to write. Why? Because it starts out by bringing back happy memories but ends as my wife Remy and I become separated. She is in Phoenix and I have now been in a series of Federal prisons.

Never the less, as I sit here in USP Atwater I am glad I wrote it and hope you will enjoy "Utah, Arizona, and Remy!."

Boy oh boy did I pick the wrong day (a Sunday) to leave Mesquite, Nevada! You will see why in just a few more paragraphs.

The drive from the Oasis Casino northward to Saint George, Utah is one of the most beautiful in the entire Southwest. It starts out at almost zero elevation and climbs gently into the foothills of southern Utah.

There Interstate 15's speed limit is like a yo-yo, going from a high of 75 MPH to a low of only 15 MPH on the sharp climbing turns. Although Saint George is only thirty-eight miles from Mesquite the trip will take well over one hour, on a good day.

Cruising along, about halfway to Johnny-D's my CB radio came alive. "Hey all yew good buddies out there, all traffic is being detoured off this here interstate into the rest area. I do hear it's a DEA drug check!"

Looking ahead I could see four or five police vehicles blocking the highway. Something was happening, but what? Okay, I'll just make a U-turn across the divider and head back to Mesquite!

Oh shit! No can do! There are cops in the turn around area and the sign says "Emergency and Police Vehicles Only." Well, the Lexus doesn't look like a police car but it is an emergency for me! I'm a dead duck; I think I am going to be sick! Calm down old man, think. I said to myself.

Cars exciting the highway were directed to park in the rest area's marked spots.

After doing so, two uniformed officers, one on each side of the car said. "Shut off the motor and have your driver's license ready when the Agents get to your vehicle."

Did he say Agents? Holy shit, I am carrying two handguns and the U.S. Marshals are looking for me! Agents? Think Frank, stay calm, and don't blow it by doing anything stupid. Calming down I ran things around in my head.

I remembered the following:

1. The license plates on the Lexus were now from Nevada
2. The car was now registered in the name of our "friend" Mr. Garofolo
3. My driver's license had a new name
4. The date of birth on the license was now 1950 versus 1940

You'll be okay, I assured myself but stay calm don't get nervous. I now had a plan. Once again as I have said many times in this book, timing and appearance are everything.

Thinking to myself—I am driving a Lexus and dressed in a suit and tie, does that fit their "drug profile"? I was calm, and I did have a plan.

So when the Agents approached the car here's what I did. Quickly I got out of the car and handing the keys to the taller of the two Agents I said.

"Sorry, but us older folks don't travel well, I need the restroom real bad! Here's the key." I didn't wait for a reply, turned and almost ran towards the toilets. Inside the building, I decided to wait there for fifteen minutes before returning to the car.

You don't know how fast fifteen minutes can be until you are staring at a wristwatch. Too soon it was time to head back. Trying to stay calm I stopped at the vending machines and bought a coffee and a Snickers bar.

Now for the minute of truth! As I rounded the corner of the building my car came into view. There were no Agents standing next to it? The closest parked car was four or five spaces away. Slowly, very slowly I walked towards the car.

The keys were visible on top of the dashboard? The agents were now down at the far end of the parking lot. Frank just jump in the damn car and haul ass out of there! Yes!

The Agents saw all the clothing hanging across the back seat and figured I was just a nice old man on a vacation. Maybe they even searched the inside of the car and the trunk?

When I didn't come back quickly they probably ran a license plate check. They found that the Lexus was owned by a Mr. Garofolo who had no police record. So, with that information and many other cars to check they just moved on to the next vehicle.

Good luck? Maybe? No, if that wasn't God watching me who was? Next stop Johnny-D's auto dealership.

At Johnny's I was warmly greeted. His first question was where did I plan on staying that night. But, before I could answer him. "Well tonight you'll stay with Marie and I, she has been busy all day cooking for you." He said with authority.

I asked him. "Who's Marie?" I thought his wife's name was Jane, Joan, Jean or something like that. His answer would make some men envious.

"Frank, Marie is my number three wife, and that's Jane that you remembered. She is still my wife." Later I found out that the rascal now had five (5) wives and a dozen or so children! Hey, who I am to judge another man's religion?

After Marie's, Jane's, Carol's Grace's, and Barbara's home cooked meal I got a good night's sleep. Their mornings started with a large and heavy breakfast in the "main house", after which Johnny and I headed for the car lot.

I asked my friend if he could suggest a place to rent an apartment in Saint George. "Why? Don't you like my house and family?" He asked with a hurt look on his face. I explained that I was the type of person who likes their privacy.

Reluctantly he wrote down the name of a well-known national hotel/motel chain, gave me directions, and the name of the manager to contact.

But before leaving Johnny insisted on showing me around his large lot. He had done well for himself; besides this lot he had dealerships in two of the area's surrounding cities.

Well, I guess he can afford those five wives and all those kids!

When my tour was done Johnny asked how I was fixed for cash. To which I replied I was set for a while. Then Johnny said something that made a lot of sense to me.

"Yeah Frank that's okay for today but every time you spend a dollar without replacing it you have a dollar less." He was trying to convince me that I should be working and offered me the job of Courtesy Driver at his dealership.

I took him up on his kind offer. "Okay boss when I I start and what do I do? And what do you plan on paying me?"

Johnny insisted that I take the rest of the week off and get settled in my new surroundings. After our talk I left to check out my new place at the Marriott Inn. I mention the name because their people were wonderful all the months I lived there.

At the Inn I asked for Johnny's manager friend and was shown straight into his office. Wow, I guess Johnny's name was a juice card.

The manager was a huge man. If you can remember the TV series Bonanza, he was a dead ringer for the character of Hoss Cartwright. He greeted me with a big smile and said.

"So you're Mr. Davis's (Johnny) war buddy from back East. I have you set-up for a ground floor room, which opens, on to our pool area. Your bill is paid in full as long as you choose to stay with us, courtesy of Mr. Davis. He is my church elder so there will be no discussion about you paying!"

All in all that day was one of the ten best days in my life. I had a new job and a place to stay for <u>free</u> as long as I wanted to stay in Saint George.

Early the next morning I bought a street index map and set out to do a little sightseeing. Did you know the Saint George, Utah was the winter home of Brigham Young the Mormon leader?

After a few days of touring the city and the nearby towns I went shopping, for groceries and new underwear. My room at the Marriott had everything needed to set-up housekeeping.

There was a stove, refrigerator, microwave, coffee maker, dishes, pots, pans and even silverware. Great job Marriott!

Before starting to work at Johnny's I had one more errand to do, get fitted for my "Courtesy Driver" uniforms.

At the uniform shop the clerk measured me for pants, shirts (lettered with "Frank") and Johnny's dealership logo and also a dark blue blazer. Oh I forgot, <u>two</u> nametags that said "Frank Courtesy Drive", one for my blazer and one for the shirts.

Monday at 6:00 AM I was "uniformed and at the car lot". What were my duties? Basically my job was to drive people to their workplace after they dropped out their cars for servicing.

Johnny's place was busy and he also had two PM drivers. They would pick up the customers I dropped off in the morning, to retrieve their automobiles that night.

I was not hired as a replacement but worked in addition to a Ms._____, I am sorry lady but I can not remember your name. Well anyway, she <u>was</u> the ultimate <u>Ms.</u>, no make-up, no bra, and no morals. That's enough about her.

The Ms. And I shuttled people in and out of the car lot, picked up coffee and doughnuts for the crew, office supplies, made trips to the post office, and the Motor Vehicle Department.

It was a great job, better than the Oasis Casino but no "Show Girls", unless you count the Ms. But, after five months I asked myself. "Do you want to stay in Saint George? Even the Wal-Mart closes early here!"

Saint George just wasn't my lifestyle, even though Johnny and the Mormons were good folks to have on my side, I needed a change.

At the six-month mark I sat down with Johnny and told him I would be moving on, preferably to Arizona. Of course he didn't want me to go but helped by finding me work in Flagstaff, Arizona, which is in the North part of the State.

A job at the Residence Inn (also a Marriott) was set-up for me, with a reference from the manager of the Inn in Saint George. Johnny had seen to that and I'll always be thankful to him for his long and good friendship.

When I arrived in Flagstaff I lived at the Inn for two weeks but soon found an apartment with a swimming pool, and except for the color of their hair, a bunch of Rebecca's! Oh no! Oh yes!

This is not a romance novel but it is non-fiction. The fact is my life got very good at that apartment complex. And then I met Remy in the year 2000 and now she and I have many plans upon my release in early 2004.

Have you had enough of this eye watering stuff? I have. So here's the rest of this chapter in a clamshell.

After my wife Remy came into my life I moved the 150 miles South to Phoenix. Once again the Marriott chain provided employment, this time in Scotttsdale, Arizona. Our life together was just starting out and then the day of reckoning happened!

Driving home from work I was arrested. How did I get caught? Good law enforcement work by the FBI? The ATF? Or how about the U.S. Marshals office? Hell no! It was a five foot two or three, lady cop, one of Phoenix's finest. If it were a male officer I would have shot him dead!

Now please don't laugh, it was just a routine traffic stop. In the course of moving from Nevada to Utah and then to Arizona my license plates had expired. I had forgotten to re-new the stupid tag!

I was carrying a .380 automatic at the time without a permit, so they arrested me. Then using the new instant fingerprint check system, they found out I was wanted by the Marshals.

The female officer called Remy in my presence and said. "Your husband has been arrested and is being held at the Madison Street Jail."

Being an escapee from the U.S. Marshals for three years, there would be no bail this time!

At the jail I was somewhat of a celebrity. It's not everyday that a lady traffic cop arrests an escaped felon, wanted by the U.S. Marshals for over three years. They (jail staff) wanted to gloat over me for at least a few days.

I finally ended up in what is called the "bull pen." There was a payphone in the cell but also about thirty (30) prisoners in an eight (8)-man cell. How could I tell it should be an eight-man cell? That's easy; there were only eight steel bunks.

Sheriff Joe Arpiao prides himself on this shit hole, also called the Maricopa County Jail. He calls himself "the toughest sheriff in America" and his jail the harshest in America. Sorry Joe, it aren't so, have you ever been to Texas?

I spent two days at the stinking, filthy, and over-crowded jail before Remy called the Marshals to please come and get me.

When the Marshals did come for me the first thing I asked was. "Why didn't you guys come for me when these fools put me in here?"

I'll never forget the young and business-like Marshal's answer. "Nobody from the Phoenix Police or the jail staff called to say they had you in custody. Your wife called us only three or four hours ago." Nice going Sheriff Joe, you and your staff get my vote for stupidity and incapableness!

The next stop was the U.S. Court in downtown Phoenix and then on the CCA, a Federal rent-a-jail in Florence, Arizona. I am getting a little ahead in my story, this chapter is over and now starts Part Two, "The Prisons!"

PART TWO

The Prisons

CHAPTER 1

CCA And Privately Owned Prisons

As Chapter 5 ended I was in custody at the U.S. Courthouse in Phoenix. After a quick "Hearing" the judge ordered me held without bail. Gee, I wonder why?

The last time the Feds sentenced me was in August 1980. a mere twenty (20) years ago. In June of 2000, I didn't know that many things about being in Federal prison had changed. Namely, the event of "Privately owned Prisons."

So, two rent-a-cops in ill-fitting uniforms, from CCA (Correctional Centers America) came to collect me from the marshals. Three hours later I was eighty miles South in Florence, Arizona.

I hope you enjoy my short sidebar about Privately Owned Prisons like CCA.

If I had a little money to invest I would buy stock in the wave of the future, privately owned jails and prisons. We inmates refer to them as "rent-a-jails". But if I had a lot of my own money I would build one. These facilities are gold mines in disguise.

However, I think I could get one built from start to finish without using a dime of my own money. Here's my idea and when you get out (I am assuming you are an inmate) you may want to give it a try. Here's my plan.

First, find an area with an extremely high unemployment rate. The inter-cities are always a best bet.

Second, drive around in the area until you find a city block or larger sized property with advanced signs of urban decay.

Third, now my scheme starts to get somewhat involved. Find out who the area's Congressman is. But stay away from Senators they want larger bribes.

From this point on in my scheme you must proceed very carefully because some parts fall within the gray area of the law. But, at least if you get caught and sent back to prison—this time you'll be a "white collar criminal."

Fourth, you will need a mailing address, not a post office box but a real street address. There are many companies that provide this service. "Mailboxes ETC." is my personal recommendation.

Fifth, I assume you already have a mobile phone? If not it's easy to get one it doesn't matter if you have <u>bad</u> credit or <u>no</u> credit. Even your bail jumping ex brother-in-law can get one.

Sixth, ASAP head for a Kinko's and have letterheads, envelopes, and business cards printed while you wait. Be sure to identify yourself as a "real estate developer" on the business cards and stationary.

Seventh, next you'll need the use of a typewriter; the same place that did your printing probably will let you use one. Type a letter to the Congressman who's name and address you found out in step three.

Explain in your letter that you are looking for a site to build a large private jail facility. Inform the politician/crook that you have already visited several properties in his district and would like to meet with him soon.

Once his greedy eyes see "real estate developer" on your letterhead he'll rush a return letter to you.

Do not call after you get the Congressman's letter. I'll bet the farm that on the ninth or tenth day your cell phone will be ringing a lot!

Can you see ahead in my plan?

Eight rent the biggest and most expensive car you can find. A Benz is best but a BMW will do in a pinch.

Ninth, call the would-be-crook and hint that you will be in his area. Ask him if you could have "no more than ten minutes" of his valuable time. Add, "to discuss a site I have in mind." You're now on your way!

Tenth, a few days later drop by the money-minded Congressman's office. At your meeting say something like this. "I represent a group investors who are interested in building a large privately-owned jail facility in your district."

Step back and watch his eyes light up with dollar signs.

That ends my numbered steps. The trap is now sprung! Here's where you get, at the movie says, Other People's Money.

Cut your meeting short saying that you are running late for another meeting. Ask him if you can meet again at the same time next week?

Now turn your cell phone over to your girlfriend or wife. However, you <u>must</u> instruct her in how she is to answer the phone. The word "Investors" should be included in their answer. Try something like, "Hello, F. and J. Realty Investors."

Let the greedy bastard politician stew and do not return his phone calls. But—do show-up at his office the following week. Think positive!

When the deal is completed you will be the sole owner of a brand new rent-a-jail.

My advice is to sell as soon as the first opportunity presents itself.

There isn't much more left to my scam but now comes the most important part of the whole deal. You must convince the Congressman that it is in his best interest to call the Mayor, and get the City to "donate" the land to build your jail on.

The site you looked at in the City was so bad that even the rats have moved out. It's safe bet that the City already owns the property due to tax foreclosures.

We're almost done with my get rich quick scheme. All that remains is to get the property's deed from the City for the legal fee of $1.00.

With the deed in hand approach the real people who build these rent-a-jails.

Offer to sell the land to them real cheap. Stress the fact that both the Congressman and the Mayor have already basically approved your plan to build a jail on the property.

Show them your deed to the property. Tell them you want to sell now due to a cash flow problem with your next project. If you ask a ridiculously low price, let's say about $50,000.00 for a place of land valued at $750,000.00 they'll bite.

My guess is they won't let you out the door before they offer, on the spot to buy "your" land. After all only $50,000.00 for a $750,000.00 building site!

Let's look at the expenses that you incurred using my plan. The cell phone, which you will now <u>keep</u> doesn't count. So this leaves the car rental, the cost of printing the stationary, which you will trash, and the few meals you bought for the bimbo who answered the phone.

It is a safe bet to say that your net profit will be about $49,500.00. You can thank me by sending a check to my publisher or agent ASAP.

After all, I am a fellow convict/author!

Next are the details of my "visit" to CCA, and I'll explain how close it comes to the rent-a-jail in the sidebar.

June 14, 2000 Florence, Arizona.

CCA is a group of concrete buildings south of no place, anywhere. Unlike the imaginary rent-a-jail in the city, CCA is in the middle of the Arizona desert.

After three fun-filled hours on the road the bus turned onto Florence's Main Street, which wasn't as long as my condo's parking lot. Looking out the cracked window all I could see were a few house-trailers and the surrounding hot, dry, and unfertile desert.

That piss poor land was of no use, unless you wanted to build a Privately Owned Prison there. Yes, Florence with its high unemployment rate and abundance of cheap labor fit the exact mode for building a rent-a-jail there.

The more I learned about CCA and Florence, the more convinced I was that my rent-a-jail scheme had been stolen! These bastards had built "my" prison there!

Just outside of CCA's front gate the bus slammed to a stop. The driver shut it down as he and the other guard hurried into their air-conditioned office. Why? Maybe to use the toilet, get a can of cold soda, call their wives, scratch their asses, et cetera.

Remember, it is June in Arizona, as in hot weather time. It was ninety (90) degrees when we left downtown Phoenix. Without the motor and A/C running it was damn hot, and getting hotter in their junk of a bus.

CCA's aging vehicle was at one time a school bus, I guessed that by the bright yellow showing thru their "less expensive" (cheap) brown paint job.

So far nothing I could see about CCA was first class, or even second or third class. Maybe last class would best describe the place.

Even the rent-a-cops weapons looked like second hand shit, possibly bought at their local pawnshops?

Nobody carries six shot revolvers these days, but the CCA staff did. Could you trust a $9.00 an hour "guard" with a sixteen shot automatic pistol? Maybe their boss knew that that's why they only had revolvers?

Our two lummoxes could be seen inside the guard post drinking soda and joking. They were in no hurry to return to the now very hot bus or the cargo of sixteen convicts.

A few of the prisoners were yelling for water and others after the long drive to Florence needed the use of a toilet badly.

I did the only thing an old man with a weak bladder can do. Yes, I pissed on the bus's already filthy floor but I wasn't the only one!

The two guards finally returned to the foul-smelling bus and were greeted with Cheers of: "You f ing assholes!"

Less than a minute later we were herded off the bus and marched to the processing unit.

With our belly chains, leg irons, and handcuffs still on we were forced into a small cell. Even in Sheriff Joe's jail (Madison Street) the "iron" is removed before they toss you in a cell. This was just a preview of the way CCA did things. Ass backwards!

The cell had no benches or bunks to sit on for the fifteen prisoners and me. Nobody said a damn word about standing around with all the "iron" still on. Nobody except? You're correct, me!

Looking over at the boss jackass's desk I said something like. "Hey you stupid bastard when are you going to take this shit off us?"

Wow! Boss jumped off his chair like somebody had shoved a broomstick up his fat ass. Pointing at me he yelled. "Get that old guy out and throw him in the shower!"

I thought to myself. "Does the B.O.P. have more idiots like Boss working in their other rent-a-jails? I hope not!"

The next moron of a guard I came in contact with was very young and had the worst case of acne on his face I ever saw. He ordered loudly. "Stand up asshole and get your ass over to the cell door!"

My reply to Pimple Face would soon become a trademark of sorts for me, one-word answers. "No!" The "no" was loud enough to get the jackass's Boss off his fat ass and over to the cell. He took charge and also ordered me to get-up.

"Listen you fat Jackass I am not going to get up and hop out the door with these handcuffs and leg irons on. If you want me out there take all this shit off first!"

Boss said, "Oh we got us a fucking wise guy here!" Then he told me if I didn't "hop" out of the cell he would get a few more officers and drag me out.

My reply, in keeping with my new trademark of one-word answers was. "So!" The word "so" was not what this fat pompous jackass wanted to hear.

The other prisoners were now cheering me on. Boss was now on the spot but he had two choices. First—he could remove the handcuffs and leg irons from me, or second—sent a goon squad in to drag me out.

To save face he chose the latter. Pimple face and three other semi-retarded guards charged into the cell. Each grabbed a limb and half carried half dragged me over to the shower.

The shower was about three feet by three feet and had bars for a door. Thinking to myself. Hey, getting tossed into a shower wasn't a bad idea, not after sweating like a pig on their bus.

I stayed sitting down as I took off my shoes and socks, then I put my watch and wallet in shoes. I could not remove the rest of my clothing because of the handcuffs and leg irons.

Getting to my feet I reached up and turned the shower on. I waited for the hot water and then took clothes "on" shower.

Try it yourself at home someday. After all aren't you going to wash the clothes you are wearing? But—you can skip the cuffs, belly chains, and leg irons!

Boss and Pimple Face looked over and saw me showering and enjoying myself.

Well, they couldn't have an old man outwit them like that, could they?

The head idiot (Boss) yelled over to me. "You think you're smart don't you? Well asshole you don't run the shit here! I do!"

With the dumb remark he just made I couldn't resist a reply. So—I said. "Yeah, I bet you can run shit better than anyone else. In fact I bet you're full of shit!"

That was the straw that broke the jackass's back! A few seconds later Pimples and the three Malamutes pulled me out of the shower.

No, I didn't turn the water off and yes they did get very wet. That will teach them not to interrupt an old man in a shower.

They put me in a cell all by myself but they did remove all the "iron". I think I won that round because looking across the room I could see the others still in iron!

If these asshole called "officers" could have their way all inmates would stay cuffed 24-7.

More than two hours later, after all the other fifteen prisoners processed, they came for me.

I was issued rent-a-jail clothing, my photo and prints taken, and then led off to a "holding unit".

At first I was celled in their 700 Unit but then moved uptown to the 500 Unit. Compared to where I had been the first few days at CCA their 500 Unit was the lap of luxury.

Now I was in a three-man cell, which had started out as a two-man cell. Most prison systems are housing three prisoners to a cell. A few years back there were only one-man cells!

What happened that caused "prison over-crowding?" The answer is not hard to explain, but at this point in the book it would throw you off the track. But—I have written about that in detail in Part Three.

A three-man cell can be laid out in one of two ways. The newer prisons have all three beds stacked on top of each other. The poor guy who gets the top bed better not roll over too far in his sleep. It's a long drop to the cement floor! I did see that happen at FCI Phoenix.

The older facilities already had bunk beds, so they just added a third bed across from the stacked two. That took away most of the "living space" in the small cell, but did they care?"

My new cell wasn't bad, I only had to share a sink and toilet with two other cellies. That was a hell of a lot better than twelve inmates using one sink and one toilet as in the 700 Unit. Gee, my life just keeps getting better and better!

At the time I had no idea of how long I would be a guest at CCA, so I just relaxed and made of the best of the situation.

Here are a few points about CCA.

Item: The Telephones

There are only three phones for the unit's 110 inmates, great planning by CCA!

Item: Personal Hygiene

CCA issued incoming prisoners only a toothbrush, toothpaste, and a half size comb. No soap, shampoo, deodorant, shave cream or razors. They sold those at their Commissary (inmate's store) at highly inflated prices.

Item: Meals

Here's the good news, at CCA they serve large portions of each meal. Now the bad news, everything tasted like warmed over dog shit.

You must keep in mind that a rent-a-jail is run differently from a State or Federal prison. Remember, they are a business and were built to make a profit for their owners.

CCA is in reality four or five separate companies who run the shit hole on a daily basis.

Correctional Centers America (CCA) built the facility but then contracted with other companies to provide the guard service, medical department, food service, and the highly profitable Commissary.

Our Federal government doesn't run their prisons with the help of four or five companies. They prefer to fuck-up everything themselves!

Because CCA was privately owned they can be sued. Remy and I did so and won! I'll explain that shortly in this chapter.

The guard staff at CCA is a bunch of overweight, under-educated, and just plain dumb "want-to-be's." If you speak in three or four letter words they'll understand you. Talk to any of them for two minutes and you'll know exactly what I mean.

Having been a guest of the Federal government on other occasions, I had a good idea of how a prison should work, or in CCA's case, doesn't work. Most of their officers would be better off working at a car wash, flipping burgers, or as a bag boy in a grocery store.

These dummies did so many things ass backwards that I could write a whole book on just them! But—I'll spare you and start on:

June 17, 2002 at 11:00 PM

A lisping female guard banged on the cell door and said: "Tucci roll it up you're thipping (shipping) out on the air-lift. Tho (So) I'll be back to get you in five minutes."

There wasn't anything to roll-up! I had been at CCA only a short time and the cheap bastards had issued me only one (1) or none of everything! I said my good byes to my Mexican cellies and waited for the rent-a-cop's return.

The lisper thoon (soon) returned after she collected two other inmates from the unit. We were then handcuffed and pushed out into the hallway to wait, and wait, and wait.

Eventually a large group of prisoners came marching towards us. I assumed they were also on the airlift, but I was wrong. Some of them had Court dates, a few were being transferred to different facilities, but most of us were for Con Air's blue and silver 737.

Here's a question for the "powers to be" at CCA. Why did their jackasses drag inmates out of their cells at 11:00 PM for a 10:00 AM Court date? I didn't know it at the time but my flight would not leave Phoenix until 2:00 PM the next day, fifteen hours later!

CCA's guard staff was truly ass backwards. In fact I wonder if CCA is short for "Classic Comedy Assholes?" You'll soon agree as you read on!

The next thing up was their strip search. Yes, the old bend and pull my ass checks apart routine. I consider these searches the most degrading of all things that I was forced to do while in prison.

These strip searched can be, and are many times done with female staff present! If you are of the Muslim faith this is an insult to your beliefs.

Some of the less civilized inmates enjoyed spreading their asses open so that the female officer could gaze at their assholes. What kind of a woman would take a job knowing that she had to look into men's asses?

With the asshole checks out of the way we were stuffed back into the small holding cell, wearing only our underwear! Also lovely was the one exposed toiled for the forty-four of us!

At 1:00 AM, four inmates at a time, we were led to the showers and then issued Federal travel clothing. Which was a tan pull over shirt, tan pants with an elastic waistband and ($1.50 a pair) blue slip-on sneakers made in China.

Why do the sneakers they handed me come from China when I am in a U.S. prison? That's a fair question. Please ask Bill Clinton for an answer.

With the above done we were again returned to the small holding cell.

At 5:00 AM, dawn comes to Arizona and so did a "bag-of-breakfast." A well balanced and nourishing meal of two hard-boiled eggs, a bruised apple and a box of outdated low-fat milk.

By George, now I see the light! That breakfast at CCA was training for a "Lock Down", which the B.O.P. does almost at the drop of a hat. You'll read more about those later in this part of the book.

It is now 7:00 AM. A full eight hours since I left the 500 Unit. The cell is now dirty and stinking badly.

Dirty from the eggshells, apple cords, and smashed milk cartons that are scattered around the cement floor. Stinking because almost everybody has "gas" from the hard-boiled eggs.

At 7:45 AM my personal property is returned, just the usual things a man carries. A wristwatch, keys, wallet and my wedding ring. But less than five minutes later I had to return everything to a second guard.

Smiling politely she asked. "Hey pal where do you want me to mail your shit?" I filled out her form with my wife's name and address in Phoenix.

Although Phoenix is only seventy-five miles north of the rent-a-jail, it would be months before my things reached home. In fact Remy had to write CCA three times via Certified Mail, her last letter was a demand prior to suing them in Small Claims Court.

The day before she was to file the suit my property arrived. Remy says God had a hand at that. I say CCA didn't want to pay $3,000.00 for "lost" property.

Unlike the B.O.P., CCA is a private Corporation which can be, and should be, sued whenever possible!

Doesn't the time fly by when you are having fun? It is now 9:00 AM. One by one were taken from the cell to be "chained" for the trip. The handcuffs, leg irons, and belly chains were applied assembly line fashion.

Guess what? After being chained it was back to the filthy cell again! How many times had I been in and out of that cell? Frankly, in all the excitement I lost count.

It is now 10:00 AM and almost everyone is starting to lie down on the floor to rest or sleep. We had been in that cell for close to twelve hours and most of us were on edge!

Then from the back part of the jail someone yelled the one word we all wanted to hear. "Bus!"

The drive to Sky Harbor Airport took only ninety minutes and I still wonder why they started to get us ready at 11:00 PM the night before? As I said early on in this chapter CCA did everything ass backwards!

When the bus finally got to the airport the stupid driver and his dumber helper took us to the main terminal! Where they looking for a sign that said "Con-Air?"

Let's use your head for a New York minute. If you were driving a bus with forty-three convicts and me, would you drive to the main terminal at any airport? Of course not! But our two rent-a-cops did.

Thank God or whoever invented the cell phone, at least one of these mental midgets was smart enough to call the Marshals for directions.

No vehicle is allowed to stop or park in front of the airport's terminal, and the air-port police did their job by keeping the jail bus moving until we cleared the facility.

Would you believe that when the driver found the Con-Air area the plane had not yet arrived?

The following is not pleasant. It is late afternoon and the temperature is 106 accord-ing to the large time and temperature signs atop the Arizona Republic building.

We are still on the bus, which has no air conditioning, even with all the windows open it is still over a hundred degrees inside.

The bus has no toilet! Some of the prisoners are now hungry and asking for food. I guess the nourishing breakfast didn't fill them up? Others are asking for water, including me.

CCA did not provide us with food or even bottled water. My guess was they were thinking more about their profit margin than our welfare. If any official from CCA is reading this, feel free to sue me for damages. See you in Court?

The plain, the plain, a little humor there. After fifteen hours of waiting the plane was an old 737, with seats for 150 cons and a Marshal's Air Service Crew of eight or ten.

Everything the Marshals did was slow but correct. We were called off the bus in alphabetical order. My last name starts with a T so I was second to the last off the hot bus.

Getting off the bus I tripped and slid down on to the runway. My leg chain had caught somewhere on the bus's stairs. A Marshal yelled out "Doctor over here quick!"

Con Air is prepared for these kind of emergencies and within seconds a nurse and the doctor were at my side. The doctor asked. "What's wrong Pop?" (When you're old they call you Pop). My one word answer was. "Water!"

The doc said I was dehydrated and gave me water and three or four salt pills. I was carried onto the plane with an I.V. in my arm. Next stop Oklahoma!

Hopefully you will never be sent to CCA in Florence, Arizona or driven to the airport by Dumb or Dumber. After all, for the $9.00 per hour these want-a-be's are paid what did I expect?

That was my true experience. Now let's see what the FTC (Federal Transfer Center) in Oklahoma City, Oklahoma is like. Maybe the over crowding and stupidity are a part of what lies ahead when I start doing my Federal time?

CHAPTER 2

The Federal Transfer Center

After I was captured in Arizona, the Feds had to return me all the way back to the East Coast for trial.

With the nightmarish <u>CCA</u> behind me, a long, long 6000 miles journey lie ahead. Its first stop would be the FTC at 7420 Macarthur Boulevard in Oklahoma City, Oklahoma.

I consider myself very lucky to have flown non-stop from Phoenix to the FTC on Con-Air. Can you imagine <u>a 1,009</u>-mile trip on <u>CCA</u>'s half-dead bus? Or worst yet, Dumb and Dumber as the drivers?

A little humor just came back to my mind. I didn't know it that June (2000) but I would become a frequent flyer and use the M.A.S. (Marshals Air Service) <u>five</u> times!

Most of the crew got to know me on sight and whenever I boarded the 737 they would ask. "Would you like your usual seat Mr. Tucci?"

Can you guess where my "usual" seat was? Why right next to the toilet, where else would you put an old man with a cane?

Now back to the travelogue.

The old plane had 130 convicts on board, including a dozen female prisoners in the first few front rows. Yes, the "ladies" also had on handcuffs, belly chains, leg-irons, and were dressed in stylish prison travel outfits.

It was plain to see the most of these women were not wearing bras! Their own personal choice? Or was it another of the B.O.P.'s cost saving ideas?

Putting that aside, as a Muslim I felt sorry for these "sisters" because the plane's two toilets had no doors. No doubt for security reasons?

Every time an officer led one of these downcast women towards the toilets the men cheered! Why? They were hoping to catch a glimpse of the female's ass as she pulled her pants down to pee. Remember, there were no doors on the toilets!

Back now to being serious. The Feds were sending me back to Connecticut, to the same Judge and Prosecutor that I jumped bail on three years back. I hope they didn't take it personal?

Our 737 put down on the FTC's own airfield, unlike Phoenix were we left from a city airport. There was no deplaning onto waiting busses or vans.

Very slowly the jet taxied to a long ramp that led directly into the facility. Glancing out the window I guessed the building to be eight or nine stories high.

The Marshals always unload their prisoners starting at the rear of the plane. That meant I would be the first one off. There were no stairs to climb up or down so I easily made it into the building.

When the last of the male prisoners were lined-up in the narrow hallway the ladies were escorted off the plane.

We were then all marched down a long dark corridor for iron removal. Ladies first of course.

At <u>CCA</u> I walked around with handcuffs, belly chains, and leg-irons on for more than one hour! But here the B.O.P. officers and U.S. Marshals had the "iron" off all 130 of us in less than fifteen minutes.

Here's how it was accomplished. First, we were formed into four lines. At the head of each line an officer would remove the cuffs and belly chains, dropping them into boxes on the floor.

Next was a short waddle over to a raised platform, which was about two feet off the floor and twenty feet long.

There were ten or twelve officers on both sides of the platform seated in swivel chairs. I am sure Henry Ford would be proud of the way the B.O.P. is using his "assembly line" idea.

The inmates climbed up the ramp and walked to the end of the platform, followed by the next inmate, and the next, until each guard had a prisoner to "work" on.

Each officer unlocked the leg-iron on his side of the inmate and they took turns tossing the irons into the nearby large boxes.

With their "irons" off first, our ladies left us for their floor in this coed prison. Good luck girls!

Very shortly we were in a large holding cell, which did have benches. CCA officials please note that!

Now the bullshit that would occur each and every time I arrived at a B.O.P. facility started. It was always in the same damn order. Here it is.

First, there were four (4) forms to fill out. Then interviews with the medical staff (some of them <u>even</u> <u>spoke</u> <u>English</u>), followed by a prison ID photo, fingerprinting and ending with a bedroll and clothing issue.

Never, no where in the entire Federal prison system was I allowed to shower before having to put on their clean but used clothing. It is very offensive to me as a Muslim having to dress a dirty body in clean clothing.

That first day ended at 7:30 PM with a "gag in a bag" (sack meal) and a quarters assignment.

A fast elevator ride took me to the seventh floor where I got my first inside look at a real Federal Bureau of Prisons facility.

Somewhere a hidden Genie buzzed the door open and a short female guard appeared. The escorting officer handed Shorty my ID photo and paperwork.

Shorty said, "Yea al cum tess whey plez." I think she said, "You all come this way please?" Welcome to Oklahoma, Frank!

Because of my age (61) and medical problems (heart), Shorty assigned me a cell on the lower tier and a bottom bunk.

Entering the cell I was surprised it had only two beds, unlike CCA where they crowded three prisoners into a two-man cell. There can be little doubt that CCA did everything with the profit margin in mind.

I dropped my bundle on the bunk and pulled it open. Let's see, what have the Feds provided me with?

A blanket, two sheets, a pillow case, wash cloth, two towels, and hygiene items of toothpaste and brush, deodorant, soap, shampoo, and a half size comb.

I grabbed the soap, shampoo, and a well-worn towel and looked for the shower. The water was hot and relaxing, it would be a long shower.

Back in the cell I laid down to sort things out in my head.

wondered who my cellie was? From down the hall I could hear the officer locking cells. It was 9:00 PM, which is when FTC locks prisoners in for the night.

A tall figure entered and the guard locked the cell. My cellie was an Indian, or to be politically correct, a Native American. However, in the prison system all Indians are called "Chiefs."

Leon, yes an Indian named Leon, gave me a run down of the facility. Here is a thumbnail sketch of what to expect if you happen to land there:

1. Cells are unlocked at 5:00 AM
2. Showers are open from 5:00 AM till 8:45 PM
3. Breakfast is at 5:30 AM
4. "Sick call" is a 6:00 AM, seven days a week
5. Telephones are turned on at 6:00 AM
6. Lunch is early, 10:30 AM
7. "Pill-line" is at 11:30 AM, everyday
8. Supper is very early, 3:330 PM daily
9. There are paperback books to read
10. Checkers, chess, cards, and board games are available
11. Clean clothing exchanges are on Monday, Wednesday, and Friday
12. Sheets, blankets and towels are exchange on Tuesday and Thursday.

The Bureau of Prisons reserves the right to change any of these items and services without notice! That's for sure.

After Leon's run down, I called it a night and tried to sleep. That didn't happen!

The FTC is not a "prison" per se and has only one function, to transfer it's guests ASAP. What hotel could do that and stay in business?

From Oklahoma you will be sent to the prison or contract facility closest to the U.S. Court having jurisdiction over your case.

After sentencing you might make a return trip to the FTC as I did. Sometimes I even get lucky.

My attorney asked U.S. Judge Peter C. Dorsey to recommend that my sentence be served in Phoenix. Arizona. The Judge agreed, but I am getting a little ahead in my story.

So—back to the FTC. AT 6:05 AM the next morning I headed to the phone area. My wife Remy didn't know that I had been shuttled off to Oklahoma. I wanted to let her know where I was and that I was one step closer to my trial.

Damn! All six telephones were dead! I went over to the unit's officer and asked. "Why are the phones off, aren't they supposed to be turned on at 6:00 AM?"

He explained that a plane (Con-Air) just took off and for security reasons, they shut the phones down. With today's terrorists having shoulder held missiles I can understand the Feds concerns.

Later that afternoon, Remy and I had a tearful conversation. My third day in paradise was the <u>Fourth of July</u>.

A large holiday meal of sorts was served at lunch time. Hot dogs, hamburgers, beans, coleslaw, potato salad, watermelon, ice cream, and the B.O.P's generic Kool Aid to wash it all down.

Sleep came easy that night with an over-stuffed stomach. But—at 2:00 AM the cell door banged open and the guard asked, "Which one of you is_____?" That was Leon's last name! He was leaving.

A few hours later the officer was back. "Tucci get ready you're leaving, strip the bed and toss everything into the bins down the hallway."

Well that told me two thing. First, the M.A.S. had more than one plane, because Leon had left at 2:00 AM. Second, Remy wouldn't know where I was again!

Everything that was done upon entering the center was now done in reverse, <u>except</u> there was no paperwork to fill-out. Thanks Allah for small wonders!

The checkout started with the B.O.P's always-popular strip search, including the spread your ass apart routine. Next came an issue of travel clothing and then into a holding cell with thirty others to hurry-up and wait!

All that remained now was to have the "iron" put on and the boarding of the nearby jet.

Soon we were told. "Six of you at a time come to the door." Yes, it was time for the handcuffs, belly chins, and leg-irons.

Here's a tip for you. Never rush out the door to have "iron" put on. Why you ask? Because you and your "iron" will seat in the next cell until the last prisoner is also in chains.

If you are last, as I was that day, they will cuff you and march you directly to the waiting plane.

The choice is a no-brainer, sit around with chains on for an hour or be <u>last</u> to get cuffed and be first on their 737.

So ended my stay at the FTC in Oklahoma. My next stop? I hadn't a clue where the Feds were flying me.

CHAPTER 3

Atlanta, United States Penitentiary

There were four of us in the last group to be handcuffed, belly chained, and leg-ironed. I had the honor of being the first inmate on Con-Air's express. Some honor?

The Marshals again seated me next to the toilets, which turned out not to be such a good location. Why? The smell would gag a maggot!

Suddenly the old jet began to move slowly down the long airstrip steadily picking-up speed. The B.O.P.'s ace pilot used every damn foot of the runway before getting us airborne.

Being a pilot of sorts myself, his take-off scared the daylights out of me. But, I am sure the officer knew "his" plane better than I did.

I looked around at the 737's aged floor and walls. The interior décor's color hinted that at one time the plane had been the property of American Airlines. But I wouldn't get any Frequent Flyer Miles this time!

Today's flight did not have any female prisoners on board. Why not? When the plane landed I would have the answer to that question.

I asked every Marshal that came near my seat. "Where are we flying to?" I got no answers, only. "Don't worry old man we'll be there soon enough." "Thanks for nothing." I thought to myself.

At first the jet was flying due east and later the pilot changed course to a Southly heading. That wasn't all that hard to figure-out. I just looked out the window and remembered, the sun rises in the East and sets in the West.

An hour or so into the flight a "piss break" was called. Here's how the officers run that.

Starting at the front of the plane, one row at a time (four inmates) were asked by Archie (the head Marshal). "Do you need to use the bathroom?" I think using the word <u>bathroom</u> in this situation is stupid—by both the Marshals and the prisoners who answered. "Yes, I have to use the bathroom."

The American Heritage Dictionary defines bathroom as: "A room equipped with a bathtub or shower and a sink and toilet." Just calling it what it is, I answered. "Yes, I need to use the toilet."

With only two toilets and over a 120 inmates on board, a "piss break" took quite a long time. Being at the back of the plane I was last. I almost didn't make it!

Try to picture this in your mind? You're a prisoner waddling down the aisle, with leg-irons and belly chains on, as the plane bounces all over the sky. Reaching the toilet you are now ready for your next challenge.

The elastic waist pants the B.O.P. issued you have <u>no</u> fly front. So you'll have to pull the pants down and your penis <u>up</u> and out of the boxer shorts to pee. Doesn't sound hard to do? Yeah, but try it with handcuffs on!

There was <u>no</u> soap or paper towels provided, and the water faucets were shut off. Worst yet, there was no toilet paper. What did female prisoners do to clean themselves?

Not being able to wash after using the toilet is offensive to a Muslim, male or female!

Back in my seat and looking out the window all I could see below was water. Where the hell are we? Calm down and think. Okay, we are headed south and there is a large body of water between Texas and Florida!

Ten minutes later we were over land as we came out of the clouds. The pilot yo-yoed the jet many times before getting us on the ground in Miami.

About half of the inmates deplaned and were led to waiting busses and vans. No Florida prisoners came on board so we were able to leave after a very short time.

Again airborne the plane headed north. I could not get an answer as to where we were headed next. But—I soon found out that "next" was last!

I woke up as the old jet bounced along the runway and with screeching tires came to a halt. Yes, the B.O.P. hires nothing but the best-qualified pilots? Yeah sure they do!

The dying plane slowed down to almost a stop and turned off the main runway. Now, I found out where we were. "Welcome to Atlanta, Georgia!", the brightly colored billboard advertised.

What the hell am I doing in Georgia? Wasn't I supposed to be sent back to Connecticut? Was I in Georgia because someone made a mistake? All of the flight's prisoners were taken off Con-Air and put on the B.O.P.'s Greyhound style bus. Where was I going?

The drive from Atlanta's beautiful and clean airport took us into the decayed and dirtiest part of the city.

I looked at the burnt-out buildings, boarded up houses, garbage all over the streets, and abandoned cars in various stages of being stripped. It reminded me of Bronx in New York.

A road sign said "Atlanta, USP 2 miles". Well that sure solves the problem of where I was going!

The bus pulled into the penitentiary's yard and you could tell you were in redneck country! The parking lot was full of pick-up trucks, most of them with gun-racks across the back windows.

A large sign came into view, it read. "Welcome to USP Atlanta," that had to be somebody's idea of a sick joke. How can someone be welcomed at a USP?

Our Greyhound stopped in front of a high overhead garage door and as the driver spoke into his radio the door crept upward. It was a long and narrow garage with a door at the other end so the bus could drive thru.

There was <u>no</u> order getting off the bus as the driver's assistant yelled out. "Everybody get up and off this here f—king bus!" I was last off.

Before we left the garage area the bus's officers removed our handcuffs, belly chains, and leg-irons.

Let's again look back at CCA. A Federal Penitentiary is where the badest of the bad are sent. Yet the three guards stood isolated from the rest of the prison as they removed the above.

Remember, at CCA on arrival, before my "shower", the two hours in chains? Or the hour and a half of being cuffed before leaving on their bus?

The whole guard staff at CCA was nothing but a bunch of woozies and they were afraid of any inmate not in handcuffs!

After being de-ironed we were led deeper into the century old prison. What would be done next to welcome us?

Food! Everyone was given two Oscar Mayer cold food trays and a box of skim milk. The trays had baloney, cheese, crackers, and a candy bar. Much better than CCA's "bag of breakfast" garbage.

With Oscar's and milk in hand we were put in a huge room, not a cell, with floor to ceiling windows. A good view of USP Atlanta could be seen from our vantage point.

Here's an example of the B.O.P.'s organization, or lack there of. It was 2:00 PM when our cold trays were handed out. Now at 3:00 PM we were marched back into the prison's main area for hot food.

The hot food line served the resident inmates first, and they took their food back to their cells to eat. There were no tables or chairs and no dining room. So—our meal was eaten sitting on a dirty floor!

What follows next the public will never hear about except in books like this humble author's.

All U.S.P.'s have only two men in a cell, not like CCA's stuffing of a third bed and a third inmate into a cell!

The airlift inmates and I were in transit to other facilities. But, because Atlanta was a USP we had to be locked in a cell overnight.

Over-crowding had already filled every cell in the unit but the B.O.P. solved the problem of what to do with forty extra prisoners!

"Okay listen-up!" Shouted a tall good old boy officer. "You all have to be in a cell so follow me."

We were now far into the main part of this monster of a place, each unit was three tiers high. Here is where the sentenced inmates are housed.

"Everybody make a f-'ing line here and get yourself a bed roll, after that go through that door over there." Pointed the officer.

On the other side of the door we were told. "You all will need a mattress for the night." With that said an inmate orderly started tossing mattresses off the third tier down to us.

One of the "brothers" asked the guard if he could, "help the old man (me) with the mattress.

So—I had a bedroll and a torn mattress, what's next? I was pushed into a cell with two of the prison's permanent residents. Where was I going to put my mattress? Did you expect one of my cellies to offer me his bed?

Atlanta is one of the oldest, if not the oldest, prison in whole B.O.P.'s chain. It's cells are smaller than the newer facilities and there is no A/C, add to that, no panic buttons in the cells in case of a medical emergency.

With my mattress laid out on the floor my head was only a few inches from the foul smelling toilet bowl. Not a very pleasant picture, an old man lying on a soiled mattress, on a filthy floor, facing a dirty toilet bowl!

At sometime during the night one of my cellie got up to use the toilet. When he flushed it was like a bass drum being banged next to my head!

I folded-up my mattress and for the rest of the night I sat up against the wall. I'll sleep some other time. I didn't know it when they locked me in the cell but I would be leaving at 4:30 AM the next morning. All praise be to Allah!

"Tucci?" The door banged open. "Grab your stuff and pull that mattress out here. You're leaving!" Said the female officer as she double-checked her list.

Soon a re-run of old events followed. The strip search, an issue of travel clothes, and the popular "bag of breakfast."

Here's a change—we were marched to the bus area without chains, only with handcuffs on! Before each inmate stepped on to the bus belly chains and leg-irons were quickly applied. Can you possibly guess who was last to get on the bus?

Once we were back at the airport the U.S. Marshals again took charge of us in their orderly manner. We were called off the bus by name, and I was last.

"Would you like your usual seat old man?" Asked Archie. For a second time there were no female prisoners on board. Maybe the B.O.P. put them on a bus instead?

There were no empty seats on the old jet and I wondered where I was going to end-up this time? After taking off the pilot headed the plane north up the east coast, to Connecticut I hoped.

Our first landing was in New Jersey and in that State the B.O.P. has FCI Fairton, Fairton-Camp (low security), FCI Fort Dix and Fort Dix Camp.

The next stop was in New York there the B.O.P.'s facilities are Brooklyn MDC, New York MCC, FCI Otisville, Otisville Camp and FCI Ray Brook. Maybe Connecticut would be the next stop?

No such luck, the plane put down in Manchester, New Hampshire! Paul (One of the Marshals) told me. "Old man Tucci this is where you get off."

When I reached the door I asked Archie. "Can I please see your off list, this has to be a mistake." But—I wasn't that lucky, my name was there. "Tucci, Francis Mario # 03836-014 to Manchester, New Hampshire."

Two of the air crew helped me down the plane's stairs, which were in the rear just under the rudder.

When we left Georgia it was eighty (80) degrees, coming down from the plane the cold forty-five (45) degree air of New Hampshire almost stopped me in my tracks. The Feds did not issue a coat or jacket for airlift inmates.

It was cold with the short-sleeved vee-neck tee shirt and the lightweight pants USP Atlanta had given us.

"Tucci walk over to that blue van and the <u>Wyatt</u> Officers will take care of you." That was a lie! I was the only prisoner that got off the 737 but after five or so minutes I was still left standing outside the van in the cold.

So—I did the "old falling down routine." During all my B.O.P. travels, I have <u>faked</u> so many illnesses and other medical problems that my dear wife believed I was really ill! But in her language. "Wala ako'y sakit!"

Take notes, because the following always works for me!

Shivering, I took a few steps forward and fell against the van's hood and let myself slid down to the pavement. Within seconds both officers were out of the van and asking.

"What's the matter old man? Are you going to be okay?" I answered. "It must be the cold air that got me dizzy, it was eighty when I left Atlanta."

If there is a doctor reading this, is it medically possible to pass-out from the cold?

One of the bozos brought me a blanket from the van and after a few minutes I was in their warm van.

It was getting confusing! The plane landed in New Hampshire, the van I was riding in had Rhode Island license plates and my case was in Connecticut?

The two guards had very sharp uniforms and weapons not like <u>CCA's</u> ragamuffins. Their shoulder patches said Wyatt Detention Center and so I asked. "Where is Wyatt City?"

That brought a chuckle from both of them as the younger officer replied. "Wyatt isn't a city it's a detention center in the town of Central Falls, Rhode Island."

Two and a half hours later I was in Central Falls and that's Chapter 4.

CHAPTER 4

Wyatt Center

My day now got worst as the short and balding rent-a-cop remarked. "Wyatt is a privately owned facility and it's not all that bad." Yes, this old man was headed to another damn rent-a-jail. Shades of CCA? God I hope not!

Driving from the Manchester, New Hampshire Airport to Wyatt's location in Center Falls, Rhode Island the van passed by hundreds of chicken coops. Poultry farming is a big business in the State of Rhode Island.

Even with my eyes closed and all the van's windows rolled-up I could smell and tell we were now deep in "Chicken Country".

Entering Center Falls reminded me of the rundown area around USP Atlanta. It had the same dead landscape of burnt down buildings, boarded-up houses, junked cars, and garbage piled all over the place.

Well Frank, were the hell did you expect to find a jail? In the best part of the town? The truth is although Mr. And Mrs. Joe Six-Pack want more jails and prisons; but they don't want them in their neighborhoods.

Wyatt Center is a carbon copy of the make-believe rent-a-jail in Chapter 1. Both are located inter-city, both are in an area of high unemployment, and both have an abundance of cheap labor to hire from.

Beep, beep, beep, Baldly sounded the new van's horn and the overhead garage door slowly went up. Once inside they politely helped me out of the vehicle and removed the handcuffs, belly chains, and leg-irons.

It was quickly beginning to look like CCA was the only joint where the guard staff enjoyed keeping prisoners in chains for extended period of time.

That day I was Wyatt's only incoming bad guy. A short Hispanic looking female (she was Portuguese) with the longest ponytail I ever saw, brought me a tray of good smelling hot food.

Soon she came back for my now licked clean empty tray and smiled. "Our medic will be in to check you and when he is done I'll finish processing you in."

Wyatt's medic turned out to be tall, black and very "gay looking". He had my B.O.P. travel medications with him and he asked. "Besides these here pills is there anything else you need?"

"Yes, my cane. It was taken when they put me in the cell." I answered him. He then replied with female mannerisms. "After she does your paperwork come to Medical and I'll have your cane for you."

I now had my security blanket back, Nitro pills, which always come in a <u>glass</u> bottle. Two days later the stupidity by a rent-a-cop, about the <u>glass</u> bottle almost cost my life! I'll explain that in detail shortly.

Ms. Ponytail came back, unlocked the cell and motioned. "Please take a seat out here, I'll be back in just a few minutes."

Wyatt's R&D area turned out to be the only one of it's kind, that I would see in all of my travel. It was a large room with rows of movie theater type chairs. A long low counter with computers on it ran across the whole front of the room.

Author's note:

Wyatt Center is a small facility that houses about 300 prisoners of the Federal Government from the States of Connecticut, Massachusetts, and Rhode Island. All of it's inmates were awaiting trial as I was.

Ponytail returned and called me up to the counter. "Mr. Tucci I have assigned you to a lower bunk in the A-Unit, which is right next to our Hospital Unit."

Next to the Hospital? Did I look ill or something? Later I found out from the "gay" medic, that the van officers had written a report about me falling down. Covering their own backsides no doubt? But, thanks anyway guys.

"Now let's go get your bedding and clothing issue." I followed her along the counter until we came to doors on both sides of it. Ponytail unlocked the door on her side and buzzed open the one on my side.

Unlike CCA, where I was issued only one of everything, Wyatt gave me two of everything! Praise to Allah! Best of all there were hygiene products like soap, shampoo, deodorant, toothpaste, etc., etc. The bedding issue included a pillow, not like some other (CCA) places we know.

When we were done she helped me carry some of my things to the A-Unit. Wow! The A-Unit was a dorm, no cells! For the first time since being re-arrested I would not be sleeping in a cell.

The dorm had twenty-six double bunk (for 52 inmates) and there were seven empty beds! What, no over-crowding here? Wyatt started to look semi-normal as compared to CCA. But, it was still like comparing garbage to horse dung. Don't they both stink?

All in all Wyatt wasn't bad, but being in a small town it's hiring policy was mostly political. It was not uncommon to see four or five nametags with the same last name on most shifts.

Here's a quick look at Wyatt:

1. Unit-A is the only dorm area all other areas have cells.
2. There is outside recreation three times everyday.
3. Paperback books are available from a library of sorts on Monday, Wednesday, and Fridays.
4. The showers are open from 7:00 AM to 10:00 PM.
5. Their food is noticeably better than most other rent-a-jails.
6. The Commissary (inmates store) is delivered to the units.

7. There are 4 telephones for only 52 prisoners, but at CCA there were 120 inmates and 3 phones.
8. Clothing laundry service is every other weekday.
9. Sheets and blankets are exchanged on Thursday.
10. Sick Call is seven days a week at 8:00 AM.

But since July of 2000, when I was a guest at Wyatt, things may have changed. For the better or worst?

On Saturday the officer found me taking a nap and asked. "Are you Tucci? You have a visitor, get dressed and let me know when you're ready to leave."

Who could be visiting me here? Oh well, I'll find out soon enough. I reported to the visiting room and there it's officer said. "Your attorney is in number three", as he pointed at the small cubicle.

As I approached the room the door was open and I was very surprised to see Attorney Weinberger (the Government's parrot) from Part One. Why the hell was he here? But, it got even worst ten days later with the same judge (Peter C. Dorsey) and the same U.S. Attorney. It was pain from the past!

"Mr. San Tuccio (Weinberger used my true name from the original arrest file) your case will be heard on July 19th, I hope you had a nice vacation! How dare you skip out on our court date? "Weinberger rattled off in rapid speech. His visit lasted no longer than five minutes.

Maybe his pride was hurt because I didn't let the Feds lock me up three years back? But—I at least had those three fun filled years to remember!

Let's look back three years and do the math. I was sixty (60) years old and Attorney Weinberger had said, "There is a good possibility that you could get a fifteen year sentence."

What do you think my chances of living to be seventy-five (75) in a Federal Prison would be? Answer: Slim to none.

My trial was only ten days away, set down for July 19, 2002, however the original arrest went way back to late in 1997. My "re-arrest" was on June 11, 2000.

Was it express justice? Within just five weeks of my rearrested I was headed to court for trial. There were many inmates at Wyatt who had been waiting months, and sometimes years, to have their day in court. Maybe by jumping bail and being on the loose for three years gave my case a priority?

There is one incident that happened at Wyatt that I think is important enough to write about. As always, please remember that the book is non-fiction.

On my return from the library to the unit an officer stopped me for a pat down (hands on search). What resulted was as dumb as it gets, even dumber than at CCA.

The rent-a-cop touched my shirt pocket and asked. "What's in the pocket old man?" I showed him my bottle of Nitro pills and he confiscated them by saying. "You can't have a glass bottle in here no matter how small it is."

Excuse me what did he say? The Federal label (from the FTC) said. "Inmate may C.O.P. (Carry On Person) at all times." Although my Nitro pills were returned quickly they were now in a small paper envelope! What's wrong with this picture?

Well for starters the factory Warning Label says. "Do not remove pills from original bottle." At the time I wasn't thinking and just put the envelope back in my shirt pocket.

Two days later I started having chest pains and reached for my Nitroglycerin. But—all the pills had melted together into a solid lump!

I asked one of the "brothers" to help me to my bed and to get the guard fast. To the officer I said. "I am having bad chest pains and my Nitro is not usable!" I then handed him the envelope with the glob of pills.

The young officer said. "Stay calm, don't move, I'll be right back with some Nitro pills!" His sister was the nurse on the shift, thank God. Remember I wrote about many members of the same family working together here.

In two or three minutes the guard and a nurse (his sister) were at my bed with a bottle of Nitro pills. I took two and laid back to rest.

The next day I called Remy and asked her to write a thank you note to the unselfish officer. However, he was reprimanded by the lieutenant for leaving his unit post unguarded! Yes, he deserted his post, to run to the Hospital Unit (right next door) for the nurse and the Nitro pills.

But the officer just might have saved my life! Does security come first? There is an old saying that cover his action. "No good deed goes un-punished!" What do you think about that?

Slowly the week passed one day at a time. I called my wife in Arizona very few times because of the cost ($14.00 for the fifteen minutes).

Did you know that the B.O.P. and your local telephone company have a sweet heart deal? Did you know also that a collect call from prison has a Correctional Facility Surcharge of $6.00 or $8.00 added to the bill?

That same $14.00 call made on our cell phone would have cost Remy and I only $1.05! At only seven cents a minute! Yes, everything is part of your punishment.

It was now Court day and in the back of my mind was the thought of spending fifteen years in a Federal Prison. Not a very pleasant thought.

At 6:30 AM before breakfast was delivered to the unit, I asked the sleepy rent-a-cop. "I am suppose to be in Court at New Haven today, did you guys forget?" I liked his answer, which was. "No, Mr. Tucci it's too early to leave yet. The day watch (first shift) comes in at 8:00 AM and they do the Court transports."

CCA management take notes from the next two paragraphs!

The night before Court I was not taken from my cell at 11:00 PM, twelve (12) hours before leaving the facility. I was not tossed into a small cell with forty (40) other inmates. I was not put in and left in chains for an hour before getting on the bus! And lastly I was <u>not</u> given a bag of sh__t for breakfast.

All of the above, as you remember from reading Chapter 1, were done at CCA in Florence, Arizona.

<u>Wyatt</u> instead served a hot breakfast of pancakes and eggs after which I returned to my bed to nap, wait, and pray. At 8:05AM the female day shift officer Said. "Get up old man and report to the R and D."

A short walk and a quick right hand turn and I was there (R&D). Now what? I noticed three other inmates seated in the room's comfortable chairs. Not in a cell or in chains like that other (CCA) rent-a-jail.

"When I call your name come up here." Yelled Ponytail from behind the counter. She then checked her inmate photos to make sure she had the right prisoner.

Two guards came around the counter and asked me. "Tucci are you ready to leave? Make sure you use the toilet because we can't stop on the way."

Yes, I used the toilet and reported back to them to have handcuffs and belly chains slapped on, but no leg irons. All praise to Allah!

The scenic drive from Rhode Island to New Haven, Connecticut would take about an hour and a half. I was the rent-a-cops only prisoner that morning, but from the Court one other inmate would be going back to Wyatt with us.

During the trip I looked out the windows remembering the towns and cities as we drove pass them. All too quickly we arrived in New Haven and the van entered the Court's underground garage.

The rent-a-cops turned me over to the U.S. Marshals who were waiting there. The Marshals were a "salt and pepper" team. Salt had the handcuffs and chains off me even before the Wyatt's had their paperwork signed.

Pepper spoke first. "Your case Mr. Tucci is on the late afternoon docket (after 2:00 PM) and your attorney is waiting upstairs to see you."

Salt asked. "I will be bringing lunch around shortly is there anything you can't eat?" Pepper rode up in the elevator with me and escorted me to the visiting room and Mr. Weinberger.

He was sitting there stiff as a wire coat hanger on the other side of the Plexiglas wall. Weinberger spoke loudly and drummed the table. "May I suggest that you plead guilty and put this long over due mess to rest!" I snapped right back with a one word reply. "Why?"

Weinberger was getting a little red in the face and answered me snobbishly. "Because I am still your attorney of record and the Judge is pissed-off about your blowing out on him for three years. In fact so is the U.S. Attorney!"

My next reply was also one word. "So?" That seemed like the straw that broke the camel's back as Weinberger just sat there fiddling with his notes.

I broke the silence. "If I plead guilty what do I get? Fifteen years? Ten years? What?" Weinberger was getting madder by the minute.

"One step at a time Mr. San Tuccio (he was still using my true name from the original arrest file). First you offer to plead guilty and then I go to the Prosecutor and see what the Government is asking for a sentence."

I shouted back. "Wrong answer, do I look stupid enough to plead guilty and end-up doing fifteen years? Here's my deal! Go to Ms. Prosecutor and see what she wants to hit me with. Then you tell me and I decide what I want to do!"

After that remark I waved to Pepper that I was done talking. Weinberger didn't return to inform me what, if anything the Government was offering.

At 2:15 PM the Salt and Pepper duo ushered me into Judge Dorsey's courtroom. There were no other defendants in the Court at the time.

The Judge seemed to be starring down at me from the bench. I knew what he was thinking! "Well they finally caught you and boy are you going to get yours today. I'll teach you not to skip-out on a Federal Judge."

<u>Weinberger</u> motioned for me to join him at the defense table. He then spoke to the judge almost with reverence. "Your Honor may I have a minute with Mr. San Tuccio before we proceed?" Judge Dorsey nodded his approval.

"Here's what it is Mr. San Tuccio, and this offer is for today only! So—if you do plead <u>not</u> guilty, you'll start all over with a new attorney. But you'll still have the same Judge and Prosecutor. Forty-six (46) months is their bottom line and I suggest you agree to that!"

I am sure I shocked the lawyer with my one word answer of. "Okay." There was no further discussions between us.

In closing Judge Dorsey asked if there was anything I would like to say be fore being sentenced.

"Yes, your Honor. Could you please recommend that I be sent back to Arizona to serve my sentence?" He did, and I was, but you'll read all about that in the Chapter FCI Phoenix, Arizona in this part of the book.

Weinberger turned and said. "Good luck Mr. San Tuccio!" and left the courtroom. The Marshals escorted me back to a cell to wait for the rent-a-cops.

On the way back to Wyatt I was in a good state of mind. I recapped in my head: the case was over, I was headed back to Arizona and Remy, and forty-six months was <u>not</u> bad, considering I had jumped bail on the Judge.

Three weeks went by as I waited at Wyatt to be airlifted back to the FTC. Then at 8:00 AM on a rainy day. "Tucci you're leaving pack it out and report to R and D."

The same two rent-a-cops who had picked me up at the Manchester Airport, now were bringing me back there for Con-Air.

Yes, I did get my "usual" seat on the plane. Five hours later we landed at the FTC in Oklahoma City, and I was a little closer to my dearest Remy.

Dry your eyes and please read on.

CHAPTER 5

The Federal Transfer Center (Again)

Author's note:

This is the shortest chapter in the book, as it should be. But, never the less it needed to be written because of the happy ending.

It was like old home week as I climbed up the rear stairs of the old Con-Air jet. The friendly aircrew, my usual seat, and Archie (the head Marshal) asking. "Well Tucci how did it go in court?"

I explained what happened with Judge Dorsey and that he had sentenced me to forty six (46) months. Arhcie added. "Hey that ain't bad time considering that you jumped bail for three years on the judge."

At twilight time the shaking old jet touched down in Oklahoma City. The unloading, iron removal, clothing issue, and their forms to fill in were a rerun of Chapter 2.

But, this time during the "processing" I was handed a Designated To Form, which showed the location of the facility the B.O.P. was sending me to.

As I read it my eyes lit-up and then my heart bounced a couple of times! It was short and to the point. "Tucci, Francis M #03836-914 to FCI Phoenix, Phoenix, Arizona." All praise be to Allah!

Quickly I ran to find a telephone and called my dear wife. "Guess what Remy? They are sending me to the Federal Prison in Phoenix!"

FCI Phoenix is on 45th Avenue and our home at that time was on 23rd Avenue, not all that far away. I ended our conversation with a good news, bad news routine.

The good news was that Judge Dorsey did not give me a ten or fifteen year sentence. However, the bad news was that I would be in a Federal Prison for forty-six months.

But be that it may, Remy and I were still thankful or as they say in her language (Bisaya) mapasalamaton!

There was no way of knowing the terror that lay ahead at the hands of Warden Ellis, or the mean spirit ness and uncaring staff there.

At 2:30AM the cell door was banged open, the light came on, and a small Ms. Guard said. "Yo, Tucci get your ass up you're on the airlift!" Wow! I hadn't even been here 24 hours and already they are flying me home?

Just as before it was the same drill leaving the FTC, the same seat on the plane but this time a different aircrew. Three hours later I was at last home in Phoenix.

Looking out the 737's window as it dropped down to land, I smiled ear to ear. Palm trees, sunshine, and the lovely hundred-degree weather. Yes, the old man was home!

The plane taxied over to the industrial side of Phoenix's Sky Harbor Airport. There were busses, vans, and a few police vehicles waiting to receive Con-Air's cargo of cons.

Dozens of heavily armed Marshals, B.O.P. personnel, state and local police, and even some military people, ringed in the hot runway providing tight security.

One hour later the bus pulled into FCI Phoenix. We had passed by the I-17 Exit (Dunlap Avenue) where my wife and condo where. I was so close, but yet so far from Remy.

Everybody dry their eyes and let's finish this chapter.

My stay at FCI Phoenix would be a long and hard sixteen (16) months before Ellis transferred me out. The official reason for shipping me out? I'll quote Warden Ellis. "The safety of the inmate." Oh really?

But, the truth of the matter is two-fold. First, the book you are now reading was a part. Second, Ellis couldn't manage or break me, so it became. "Get Tucci out of my prison!"

The next chapter is a long one, with many sidebars but a true one. Chapter 6 F.C.I. Phoenix!

CHAPTER 6

FCI Phoenix, Arizona

Author's note:

Judge Peter C. Dorsey had recommended the facility where I would start serving my Federal sentence. The word "start" is underlined with good reason, which will become clear in this chapter.

Hopefully your sentencing judge will suggest where you are to be incarcerated, but remember the B.O.P. always has the last say in the matter.

So with that explained, as Paul Harvey says. "Now the rest of the story!"

July 17, 2000

My arrival at FCI Phoenix was different from all the other Gray Bar Hotels on this happy road trip. Their new bus didn't drive us into a fortress type garage but instead jerked to a stop in the parking lot.

Some things never change, as the guard yelled his profanities at us. "Alright everybody get off your fu_king ass and down off the fu_king bus! Move, move!"

Question? Are there B.O.P. classes in how to order inmates off a prison bus? I am positive there are! You ask why? Because the officers always make sure to use the "F" word two or three times in their orders.

It doesn't matter what State the B.O.P. facility is in, it's always the same. "Get off the fu__king bus, or get off of your fu king asses!" Well you get the idea.

Forty-three (43) prisoners and I waddled down off the air-conditioned bus and into a blast of Arizona hundred degree heat. Yes, the old man (me) was home and all praise to Allah!

Dragging the heavy leg-chains we went through the Visiting Room and ended up in FCI Phoenix's R&D area.

"What's next pops?" A light skinned brother asked me. "Let's wait and see?" I answered. But, I knew what happens next depended on what time it was.

Please keep in mind that in America Federal prisons are a big business and as such most of their employees work on the first shift. Arrival at 8:00 AM would have been ideal, but the odds of that are slim to none.

The first thing the inmates wanted was to get the damn handcuffs and chains off. But, that didn't happen as we were herded into a holding cell. How long we would remain cuffed depended on how many officers were working that shift.

I have always considered any R&D to be the worst part of a prison. There areas are not just dirty, but filthy! The cells are built to hold eight or ten prisoners but we are usually packed in thirty or forty, as we were today.

There was one exposed toilet for the needs of all. If there is a toilet paper you can be sure that an inconsiderate inmate is using it for a pillow. You'll see all kinds of things in prison that you never knew existed, till then.

After what seemed like a long wait a good old boy guard unlocked our cage, and with two others started removing the chains as we exited the cell one by one.

One of these officers could pass for Lurch of the old TV program "The Adams Family." The second guard looked like a moron, but on closer examination I changed my mind. Maybe he is just a case of arrested development? But the third cop was a midget! These people are entrusted with my safety?

Put into our next cell we were served a B.O.P. gourmet meal. Let's see what's in the bag Lurch just tossed at me? Wow! FCI Phoenix has spared no expense; there were two bologna sandwiches, each with a slice of make-believe cheese. In the bottom of the sack, a fruit bar, a box of milk, and a smashed pear.

But, compared to the bag of sh_t I had as a last meal of CCA, this indeed was a feast! Now that we have been so called "nourished", what's next?

The answer came as the Midget unlocked the cell door and yelled in over the noise. "Listen-up, when I call your name come out and over to the counter." Well, that answered what was next. Processing.

Sometimes processing can take hours, or even days, that depends on how many inmates need processing and the number of guard staff working the shift.

Processing again (my sixth time), the same stupid B.O.P. forms to fill in again. Don't these people have computers? Also, the same dumb questions to answer for their ad hoc medical staff. Again an ID photo and finger printing. Maybe the B.O.P. thinks I changed fingers on the airlift to Phoenix?

My happy hour ended with Lurch saying. "Tucci you're assigned to Yuma unit, we'll be leaving in a few minutes."

The last thing the B.O.P.'s trio of misfits did was a clothing issue of sorts. Of sorts? You'll understand as you read the following: One tee shirt, one pair of boxer shorts, one pair of socks and one pair of B.O.P. tan trousers with a stylish shirt to match.

Hey, just like CCA—one of everything! I questioned the Moron. "Officer is this the only clothing I get?" Lurch, hearing my very loud remark came to Moron's aid. "Old man if you are designated to our fine facility you'll get a full issue of clothing and work boots on Monday."

I couldn't control myself and shot back with. "You're telling me that I have to wear the same underwear for three days in this hot weather?"

Lurch's sarcastic reply didn't surprise me. "Yeah, pops no clean drawers until Monday."

Yes, my arrival at FCI Phoenix was a case of bad timing. At ll:15 PM a sleepy female officer showed us to our pool side suite. As my wife Remy would have said. "Lain na usab nga adlaw ugma!" That's Bisaya for "Tomorrow is another day!"

In the Yuma Unit an inmate orderly handed out our bedding: Two sheets, one blanket, one pillowcase (but no pillow), one towel and one washcloth. We also get an overnight hygiene kit with soap, shampoo, a half size comb, and toothpaste and brush.

The next morning I found a shower that no one was using, the <u>only</u> one nobody was in. I soon found out why? Its water came out more cold than hot, and the spray from the showerhead could best be described as a trickle.

After the shower I had to put back on the same smelly clothing and underwear, there was no alternative! For a Muslim it is very distasteful to put dirty clothing on a clean body.

Yes, everyone was looking forward to Monday's issue of clean clothing, but I realized that everything bad in Federal prison is a part of his or her punishment!

Until Monday morning I was free to walk the unshaded, hot, and dry grounds of FCI Phoenix, unless I got tossed in "the hole", as a friend was on arriving here.

It was too hot this morning for walking around (102 degrees), so I went over to their indoor recreation building, which also housed the library and the Law Library.

FCI Phoenix's Law Library is up to date with their new 1996 books, well that was the <u>newest</u> book I could find? Hey folks, that's only four years behind times, that's good for a prison library I am told.

If library activities don't strike your fancy you can watch mindless TV, or catch-up on your sleep.

Now let's get serious. Pretend that you are here with me in FCI Phoenix and the day is a Monday morning. Chisel into your mind that you are about to start on a prison routine that never changes. Every day will be the same, every week of every year of your sentence.

You will very quickly fall into the B.O.P.'s daily pattern as your Monday through Friday stay the same. Some change comes on your first Saturday and Sunday, but even those two days will be the same the following week.

If your sentence is a lengthy one your are in great danger of becoming "Institutionalized". Hopefully, that will never happen to you and I personally wish that on no one.

But some of the facility's inmates who have been down a long, long, time, do mirror the famous "Rat Test".

The test was done using hundreds of rats and was very simple. A lab technician would ring a bell, the rats would run towards the sound of the bell, and then the rats were fed. After a few months of being "conditioned" to the sound of the bell, the rats were ready to be tested for results.

The bell was rung and the rats raced towards the sound of the bell, but his time no food was offered. However, because the rats were "conditioned" that the sound of the bell meant food, they started chewing with empty mouths.

It hurts me to say it but there are inmates here "conditioned" just like the rats. At the ends of the chapter are fifteen questions to help you determine if you are headed towards becoming "Institutionalized"?

Back to now, July 17, 2000. Let me walk you though your first fun-filled day at FCI Phoenix, Arizona, or it could be any other of the Bureau's FCI's. You're going to love it here, lots of fresh air, palm trees, plenty of sunshine, and one hundred degree weather six months of the year.

The first facility movement of the day is the breakfast "main-line" call. I didn't make-up the term "main-line", the B.O.P. did many years ago in 1937. Three times everyday the loudspeakers blare out. "Yuma Unit to main-line!"

My American Heritage Dictionary says. "Main-line, to inject narcotics into a vine."

Doesn't that seem like jailhouse humor to you? Why? Because I am in a Federal prison, and at least 60 percent of the inmates are here for drug related crimes, and the B.O.P. insists on using the drug term "main-line".

Leaving the unit you'll see your first Arizona sunrise. I was living in Phoenix before my arrest and believe me the wonders of nature here are unequaled in the rest of America. Okay we are not doing a travelogue, so back to your first day.

Here's the bad news first. Your Monday breakfast will be the same next Monday, and every Monday after that. The same goes for Tuesdays, although a different breakfast from Monday's every Tuesday will be the same breakfast. Are you getting the idea?

Look at the bright side of it, once you have memorized the seven breakfast meals you'll never need a menu. But the good news is that the lunch and supper meals do change daily.

You want to know what your Monday breakfast is? Here it is: Fresh fruit, hot farina, creamed beef, home fried potatoes, toast, butter cups, (5) sugar packets, milk or coffee. Sounds good? You'll find out!

I hope you liked it because it's yours for the length of your sentence, every Monday morning!

The posted unit memo said. "In this facility you will leave the cells as a unit, at the designated time, to the announced activity." If that's not enough to confuse an old man what is?

The unit's door is never left unlocked to come and go as you please, this was very confusing at first. Here's why.

To get into the Law Library, which opens at 9:00 AM, I had to leave the unit a half hour earlier at 8:30 AM. Or I could get there a half hour later at 9:30 AM. Why? All weekday movements are done on the half hour, 7:30 AM, 8:30 AM, 9:30 AM, etc.

That is until 12:30PM, after that the movements are done on the hour, 1:00PM, 2:00PM, etc. Isn't prison fun? Just when I had mastered the weekday movement times it was Saturday and time for the weekend movements.

On Saturday, Sunday and Holidays all moves are made on the hour, day and night. Without a wristwatch I was lost!

Back again to your Monday. After breakfast, because you are designated to FCI Phoenix you will next report to Arrival and Orientation (A&O) Classes in the Chapel. There was one inmate who refused to attend A&O because the classes were in a Chapel. Maybe he was an Atheist? He was not a Muslim.

The classes last two or three hours and run for three days. When they (the classes) are finished all your questions about the B.O.P. and FCI Phoenix will be answered? You'll also know everything in the Inmate Handbook, which you get to keep. I mailed mine home to Remy.

Staff from each of the facility's services and departments will speak and try to answer your questions? These B.O.P. people spoke:

The Assistant Warden, the Safety Director, a Recreation Department Specialist (these people have titles), or Commissary Officer, the Medical Services Director, a teacher from the Education Department, and last was the Assistant F/S (Food dis-Service) Director.

You can always tell at an A&O the inmates who are in prison their first time. How? That's easy, because they always ask the dumbest questions. However, their questions may not be dumb to you, if you are a "first timer".

Here is a short sample of "first timers" questions:

1. How many books can I take out of the library at one time?
2. Do you have kosher food here?
3. Can I write to my brother who is also in Federal prison?
4. Does FCI Phoenix allow conjugal visits?
5. Can I have my Reebok's sent in from home?
6. Does the cable TV have HBO?

That should be enough for you to get the idea.

Recapping: You have been to breakfast, and sat through a three-hour A&O Class. But now comes the highlight of your day. The clothing issue! Hi ho, hi ho, it's off to the laundry unit you go!"

Yes Mr. Convict you are about to trade in your dirty shirt, pants, socks, and smelly undies. Also those stupid looking blue pull-on sneakers that are made in The People's Republic of China. Thanks for the "cool" shoes Mr. Clinton, you Commie Bastard!

After your three days in the same clothing and Arizona's 100-degree heat, it's no small wonder that the next prisoner in line is keeping his distance! You really do stink!

At last, your clothing "issue"! First, comes the most expensive part of your new outfit, the steel-toed work boots. These cost more than everything else you'll get added all together. Why is that? Because the boots are not made in Unicor, which is the B.O.P.'s in house prison industry.

Now your "whites", hang on to them socks because you are issued only four pairs every three months. You'll also get four tee shirts and four pair of boxer shorts. If you never wore boxers before you are in for a rude awakening. It is damn embarrassing to keep reaching inside your pants to put "it" in place.

They'll finish dressing you with their B.O.P.'s "prison tans", three trousers and three shirts, and a thin web belt to complete your new outfit.

Hold on, you are not done yet! Last of all is your own personal bedding, yours to keep and wash to whenever. The items: Two sheets, one blanket, one pillowcase with a pillow to put in it. There's still more: Two washcloths, two towels, and to top it off you even get a drawstring laundry bag to carry everything in!

Just think. If you had to buy all that stuff, except the boots, at a K-Mart or a Wal Mart, you could expect to pay at least ten (10) dollars?

Two things remain before the B.O.P. can insert you into FCI Phoenix's daily routine. One is a visit to the Medical Department, the Government wants to make sure you are alive and can perform cheap labor for them.

The other thing is finding you a prison "job". At first they will assign you mindless labor but later you can find something more to your liking.

The Medical Officer finds it okay for you to work in prison. After all, you are still breathing and no one is pushing you around in a wheelchair, yet.

Your luck just went down hill! You have been assigned to work for "Lands In", which are the prison's grounds keepers. But, don't worry it never stays at 125 degrees for more than two or three days!

Welcome to FCI Phoenix. I'll see you daily where I appear at the facility's Food dis-Service (F/S)!

Here as promised is your list and test. Are you becoming "Institutionalized"?

1. When another inmate asks, where are you going? Is your reply "home", instead of saying back to your cell?

2. Do you try to be first in front of the locked unit door, ten minutes before it is unlocked?

3. Do you run from the unit to the mess hall just to be sure you eat before they run out of food?

4. When a guard tells you to do something do you do it, even when you know the officer is wrong?

5. Do you tell other inmates how much money you have on the street and then ask to barrow a postage stamp?

6. On your prison job do you refer to the equipment as "my" mop, "my" rake, or "my" broom?

7. Have you become Officer (fill in your name) by telling other inmates not to do this or that?

8. Do you eat your meals quickly and hurry back to the unit only to be locked in that much earlier?

9. If you need something done by the Counselors are you afraid to ask?

10. Do you make your bed before 5:00 AM and then stay in the cell all day?

11. Do you go to religious services more than three times a week?

12. Do you wear your prison shirt with the top button buttoned?

13. Do you shine your boots and press your clothing for your job in the kitchen's dish room?

14. Do you go to the telephones and make believe you are talking to someone on the other end?

15. Do you talk about things that happened five years ago while you were in prison?

If you answered yes to more than three of the test questions you are a borderline case of "Institutionalizations". Do something fast before the B.O.P. turns you into a lab rat!

Coming up next are survival topics I wrote about during my sixteen (16) months at FCI Phoenix. Please remember that after 911, I was really "A Muslim Surviving the Federal Prison System."

As salaamu alaikum.

The Telephones

Trying to keep your family strong and together during an incarceration is a difficult challenge. The Government will try their best to destroy your family's spirit, and maybe even their well being.

The telephone will become a very important part of your prison life. But remember, it is not so easy to reach out and touch someone from inside a Federal prison.

The Maricopa County Jail in Phoenix, where I was a guest at the beginning of this book, had pay telephones in their holding cells. But who had any quarters?

If you are locked-up in a State prison system the rules will vary from state to state but most States have adopted parts of the U.S. Bureau of Prisons restrictive rules on telephone usage.

Yes the B.O.P. will let you use the telephone, but not until they have delayed you for ten or fourteen days!

In the B.O.P.'s system you must first submit a form, "Telephone Number Request", before you get to use the phones. You must provide complete information as to the following:

1.   The area code and phone number(s).
2.   Whose name the phone is listed in.
3.   Their relationship to you, if any.
4.   Street address, City, State, Zip Code or Country.

B.O.P. policy states. "A phone number will not be approved if any information is left out, i.e.—street number, city, etc. You can't write:

John Smith

Wilson Street

Phoenix, AZ 85021

Without the actual street number Mr. Smith will not make it on to your list. Don't think that the sadistic employees in the Telephone Office will call 411 on your behalf.

In a week or ten days, some inmates have waited much longer; you'll be able to make telephone calls. But only to those who are "approved" on your list. The next sentence is off the B.O.P.'s telephone form.

"You will be notified by a member of your unit staff if a telephone number is not placed on your telephone list."

When and if you "approved" list comes back you will also be assigned a P.I.N. (Prisoner Identification Number), which you must punch-in before making a call.

The remaining parts of this chapter were not allowed out of FCI Phoenix when I wrote it there in late 2000. Maybe Warden Ellis didn't like the idea of me helping other inmates?

Trust me on this, we inmates are not dumb even though the guard staff has been led to believe that by the B.O.P. and their Warden.

Case in point, how to get around the ten day wait before the B.O.P. allows you to use a phone. You can use the telephone the same day you arrive at any facility. Here's how to do that!

If you are a gang member that now becomes a plus in prison. Let's say you are a member of (fill in your gang's name) and are in the B.O.P.'s new home for you. Take a look around for some of your homies. Or find someone you knew from the street.

Explain to your homie that you just got off the bus and would like to let your family know where the Bureau has dumped you. If he is a solid homie he will write down his P.I.N., and his old lady's phone number for you.

Next call the homie's woman and tell her that you are her guy's best friend, and then ask her to contact your family. See, no ten-day wait.

I am not giving away a secret but don't many people have three-way calling as a part of their telephone service?

Call your homie's lady again but this time ask her if she can make a three-way-call to your family? Hopefully she has that as part of her telephone service.

There is a downside to making three-way calls, they are not allowed in Federal prison. If detected your call will be terminated and the unit team will impose sanctions on you. More than likely, a loss of your telephone privileges!

But, again I will come to your rescue and there is a way around the B.O.P. detecting your three-way call. This time I am giving my secret away!

Do you know anyone who has a cellular telephone? Good, now here's what you need to do. First you'll have to get the home phone number of the cell phone owner on your calling list. This means a ten-day or longer wait.

However if there is someone already on your phone list who has a cellular phone your troubles are over! So let's do it!

Call the cell phone's owner on their home telephone, and then ask them to dial-up the number you want on their cell phone. Now place both phones on a tabletop, counter top, or whatever. Make sure the phones are close together facing each other.

You can now enjoy your conversation; you have just screwed the B.O.P. and their three-way call detector! There is a huge plus if you make calls this way. First, you can call phone numbers not on your "official" list, and second, the Feds cannot trace whom you are talking to.

I have one more trick up my sleeve. I have not tested it myself but my Muslim brothers swear it works. Here's the question. How can an inmate in FCI Phoenix talk to an inmate in a different facility using the inmate telephones?

How is that possible? Read on please, I hope I am hindering the B.O.P. and helping other inmates.

I labor in the Food dis Service and everyday I get to see inmates from all of the facility's units. Here's how to test the inmate calling inmate theory.

If a "brother" is being transferred to a different prison he can come up to me and say. "Pops, I am being moved out, get this note to my friend Marty."

The "note" will have his P.I.N. and his mother's telephone number. At the next meal when Marty comes by me in the serving line, I'll pass him the note from his homie.

"Thanks, old man, I owe you one." Marty smiled and said. These are good i.o.u.'s to have because one never knows when you'll need a favor in prison.

In a day or two later Marty will call his "home boy's" mother and say. "The next time your son calls tell him I will be calling you on Saturday at 7:00 PM." Have you figured out how it works?

What Marty said was code for have your son call at 7:00 PM on Saturday. Now have you guessed how it works?

Sure you have, yes that's right! Marty and his homie will both call ma at 7:00 PM on Saturday! Because mom has Three-Way Calling and Call Waiting she can switch them on to each other!

That is not a true three-way call because ma called no one, both of her calls were incoming. How can the B.O.P. blame or punish Marty and his homie for that? They can't!

In closing this chapter I have a couple more telephone tips.

Find a homie that you can trust and ask him to put your wife or girlfriend's telephone number on his phone list. This is allowed by the B.O.P. On his phone list request, where it asks relationship, he can write "a friend".

Having your wife's phone number on another inmate's list will help in many ways! Later in the book's Part Three you'll learn how I used the telephone almost daily, after USP Atwater suspended my telephone privileges.

Also in case of an emergency, like getting tossed in "the hole", as I have been all too many times, your family will know what's going on when your homie calls them.

The other big plus is the extra minutes you'll have by also using your home boy's P.I.N. The Feds only allow each inmate 300 calling minutes each month.

I sincerely hope that what I have written about the telephones helps you to reach a loved one today.

In Federal prison success means that I get-up one more time than the B.O.P. kicks me down.

Your gang buddy helped you out with the telephone problem, now let's see what else happens when gangs are together in prison? "The Gangs!" are the next chapter, also written at FCI Phoenix.

The Gangs

The B.O.P.'s website will inform you that sixty percent of the inmates in Federal prison are there for drug-related crimes. Yes, the manufacture, distribution, and selling of drugs in America is a "gang thing". The end result is the hundreds of "homies" who have been shipped off to State and Federal prisons.

Federal Sentencing Guidelines for drug crimes are tough with ten, twenty, or more years common for even a first-time offender.

While back East awaiting my trial, I met a nineteen year old ganger who got a thirty (30) year sentence for the manufacturing of designer drugs. Thirty years? Maybe because the Government has to justify the existence of their huge bureaucracy known as the D.E.A.?

The Gangs do have the attention of administrators in all of America's prison systems. Upon my arrival in R&D a snotty officer asked me. "Are you a member of any gang or organization like that?" You do remember that I am 62 years old? I mentioned my advanced age to officer Snotty who just shrugged his shoulders and yelled back. "Well, you old bastard you could be a gang's president or something like that!"

I had more to say and my next remark to Snotty was. "Do you people consider the Mafia a prison gang?" He quickly answered back. "Old man, the Mafia is not a prison gang!"

My final jab at Snotty was. "Then why does the F.B.I. arrest Italians and claim that they are gang members of the Mafia?" He didn't try to answer that question, gave me a dirty look, and then called the next inmate up to the desk.

Personally I don't think anyone should rush to join a gang on their arrival in prison. But, if you are a ganger find your "home boys" and hang with them. Your street buddies could be the difference between you being beaten, raped, or even killed in here!

Gangs are dangerous enough on the streets, but when locked up with long sentences they become twice as dangerous in the prison system!

In today's prisons, County, State or Federal, the gangs are highly visible and recruit openly. Although the Feds have made a very strong attempt to stop, or at least control the gangs, it has not worked.

The prison system is my home State thought they had a solution for containing and controlling their prisons gang populations. The State stupidly locked up all the gang members in a "Special Gangs Unit" (SGU).

To the sleeping public it seemed like a great idea, but it turned out to be a huge nightmare. Can you just imagine a whole unit with nothing but young gangbangers housed in it? Isn't that like tossing gasoline on a bonfire?

The SGU's inmates are not all from the same gang, there maybe four or five different clubs represented in the unit. But, due to prison over-crowding all empty cells in the SGU will be filled in.

Would you care to guess who the staff puts into those empty cells? The answer is so dumb it may shock you? Other rival gangs will get those SGU cells! Like I said before, gasoline on a bonfire!

Here's a question for all the prison "powers to be". Do you still think it's a good idea to put so many gang "homies" together? If they were robbing and drugging together on the streets, isn't it safe to bet they'll do the same in prison?

But what do I know? The B.O.P. says. "Tucci is just a crazy old man writing a stupid book!"

Let's go back in time and trace one gang member's life, and how he got to Federal prison. My thumb mail sketch of Eddie is true but it could describe almost any ganger in here.

Most gangers come into prison penniless and will leave here the same way, if they live through the experience! I can't help but wonder what happened to the thousands of dollars they made selling drugs?

These "youths" have very little education, they didn't quit school, the schools quit on them. Yet they still don't care to obtain a simple G.E.D. while in prison.

Don't foreigners come to America speaking little or no English and yet they get a G.E. D. quickly? How hard can it be for can inmate to get his/her G.E.D.? The B.O.P. even has a policy of sorts regarding G.E.D.'s.

"If you enter a facility without a High School Diploma or a G.E.D., you will be paid only $5.25 a month, until such time as you do obtain a G.E.D." The gangers could get out of the $5.25 a month rut, but they can't find the time for classes and scoff at their homies that do.

Eddie lived in public housing with a mother who loved children so much that she just kept having them, one after the other. The fathers/men in his mother's life didn't stay around long.

Looking back we'll find that these "fathers" never worked at any job, but still they always seemed to have money and lived well. It's a safe bet that most were pimps and/or drug dealers.

Eddie's two sisters turned to prostitution, after all wasn't Mama doing that with all the "fathers" that came and went? Didn't Mama always dress well and drive a new car without having a job?

Is it any wonder that about seventy (70) percent of these troubled youths become street punks, and have never worked at a real job on the outside?

Eddie's first taste of the good life was his shoplifting to order. That's when somebody tells you what they want, and then you steal it for them

At some point shoplifting become dull so he took up breaking and entering. Eddie grabbed the usual things. TV's, VCR's, cameras, jewelry, etc., which were a quick and easy sources of pawnshop money.

Next the homie turned to armed robbery, gas stations, convenience outlets, liquor stores, and the defenseless Ma and Pa stores.

Then one day somebody said. "Fu-k it, let's rob us a bank!" They tried too but killed two people in a botched "take over" attempt. One of those killed was female police officer! It took Eddie only ten years to go from shoplifting to cop killer.

He will do well in Federal prison because there is a pecking order here, your status is determined by the crime you committed. The young gangbangers in here idolize cop killers!

Do you remember this saying? "Birds of the same feathers flock together?" In prison the saying changes a little. "The eagles are being flocked to by the sparrows." Of course the eagles are the cop killers, and the sparrows are the young gangers.

The eagles will have no shortage of jailhouse admirers, and they will exploit their homies who keep asking the same dumb question. "Yo, how did it feel to kill a cop?"

Wouldn't the B.O.P. be pleased to know that the street punks are finding friends, big brothers, father images, and excellent role models here in Federal prison?

Federal prison to any gang member is just one big friendship club, and also a trade school to learn how to do "better crimes". Your tax dollars at their finest! The sad part of all this is the reality that boys do become men in prison!

To the parents, here's what the politicians and prison hardliners are saying. "Let's teach these street gangs a lesson! If they do a man's crime they'll be punished like a man! If that means tossing them into a penitentiary so be it!"

Are you a parent of a young ganger who is currently locked up? Please ask yourself the following:

"Why did the Federal Government put my child in a prison with older inmates, cop killers, mass murderers, and those who have committed sex crimes? Wasn't my kid's only crime selling a small amount of drugs?"

Now here's how the gangs survive and recruit in America's prisons, I'll start with a very short list of the many found inside any B.O.P. facility.

Skin Heads, White Power, Border Brothers, Picis, Peckerwoods, Asian Nation, Mexican Mafia, L.A. Mafia, Crips, Bloods, Latin Kings, Texas Mafia, Texas Syndicate, and the Wise Guys (the real Mafia). The gang list is endless!

How do they recruit in a prison? First, I would like to state. "I can not, and will not name any gang as being here in FCI Phoenix. To do so would betray their trust in me. But isn't the B.O.P. really suppose to know what gangs are where?"

In this facility the gangs compete for new blood strongly and here's how they may come after you.

I'll start with the obvious. If you are a Black the White Power gangs will not seek you out and vice versa if you are a White. However, there is one exception to the Black and White rule, but only one! Case in point, me!

Islam is colorblind and I am the only White among this facility's Black Muslim population. All praise to Allah!

When an inmate gets off the prison's bus he has no personal property with him, in fact he has nothing! But anything a newly arrived prisoner needs he can get quickly from a "homie" or a "ganger".

Most gangs will give you things with no questions asked, but all too soon you'll find out that you have joined their gang. What would a new guy need? Didn't the R&D issue him one of everything and a hygiene kit good for at least three uses?

Well just for starters how about a change of underwear? Remember it's Friday and he'll get no clothing issued until Monday.

Also the "hygiene kit" didn't have any shave cream, shampoo, razors, or deodorant in it. Maybe the hard line prison officials don't use items like those? That's why they were not included in the "Welcome Wagon" package?

In "The Telephones" the ganger hooked up with a homie and contacted his family. The next most important thing also involves contacting home, postage stamps. With stamps he can write home and ask for money!

Good news, if he has no money on the prison's books he can get five free stamps each week from the unit counselor. Bad news, the stamps are passed out on Thursdays and today is Friday! But, he can ask around and somebody will loan him a stamp at two for one.

That means you barrow one and pay back two, or else! Hey buddy that's not a bad interest rate, seeing you have not establish credit here yet!

At age sixty-two I didn't join a gang, the Muslims joined me! The elderly are highly respected among this FCI's Muslim community. Contrary to the B.O.P.'s and public beliefs, the Muslims in Federal prisons are not a gang.

Here's what could happen to you. An inmate may come into your cell and say. "Hi, I'm Ted Smith and I noticed you just got in." His next sentence should set off flashing red lights in your head. "Do you need anything?"

Think now—you don't know a soul here, and just out of the blue Ted comes up to you and offers to get you anything? Is Ted a "home boy"? He could have found out where you are from via the prison's grape vine.

Is Ted a ganger trying to latch on to you before another group does? Or worst still, is Ted a homosexual looking for a new friend? Use extreme caution if Ted is a different Race than you!

My message to you is yes join a gang for protection, remember not everyone can fight like a Mike Tyson. If you are weak and try to go it alone you won't last long in prison!

The brutal stories you hear and read about prisons are true! Inmates and even staff members are beaten, raped, and/or killed almost everyday in America's prisons.

Here is an example of what I mean, involving inmates attacking inmates. Recently a Black gang member had a serious disagreement with a Cuban inmate. It was a classic mismatch, the Black's six foot, and 200-pound frame, against the tiny five foot six inch, 140 pounds of the amigo. The Cuban didn't do so good and suffered a broken nose and lost a few teeth.

Here in FCI Phoenix, the Hispanic groups tend to only fight each other. But when the need arises the Mexicans, Cubans, Puerto Ricans, and the other Hispanics will join forces.

About ten or fifteen, depending on whom you ask, Hispanic's did a "pay back" the very next day. The "brother" wasn't just beaten up, he was badly cut-up!

The "cutting" took place in the Navajo Unit and resulted in a six-day total Lock Down of FCI Phoenix from 1-05-01 to 1-11-01. There never was a "pay back" by the Blacks that would have been fruitless, they being outnumbered by at least five to one.

A day later the broken nosed and less toothed Cuban was bussed off to parts unknown. The Black died at the outside hospital.

No person(s) was ever charged for the "slice and dice". Question, what's the main reason inmates join a gang in prison? Answer, for protection!
Author's note:

Toothbrush razors were used in the attack. These are easily made in here by first removing the bristles from a toothbrush, and then smashing a Bic razor. Then you glue the razor blade to the toothbrush.

Where do you get Crazy Glue in prison? No problem, FCI Phoenix has a Unicor (inmate factory) facility. But remember, it is a good idea to let the glue set for 24 hours before trying to cut someone.

Wow! "The Things I have learned In Prison". That could be the title of my next book?

Gang violence by inmates on each other happens everyday in Federal prison, it's no big deal. In fact many of the sadistic guards enjoy watching us trying to kill each other. But, when a prisoner assaults a staff member there is hell to be paid!

I witnessed the murder of a guard, the futile attempt by a lonely inmate to try and stop the guard's killers and the death of that well-meaning inmate. Sam's death was written in as "due to the confusion at the scene", on the S.I.S.'s Official Report.

The following is a true chain of events. Yes, another example of "The Gangs" in prison.

A young and problem causing White officer was supervising a work detail of six Blacks. When suddenly one of the "brothers" cracked the officer over the head with a shovel! The officer fell down bleeding and the rest of the crew joined the assault, kicking and beating their "boss".

Big Sam raced across the rec yard and started pulling and pushing the attackers off the badly bleeding guard. As the mayhem continued all six turned on Big Sam. My guess is that the "brothers" didn't like the idea of Big Sam, who is Black, helping the White officer.

I watched in shock as Big Sam was repeatedly cut on his arms, face, and back. He soon fell to the ground with blood all over his body! Then just like in the movies, the riot horn blared loudly!

The murderers, many onlookers, and I ran quickly and scattered from the area. The officer was already dead before the Goon Squad (riot armed officers) burst into the yard.

But, Big Sam was still alive, however none of the squad's attention was directed to helping him. After all, Big Sam was just another Black convict; their only concern was for their fallen comrade. Big Sam did not receive medical help, and as result died in a pool of blood where he had fallen.

There was a five-day Lock Down of the whole facility and a massive investigation was done. No one was ever charge with the murders of the officer and Big Sam. This place does not have surveillance cameras in the yard, so nobody was caught "on camera" for the crimes!

So much more could be written about "The Gangs" here in prison. Maybe still another book?

Always remember, it doesn't hurt to be a gang homie in here, but it could hurt not to be one! I hope you get my meaning?

The next chapter, "Visitation" was also written at FCI Phoenix. A small part of the chapter was my wife Remy's first attempt at writing. We both hope you enjoy our chapter.

Hinaut unta nga makaayon o ganahan kamo!

Visitation

Author's note:

"Visitation" was written during happier times when Remy and I were still allowed visits. But shortly there after I would be in "the hole" (Segregation), denied visits, and write the book's "Introduction". Warden Bernie C. Ellis retaliated by shipping me 700 miles away, to FCI Sheridan in Oregon.

Yes, the mail and the telephone are two important things that can help an inmate keep in touch with his family. But visits are the main and necessary foundation that will hold a prisoner and his loved ones together.

Here in FCI Phoenix, just as with the telephone, a lengthy form (Visitor Information) must be submitted. The B.O.P.'s form has fourteen (14) questions for your would be visitor to fill in and mail back. Each "visitor" must be on a separate form. One form, one envelope, and one postage stamp.

Please explain that? Okay, <u>you</u> mail out the visiting forms at <u>your</u> expense providing the stamps and envelopes. The hopeful visitor will fill-in the questionnaire and return it to your counselor.

Well that was the fast and easy part. The rest is not fast, when the counselor gets back the forms he will record the information in the unit's files. Days later he will pass the forms on to the Visitor Room Clerk. Approval can take weeks or even longer as the Clerk forwards the "Visitor Requests" on to the F.B.I.

However, if any of your intended visitors are family members, wife, sister, mother, father, brother, etcetera, they can visit long before your request list becomes official. But yes, there is a B.O.P. "Catch 22". Your family visitor must be mentioned in the P.S.I. (Pre-Sentence Investigation) done by the U.S. Probation Department.

In the County jails and some State systems there are no lists on forms needed. Anyone can visit you seven days a week in those two types of facilities.

For those of you lucky enough to be imprisoned within driving distance of your loved ones or family, count your blessings.

If they put you in a <u>Federal</u> prison. "You will be placed within 500 miles of your legal address at the time of your arrest." But you better not believe that!

As you read other chapters you will find out that many of my Muslim friends are thousands of miles from their homes. Allah was indeed smiling—<u>He</u> put me only a taxi ride away from my home and Remy.

What kind of visits will you have? The County jails are the worst places in the whole American prison system for visitation. In a "jail" you will be behind a glass wall and use a telephone to speak with your visitor. Haven't you seen that many times in the movies or on TV?

Isn't it a sad scene as the inmate and his visitor/lover touch hands on the glass? When I was in CCA (Chapter 1) I asked Remy not to visit because of that type of visiting.

Did I want my frail wife to see me in a glass cage looking like a frighten animal? No, of course not! Would I be happy to have Remy see me in dirty jail clothing while she cried her eyes red? No!

So we just prayed and waited for the time when we would be able to see each other, sit together, and tightly hold hands. It turned out to be a long four months before Remy and I had our first prison visit.

I can still remember the tears of joy running down her smiling face that happy Saturday morning! My eyes were also wet, but I held my head up and insisted that the tears were just my allergies acting up.

Yes, in a F.C.I., you can sit together, hold hands, and cry!

Visiting days are special days to every inmate. Please don't tell us that you are "coming to visit", and then don't show up. Anyone who is reading this book and has a loved one in prison please, please keep your word in regards to visiting. Also, don't tell us, "I'll be there at 10:00AM", and then arrive at 2:00 PM!

Remy has a routine that she follows before, during, and after our visits. I have asked her to write about that in her own words. But I knew she would because Remy is always telling me to write about this or that for our book.

First, here's what I do to get ready for her visits. Remy can only visit on a Saturday, so Friday night I make sure I have a clean set of prison clothing and my work boots shined.

Saturday morning I will not leave the housing unit, not even to the mess hall to eat! Why not? Because I want the unit officer to know that I am there waiting to go to the Visiting Room.

When my Muslim brothers see me standing around "dressed" for a visit, they do not ask me to join them in any activities that day. Sometimes even my non-Muslim friends will shy away from me on a Visiting day!

And there are those who seeing me happy as I wait for Remy's visit, are reminded of the sadness of never having a visitor. Some inmates react in strange ways to the good fortune of others. Or is it to their own misfortune that they are reacting?

Visitors, if you are planning a surprise visit to your loved one, the surprise may be on you!

When you (a visitor) first enter the prison you are asked to fill out a form for the inmate you wish to visit with. The officer will then check the B.O.P.'s frequently "down" computer to see if your inmate is still at the facility. He will also check to see if you are on your "Eddie's" list of approved visitors.

If Eddie is still at FCI Phoenix and you are on his visiting list you can now enter the Visiting Room. What follows next is how your good intended surprise visit turns into a daymare!

Once inside the Visiting Room you'll hand your "Approved Visitor Form" to the desk officer. He will then look up what housing unit Eddie is in and call the officer there.

At the unit the officer will send an inmate orderly to your Eddie's cell to tell him you are waiting. But, because Eddie was not expecting a visit he is out somewhere in the recreation yard. Let's say that it is now 9:00 AM, just so that you can get an idea of the time frame involved.

If the unit officer knows your inmate he might get off his ass and walk around looking for him. But don't count on that. The longer a B.O.P. employee is in the system the less they do!

Not finding Eddie in his cell or in the unit the bright officer will now go to "Plan B", the computer. He will check to see if Eddie is working at a prison job, if so the search is over. If he is not, their search is on!

The good news is, yes FCI Phoenix does have a P.A. system. The bad news is, as of today's date (4-05-01) it is not working, nor has it worked for months. So there will be no loudspeaker saying. "Inmate Eddie, number 1245-678 report to Visiting." Remember, the clock is running and it started at 9:00 AM.

Today is an almost lucky day for you and Eddie. He was playing tennis and stopped at 10:00 AM and returned to the housing unit. When Eddie got inside a homie told him. "Hey man the stupid cop was looking for you, it think it was for a visit."

Eddie ran around looking for the unit officer, found him, and asked if he could call Visiting to see if you were still there. Are you now starting to understand why a surprise visit is not such a great idea? It is 10:15 AM as the desk officer informs you that they have "located" Eddie.

There will be a longer wait, as Eddie, who was playing tennis, needs a shower and a change of clothing. Finally at 10:45 AM a smiling Eddie enters the Visiting Room, one hour and forty minutes after you got there!

Next time will you make a "surprise" visit? No. I didn't think so!

There are no surprise visits for Remy and I. She can only come on a Saturday and only once a month. Visiting starts at 8:00AM, but I am sure she is there even before they unlock the doors.

A Recap for Inmates:
1.   Have a clean uniform and shined shoes, and be ready;
2.   Stay in the unit;
3.   Tell the officer you are expecting a visit and will be there in the unit.

A Recap for Visitors:
1.   Arrive at the promised time;
2.   Always show up if you say you are coming to visit;
3.   Please try not to make a surprise visit!

Author's note:
Next is my wife Remy's heart-filled message written in her own words. She is a native of the Philippines and some of her English may be a little off, but after reading it I choose not to correct or change a word of it.

Now, here's Remy's message:
Once Frank and I agreed on a visiting day, I would make an arrangement with my taxi driver—hiring him five (5) days in advance before the visiting day. I would always ask my taxi driver to pick me up before 8:00 AM from home and to come back for me at 3:00 PM, homebound.

When visitation day arrives, I am up at 4:00 AM and around 7:30AM, I would always call up FCI Phoenix first to verify if it is okay to visit just in case there is a lock down in progress. Then, I would dress up according to the dress code given by B.O.P., which is no sleeveless tops, no blazer, either! Short shorts and mini-skirts are no-no! Open-toe sandals and tongs are not allowed either! It's pitiful sometimes when I witnessed most visitors crying in the lobby just because they are not dressed properly and are not allowed visitation. That would be really devastating for me if it happened on me since I don't drive and would have to call my taxi-driver to pick me up! Worst scenario is—there is no public phone at the waiting room and you are not allowed to carry cell phone!

My taxi-driver would make sure I get in okay at the waiting room before he leaves due to sometimes lock down where visitations are cancelled! I can not rely on the phone assurance regarding FCI's facility status because there is no visitation due to lock down once we get there!

It is always delightful feeling when I can see the normal waiting room ready for processing visitors and would always be the first in line to fill up the visiting form and submit it right away to the C.O. in charge of that visiting day. Next, I would take a seat (there are two L-shape bench next to the glass wall of the building's main entrance) after depositing my big purse in a designated locker. You must ask for a token to close the locker. This was the status during my first few weeks' visitation but was changed after several months! There were no lockers assigned for visitors like me that does not drive and have to carry all the necessities in my purse. For those that drive, they must leave all their personal things in their car except for their ID and car keys.

It would only take at least between five to ten minutes to process the paper—if everything is working ring. Sometimes it takes almost an hour to process several papers especially during holidays where there are lots of inmates visiting families and loved ones! Computer-malfunctions for one! The C.O.'s would manually check and/or verify visitor's status! This takes half an hour against the five minutes time frame! The pain of waiting! Sometimes it seems forever!

When my name is announced, I would proceed to the counter for the officer in charge and submits my clear-plastic purse with my ID and US passport plus the $25.00 cash in one-dollar increments only to purchase foods at the vending machines.

We then would be told to submit to metal detector test (just like in airports) then after being stamped on the left hand, would wait again for the actual admittance after signing the "Visitor's log book" stating the exact time and date, listing Frank's name and register number as my Inmate to visit.

I would always make sure that I will be among the first five (5) of the visitors to be escorted when the Admitting Officer shows up and open the gate for the main visiting building.

Once we are admitted in the main visiting building, we then would submit the completed and approved visiting form to the C.O. at the front desk. The C.O. would double-check our forms and again check our ID and would direct us to take a seat and wait for our loved ones! However, we are ordered not to take the "Reserved Seats" for the Segregation status inmates next to the C.O.'s front desk for monitoring purpose!

Like every body else in the visiting room, I would go to the coffee and hot cocoa machine to buy our cup of coffee and cup of hot cocoa! There were no plenty of selections—we just have to buy what's offered in the vending machine! Doughnuts and candies were not really appealing and very costly too! But, I want to give the best to my loving husband—I want to please him. It always makes me happy when I see my beloved husband eat! He is good cook and would always prepare balanced meal—it was awkward to give him vending machine food but I did not have any choice! Wouldn't it be nice if we can bring them a home cook meals at least during holidays?

At around 8:30AM, Frank would show up with some of his co-inmates. I can't describe the exact words to express the happiness I feel! Seeing him in person, with his smile and then big hug makes my day!

Sitting side-by-side and holding hands, more often than not wiping tears in our eyes and all that unexplainable emotions we both felt for each other! I would always have lump on my throat and would always ask for his welfare! I want to ask him million of questions but decided against it. Being with him, sitting side by side was the most we can enjoy at the moment!

Of course, we have to comply with rules and regulations with B.O.P.'s regarding visitation. The visitor, and our inmates are not supposed to embrace and kiss—we can only embrace and kiss during the arrival of the inmates at the beginning of the visit and during the visitor's departure.

I always look forward to "Visitation Day" where Frank and I could hold our hands, sit side by side and eat together. I would just pretend we are having an indoor picnic eating what is sold at the vending machines—his favorite beef or roast sandwich while I choose the Buffalo hot wings!

The most important part of our visit is reassuring him that I will be waiting for him when he gets out and gives him positive moral support, spiritually and emotionally, the best I know how!

Laughing and caring for each other during our visitation is always a happy time for both of us and I would always wish it wouldn't end! I wish we could visit everyday!

At five minutes before 3:00 PM, the C.O. will announce that visiting is over! It was very hard to accept but rule is rule—visitation is over for the day! We have to give each other a good-bye embrace and good-bye kiss! The inmates would then be ordered to stand on the other side of the room while we, the visitors would be escorted to the door back to the main entrance of the admitting lobby in groups of ten.

We had to show our ID again and our left hand laser-scanned (stamped earlier) we are then allowed to leave!

If only I drive! I would be visiting Frank every weekend instead of a one-day on a monthly basis! It would be nice spending the weekends with him but—right now it would just be wishful thinking!

Well, anyway, once I reached home, I would look forward to his call—at 6:30 PM to check my status (if I reached home safe, etc.) that is really sweet and so caring for him to do so. If I could make calls to let him know if my safe arrival, I would do so!

Author's last note:

Well readers, what could I add after Remy's thoughts? Only, that Allah has blessed me with a loyal and wonderful wife!

The next chapter is "FDC Dublin".

Chapter 7

On To Dublin!

Author's note:

Yes, the time to leave FCI Phoenix had come at last! But not before I had spent ninety-eight days in a punishment/segregation cell for Warden Ellis, A.K.A. the Jackass.

My thoughts at the time were mixed and uncertain. What lie ahead for my wife Remy and I? There were other questions dancing around in my head, but the B.O.P. would answer all of those soon enough.

October 9, 2001 at 2:30 AM.

Without warning the dull 75-watt bulb in my roach-infested cell blinked on. Seconds later four officers rushed into the cell, that didn't leave much room for the fifth officer who pushed a wheelchair in.

"Tucci, you're fu—king out of here! Pick up your shit and let's go!" Said the rotund Lieutenant Renskowski. He was the same idiot who signed my Lock Up Order way back on July 4, 2001!

I yelled at the big dummy questioning him. "Show me the paperwork! Then may be I'll try to get up!" Well my remark didn't go over to good with the obese Renkowski, or the four other sadistic officers in the cell.

Oh, I forgot to mention a sixth officer, (Ms. Ventura) who was using a video camera to film the epic event. Was her videotape for future generations of B.O.P. guards to use as a training film?

Included on the film is the "famous" Federal prison "bend and spread your ass" routine. Remember that the scene was being video taped by a female officer?

Ms. Ventura is rumored to be a lesbian and probably wasn't looking at my genitalia with lust. But, never the less a woman was filming me naked! As a Muslim I find this totally un-excusable!

Gee, I wonder if I could get copies of that x-rated tape for the public? I am sure you would like to see how they treat a non-violent, 60 year old man in Federal prison.

The two biggest of the five male Apes pushed me into a straight-up position on the steel bunk, and someone threw a set of travel clothes at my head.

One of the "get Tucci out of my prison" crew, hurriedly tossed my few possessions into a pillow-case. Soon I had all of my wrong sizes of travel clothing on, including one size 9 shoe and one size 11 shoe (the left foot). Everything, even little things, becomes a part of the B.O.P.'s punishment.

Now the same two Apes dumped me into the wheelchair, they knew I was very weak from my on-going sixteen day hunger strike. So, no walking for me.

A light came on in my head. I'll bet that's why the M<u>s</u>. Was filming this, FCI Phoenix was just covering their own fat asses!

Again the two Apes, one pushing the chair, and the other walking alongside holding me back from sliding out of the wheelchair, hurried me over to the medical building.

A nurse was called in at 3:00AM, most likely on Warden Ellis say-so, and waiting to "okay" me for the long bus trip. She signed some papers and handed them back to Ape #1 but Ape#2 asked. "Are you sure Tucci is okayed to travel?"

Her answer wasn't a surprise. "Yes." She said quietly, almost not wanting me to hear.

I couldn't just sit there without saying something. "Excuse me! Hello! I am on the sixteenth day of a hunger strike, weak, dizzy, and dehydrated and you say I am well enough to travel? What school of Veterinarian Medicine did you attend? Because you don't know shit about humans!"

Doesn't that explain to you a little about the quality of health care the B.O.P. provides? Or could it be that lard ass Ellis just wanted to "get that old Muslim bastard out of my prison!"

I remained at the hospital unit for over two hours as the other "bus" prisoners were taken to the R&D for their travel clothes.

At 5:30 AM the nurse, pushing the chair and with Ape #2 escorting us, headed over to bus area. A few minutes later a shiny new B.O.P. bus arrived. The nurse using her best wheelchair skills speed pushed me over to the bus.

Then a small problem came up, there were three steep stairs leading into the bus, this was <u>not</u> good to say the least! Your convict/author has surgical pins in both legs and a helpless case of arthritis in both knee joints.

The two Apes solved the problem. These officers could pass for pro weightlifters. They lifted me out of the wheelchair, up the three steps, and dumped me into a rear seat on the bus.

Wasn't I handled with care or what? After the "old man" was seated the other twenty-four inmates clanged onto the bus with their chains dragging.

The last inmate to board the bus had <u>no</u> handcuffs, belly chains, or leg irons on. He would act as the trip's food orderly. Most likely he was a "snitch" or a "queer."

As our B.O.P. taxi departed he started passing out two pieces of Danish pastry and a small four-ounce cup of some kind of juice. He insisted on leaving a double order of both with me. I didn't know why?

In my mind were these questions. "I am leaving FCI Phoenix and Warden Ellis behind, should I start eating? Or maybe I'll just drink the juice?" The good news was that I quickly decided to eat and drink. The bad news was the pastry and drinks were still frozen solid! They remained that way for hours on the empty seat next to me. All praise to Allah!

Here are my final words about FCI Phoenix.

"I have been in far too many prisons at other times in my long life. Please do believe me when I say that Warden Ellis, Captain Miller, and most of the staff and officers are nothing short of just plain mean spirited!"

The driver pulled out of the parking lot and down the I-17 ramp heading south. Soon I saw the sign, "Dunlap Avenue Exit" (my home was there) and I thought of my wife Remy asleep as the bus speed by. To myself I said. "I love you Remy!"

Three hours later the GMC bus pulled off the freeway and into a Burger King parking lot. All three of my "hosts" left the vehicle to smoke, stretch their legs, and buy coffee. No, they didn't bring me back a coffee.

Before continuing on our holiday outing the food orderly/snitch/queer, passed out box lunches. Yes, I did eat some of it. What was in the box? There were four slices of stale bread, foil packs of peanut butter and jelly, a large foil pack of cheese spread, which was labeled "U.S. Government Surplus, Not for Resale—08-1986." Aren't we now in the year 2001?

Rounding out the box lunch meal were also a small bag of chips and a fruit bar. However, there wasn't anything to drink with this B.O.P. five star meal. Oh, I get it now! That's what the frozen juice, now thawed out, was for! Thanks B.O.P.!

The shotgun guard and the driver had changed positions. Lieutenant Renkowski would be able to keep on sleeping. Do you think he got that obese from over working?

I kept looking out the window and thinking about the heavy price I had paid for this trip. There would now be no visits from Remy as they were taking me far away from her.

God I wished I had taken the time to teach Remy how to driver our car. Also, my personal property was left behind at FCI Phoenix to be shipped to my new facility. But who knows when or if I would receive it?

The miles and hours slowly went by and finally the GMC stopped again, this time to refill the bus's double tanks. Guess what? A second box lunch was passed out with the exact fare as the first one. Thanks a second time B.O.P.!

Before getting on the road the last change of musical chairs was done. It was Rotund Renkowski's turn, and he would drive the last leg to Dublin.

More miles, more hours, and more staring out the bus window at the never changing scenery. Then! A large overhead freeway sign said "Dublin 5 Miles". Well, at least I know where I am now headed.

FDC Dublin is just like the FTC in Chapter 2, it is the Western Region's Transfer Center. If they (the B.O.P.) sent me here, it meant two things. First, I would be imprisoned somewhere in the West. Second, I would not be staying long in Dublin because it is a transfer hub.

The bus turned off at the Dublin exit and I noticed that FDC Dublin was not far from the main part of the city. FCI Phoenix is isolated and thirty miles from downtown, and without public transportation to the FCI. For sixteen months Remy would taxi to our visits.

Our bus passed through the outer gates of FDC Dublin, the inner gates and came to a halt in front of the receiving area. Each inmates name was called and they exited the bus, except one, me.

I didn't even try to stand up and requested medical help. The Phoenix officers, who were in a damn hurry to turn the bus around and head back, carried me into the hospital unit.

My cane was handed back to me, but there would be no wheelchair for me to sit in yet. Looking around I saw a clean, well-lighted facility. There were no dirty floors, pealing paint, or roaches, as was the case in FCI Phoenix.

Before going to the R&D for clothing and processing a doctor came to check all my vital signs. He said I didn't look so good and asked. "Who was the idiot who signed you off to travel?" I smiled and replied. "Oh, some asshole named Ellis!"

The doctor called "custody" and I was wheel chaired over the R&D. Next, as always when entering a B.O.P prison, I was strip-searched. Hey, with all the stripping I was doing if I were a younger man, I would make a post-prison career of it! Those ladies pay big money to watch male strippers!

Now a clothing issue. Here I go again. One tee shirt, one pair of boxers, socks, pull-on blue sneakers, and a damn red jumpsuit! The same clothing and the same colors as my ninety-eight day stay in "the hole." Some things never change!

After changing into the chic designer outfit, paperwork would be next. But, Mr. Rivas (a guard/counselor) asked me to follow him back to the clothing issue area.

He handed me a size 2x <u>green</u> jumpsuit to now change into. I was shocked and asked him. "Why am I getting a green jumpsuit?" Rivas replied. "Mr. Tucci a green suit means you are going into our regular population here." After many long days in Segregation I didn't know what to say except. All praise to Allah!

My "processing" ended with a jail photo and signing one last B.O.P. form. There were only two questions on the form. "Do you have any fear for your safety?" And, "Is there any reason why you should not be placed back in population?" My answer to both questions was, of course, no!

With that done the last thing to do was to find me a cell. I was taken to J-2, the "J" means <u>jail</u>, and assigned to #218. The jail was just like the other parts of this FDC, clean and well lit-up.

Wasn't call #218 on the second tier? Yes it was, but here in FDC Dublin they have a wheelchair lift. All that I had to do was wheel-in and press the button!

My new cellie was Steve who had the cell to himself and the <u>bottom</u> bunk. I really felt bad about him having to move to the top bed, but what could I do? I could not climb to the top bunk with my bad legs and heart problem.

Never the less, Steve and I became friends, exchanged home addresses, and promised to write each other when we got to our final destinations.

The great news here in FDC Dublin is their food, it is ten (10) times better than any other facility I have been in. Starting on 11 June 2000 until today, 21 October 2001, I have been in seven (7) B.O.P. prisons! Yes, writing a non-fiction book about the B.O.P. will get you moved around!

In closing, there is nothing bad about FDC Dublin that this convict/author can say. There <u>isn't</u> one staff member here that even remotely could be called a jerk. These officers and staff are a credit to the Bureau of Prisons.

Hopefully you too may at sometime be sent here to FDC Dublin, California. Soon I will be leaving here but if asked where I would like to do my time, my answer would be a loud Dublin! My next stop? Agad-agad? That's Bisaya for "Let's wait and see?"

CHAPTER 8

FDC Sheridan

October 23, 2001

At 2:50 AM (the B.O.P. never sleeps) a female officer unlocked the steel door and yelled with a extremely loud and squeaky voice. "Hey, are you Tucci?" She was probably heard at least ten cells down the tier. I didn't answer Squeaky because I thought it was a trick question.

And why would I think that? Maybe because I was the only inmate in the cell? Or, could it be because of marker outside the cell that said. "Tucci, Frank #03836-014."

Squeaky added. "Roll your shit up old man, you're out of here, bus time!" You can be positive that when B.O.P. officers are being trained for this "Kodak Minute", they are instructed the following: "Always refer to the inmate's personal property as shit.".

Being in a "transit status" all I had was ten postage stamps, a small nail clipper, and a tube of denture adhesive. But I wasn't even allowed to take those on the prison bus, even though I just bought the stuff in FDC Dublin's commissary.

The B.O.P. mailed everything home to my wife Remy in Phoenix. Yes, your Federal tax dollars at work! What was the cost of their package? Maybe around two dollars? But don't sell the Bureau of Prisons short, they know what they are doing!

If you look at it from their side, you will learn just how slick they really are. Here's their scam. The postage stamps cost $3.40, the nail clipper only 60 cents, but the Effergrip was overpriced at $3.25.

Adding those three items up it comes to $7.25. So even with the two dollar cost of the mailing the Feds are still $5.25 ahead. Why? Because I will have to buy those same things again at my next facility for $7.25.

There were twenty-three others leaving FDC Dublin with me as the unit officer told us. "You guys are on the bus to Sheridan (Oregon)." All praise to Allah, this time I knew where I was going before getting on the bus!

A cold breakfast was offered us at 3:30AM and we waited in the "day room" until 5:00AM. I am sure you can guess where the next stop would be, yes, that's right, their R&D area.

At the R&D our happy group was split in two and stuffed into holding cells. Once again I was herded with eleven others into a four-man cell. Yes, twelve inmates packed into a cell designed to hold <u>four</u> prisoners!

Why do I say the cell was built to house only four inmates? Here is the simple answer—there were only four steel bunks in the cell! I rest my case! It was standing room only, again.

Soon came the fun part for the "good old boys" of the B.O.P. Now they get to slap handcuffs, belly chains, and those damn awful leg-irons on their "scum" prisoners. Gosh, these people even whistle and smile as they go about their work!

In charge of the bus was a tall, well groomed and soft speaking lieutenant who was Black. He insisted that I should have leg-irons put on. "Just like everybody else on the fu-king bus!" He looked at me and shouted.

Leg-irons were a first for this old man! Remember in Chapter 1 (CCA) when I tripped on my chains getting off their junk of a bus? You'll also recall that the doctor on Con-Air ordered my leg chains removed. Well, the doctor wrote "no leg restraints" into my B.O.P. medical file.

I asked the lieutenant. "Would you please check my medical file, it says no leg restraints!" His all to quick reply was right in tune with the B.O.P.'s mentality. "Old man where the fu—k am I going to get a copy of your medical file at five o'clock in the fu—king morning?"

I thought for a few seconds and then replied smartly. "How about calling the medical department?"

Well, my remark went over like a lead balloon! Shortly after 6:00 AM, in chains, we were led out to the waiting bus. Yes, I had leg-irons on! I can only guess that the Black lieutenant felt good about putting White folks in chains.

The bus ride would last for twelve long hours, with stops only for the officers comfort and to take on fuel.

Our travel meal was again a B.O.P. box lunch, which was almost the same crap as on the trip in from FCI Phoenix.

Six hundred miles later the chugging prison bus came to a dying stop at FDC Sheridan, Oregon. Damn it was cold! On October 9, 2001 it was 103 degrees when Warden Ellis ran me out of FCI Phoenix.

At FDC Dublin when we left that morning it was a sunny 75 degrees. But, now getting off the bus, my system almost went into a shock at the 40-degree Oregon weather!

What a difference two weeks and the B.O.P. can make in a convict/author's life. The bus was quickly unloaded and the inmates rushed into FDC Sheridan's receiving area. I was last off their trolley as the officers carried me down the steps.

A semi-new wheelchair was provided for my grand entrance into FDC Sheridan. Although I didn't know it as they speed wheeled me in, the rest of my day was headed straight down hill!

You already know all about the R&D and "processing" so I won't bore you with repeat details. Except to again voice my objection as a Muslim, to female B.O.P. staff being present as I am ordered to. "Lift up your balls, now bend forward and spread your ass!"

Author's question for the B.O.P.

Are some of your guard staff sexually perverted? Or are they just border-line homosexuals? Next, I may confuse you with these facts:

At FDC Dublin before being issued "bus clothing", I was strip searched using the "bend and spread" routine. After I was clothed came the handcuffs, belly chains, and leg-irons, followed by a quick march on to the bus.

I remained on the noisy bus for more than twelve hours before its arrival at FDC Sheridan. When off the bus I was rushed directly to their R&D area and the first order given to me was "Strip, bend and spread 'em!"

Why? What legitimate reason can there be for a repeat "strip and bend"? Was it that the receiving staff just needed their cheap thrill for the day?

The last and down hill part of my first day in FDC Sheridan was the clothing issue. Jumpsuits are the style here and they come in three different colors.

If they issued me a green suit I would be sent to their FPC (Federal Prison Camp) but there was no chance of that.

If they issued me a blue suit it would be a short drive over to their FDC (Federal Detention Center). Then a few weeks later, a welcome move over to their FCI (Federal Correctional Institution). All three facilities are here in Sheridan, Oregon.

Guess what? The old man didn't get a green or a blue suit. Well, that left only one other color. Orange! Oh shit, I was headed back into the SHU, Segregation, "the hole"!

After being out in population for two weeks at FDC Dublin why was I being tossed back into Segregation? It was déjà vu of my ninety-eight days in FCI Phoenix's SHU!

That night I was celled with a Hispanic named Rolando who was being released from "the hole" in the morning. He was happy about that and sang the night away until dawn.

After breakfast they took Rolando out. All praise to Allah, now I can get some sleep?

But I was wrong! A guard switched on the cell's light, in the SHU the switch is outside the cell, and opened the small trap in the door.

"Tucci the Looney Tuner wants to see you now!" He said impatiently. I was only guessing but I thought he meant the Psychologist, sadly I was right.

Doctor Boelgrin is a heavy man, bifocal, quiet in speech, and very slow in his movements. He opened our dialogue with a question. "Mr. Tucci what's this I hear about you being on a hunger strike?"

At once I knew why I was in "the hole!" The three successful hunger strikes at FCI Phoenix had come back to haunt me here!

The doctor's next question was a little more direct. "When was the last time you ate Mr. Tucci?" The truth was that I had not eaten in two days, but only because I was trying to cut back after over-eating at FDC Dublin.

When Warden Ellis completed the B.O.P. paperwork he got in one last slap at me. He added to the transfer file. "Inmate is currently on a hunger strike."

I was sure I would be in "the hole" for some time to come as a result of Ellis's meanness. Doctor Boelgrin's next question "Mr. Tucci what's it going to take to get you off this hunger strike?"

Wouldn't it be useless to try and explain that I was not on a hunger strike? Didn't the doctor have Warden Ellis comments and the file from FCI Phoenix in front of him?

So I played the hand I was dealt and answered Boelgrin. "Put me back in population doctor and I'll eat the next meal!" He replied. "Mr. Tucci I'll get back to you." Less than 24 hours later I was out of "the hole" and back in population of "sorts". Thank you Doctor Boelgrin!

But I wasn't out of the woods yet. They didn't drive me over to the FCI but instead dumped me in their "jail" (the FDC). Being in the FDC was only a slight step up from being in Segregation.

One last paragraph about FCI Phoenix and Warden Ellis. Often during my 98 days in the SHU Ellis would tell me. "Tucci, you'll leave this facility over my dead body!" Well I assume he is dead because I am here in Sheridan, Oregon!

The following facts are from the B.O.P.'s policy statement on "Inmate Hunger Strikes". Are there maybe also "Staff Hunger Strikes?" Shouldn't they have just labeled it "Hunger Strikes?"

You also read "the facts" in the long Introduction, but I think they are important enough to review again.

Remember please that a prison hunger strike is not like you see in the movies or on TV. Those always show the prisoner in a clean hospital bed with a nurse, doctor, and clergy member at bedside. Trust me, that's not the way it is in Federal Prison!

1. If you do not eat for 72 hours (miss nine meals) you are then considered on a strike.
2. You will be put in a separate cell away from others (this was always a plus as most cells in the SHU had three or four inmates).
3. The water to the cell's sink and toilet will be shut off.
4. If you want a drink of water, which is allowed while on strike, you must ask the offer. He will bring you one cup at a time which will be logged into your "strike file".
5. You are not allowed a blanket, sheets, or a pillow, only a mattress.
6. All hygiene items, even toilet paper will be taken away from you. If you should need toilet paper, the guard will roll off a small amount for you.
7. All medication is taken away from you except Nitroglycerin pills. The medic will bring your needs to you one pill at a time.

That's what faces any inmate going on a hunger strike. The B.O.P.'s rules are meant to punish you and force you to end your strike quickly.

But if this sixty-two years old man can do it, so can you. Put the mind in gear and the body can do anything.

My first staff contact at FDC Sheridan was a gawky looking Asian named Mr. Fuji, probably short for Fujiyama, who assigned me to cell 111.

Entering the over-sized broom closet I saw a set of bunk beds on the back wall and a single bed on the left wall. Damn it, a three-man cell again!

An inmate was lying in the bunk bed's lower reading a pornographic magazine. The cell's other inmate was out on "sick-call". Fuji informed Porno. "This old man has a medical order for a lower bunk. Which one of you two guys has been in the cell longer?"

Yes folks the prisoners have a seniority system in your Federal prisons. Porno had been there the longest so Mike, the inmate at medical would now have to move to the top bunk.

I never like running a fellow inmate out of their bed but there is no way I can climb up to a top bunk.

In prison all things are done with a certain protocol and every inmate learns that quickly, or he gets hurt!

Even though Fuji had assigned me the lower bunk I just couldn't strip off Mike's sheets and blankets. So I took a seat on the cold hard floor and waited.

A half hour later, Officer Fuji returned with Mike and a surprise. Mike now had a medical order "for a lower bunk". Porno had more time in Cell 111 but he would be the one climbing to the top bunk.

There would be one last surprise for the day. Officer Shaw, the second shifter, came to the cell with what was good news to me! Porno was told. "Roll it up you're moving to another cell."

Was it Allah's doing, taking Porno and his filthy magazines out of the cell? I chose to believe that it was.

Reading the "Admission and Orientation Handbook" I found some bad news.

"Movement from the FDC to the FCI Inmates housed at the Federal Detention Center awaiting transfer to the Federal Correctional Institution will wait an average of eight weeks."

That meant that for eight weeks I would be locked in my cell twenty-one hours a day, versus being locked in for only six hours a day at the FCI!

Why? I was designated to FCI Sheridan not this "jail" called an FDC! I have already served sixteen months on my sentence and there is no reason why I should be placed in a FDC!

Mr. Hollingsworth, the jail administrator had the following answer about my detention. "We are waiting for bed space over at the FCI for you, Mr. Tucci." His answer is just plain old bull sh—t!

Here's why, and how I know that. The facts are that the B.O.P.'s super smart computers would not have moved me from FCI Phoenix to FDC Dublin to here in Sheridan, Oregon unless there was a bed waiting for me!

If the B.O.P. moved me without bed space ready and waiting for me, it can be called only one thing. "Gross mismanagement!"

October 29, 2001

It seemed like I had been waiting for weeks at FDC Sheridan to be moved a few hundred feet over to their FCI. But, it had been only six long days.

My wife Remy's letters and faxes to Warden Hollingsworth had worked! She had pleaded to have me moved closer to the Hospital Unit, which was inside FCI Sheridan's grounds. Salamat my dear wife!

Last night after the supper meal, officer Shaw came to the cell and said quietly. "Mr. Tucci you will be leaving about 7:30 AM, check with the day watch officer."

Well there's a first, any staff member has never informed me politely of a move. Remember my moves from FCI Phoenix and FDC Dublin?

I could not sleep the whole night as I thought about the freedom movement I would soon have at the FCI.

Dawn came, and then quickly it was 6:00 AM as the cell door popped open for breakfast. Mike and I said our farewells as I ate my last meal at FDC Sheridan.

Finished with the meal I returned to Cell 111 for the last time, stuffed a pillowcase with my few belongings and returned to the "day room".

There were only eight of us being moved across the yard, some of the inmates, like the Handbook said, had waited weeks to be moved. But, I had waited only six days, and again thanks to my Remy.

Do you like re-runs? Here I go again! The R&D for a strip search, clothing, and a sack lunch. But, this time only eight of us were stuffed into a four-man cell. I guess you could call that progress of a sort?

Only three hours later our jailer returned and yelled at us. "Let's have two of you bad guys out here at a time."

Next came the B.O.P.'s ever popular "iron". I wondered if handcuffs, belly chains, and leg-irons were needed for a trip of only a few hundred feet?

Like always I was the last inmate out of the cell and the last one to get "ironed". Isn't it dumb to rush out of the cell to be chained? I have tried to explain that to the "youths", but I guess they really like sitting around chained up.

On to FCI Sheridan, but not in a bus this time, two new GMC mini-vans were used. The short three (3) minute ride ended at still one more R&D area, and a reverse of the prior R&D's outgoing events.

There we waited to be put back "on the yard", and waited, and waited. But I didn't care about this wait, at least I was at FCI Sheridan!

CHAPTER 9

FCI Sheridan

Author's Note:

This chapter has sub chapters within it that were written while I was in FCI Sheridan. To judge FCI Sheridan against FCI Phoenix is like comparing a lovely wife to a prostitute! Yes, they both can do the same job, but which one was better for you? I used a prostitute as an example because frankly, the B.O.P. screws you in so many different ways! Some places in the chapter I may say "better" than at FCI Phoenix, but the "better" is only the way things should be. To be curt, FCI Phoenix and Warden Ellis were ass backwards!

October 19, 2001

It is hours later and I am still locked in the SHU at FCI Sheridan, but only minutes from the freedom of the facility's yard.

Clunk, clunk, our jailer finally returned, unlocked the cell and yelled at us. "Off your asses, time to go!" It sounded like a female voice, well I thought the jailer was a woman? But never the less the turn key could play offensive line for the New York Jets.

"Everyone line up against that wall!" The Jet instructed and then added. "Grab a bed roll out of that bin, state your name and number and I'll tell you what unit you are assigned to."

So I pulled out a stylish and tightly wound bed roll and spoke up. "Tucci, 03836-014." The Jet replied. "Tucci? Are you the one who is supposed to be writing a great book? Well, sir, you are in Unit #4."

I am a non-smoker so I was assigned to Building #4, which is the only non-smoking unit at FCI Sheridan. Reaching the unit I reported directly to the officer who led me to a cell. It turned out that I had a top bunk in a three-man cell!

I was a little irate as I informed the officer. "I have a medical order for a bottom bunk!" The guard claimed that he wasn't notified of that and I should see the counselor to straighten it out, or. "Just shut up and take the fu—king bed."

There was a long line outside the office because it was a Team Review day. After only two hours I was able to speak with the Counselor, Mr. Hawks. He said. "Just sit tight and I'll find you a bottom bed." Hawks was back quickly and walked me over to cell #124 and a lower bunk.

My latest cellmates were Dennis, an old timer (bank robber) and a Mexican who's name I never got, he left for home the next morning. So as of today there are only two of us in a three-man cell, but I am sure that will change soon.

After making my bed, neatness doesn't count, and tossing my things into the locker, I left the cell to check out the rest of Building #4.

The unit is three tiers high, almost clean, and has a wheel chair lift that only goes as high as the second tier. Walking around I also found the TV rooms, the <u>three</u> telephones, and the Laundry Room with three washers and three dryers.

Of course the Laundry Room was on the third/top tier! So, if you are totally wheelchair bound (I am not) you can not get to the Laundry, because the wheel chair lift only goes to the second tier. Good planning, B.O.P.! Couldn't the Laundry Room have been built on the first floor?

"Count time, count time, everybody get in your house!" Shouted the baby-faced officer. "House", is the term inmates who have been down too long call their cells. The officers use the term to insult us. It was now time for the 4:00 PM Standing Count.

For those of you who have never been in a Federal prison I'll explain the "Count" and why it is now a B.O.P. mandate.

Everyday at 4:00 PM you must return to your cells to be locked in, and to stand up! You will remain standing until two officers, in case one counts wrong, tour the unit counting the standing inmates. Hence the B.O.P. terminology, Standing Count.

Rumor has it that the Count came into being in the 1930's of the B.O.P.'s early days. Back then the Feds only housed one inmate to a cell. Without a Standing Count in effect an inmate was found dead in his bunk after a few days!

If a Standing Count were in effect they may of found the inmate dead a whole day sooner?

After the Count and roaming around I found the unit's wheel chair and took possession of it. My next exploring was to find the mess hall, which turned out to be far, far, away from Building #4. Just as was the case in FCI Phoenix, I was in the unit farthest from the chow line.

I was slightly hungry so with my cane in hand I set out to find food. When I got there the mess hall was full and overcrowded and after getting a tray I limped around looking for a seat.

There were two empty tables in a back area so I went there and sat down to eat. But, a skinny white inmate came over and told me. "You can't sit there old man, the tables are reserved for the N.A.'s. You better move before one of the Chiefs kicks you the fu—k out!"

I was considering telling the N.A.'s that I am one ninety-seventh Indian on my great, great, great grandmother's side.

As I sat there filling my face I noticed most of the guards looking at me. I guess they were thinking one of two things. First, maybe they were watching to see if the Indians would run me off!

Second, they might have been thinking. "That old man really has balls!"

Well it wasn't so much "balls", but the facts that I was tired, hungry, and not going to keep walking around while balancing a food tray!

After the meal I walked slowly back to the unit and was lucky to find a telephone not being used. Remy was home now? I hoped! Yes, and it was wonderful to hear her sweet and accented voice.

"Yes, mahal (Bisaya for dear) I am at the FCI!" So ended my first day at FCI Sheridan and the start of a torrid eight month stay there! But I am getting ahead in my story.

Once the B.O.P. considers you a "trouble maker" your life in Federal prison will become a living hell! Case in point: FCI Phoenix and Warden Ellis.

For the thirteen months that I remained in that prison's regular population I never received a serious Incident Report. But, during my ninety eight (98) days in "the hole" they wrote so many "shots" that I stopped counting at number ten.

Next, "The Ghost of Phoenix Past!" It will explain just how a "troublemaker" gets treated as I arrived in yet one more B.O.P. facility.

The Ghost of Phoenix Past!

November 3, 2001

Yes, Warden Ellis and FCI Phoenix can still reach out to interfere with my life, ruin my days, and continue to punish me! At 10:00 AM officer Herber strolled over to the cell. "Tucci, the lieutenant wants to see you in his office." As you know, the lieutenant doesn't send for inmates to pass the time of day, or to have tea and cookies with.

I dressed quickly and found one of the "brothers" to wheelchair me up to the lieutenant's office.

I tried to get my mind to focus on what I could have done. Nothing came to mind as I had been in FCI Sheridan less than a week.

A lieutenant with a crew cut stuck his head out the door and said. "Tucci, inside!" There were several other inmates also waiting to see him, how did he know who "Tucci" was? Maybe my inmate photo was on a dart board somewhere at the facility?

His very first sentence answered all my questions.

"Mr. Tucci I have an Incident Report with two charges against you." Next came his official B.O.P. speech. "You have the right to, etc., etc., do you understand the rights I just read?"

I wished he would stop with the required bull crap and just read the damn "shot." Finally he did. "First is the charge of, Use Of The Telephone For Abuses Other Than Criminal Activity. Second is, Refusing An Order Of the Unit Disciplinary Committee."

With that done Crew Cut next read the Incident Report to me. It is printed exactly as Officer G. Martin wrote it.

"On 11-3-2001 at 9:50AM I became aware that inmate Francis Tucci, #03836-014, had made seven phone calls while on telephone restriction. The Admission and Orientation handbook clearly states that inmates must not attempt to use the telephone while on restriction.

The Unit Disciplinary Committee sanctioned inmate Tucci to loss of telephone privileges from 09-27-2001 to 11-25-2001. Inmate Tucci refused this order my making seven calls during this time period. Inmate Tucci's last completed call was at 5:22 PM on 11-02-2001."

When Crew Cut finished reading the report he didn't ask me if I was guilty, or not guilty. Why not you ask? Because the B.O.P.'s mind set is. "That an inmate is always guilty or the good officer would not have written an Incident Report."

Also I would like to mention, that all the time I was in the office he kept trying to get me to lose my temper. At some point I did raise my voice just a little and was told. "Tucci one more fu—king word out of you and I'll toss your old ass in Seg!"

Crew Cut's last attempt to press my button came quickly as he pushed the Report (my copy) across the cluttered desk and on to the floor in front of me.

Was I supposed to bend forward in the wheelchair and try to pick it up? Or was I suppose to ask the jackass to pick it up for me?

To be on the safe side I did neither. I had the last word as I turned the wheelchair around to leave. "If I am on telephone restriction how come my P.I.N. worked for seven, not one or two, but seven calls? It didn't work for me at Phoenix or Dublin!"

Damn the B.O.P. don't these mental midgets ever get anything right? To explain what was happening I'll have to "Ghost" back to FCI Phoenix. Starting on.

September 25, 2001

While in Segregation I received an Incident Report for "Disobeying a Direct Order", the first of many. What was the Direct Order? Here is what officer Johnson wrote in his stupid and self-serving Incident Report. "Inmate Tucci, #03836-014, refused a direct order to allow another inmate to be celled with him."

So why did I refuse? Simply put, because Warden Ellis had locked me up in P.C. (Protective Custody), on a whim, and then used an elaborate hoax to keep me in there for 98 days!

What fabrication of fact(s) did Warden Ellis was to dump me in the "hole"? Well, Ellis claims that an anonymous note was dropped into the unit mailbox that said. "Tucci's cell will be fire-bombed with him in it."

Trust me that was a truly big lie! Second only to the Feds, "the check is in the mail." There was never a note or a threat! But, that's in the past, now back to the "Ghost".

The result of officer Johnson's "shot" was the U.D.C.'s sanction of,"sixty days loss of telephone privileges." When I arrived at FDC Dublin the telephone sanction was still in effect and my P.I.N. would not allow me to make calls.

But when I got to FCI Sheridan I tried the telephone and my P.I.N. worked! Hello Remy! Hence, the seven calls I made as in officer Martin's report.

Is it my fault their computer allowed me to make seven phone calls? Or maybe the <u>B.O.P.</u> thinks I had someone on the outside hack into their system and turn my P.I.N. on?

Here's a short recap of my last few days at FCI Phoenix.

1.   I had been in Segregation for 98 days.
2.   A third hunger strike was now on day number fifteen.
3.   Was a transfer to a new facility getting close?
4.   I didn't care about getting Incident reports and kept refusing cellies.
5.   I stopped caring about the loss of visits, telephone, or commissary.
6.   The only thing I cared about was getting moved out of FCI Phoenix!

Well that brings you up to date as I sit here in FCI Sheridan waiting to be kicked to the curb again. But, let's see what an old man can do against the mighty B.O.P.?

Damn, I wouldn't be able to call Remy and let her know about the "new" telephone set back. She would without my calls panic, or as she and I say, go Lucy, Lucy"! It was time again to fight back.

Sunday, November 4, 2001

I stayed up all night planning a battle strategy. The first and most important thing to do was to let Remy know why I didn't call the night before. Only one of the office staff would be in on a Sunday, Mr. Jbour the Case Manager. He was due at 7:30 AM so at 7:32 AM I was outside his office.

With a pained look, I knocked lightly and he politely waved me in. "Mr. Jbour, I need to make a telephone call home, because yesterday I was placed on telephone restriction." I handed him the "shot", he read it and then asked what phone number to dial.

Remy answered on the second ring. I explained everything about the latest "shot" to her, thanked Jbour and left to plan the rest of my one-man attack.

The plan was simple, but anything could happen to derail it. First, I would write out an "Inmate Request To Staff" for Warden Hood, explaining the "shot" and the telephone problem.

Second, I would seek out the Warden and personally deliver the Request to him. The bad news was I didn't know if Warden Hood was at the facility that day. Also, I didn't even know what the Warden looked like, having never met him.

So when I got to the dining room (all Wardens are there for the afternoon meal) I asked an officer. "Hey, which one of the suits is Warden Hood?"

He was well dressed (a suit). Extremely well groomed, about fifty years old, and with an air of confidence about him. As I pushed my wheelchair towards him, I thought. "Oh well, here goes nothing!"

I stopped in front of him and in an low voice said. "I would like to leave a written Inmate Request with you." He replied. "Please take it out of the envelope and hand it to me."

He quickly read it, nodded his head a few times and then said. "I know who you are Mr. Tucci, Warden Ellis mentioned you to me. I have also heard about your book."

Oh shit, I am a dead duck! Warden Ellis strikes again? Our conversation lasted about five minutes and I left with the impression that Warden Hood was a decent man who would help me.

But in the meantime I still had the "shot" and the Unit Disciplinary Committee (U.D.C.) to deal with.

November 7, 2001

"Show Time!" Counselor Hawks has just said. "The U.D.C. is waiting to see you Mr. Tucci." So, off I go again into harm's way again, or is it still?

"Things will be different for you here than in FCI Phoenix!" Said Ms. Angus, yes, that's her real name. I almost believed that, until she and the U.D.C. referred my Incident Report on to the next step towards punishment. The Disciplinary Hearing Officer (D.H.O.).

The U.D.C. was recommending a one year loss of my telephone usage! It really didn't matter that the B.O.P. screwed up and their computer allowed me to make seven telephone calls to my wife!

That's were things stand right now and I will write an update for this chapter after the D.H.O. hammers me.

Update: December 7, 2001

Warden Hood has expunged all Incident Reports given to me while in the SHU at FCI Phoenix. His action had a double effect.

First, it removed all the sanctions that had restricted my visiting, commissary and telephone usage. Second, it nullified the Incident Report, which you read at the start of this chapter. Yes, officer Martin, sometimes there is justice!

I am only guessing but Warden Hood may have used the following reasoning. The sanctions placed on my privileges, while Segregation at FCI Phoenix, were all done against B.O.P. policy. The sanctions should not have been in place when I arrived at FCI Sheridan.

Therefore, with no sanctions in effect, there could be no action on the Incident Report. Sorry about that Mr. Martin!

Always remember that FCI Phoenix's Warden Ellis did what he wanted, when he wanted, to whom he wanted. Following B.O.P. policy never was his strong point!

It is my personal belief that the only reason the Bureau of Prisons has books and books of written policies is to show the public! They never play by their own rules!

Next up is "Sheridan's Monster—Their S.I.S.!" Or it could have been entitled "Get Tucci For Something!"

Sheridan's Monster—Their S.I.S.

In the last chapter, "Ghost", you read how Warden Ellis was able to reach out and influence my new jailers into punishing me still further. But Ellis could not have succeeded without the help of "Sheridan's Monster—Their S.I.S."!

The letters of S.I.S. in Bureau of Prisons language stand for Special Investigative Services, but the inmates have their own slang for those three letters. The most common, and the words I like best, are Stupids Investigating Shit.

Also popular sayings are Sending Inmates to the SHU, Sadistic Indifferent Staff, and Screw Inmates Severely. Most B.O.P. facilities have their own local slang for this Gestapo part of "the system".

Those within the S.I.S. work with great enthusiasm and refuse to rotate to other posts, units, or jobs, as their co-workers do. Are you wondering why? To put it bluntly, they enjoy working as a F.B.I. "want-a-be".

Here, in only one month I have been slapped with three Incident Reports. All three are the product of Sheridan's Monster and her offspring, G. Martin and T. Leitch. What does that tell you?

Well for starters, the rest of the facility's officers and staff do not have any problems with "the old Muslim". Only the Monster does!

Remember S.I.S. Technician Martin's Incident Report in "Ghost"? The Update at the end was a happy ending for me but a loss for Martin and the S.I.S.

As you read on there are many references to the mean spirit ness of the S.I.S. Remember Mr. Barton, the head of the S.I.S. in FCI Phoenix? Read back on the "Introduction" and you'll see how he did nothing to investigate on my behalf.

Is it paranoia, senior dementia, or sour grapes on my behalf? I don't think so! Read on and then you judge.

Less than a week after his first "shot" at me, officer Martin switched from listening to my telephone calls to reading my outgoing mail to Remy.

Author's note:

At FCI Sheridan, according to the B.O.P.'s last Population Report as of 12-31-01, there are 1,428 inmates, or as the S.I.S. says. "Tucci and 1,427 others!"

Martin's next Incident Report was for Unauthorized Use of The Mail, B.O.P. Code #406, a low to moderate category offense. Soon, the B.O.P.'s usual bull crap was put into gear again.

Just as with the first charge I was summoned to the lieutenant's office via the unit officer's telephone. However, this time I didn't allow Ms. Paine the shift lieutenant, to start the usual routine of "do you know your rights? Etc., etc."

Wheeling into her office I let fly with a monologue. "Lieutenant Paine you have three choices. You can cut to the chase and toss me in Segregation! Or if you're not going to lock me up, I'll listen! Also, you could listen to what I have to say and then lock me up! Which one is it?"

Quietly she said. "Mr. Tucci why are you so damn hostile? I am not going to lock you up! I only want to read you the charges."

Very calmly and not so loud I replied. "Don't bother to read it just hand it to me and I'll read it during my morning bowel movement."

So, with the unread report under my ass, a good place for it, I wheeled back to "Building #4. The next step would be an appearance before the U.D.C. again.

Mr. Martin's charge against me was as dumb as it gets. Yes, I was guilty of spelling all the words in a long letter to Remy, backwards. Or as the S.I.S. says. "Code #406, Misuse of the Mail by writing in a code."

I was testing the mental retardation status of the S.I.S.'s personnel, yes the are!

How's this for a defense? "My wife has Dyslexia and unless I write my letters to her backwards she can not read my mail." It was a pissing contest between the Gestapo (S.I.S.) and I.

Three days later the U.D.C. sent for me. Upon entering the office I noticed Ms. Angus, the Unit Manager and Mr. Jbour were in almost a lighthearted mood?

She greeted me with. "Mr. Tucci we are dropping this latest charge against you and I hope this type of behavior between you and the staff stops!"

Are you keeping score? With that "shot" dropped it is now Tucci two and the S.I.S. zero. But, let's not sell those people short. The rest of the chapter explains what happened next and shows their resourceful two out of two Mr. Martin lness.

After losing no doubt left with a bad taste in his mouth. So, using his <u>B.O.P</u>. mentality he did what any idiot would do, he got help from a <u>c</u>rafty fellow idiot. Enter a second S.I.S. Technician, T. Leitch.

Between Martin and Leitch on a good day, maybe they had one full pocket sized brain. Never the less they did come up with two new charges against me, which I admit I was guilty of.

November 27, 2001

"Tucci, 03836-0l4 report to the lieutenant's office now!" Sounded over the P.A. system. Question: Why no phone call to the unit officer as was done with the prior two Incident Reports? Answer: Because part of the B.O.P.'s punishment is to embarrass and inmate whenever they can.

Maybe I was beginning a new career as a designated "Incident Report Receiver?" Yes, a third trip in as many weeks to the lieutenant's office.

Here is the gruesome two some's (Martin and Leitch) report as they finally, "got Tucci for something".

11-27-01 at 10:06 AM

"On the above time and date, while monitoring recorded telephone calls, I noted that inmate Tucci #03836-0l4 directed the other party on the telephone to send money to another inmate. Specifically, he asked the party at (602) 997-8000 to send $20.00 to Richard Biswell #63734-065. This is a prohibited act in that he is giving something of value to another inmate, as planned over the telephone. This call was placed at 5:44 PM, 11-26-01."

There were many mis-spellings in their Report, but Remy's computer has "Word Perfect" and corrected Martin and Leitch's lack of education.

In B.O.P. language, they charged me with a Code 328—Giving Something of Value To Another Inmate Without Staff Authorization. Also, a Code 297—Use Of The Telephone For Abuses Other Than Criminal Activity.

The Code 328 charge was minor and I didn't concern myself with it, but the Code 297 charge was a major problem to face. The U.D.C. cannot hear or issue sanctions on a Code 200 series offense; it must be referred to the D.H.O.

Please look back at the Incident Report, I would like to explain a little more about it to you. It might be called a "rush to judgment".

From the text of the Report. "Time staff became aware of incident 10:06 AM. Time and date of reporting employee 10:20 AM on 11-27-01." Your tax dollars getting a bang for the buck, only 14 minutes to express justice!

Because I asked Remy to send $20.00 to a relative, who had no money for stamps or commissary, I am on my way to another D.H.O. hanging. If FCI Sheridan's D.H.O. is anything like the bastard back in FCI Phoenix, I am in deep shit!

As I said, this time I did the crime and admitted that to the D.H.O. But why should there be sanctions for giving only $20.00 to a blood relative? Richard is my uncle Louie's youngest son.

The D.H.O. ruled the following:

Code 297: Disallow 27 Days Good Conduct Time.

Loss of Telephone Privileges for Six Months.

Code 328: 10 Days Disciplinary Segregation, Suspended Pending 110 Days Clear Conduct.

You could say I bought all of the above for $20.00! But, I have appealed to the Regional Office to have my "Good Time" restored and telephone sanction reduced.

So now Remy and I wait, and wait, and wait for Region's reply.

Update: January 12, 2002

"Appeal denied, all sanctions upheld".

The next two writings "The Old Man In The SHU!" and "The Old Man In The SHU, Again?", close out my rocky nine months at FCI Sheridan.

These are long chapters but needed ones as they explain how I ended up in Segregation without sanctions or a D.H.O. hearing.

"The Old Man In The SHU!"

March 24, 2002

SHU is pronounced as shoe. It's proper name is the Special Housing Unit or a.k.a. "the hole". Was I yet to have one more flashback of FCI Phoenix?

My day started out just like any other Sunday here in beautiful and scenic FCI Sheridan. It was a go to church day, and a day to report at the FS (Food Service) for my assigned prison "job". My normal Sunday would soon be shattered and replaced with two days of physical pain and mental duress. Courtesy of Officer J. Hillary.

Warden Hood and his administrative staff are good and decent people. However, it's the few bad apples in the guard staffs that give FCI Sheridan a black eye and leave an ugly mark!

In less than one hour I was slapped with three "shots" (Incident Reports) and became a guest in the facility's SHU.

Now I'll explain the why, where, when and who, so that it all will make sense to you.

There were three officers involved in throwing "The Old Man In the Shu!" And also one innocent bystander, the shift's lieutenant. In this chapter the main characters are:

B. Bong, a male nurse with the Public Health dis-Service. His baldhead and bad breath are his best features. It is strongly rumored that he may be cross-addicted to drugs and alcohol. But I am sure in my opinion that he is a homosexual.

J. Hillary, a guard. He is a six foot mental midget, and never without a "chew" in his mouth. He has the personality of a wire coat hanger and the good old boy I.Q. to match. Readers trust me on those remarks.

D. McClellan, a Senior Officer Specialist, I made many inquiries as to what he was a Specialist at, but got no answers. Because he has repeatedly told me. "I don't like your mouth, your attitude or care about your fu—king book!" I'll speculate and say he is a Specialist at being mean spirited, and a drunk.

E. Gendreau, the shift lieutenant was the innocent bystander. He said. "Tucci I personally have no problems with you but Hillary wants to lock you up." So—he signed my Administration Detention Order, for the SHU.

Now as Paul Harvey says, "the rest of the story". What follows is a true account of my "crime" and the action taken by the officers.

My FS workdays ended at 5:00 PM. Here in FCI Sheridan the dining room has two doors, a North door and an East door. Why they are called North and East I don't know, but they are referred to as such.

I started to leave by the North door but changed my mind as I observed it was being guarded by Chew. Yes, there he was as big as life with that familiar bulge in his cheek.

There was no way I would cross his path this day. For the last two days he has "shaking" (patting) me down. "Chew" lives just to shake down inmates. Sometimes I bet he even finds contraband.

Here's a sidebar about prison contraband for those of you who have never "done time".

At breakfast you are given five (5) packets of sugar. If you try to sneak out a few packets for a cup of coffee in your cell later, you are carrying contraband. Wow, shouldn't the B.O.P. add time to your sentence for that?

For the noon and supper meals sliced bread is served, sometimes even whole wheat. Two (2) slices are put on the plate, most times under the food. However you can get extra bread by asking the food servers. Sneak the bread back to the housing unit and it becomes contraband.

Why would an inmate want to steal bread from the mess hall? I am so glad you are asking that.

The prison's Commissary (inmate's store) sells peanut butter, jelly, tuna fish and other food items that go on bread. But—the store doesn't sell bread. Have you ever tried to make a peanut butter and jelly sandwich without bread? I rest my case for stealing bread from the dining room.

You "Conservatives" out there are probably saying. "Cry babies, why can't them felons just bring the peanut butter and jelly in the dining room and make their damn sandwiches there?"

No can do! The B.O.P. says "No personal cups, bowls, or food containers maybe brought into the dining room." As my wife Remy says: "Everything is part of your punishment." And that's the end of my sidebar.

Now back to Chew. So, not wanting to have conversation or contact with him or his chew, I went out the East door. Here's the part where this gets good.

Mr. Chew, seeing me exiting at the door he was not guarding, left his post, and ran to get to the metal shack ahead of me.

The "shack" separates the housing units from the rest of the facility's buildings. All inmates must pass thru the shack to get back to their quarters. It was no contest as Chew's six foot six strides beat my cane and arthritic knee joints, he got there first!

There he was, waiting with a chew induced smile and his standard greeting for me. "Tucci, shakedowns take off your coat!" This is a non-fiction book and next to the complete text of officer Hillary's Incident Report:

On March 24, 2002 at approximately 5:20 PM I stopped inmate Tucci #03836-014 for a random search. I instructed Tucci to allow me to pat search him. Inmate Tucci stated, "You are going to regret this". I ordered inmate Tucci to remove his coat which he stated "no". I ordered him two more times to remove his coat before he did remove it. I conducted a pat search of the inmate. I then ordered him to come with me to the lieutenants office, he stated "no", I ordered him a second time, he said, "I'm not going". Inmate Tucci then began to walk away. I proceeded to get directly in front of Inmate Tucci. I again ordered him to come with me to the lieutenants' office. Inmate Tucci followed me to the office. It should be noted that throughout this entire incident inmate Tucci was threaten me with a BP8, telling the Warden on me and was using profanity towards me."

Okay that's Chew's side of what he said happened? Now mine, as I explain sentence by sentence what really occurred. Here we go.

"On March 24, 2002 at approximately 5:20 PM I stopped Inmate Tucci #03836-014 for a random search."

Answer: A random searches my ass! How is it random if the same officer is shaking me down for a third day in a row? Come on Chew my readers are not dumb.

"I instructed inmate Tucci to allow me to pat search him."

Answer: Yah sure he did. Can you just see it now? "Excuse me inmate Tucci will you allow me to pat search you?" Bull shit! Chew's exact words were: "Tucci, shake down, take off your coat!"

"Inmate Tucci stated you are going to regret this."

Answer: Yes, I did say that but Chew just forgot to mention what he did before I made my statement. Mr. Hillary, while pat searching me grabbed my private parts very firmly.

"I ordered inmate Tucci to remove his coat which he stated no."

Answer: Chew's English is as bad as his memory.

At this point I'll cut the chase. The first "order" I was given was, "Tucci take off your coat." My reply was indeed no, three times before I took off my coat and dropped it to the floor. If he wants to look in my coat let him bend his ass down and pick it up.

Next Chew started running his hands from my shoulders down to my wrists. How stupid was that? I was wearing a short sleeve kitchen work shirt! He could see from my elbows to my writs. Maybe he thought I had something surgically implanted under my skin? Or could it be he gets turned on touching old men?

He moved along and ran his hands from my waist down over my buttocks, pausing to give an extra "pat" at each back pocket. I was then "ordered" to turn around and face him.

Now come the worst part and the basis for my filing a Sexual Harassment complaint against Hillary.

As I said earlier I had just left FS and was wearing my "kitchen whites", a pullover shirt and pull-on pants with an elastic waistband. The pants have no front pockets to discourage FS workers from stashing items.

The ever-observant officer Hillary noticed what he thought was too large of a bulge in my genitalia area. Can you guess what he did next?

Hillary grabbed my penis and patted the surrounding area! Did you guess that? Why not? Nothing these people do should surprise or shock you.

When his groping was done I let off a loud string of profanities. I called him every dirty name that came to mind. At that point I did yell at him. "Your are going to regret this." Hillary has my words right but in the wrong order in his report.

For his actions didn't he deserve my insults? Maybe his sexuality should be questioned? But—he is the correctional officer and I am the inmate.

It was now Chew's turn to shout. "Tucci your old ass is on the way to the SHU!" He did order me to the lieutenant's office and I did refuse to go there, three times. But— "Inmate Tucci followed me to the office", doesn't tell what really happened.

Hillary doesn't write that he grabbed me forcefully by my arm (not the arm holding my cane) and pushed me towards the lieutenant's office. They always leave the "little" details out of their reports.

The last sentence of Chew's report says. "It should be noted that throughout this entire incident inmate Tucci was threaten (sic) me with a B.P. 8, telling the Warden on me and using profanity towards me.

Doesn't Hillary sound like a little boy caught by big sister after he dropped and smashed the cookie jar? I bet he would have said. "Mommy, the reason I dropped the cookie jar is I got nervous when sister said she would tell you I took the cookies!"

So, using Hillary's reasoning, he was right to send me to the SHU for yelling and swearing at him after he Sexually Assaulted me?

At the office I started to have chest pains and Lieutenant E. Gendreau ordered, enter the next character, D.McClellan to "walk", yes "walk" me over to the hospital unit even though I was having chest pains—no wheelchair!

So this old man who was still having chest pains, with rheumatoid arthritis in both knee joints and cane in hand, started the long walk to the prison's hospital.

Once inside the building my second "shot" would be written by the next character in this chapter. Mr. R. Bong an unlicensed R.N. with the P.H. dis-S.

In Part Three you'll read about how B.O.P. or P.H. dis S. medical staff are not required to be licensed in the State where the facility is. Nor are they every subjected to re-testing while employed by the Government. Isn't that swell? It's like a tenured college professor who has out-lived his usefulness.

Here are just a few of the sentences in "ding-dong" Bong's report.

"When I first greeted Tucci, he did not acknowledge my presence. When I continued to attempt to get his attention, inmate Tucci stated that I was an incompetent asshole and a poor role model for my profession".

What did Bong want me to do to "acknowledge" his presence? Bow? Or, maybe I should apologize to "ding-dong?" Okay, here it is, "I'm sorry Mr. Bong is an asshole, and incompetent! Gosh I feel better already!

In Bong's closing sentence are my thoughts exactly, as he says. "Tucci stated he would rather die than get care from me." I guess my statement hurts his fragile feelings and he too wrote me a "shot" for Insolence Towards A Staff Member. But—damn it was well worth it!

March 27, 2002

I wrote an Inmate Request to "ding-dong" asking only one question. "In what State are you a licensed R.N?" Bong never answered my request. A computer check by outside sources found that Bong is not a licensed R.N. in the State of Oregon, where this FCI is. In my "book" I think that makes him incompetent.

D. McClellan is the last character in this chapter and he also wrote me a "shot" with two charges, Refusing to Obey An Order, and the ever-popular Insolence Towards A Staff Member.

I call him little Mac   because he is short, and like many short men he has the "Napoleon Complex". However, his report is the longest, as most short people always have a lot to say. I picked out a few of his outstanding sentences to share with you.

So here's what little Mac had to say: I was instructed by the Operations Lieutenant to escort inmate Tucci to Medical for an evaluation, then to escort Tucci to the Special Housing Unit.

Does McClellan report mention that I was having chest pains? Of course not! That's why the lieutenant ordered him to take me to the Medical Unit! Go back a few paragraphs and you will read how they even made me walk to the hospital.

The prison's medical history, for me as a heart patient, never entered their pea-brains! One of the reasons an inmate dies in Federal prison is the guards' stupidity! Going on—little Mac said. "Inmate Tucci told P.A. Bong has was an incompetent ass-hole and continued calling the P.A. a Bald Piece of Shit and refused treatment."

Yes, I said all of that. But—it seems McClellan has promote Bong to a P.A. (Physician's Assistant). The "ding dong" signed my "shot" as R. Bong, RN/LT/PHS. A P.A. is a higher rating than an R.N., but maybe next week Bong will start calling himself a P.A.?

The next couple of little Mac's sentences are my personal favorites. "I asked inmate Tucci to stand and submit to hand restraints. Inmate Tucci told me you just made my book, I just haven't decided if you are an alcoholic or a homosexual."

I found it interesting that McClellan didn't spell alcoholic correctly but got homosexual right.

Mr. McClellan you are what you spell, think about that!

"He twice more refused my order to stand and said he needed his cane to stand. I ordered Tucci to put his hands behind his back, three times Tucci refused. I took inmate Tucci's left hand, and placed it behind his back, inmate Tucci finally complied to hand restraints. I lowered Tucci into the wheelchair and proceeded to the Special Housing Unit."

Truth is stranger than fiction. What really happened, versus what the little Mac said happened?

"He twice more refused my order to stand and said he needed his cane to stand."

Here they go again, he has what I said correct but in the wrong order in his report. The truth is McClellan said. "Tucci stand up and put your hands behind your back you're going to the SHU!"

Yes, I questioned him. "How am I going to use my cane with my hands cuffed behind my back?" I did refuse to stand many more times than the twice that he reported.

When I finally did stand McClellan ordered, "Tucci take of the damn coat!" He then searched the pockets removing my Rag wool gloves, I.D. holder, my prison I.D., and a photo of my wife Remy and I.

But—on my release from the SHU the gloves, I.D. holder and my wife's photo were to turn up missing. Yes, I could again buy the gloves ($5.00) and the I.D. holder (15 cents) at the Commissary but I could not replace the "lost" photo.

Things end up missing all the time in any prison. The officers steal much more from the inmates than the inmates steal from each other. Or, maybe someone in McClellan's family just needs a new pair of winter gloves?

Because the convict/author is not one to just let things slide by, I wrote an Inmate Request to little Mac. I asked only one question. "Where are my gloves and other items that you stole from me at the hospital unit?"

McClellan's answer was: "All you had in your pockets was an empty pill bottle and your I.D."

"I took inmate Tucci's left hand and placed it behind his back, inmate Tucci finally complied to the hand restraints."

Well it wasn't exactly kindly the way he "took inmate Tucci's left hand and placed it behind his back." It was more like twisted than "placed".

"Inmate Tucci finally complied to hand restraints."

You would have complied too if some buffoon was twisting your arm and you needed to hold on to the chair with your other arm to keep from falling down.

"I lowered Tucci into the wheelchair and proceeded to the Special Housing Unit."

Lowered? It was more like shoved into the wheelchair and held down.

"P.A. Bong told inmate Tucci that he would come to S.H.U. and see if he needed anything. Inmate Tucci stated "Fu-k Off".

The truth is I didn't say "Fu-k Off" to Bong. I said Fu-k You!

Picture the following in your mind's eye. A bearded old man, being pushed in a wheel chair, hands cuffed behind his back, with no coat on, out in a cold February night in Oregon. Remember, McClellan took my coat before he cuffed me.

Yes my dear wife Remy, everything is part of the B.O.P.'s punishment. As little Mac pushed the chair towards the SHU "ding dong" Bong yelled to me. "Tucci I'll be over to check on you later!"

Again please picture this—Bong is yelling to me and McClellan is pushing the wheelchair as we hurry by a large group of inmates. I turned in the chair and looking back at Bong I shouted. "Go fu-k yourself you bald headed piece of shit!"

Little Mac didn't lie in his report; I did say all of that!

It was only about a hundred feet from the medical building to the SHU. My mind raced ahead and got there far ahead of McClellan's wheelchair pushing.

Plan, think, plan, think, and take charge of what's happening to you! I replayed the ninety-eight (98) days in FCI Phoenix's SHU in my mind.

The door was buzzed open and I was pushed into a well lit and surprisingly clean SHU. It was unlike the dark dungeon of FCI Phoenix, but it was still a place I would rather not be.

From this part on you'll see just how mean spirited these people are. I was ordered: "Get the fu-k out of the wheelchair, and stand up!" As always, I said, "No, not without my cane, I need it for balance."

The officer in charge almost sounded intelligent as he asked. "McClellan where's his fu-king cane?" I think the use of the word fu-king is a mandatory part of all correctional officers training.

McClellan did a quick shuffle back to medical to retrieve my cane. He returned and presented it, almost as if it were a trophy, to the SHU lieutenant.

All that happens next you can expect if you ever become imprisoned here in FCI Sheridan. I am sure you know that these officers are not hired for their mental ability.

"You got your damn cane so now stand up!" Excuse me? Didn't the big lummox notice that my hands were cuffed behind my back? Talk about dumb, this guy get's my vote.

There we were, three SHU officers, little Mac, the SHU lieutenant, and Lieutenant Grendreau, who just joined the "Tucci's in the hole group".

Finally, one officer said. "I'll redo his cuffs to the front so that he can use his cane." Gosh, who ever said they didn't hire intelligent officers here?

Okay, the cuffs are in front of me, I now have my cane and stand up. "Tucci just walk over and get into that cell and hand me out the cane." Said the Lummox.

Well, that sounded reasonable so I did it. Once inside the cell my handcuffs were removed by putting my hands out the small opening between the bars.

"Strip!" I was ordered. Now my mind went into high gear, SHU mode, and "El Viejo" (the old one) came to life! I yelled back. "You bring me some damn clothing first and then I'll strip."

Seeing Lieutenant Grendreau still there I asked him to cover over to the cell door. I informed him. "Hey do you guys think I am stupid? In Phoenix they stripped me, took my clothes away, and left me bare ass naked for more than an hour.

Almost shouting I said. "You have two choices, either bring me some clothing before I strip, or come in the cell and beat me to get these clothes off!"

Lieutenant Grendreau nodded to the officers and said. "Just get him the clothing." Take charge I kept telling myself, don't give them one inch, fight them tooth and nail.

An officer, let's call him Bozo, returned with my SHU clothing. The usual B.O.P.'s red jumpsuit and blue pull-on sneakers. I took the clothing and put it in the rear of the cell out of the Lummox and Bozo's reach.

I then started to "strip" as ordered. I hope you will never have to deal with what I call the B.O.P. strip, bend, and spread'em routine. It is the most demoralizing and degrading things that goes on within a prison.

If you are a modest person you will soon learn to forget about that while in prison.

It makes no difference if the guard is a male or female—they both enjoy ordering you to, "spread your ass" or "pick-up your balls." Inmates have been known to hide things up their ass, but how do I hide something under my balls? B.O.P., an answer please?

Finally dressed in my wrong size, worn-out and with buttons missing jumpsuit, Bozo gave the next order. "Tucci you'll have to give me your wrist watch to put with your property." Kiss that watch good-bye I said to myself.

As if by magic the tough side of me took over. "Hey Bozo, (yes I did address the guard as Bozo put this in the log book—Tucci is declaring a hunger strike and refusing all food or water. And for your information that means I am to be celled alone!"

Well Bozo must have been confused as he looked at me, and then back to Gendreau who was still there, and then back to me again.

Plan, think, plan, think, stay in charge Frank!

Next the lieutenant spoke up. "Yeah, he's right he get's a cell to himself if he is on a hunger strike."

"Put your hands behind your back and out the bars." The Lummox said. Well here we go again! "Look you jerks I can't walk with my cane if my hands are cuffed behind me, and I can't walk without my cane!"

This time all the officers look to the lieutenant for help.

Gendreau answered very loudly. "Just cuff him in front and give him the cane or else we'll be here all night."

Plan, think, plan, think, stay in charge Frank. Break their rhythm. So far I did just that by:

1.   Refusing to stand or get out of the wheelchair.
2.   Being able to get my cane back.
3.   Refusing to strip until they brought me clothing.
4.   By giving my watch to Gendreau instead of Bozo.
5.   Refusing to be cuffed "behind".
6.   Refusing to leave the cell without my cane to walk with.
7.   By declaring a hunger strike.

So far I was taking charge, but read on and you will find out just how resilient and strong-minded a 63 year old can really be.

Plan, think, plan, and think! I was sure that perseverance would make the difference between my success and their failure.

It was close to eight PM when they finally put me in my assigned cell. The Lummox tossed in a bedroll, which was: two sheets, two blankets, a pillow case (no pillow), and a towel. There were no hygiene items or even toilet paper included. Why didn't that surprise me?

I would not give these people the satisfaction of begging for a toothbrush, soap, toothpaste, or even toilet paper. They knew those items should have been given to me.

Tomorrow would be Monday. I was sure that Warden Hood would send someone, or come himself to spring me. As it turned out I was wrong. It would not be until Wednesday before I left the SHU.

That first night in the SHU was spent on the floor in the far corner of the cell. I would not make-up the bed that night nor for the rest of my time in their SHU.

Later that night I stopped Bozo as he was making his rounds. "Hey Bozo could you kill the light?" Yes, I did call him Bozo. Well, anyway, he did, but the third shift moron turned the light back on.

I knew that they made their rounds every thirty minutes so I waited at the cell door for the moron's return. "Officer, could you please shut the light?" His smart-ass reply was. "I could but I ain't."

See what happens when I try to be polite? If I had said: "Hey, asshole shut the fu-king light!" He more than likely would have.

No problem. I had long ago learned to ignore the light being on all day and night. Warden Ellis and his SHU crew at FCI Phoenix had trained me for that. Thanks, Phoenix!

The breakfast meal would be the first test for me. It was still dark outside my cell window as I heard the "trap" (slot in cell door) being unlocked. Quickly I got over to the door.

"Hey numb nuts, no food or drink I am on a declared hunger strike, don't leave anything!" My guess was he didn't believe me and left a cup of milk, coffee and the breakfast meal tray on the trap's ledge.

Later, when he was back to collect the trays he remarked. "Tucci, you didn't eat but I see you drank the milk. Well there goes your hunger strike. You drank the milk so you ain't on hunger strike no more!"

His stupid remark caused me to "lose it". I let fly a few profanities followed with. "What the fu-k are you talking about? I didn't touch the food tray or drink anything. Are you on drugs or something?"

He shouted back with "Tucci if I tell the lieutenant you drank the milk, you drank the milk."

I could see what their plan was to be. If they read my "record" they knew that I had three hunger strikes to my credit while in FCI Phoenix.

Lummox, Bozo and the Moron's mindset were: "Hey, if we say Tucci ate then he ate, and he can't cause us problems with a hunger strike."

"Wrong answer guys!" Plan, think, plan, and think, okay, I now have a plan.

The shift lieutenant, the Warden, someone from my unit's team, and the P.A, visit the SHU daily. I was hoping to see anyone except "ding-dong" Bong, remember, he is the ad hoc P.A.

My luck was good, after the midnight to eight AM shift change the morning lieutenant was making his rounds.

"Sir, could I please speak to you for a minute?" I spoke out the little mouth hole in the cell door. I always try to be respectful at first but if they don't respond, my next greeting will not be a polite one. In fact it would be profanities.

The lieutenant was a tall Black man, who was referred to as an Uncle Tom by the "brothers" in the SHU.

He bent down to speak into the door's small round opening. "You're Tucci, aren't' you? What's the problem?" So far so good I thought to myself. At least he stopped and is talking to me.

Lieutenant, I am on a hunger strike, you know, no food or drink. The officer on the third shift said I drank the milk from the breakfast meal but I didn't. He's lying!"

His answer was right out the B.O.P.'s official lesson book. He said. "Why would my officer lie?" You don't have to be a genius to see their answers coming. I had a few pre-selected quotes ready for his reply.

I shouted these two at him. "Hey, your officer's mouth ain't no prayer book!" And "Just because your officer said it that doesn't make it gospel!"

Try as I might to explain why the jerk guard on the third shift would want to lie, it fell on deaf ears and a dumb mind. Okay, if that's the way these assholes want to play it, just wait and see what I do with the next meal.

The lunch meal is delivered to SHU guests between eleven and eleven thirty. Click, clack, the door trap was opened and a tray of food and something to drink was placed on its ledge.

A good way to anger these morons is to call them "guard". In their tiny minds they are Correctional Officers. I yelled out! "Hey guard, I am on a hunger strike and the other guard said I drank some milk. So this Bud' for you!"

After that choice comment I kicked the food try and drink cup to the floor. I finished-up with: "Now, run and tell them I ate that meal!"

Well that left a real mess and because the hallway was narrow, the guard had to tip-top over it to get to the next inmate's cell. The rest of the day no one came to my cell, not until four P.M.

The B.O.P. has what they call, the "Four PM Standing Count". It is just as it says; You must stand by your bed at that time. If you don't stand-up you'll get a #302, Failure to Stand Count "shot" (Incident Report).

At the appropriate time, four PM, the prison's P.A. system announced. "Four PM Stand Up Count!" The rule applies even if you're in the SHU, except if your name is Tucci.

I was sitting on the floor in the far corner of the cell when I heard, bang, bang, kick! Sounds like someone is at the door? Yes, two some-ones, I'll call them Huey and Louie.

Huey said. It's four PM!" I replied. "Why thank you for telling me the time!"

Louie quickly spoke next. "That means Stand Up Count you old asshole!" My answer was very polite. "No, I don't think so, I am not in the mood today."

So. Huey and Louie stormed off to try and scare some of the other SHU inmates into Standing Count.

Compared to the officers in FCI Phoenix, SHU where I spent ninety-eight (98) days, these guys were like a couple of Snow White's dwarfs.

Huey spoke again. "I am giving you a direct order, stand-up!" Borrowing a line from George Bush, Sr., I said. "Read my lips—no!"

Later that night I was presented with three more Incident Reports. They were for Failure to Stand Count, a #302, Refusing to Obey an Order From a Staff Member, a #307, and Failure to Follow Sanitation Regulations, a #317. The last one was for not making up my bed.

Are you psychic? Guess what happened when they brought me the supper meal tray? That's right! More floor food!

That ended my first full night in the SHU. Plan, think stay in charge Frank.

Break their rhythm! My mind was in high gear.

If you are "Doing Time" and reading this book always remember the following. Never stop fighting them, even when you are in the SHU, especially in the SHU! These bastards just love to kick you when you're down. So why not kick them back?

Tuesday 26 March 2002, 0600 hours.

Its only day two in Segregation but who's counting? In the SHU you are allowed one hour of outside recreation five days per week. The other twenty-three hours will be spent in your cell.

At 6:05 AM the "snake" started banging on cell doors, yelling only one word. "Rec?" If you answered yes he would put your name on a list for the day watch officers. They will supervise your "rec."

Bang, bang on my cell door. "What do you want asshole?" I asked. He smiled showing missing and yellow teeth said. "Rec?" I felt no need to reply to the question.

I have a quick question. With all the money these people make (almost $20.00 an hour) and with medical and dental plans, why didn't "snake" have his ugly teeth fixed?

A short time later, click, clack, the cell's door "trap" was opened and "snake" poured a cup of coffee and a cup of milk and left them on the tray's ledge. He moved on to the next call and did the same.

I could see no point in kicking over just the milk and coffee; I'll wait for the breakfast tray too. Have you guessed the plan? "Hey, stupid, didn't I tell you yesterday I was on a hunger strike?" I shouted at "snake".

He looked into the cell and replied. "Yeah, but Tucci you drank the milk yesterday don't you remember? Do you have Alzheimer's or something?"

At that point I lost it! "Here drink this!" I said as I kicked the tray and drinks to the floor. Damn if that didn't make me feel good!

By trashing the food and drink I would take away the temptation to eat or drink any of it. An old saying says it best. "Out of sight, out of mind"

A hunger strike gets very painful after only a few days. It's not for everyone but as you read in the "Introduction" it works for me.

A few hours after I dumped "snake's" food three guards were at the cell's door. "Tucci cuff-up!" That meant they wanted me to put my hands out the "trap" to be handcuffed.

I questioned the order. "Why the hell for?" I said as I sat on the floor in the cell's far corner.

We need to search the cell for food because you're on a hunger strike". "Skinny" said. Is it just my opinion or are these people really that stupid?

Where the hell did these morons think I was getting food from? The "food fairy?" Once again came the order. "Tucci cuff-up!" Followed by a one-word answer from me. "No!"

They didn't ask me a third time as all three stormed into the tiny cell. "Stay in the fu-king corner and don't move!" Were Skinny's exact words.

They of course found no food and I never did cuff-up. Scored one for the old Muslim.

But—sometimes later that afternoon, guess what? They're back!

"Tucci cuff-up!" Oh well, here we go again. Always question every "order" they give you. I yelled my one word reply back at the guard. "Why?"

Duncan's answer was. "The Assistant Warden and the Captain want to see you." Without even thinking I answered. "So, hey, tell them to come and see me here."

The guard was showing a bit of temper as he added. "Tucci you will cuff-up!" The pissing contest continued as I spoke again. "If you want cuffs on me come in here beat me down, and put them on me!" He did now answer but turned and left taking the other two idiots with him.

Bang, bang, bang! Now what? Don't these people understand that I never change my mind? A no is a no is a no?

Without looking towards the door to see who was there I yelled out. "What do you assholes want now?"

"Mr. Tucci we would like to talk to you outside of the cell." Well when I heard "Mr. Tucci", I looked up at the cell's small window to see Captain Smith and the new A.W. Mr. Ives.

The captain spoke first. "We would like to see about getting you out of here today. Cuff-up so that we can talk in a room out here." That sounded like an offer I could not refuse, but I said.

"If I am going to leave why do I have to be handcuffed to leave?" Captain Smith answer was. "Tucci you have been around long enough to know the rules in the SHU."

Slowly I got up and made my way over to the cell door. But just at that minute, as luck would have it, my hearing aid sounded a sharp note.
Author's note:

I forgot to mention that I wear a strong hearing aid in my left ear and that my right ear is completely deaf.

At the crack in the cell's door I said loudly. "My hearing aid battery is dead and I won't be able to hear you!" With that said I sat back down on the floor. Maybe they would be back? I did want to get out of the SHU.

After a very short time. Click, clack, the trap in the cell door was opened. I looked up to see that one of my guests had placed a hearing aid battery on the trap's ledge.

I got-up, put the battery in my hearing aid and spoke, "Hey, I am not going to leave here for a couple of days and then get tossed back in here. No thanks! "I'll just wait for the D.H.O.
Author's note:

In Warden Ellis's SHU at FCI Phoenix, I waited nine (9) days to be heard by the D.H.O. The catch? Those nine days didn't count towards the fourteen (14) days he sentenced me to spend in D.S. (Disciplinary Segregation). So, I stayed in there twenty three (23) days on a fourteen-day sentence!

Back now to the present time and FCI Sheridan. Yes, Ms. Angus and Warden Hood, things are indeed done differently at FCI Sheridan?

Cutting to the chase. The A.W. and the Captain did speak to me outside of the cell. I did not cuff-up, and I left the SHU after the four PM count, which I did not stand up for!

When Bozo, Lummox and a third guard came to "release" me, I got the last words in. "I can't leave the cell without my cane, I need it for balance!"

Bozo turned to the Lummox and said. "Where's his fu-king cane? Let's get him the fu-k-out of here!" The third guard left in search of my cane and returned quickly with it.

Bozo spoke again. "Is there anything else Tucci?" Okay now cuff-up." Are these people gluttons for punishment? "No," I am not going to cuff-up. If you are releasing me why do I have to be cuffed?"

The Lummox put his two cents in with. "If you don't cuff-up you'll stay right here." Not to be upstaged I said. "So! I'll just stay here and wait for the A.W. and the Captain to look for me!"

Well that did it! I guess they never had an inmate refuse to cuff-up when told they were leaving.

"Fu-k it just open the cell and get him out of here." Said Bozo with a tone of defeat in his voice. Yes, I held firm and pissed these people off beyond belief.

There were more kicks and giggles awaiting me back at the housing unit.

Officer Taylor, tall, bald and semi-intelligent, was the guard on duty. He and I have had several go-rounds prior.

Taylor's face was angry and flushed with red as I entered the unit. It was plain to see that he was not happy with my return. Oh well, screw him if he can't take a joke.

Later I found out from the Muslims that the day before at "mail call" Taylor had said. "For your information Mr. Tucci will not be coming back on the compound, he's on the bus!"

Translating that—I would not be coming out of the SHU and I would be moved to another B.O.P. facility. Very wishful thinking on Taylor's behalf.
Author's note:

When I was put in Segregation it was Taylor who removed and inventoried my property. Seventy-two ($72.00) dollars worth of items were missing and I have filed a claim for them. What is with these guards? First McClellan steals my gloves and I.D. holder and then Taylor loses seventy-two dollars worth of my property!

Maybe it's a new part of B.O.P. training. "If you need something just take it." Well be that as it may, back to my story.

Mr. Hawks, the unit's "A" side Counselor found me and said. "They want you back at 6:30 PM to pick-up your property."

The unit is locked-in at 6:30 so Mr. Hawks informed Taylor. "Tucci needs to be let out at 6:30 to pick-up his property at the SHU."

In the meantime Taylor spread the word. "Anyone who helps Tucci gets a shot (Incident Report)." I indeed needed help; I had a lot of property to bring back to my cell. With one hand using my cane I couldn't carry a hell of a lot with the other hand.

Try as I might I could not find an inmate to help, at the risk of their getting a "shot". Yes, I could understand their reluctance.

Most inmates worry about losing their "good time credit", but under Federal Guidelines they will do ninety (90) percent of the sentence anyway. The ten (10) percent they give you is not worth taking shit from these people. So I fight them!

The B.O.P. screwed-up by taking almost all of my "good time" very early in my sentence.

Here are a few true facts to consider when you ask why a 63-year old man fights these B.O.P. mental midgets.

1.   I was transferred from FCI Phoenix, 1,200 miles away from my home and wife Remy.
2.   They have taken my telephone privileges for one full year. The restriction ends on December 10, 2002.
3.   I have no "good time credit" and will do all of my sentence (max out) as the inmate slang says.
4.   There are no visits due to the 1,200 miles and the fact that Remy does not drive.

It was almost 6:30 and I had not found a helper yet. Taylor had done his dirty deed well with his "threat".

Okay, so there's no one to help. Think Frank! The unit has a small cart, similar to what you would find in a grocery store, I'd use that to bring my property back. But—if I ask Taylor for the cart's use his answer will surely be no.

Inside the counselor's office. "Mr. Hawks, Taylor says anyone who helps me get's a shot. I don't want that to happen. May I use the cart to haul my stuff back from Segregation?

Hawks said that was okay by him, but one more call had to be made. "Could you please let Taylor know that I'll be using the cart?" I pleaded.

At 6:30 I hooked my cane to the side of the cart and started the long push to the SHU building.

Arriving there I pressed the buzzer to let them know I was outside. Five minutes went by, nobody home? Again I buzzed!

They have a video camera above the SHU entrance, not only could they hear the buzzer but they could also see me on TV! They most likely said. "It's only Tucci, fu-k him let him wait."

After being such an unruly guest in their SHU did I really think they would hurry to open the door?

But—sometimes even I get lucky. Coming towards me was the shift lieutenant making his rounds. He asked. "Tucci why are you standing there?" Hey, it was a dumb question but I played the game and answered. "I'm here to pick-up my property."

He spoke into his radio and like magic the door buzzed open.

Inside the door I was asked. "Tucci did you bring laundry bags to put your shit in?

There's that consistency in B.O.P. training again, always call an inmate's property "shit".

It took me a long time to take my shit out of the SHU's plastic storage boxes and into the bags. No, the guard didn't lift a finger to help or even offer to.

Twenty minutes later, at the metal shack, "Tucci where are you coming from?" The compound is closed!" Said the dragon lady (a.k.a. Ms. Kline).

Nobody could be as dumb as they look, but in Ms. Kline's case I'll make an exception.

Please picture in your mind's eye. An old man, pushing a cart piled high with three bags of "shit" headed towards the housing units.

There was no possible way Ms. Kline would not have known I was coming back from the SHU. Remember the lieutenant using his radio to get me into the SHU? Well, I am sure she heard the call on her radio!

Where did she think I got the cart piled high with three bags of shit,? Ah yes, let's not forget Ms. Kline was in the metal shack as I pushed the cart thru on my way to the SHU.

Maybe Ms. Kline was just trying to make conversation? Anyway, back at the unit it was home sweet home, even if it was cell #124!

The Old Man In The SHU Again?

Author's note.

In Chapter 9 you read about my first experience in FCI Sheridan's SHU. This chapter deals with my last! What follows is a true account of my twelve (12) day hunger strike, B.O.P. stupidity, and the meanness by some of the individual officers. Remember, the truth doesn't always win!

I was sitting in the unit's common area working on this book when this latest trip to la-la land (Segregation) came my way. Hopefully, this chapter will help a Muslim in "Surviving The Federal Prison System."

Denis Kretzschmar (B.O.P. #06663-046) came up behind me and poured a large cup of water over my head. There was some debate later as to the temperature of the water but all I can remember was that it was wet!

Then he ran around to the front of me and yelled. "'What the fu-k are you going to do now asshole?"

Try to picture this in your mind's eye. A sixty-three year old man (me) dripping wet, sitting in shock as a demented racist starts to attack you! My reflexes took over as I picked up my cane to ward off this loony's charge.

But that didn't work as Kretzschmar grabbed hold of my cane, refusing to let go I was quickly pulled to my feet.

At the time of the "Incident" all of the "Brothers" were not in the unit but out on a recreation period. If the "Brothers" any of them were there Kretzschmar would have been badly beaten!

There is no group of inmates who respect the old more than the Muslims.

The noise as Kretzschmar kept yelling filth at me, and myself yelling, "Help, this guy's going nuts", brought some of the office staff to the scene.

Mr. Jbour (case manager) and Ms. Boston (the unit secretary) got there first followed by about a dozen guards. As the two (Jbour and Boston) started yelling—"freeze, stop", or something like that, I was distracted and Kretzschmar wrestled the cane from me.

When the two office workers reached us the lying bastard Kretzschmar started shouting. "Tucci attacked me with his cane—he's crazy!" Kretzschmar then handed my cane to Jbour and looked at me with a stupid grin of his face.

A second or two later I was handcuffed with my hands behind my back by the lovely 250 pound Ms. Boston. Her official title is "Unit Secretary" and her job description reads, "To perform clerical and administrative duties." But in reality she is a Correctional Officer want-a-be!

She ordered me to, "shut the hell up and face the fu-king wall!" Well it's de ja vu all over again! I told Boston "Hey, I can't stand without my cane!" Well it didn't matter now because four officers were holding me up against the wall.

Ms. Boston was in such a hurry to get her handcuffs on me that she forgot to "lock" them in place. The result was every time I moved my hands the cuffs got tighter. Two days later I still had marks on my wrists.

Trying to reason with any of them was useless! But I kept yelling. "I didn't attack that lying Nazi bastard, he poured water on my head, how do you think I get this wet? He attacked me I was only trying to defend myself!"

Okay, Tucci start walking your old ass out of here!" Said one of the guards. I pleaded "I can't walk without my cane and I can't use it with my hands cuffed behind me!"

Boston, being the lady that she is, spoke. "Just pick him up, drag him, or whatever, out of here." That's what they did! Drag! At the half waypoint to the SHU, the out of shape, beer bellied guards, called for the electric cart to bring me the rest of the way.

While waiting for the cart they just laid me flat on the ground, wet clothing and all. The golf cart arrived and what happened next could have been right out of an old Keystone Kop movie.

The four guards one at each arm and leg, started to lift me off the ground. But— one of them slipped causing the others to drop me back to the ground.

The script continued as they banged the top of my head putting me in their stupid cart. Then, I feel over and out of it! So—instead of going to Segregation I was rushed to the medical department to be checked out.

At the facility's hospital the officers were told. "Tucci's fine he doesn't need anything from medical, he can be taken to the SHU!" Later in my cell I could feel the bump on my head swelling up. Gee, thanks, doctor!

The SHU door buzzed open and I was dragged in roughly and dumped in a cell. A few minutes later, the Bozo from the prior chapter came and removed the handcuffs.

"Okay Tucci strip-off your shit!" Well here we go again, or is it still? My one word reply was, "no". My argument was the same as in my last SHU visit. I wanted SHU clothing before I stripped.

Getting tossed in the hole on a weekday has its disadvantages because all the powers to be are at their jobs. This time they would add a new twist to my experiences.

First came a lieutenant, then Captain Smith, Mr. <u>Ali</u> the Assistant Warden and last of all the loony tuner (psychiatrist). They all ordered this old man to strip!

Mr. Ali came back a second time and said. "Tucci, I am ordering you to strip for the last time! If you don't we'll have to get it done some other way. What's it going to be?" My answer was the same. "No!" Ali spoke into his radio. "Team up!"

In less than a minute five (5) riot dressed guards charged into the small cell. It looked like a scene from Star Wars.

They were all dressed in black, wearing protective headgear with clear face visors, heavy gloves, and baseball type shin-guards.

I was knocked to the ground as each one of them had an assigned part of my body to grab and hold. First my shoes and socks were pulled off, then my shirt and pants, and lastly my underwear.

The only clothing they put on my (yes, they dressed me) was a tee shirt and a part of boxer shorts. No socks or even shoes. Later in the cell I noticed that the boxers were on inside out. I guess the guard's mother never told him that the "tag" goes on the inside of underwear.

Again, with one officer at each of my limbs, I was carried off to a cell #308-C. This would be my home for the next twelve (12) days and the cell was at the very end of the block.

In my last stay I had yelled insults and swore at the guards and administrative staff as they passed by my cell. So—they put me where no one would have to pass by.

I was dropped on to a green rubber mattress. On the floor were dirty sheets and a blanket from the prior guest. Nothing was given to me. I won't rehash but go the last chapter for a list of items not provided me.

This cell was damn cold my guess was about 62 to 65 degrees! It became even colder as night fell. To a sixty-three year old man only in his underwear it was very cold.

I would not use the dirty sheets from the floor or the blanket. That first night I sleep with the mattress from the top bunk as my blanket. A Muslim does not beg!

Morning came and so did Huey and Louie, also from the last chapter. "Hey, jerks guess what? I'm doing my hunger strike thing again, you all have a nice day!" I shouted at them.

The breakfast, noon and supper meals were kicked to the floor that first day. No staff or medical people visited that day.

June 5, 2002

Day two, I was given a Code 312 Incident Report for Insolence Towards Staff". Hey, what else is new? D. White, Senior Officer Specialist wrote the following.

"On 6-5-02, at approximately 11:35 AM Inmate Tucci was receiving the noon meal. Inmate Tucci stated that he was not going to eat! Tucci was then informed that he was to receive his meal per the Special Housing Lieutenant. Inmate Tucci then moved up to the meal slot and threw the trays onto the floor outside of cell #308.

The next day came and brought. "Tucci cuff-up!" Said Lieutenant Ierrulli. My answer was. "Why?" His reply was. "Never mind why just do it damn you Tucci!" After a few seconds I answered. "Not today I'm not in the mood, if you want cuffs on me call the goon squad back. I am not going to cuff-up." Those were my last words.

Well shortly there after I was again given the Men In Black treatment and ended up in Ierulli's office. He told me he had to read the charge(s) against me. They were as follows:

Possession, Manufacture or Introduction of a Weapon a Code 104, and Fighting a Code 201, Mr. Jbour's report said.

"On June 3, 2002, at 1:05 PM, I heard a loud noise associated with a fight. I stepped out of my office to investigate the commotion. I observed inmate TUCCI swing his cane at inmate KRETZXCHMAR. Inmate KRETZSCHMAR managed to take the cane away from inmate TUCCI and backed away. Inmate TUCCI proceeded to attack inmate KRETZSCHMAR after he backed away from him. I ordered inmate TUCCI to stop attacking, however he proceeded towards inmate KRETZSCHMAR with his fist closed in an offensive manner. Inmate KRETZSCHMAR handed me the cane and stated. "He was attacking me with his cane and I took it away from him."

"Okay Tucci what do you have to say?" Ierulli questioned. I told him my story short and sweet. "It's a lie, Kretzschmar came-up behind me and poured water on my head, and then he started to attack me!

I really think the lieutenant did believe me but he was in no position to help. His only function was to get a "statement" for the record.

Later that same day, the moronic guards were back. "Tucci cuff-up!" I snapped at them. "No I don't think so, get the goon squad back!" Huey asked, "Why always the hard way Tucci!" My one word reply was, "Because!"

Not to be repetitious I'll just skip over the next event. The goons this time took me to the SHU's law library for a U.D.C. (Unit Disciplinary Committee) hearing.

Ms. Angus and Mr. Wait was the UDC committee. My statement to them in regards to Jbours report was as follows:

"All of Mr. Jbour's report is true but that's all he saw. Proceeding this, inmate Kretzshmar snuck-up behind me while I was sitting on the flats and poured hot water over my head. He then ran in front of me and came at me. I warded him off with my cane—that's when Mr. Jbour came in."

I don't know if they believed me but it didn't matter anyway! What they did was, "referred to the D.H.O. based on severity of charges and numerous suspended charges."

The next day I refused meal number nine (9) and the B.O.P. hit a new low.

"Tucci cuff-up!" I was so tired of those three Damn words! Yelling I said. "Hey don't even bother to ask me a second time, just get the ugly bastards in Black!"

After all was said and done I found myself in a "dry cell" (no toilet or sink) on the first floor. The move was good news for two reasons. First, it was warmer downstairs and second, I was finally given shoes, socks, and the stylish and ever popular orange jumpsuit.

Why the clothing after days of having none? My guess was they (SHU guards) didn't want other staff members to know I was dong time in my underwear!   The "dry cell" had no bed. What it did have was cement slab about three feet off the floor with urine stained mattress on it. In each corner of the "bed" was a metal hinge to which handcuffs and leg irons could be attached.

That is called "four pointing" in B.O.P. lingo. To explain that—an inmate is laid flat on his back and his hands and feet are cuffed to each of the "four points." They didn't do it to this old man but it was in my mind as a possibility.

Choosing not to lie on the bed, I tossed the mattress on the floor, and with the blanket and pillow Snake gave me tired to rest up.

Snake handed me a plastic urine bottle and said. "Tucci if you need to piss use the jug!"

Oh I forgot to mention, the cell had no door but rather bars which meant that the officers could look in and see me easily at all times.

So—when I needed to piss, I walked over to the bars and pissed out onto the floor.

Snake returned shortly and seeing my urine on the floor starting laughing. When he did stop laughing he walked closer to me and said. "Tucci at first I was against you but with your hunger strike and the elephant balls you have, I am now with you!"

And so started a strange friendship with the Snake, a.k.a. James Horvak.

Day five (5) of my hunger strike was a very good day! Horvak rushed in to me with some news. "Tucci the medical director (Doctor Saltzberg) himself is here to see you. I know where he lives and he drove at least an hour on his day off to get here (it was a Sunday)."

Huey and Louie now joined Horvak in front of my cell. "Tucci get ready, you're going over to medical to see Doctor Saltzberg". Said Huey. What, no cuff-up Tucci this time?

"Why?" Was my response. "The doctor didn't tell us why, Tucci," Louie chimed in.

"Wrong answer jerk, I am refusing all medical treatment at this time. Tell the good doctor to go screw himself!"

Huey and Louie left in a huff but Horvak stayed, smiled, and said. "Tucci I like the way you are running these people around in circles." Then he left too, leaving me to my thoughts.

My new friend was right; soon he (Horvak) was back with a grin on his face and said. "Guess what? Saltzberg just came in the building and he's coming to see you."

Doctor Saltzberg, with Huey and Louie joined Horvak in front of the cell.

Next came a surprise. The doctor told the three officers he didn't need them and walked them to the end of the hallway. He then closed the door and came back.

"Mr. Tucci I'm here because of your hunger strike, is there anything I can do to get you to start eating?" After thinking for a few seconds I answered his question.

"Yes, sure have these smucks (I used a Jewish term because his last name was Saltzberg) move me out of this shit hole and back to a regular cell."

The doctor asked. "If I can do that will you start eating?"

Think, plan, think, plan, and stay in charge Frank! I answered him. "No but if you get me moved back upstairs I'll start drinking liquids (to push the envelope I had been refusing all food and water)."

Saltzberg said he would be right back and left quickly. Well old man, I said to myself, these people are not going to give-in this time.

With that thought in my mind I almost wanted to say the hell with it, and start eating.

But just then I heard a voice in my head saying. "Hey tough guy why are you even thinking of giving-up? You've got them on the run, don't give-up now!"

Saltzberg was back and informed me. "Mr. Tucci here's the deal. I can get you moved back to a regular cell but you have to drink something other than water at each mealtime. That won't break your strike but at least you'll have some liquids in your system."

Always push the B.O.P. back just one more step when you have them giving in to you.

"Okay, I'll have a juice, cranberry only at each meal time. Also, I want a water pill (Forosemide) to get my one good kidney working again. But—first, move me back upstairs!" That was my long and firm reply.

Less than five minutes later I was back in cell #308-C, drinking cranberry juice as I swallowed a Furosemide pill. Yes, the old Muslim had won still another battle.

But—early the next morning. "Tucci cuff-up!" As always, my reply was. "Why?" Bozo told me that Doctor Saltzberg wanted to weigh me and take blood and urine samples.

"Hey asshole, I am not cuffing-up or going to medical, I am refusing! Screw you and the horse you rode in on!"

Doctor Saltzberg was not about to accept my refusal and he and a lab technician were now at the cell door.

"Mr. Tucci why won't you let me weigh you and take specimens?" He almost was pleading. I was calm and this time respectful of the doctor as I answered.

"Doctor I am so tired of being ordered to cuff-up four or five times every damn day. All I want to do is rest, being on a hunger strike is not funny you know."

He nodded. "Yes, Mr. Tucci but that's your choice and I have to keep a record of your health. Just in case we need to send you to an outside hospital. If I can get the lieutenant to let us in the cell will you give me my samples please?

"Yes, if he (the lieutenant) lets you in and I don't have to cuff I'll give you whatever you need!"

As luck would have it Lieutenant O'pry was standing out in the hall with the doctor.

The cell door banged open and in came Doctor Saltzberg, the lab technician who would draw my blood, Lieutenant O'pry, Huey, Louie, and Horvak bringing up the rear with a scale under his arm to weigh me on.

Being on a hunger strike I was very dehydrated and the lab lady had a hard time finding a vain to draw blood from. It took three "holes" before she was able to draw blood.

Last, Horvak put the scale down and helped me to stand up on it. "Shit look at the weight I lost!" I said to myself.

With their work done they all left except Horvak. He was hanging back to give me some information.

"Tucci the D.H.O. will be here early tomorrow morning to see you." "So!" I answered. Just then I thought of a fun thing to spring on the D.H.O and the B.O.P.

"Hey Horvak, I want you to be my staff representative tomorrow at D.H.O." This is allowed under B.O.P. policy. It states, "An inmate may have a staff member represent him before the U.D.C. or at a D.H.O. hearing."

I asked Horvak if he ever heard of an inmate asking a SHU officer to be their staff rep. His smiling answer was. "None the fu-k that I can remember!"

"Okay let's do that if you don't mind?" I asked him. He agreed and the next day the shit would hit the B.O.P.'s backwards-running fan.

June 10, 2002

Horvak brought me my morning cups of cranberry juice (I was still on my hunger strike) and reminded me that the D.H.O. would see me at about 9:30. I drank the juice and sat down to think, plan, think and plan. But—I fell asleep.

I was awakened by kicking and banging on the cell door. Huey, Louie and Horvak were back. This time Horvak had a wheelchair with him and there was no "cuff-up" Tucci ordered.

"Tucci let me help you into the wheelchair, then we'll cuff you and go downstairs to the D.H.O." Horvak said almost too quietly.

When we arrived at the hearing room Mr. Griffith, the D.H.O., was already in place. He was eating a doughnut and drinking good coffee. Was it a late breakfast? No, it was just part of my punishment!

"Good morning, Tucci if you weren't on a hunger strike I would offer you a jelly doughnut." Said Griffith, with a phony smile. He finished his doughnut, wiped his hands and took a long sip of coffee.

His remark was. "Mr. Tucci you're looking at least fifty (50) days in "the hole" before I even gets to your latest charges." He again put that phony smile on his face.

I cut lose with. "Hey buddy kiss my Muslim ass! I don't have any good time left for you to take so ha, ha, the joke's on you!" With my remark he pulled closer to the desk.

But I wasn't done yet. "All you can do is give me more time in the SHU and that always costs the B.O.P. lots of money!" I was of course referring to my trips to the outside hospitals for forced feedings and other medical problems.

"I get no visits, my phone privileges are suspended for six more months and I already know that I will not be offered a halfway house. What the hell does that leave you to hammer with? Nothing!"

While I was yelling and swearing Horvak was trying to keep a straight face but not succeeding. Later in my cell he told me that he had never heard anyone "get" off on Griffith like you did.

The D.H.O. always has the last word, putting down his coffee he said. "Tucci you get the fifty (50) days in Disciplinary Segregation for your previous Incident Reports, which I suspended the last time I saw you."

This guy (Griffith) loves his job, I could tell by the way he was taunting me.

Going on he added. "Now the charge of Fighting a Code 201 is changed to a Code 224 a more appropriate charge of Assault, because you assaulted Mr. Kretzschamar!"

Well I lost all control after that stupid remark and shouted at Griffith.

"Are you fu-king crazy? That lying bastard Kretzschmar is the unit's snitch. He poured hot water on my head and then attacked me and I get charged with assaulting him?"

My face was red and I could not stop myself. "You know what Griffith, you would-n't know the truth if it bite you in your big fat ass!"

Griffith shot-up from his chair. "Either you shut up now or you're back in your cell and this hearing is over!"

Think, plan, think, plan, Frank! I stopped yelling because it would be better to know my entire sentence than and there, versus reading Griffith's report in a week or so.

Then he continued. "On the second charge, the Code 104—Possession or Introduction of a Weapon, the Code stays the same."

I cut in. "What weapon are you talking about? Do you mean my B.O.P. issued cane? Boy you people sure know how to write your shit! Why don't you mention in your report that my weapon was a cane that I need for walking?"

"That's it Tucci! One more outburst from you and you're out of here! Then you can read about my findings when you get my report a few weeks from now."

Horvak looked at me and put his finger to his lips; he was trying to calm me down.

Griffith next summed-up my trumped up punishment. "On the Assault, Code 224 you get 15 days in Disciplinary Seg. Forfeit 27 days Good Conduct Time, and I am recommending a Disciplinary Transfer to a USP (Penitentiary) where you can't go around assaulting people!"

My will power was being tested more and more as he read on, smiling at my misfortune. Just wait until the son-of-a-bitch get's done. I thought to myself.

"For the Code 104, the Weapons charge, 30 days Disciplinary Segregation, and a forfeit of 40 days Non Vested Good Conduct Time. You have a nice day Tucci. Officer Horvak get him out of here!" Griffith was laughing and all smiles.

He was done, I wasn't! I really can't remember all the filth and my exact words that I yelled at him, but here's most of it.

"You are the dumbest bastard I have ever seen working in the B.O.P. How did you get your job? Did your wife screw someone for you? She must have been a good lay or you wouldn't be here today! Hey buy my book you'll just love it when I mention your penis sucking wife in it!"

Looking behind the wheelchair at Horvak, I said. "Home James!" The last few lines of Griffith's B.O.P. self serving report shows just how good he was at putting a "spin" on the truth.

"The possession and use of a weapon has the potential to cause to harm to staff and other inmates. Inmates possess weapons for one reason, to hurt another person." M. Griffith, DHGO, 6-13-02

The B.O.P. issued me the cane. If "possession and use of his cane as a weapon is against the law", why didn't they let me keep my wheelchair instead of giving me a "weapon?"

But—after thinking it over, I figured it out. The wheelchair would have been a bigger weapon. I could have maybe picked it up and hit Kretzschmar with it? Yeah sure.

Back at #308, I added up the time I would have to do in the SHU. Starting with the fifty (50) days left over from my last crimes. And then adding the times of the new charges. So—50 added to 30 plus 15 meant 95 days as a guest at FCI Sheridan?

Or would I be transferred before? Would I end up doing my time in a filthy SHU elsewhere?

My questions were all answered nine days later and you'll read about that in "Arriving At USP Atwater!"

This chapter closes out my nine-month stay at FCI Sheridan, Oregon.

CHAPTER 10

Odds And Ends!

Before closing out Part Two here are a few "Odds And Ends!"

Some are funny and some are sad. It really doesn't matter at which B.O.P. facility they occurred, as all 102 of their prisons are run the same chaotic way.

Remember, when dealing with B.O.P. staff, their employment is not just a job; it's a "mind set"!

First up is "FCI Sheridan's Commissary".

FCI Sheridan's Commissary

(A Jones Enterprise?)

I bet you are wondering what the sub-title means? I'll explain that in just a few more paragraphs. If you don't know what a prison Commissary is, think of it as the inmate's WalMart.

FCI Sheridan is the ninth facility I have been since being sentenced eighteen months back, and that seems like a lifetime ago! Maybe the Bureau of Prisons just wanted me to visit some of its different commissaries to get a better insight for this chapter?

So if you like to travel start writing a non-fiction book about the prison you're in, and see if that doesn't get you "on the road".

The Commissary has everything from postage stamps to peanut butter, sweat-pants to squeeze cheese, but at highly inflated prices. The B.O.P. believes. "If an inmate can afford to buy at the Commissary let's gouge him as part of his punishment." B.O.P. policy "suggests" that the Commissary be run on a "cost plus ten per cent" basis. There's a laugh for you!

Why does anyone buy there if the prices are so high? Remember the old saying that says. "It's the only game in town!" Also. "In the Devil's county nothing is given cheaply. Everything must be bought at a terrible price!"

After you price one or two of the "goods" you'll get the idea real quick. Everything at the Commissary is overpriced, as compared to a K-mart, WalMart, or even your local grocery store.

The following are a few examples for those of you outside to price out.

1.	Tide Laundry Detergent	33 ozs.	$ 5.50
2.	Seasodyne Toothpaste	3 ozs.	$ 5.70
3.	Flax Seed Oil Gel caps	120 Ct.	$ 7.15
4.	Rubbermaid (bowl)	1.5 qt.	$ 2.80
5.	Taster's Choice Coffee	9 ozs.	$ 8.25

When I first looked at the Commissary's list of items, I was sure the prices were in Yen (Japanese dollars) because being that high they couldn't possibly be in U.S. dollars!

Mr. M. Jones at the Commissary hasn't yet figured out how to charge the inmates thirty-five cents for a thirty-four cent stamp. But you can bet he is sure working on it! Oh yes, he's the Jones in the sub-title.

Now here's my sad story and once again it goes back to Warden Ellis and FCI Phoenix.

When I arrived at FCI Sheridan I still had sanctions against me from Ellis. You'll remember, no telephone, visits, or Commissary privileges. Ms. Angus, the Unit Manager here suggested that I "Appeal" to Warden Hood and try to have the sanctions expunged. I did and he did!

December 10, 2001

I received Warden Hood's notice restoring my Commissary privilege. Tomorrow is the unit's day to shop, my good luck and great timing you would think. Wrong! Never forget where I am, in Federal prison.

It had been almost ninety (90) days since I was last allowed to buy at the store and there were badly needed hygiene products I had been going without. May I remind you once more, this is a true story.

If you are old and wear dentures as I do try to stay out of prison. My dentures had gone from white to yellow and then almost brown, because on "Commissary Restriction" I could not purchase denture cleaners.

Here's something else you may find hard to believe. I wasn't able to even buy denture adhesive also because of the "restrictions." After biting into a sandwich and having my dentures come out on the plate I gave up eating solid food!

It's now 6:30 PM and time to go to the Commissary. With list in hand, and a "brother" to push my wheelchair I happily headed up the slight hill.

After a short wait in the rain I was called over to Window #1. "Sorry buddy, you are on Commissary Restriction and can only buy postage stamps!" Said Mr. Jones. Well, let me tell you that caused me to go off!

I tried and tried to explain to Jones that I had a written notice dated yesterday from Warden Hood, stating that I could shop. Jones only reply was. "It's not in my computer!"

Needless to say, I got nothing! So, I just wheeled myself downhill back to the unit. Another victory for the B.O.P., Mr. Jones, and their damn computer! The following week I returned with a longer commissary list and the memo from Warden Hood in hand. If Jones pulled the, "it's not in my computer" routine, I had the memo.

There are two shopping windows but as luck would have it I got Window #1 and Jones again. Well, never being one to hold my tongue, I got up from the wheelchair and passed the notice from the Warden in to him.

Jones commented. "What the hell am I suppose to do with that?" I answered. "Read it, it proves that you should have given me commissary last week!" Then things got ugly and Jones said. "You're done for tonight!" I shouted back at him. "But I only have part of my order!" He repeated himself and added. "Sign the sales slip and get out of my window!"

I always try to get the last word in so I told him. "I am not signing the sales slip!" Jones, not to be upstaged in front of the other inmates yelled. "Good I'll just keep your I.D." That didn't worry me and I yelled back. "Keep it I'll get a new one!"

I won that round as Jones last reply was. "Sign the slip and I'll pass out your I.D.!" This old man is no fool. "The I.D. first!" I said. True, I did get my I.D. back but I had only a few of my needed commissary items.

Once more the Jihad in me was needed! War again! Who was right? Jones and the computer or Warden Hood and I? You can think about that while you read what I did.

First, I wrote an Inmate Request to Staff for Warden Hood on December 19, 2001. I explained what happened and how officer Jones stopped in the middle of my order. He didn't answer, so on January 1, 2002 I took the next step.

A request for Informal Resolution or as it's called here a form B.P. 8. That request was answered quickly on January 4, 2002, signed by both my Unit Counselor, Mr. Hawks and the Unit Manager Ms. Angus.

Here's what they had to say. "Mr. Jones felt that you had become disruptive in line and discontinued your shopping. Mr. Jones had the option of writing an Incident Report but choose to try and resolve it verbally."

I didn't agree with their answer or Mr. Jones action so I wrote a B.P. 9, the next form in the prison paper trail. It would go directly to Warden Hood's office. I'll cut to the chase, this is what I wrote. "If I said or did anything wrong the officer had the option of issuing an Incident Report. He does not have the right to refuse me service without a sanction in place."

As of today, January 20, 2002 the Warden has not answered my request but I will up-date this chapter when he does.

In closing this chapter I have a few more thoughts to share with you about the Commissary.

What do the politicians say about the Commissary? The "Liberals", I am sure having the following mind set. "Yeah, let's cuddle them inmates and their families and friends then they'll send in lots of money! Then they can buy the fancy food, tobacco products, sports clothing, watches, radios, and maybe even our high-priced $75.00 Addidas Cross Trainers. We're overcharging them but the profits keep coming in!"

On the other side of the coin we have the "Conservatives", whom I am sure have asked the following questions. "Why do these convicts even need a Commissary? Doesn't the prison give them everything they need while we have them locked up?"

That's enough from the morons on both sides of issue.

The truth is most inmates do not have any money being sent in! I am blessed; rumor has it that I have a stash of 1.4 million U.S. dollars. I have always said. "Crime does pay but you have to save some of the pay!"

Update—January 25, 2002

Warden Hood has agreed with the Unit Team and added "loud" to his report to go along with my being disruptive. Hey, in Federal prison "loud" is anytime an inmate tries to talk to a staff member, and "disruptive" is when the officer doesn't want to listen to you!

So, I have filed a complaint to the next level, a B.P. 10 for the Western Regional Office in Dublin, California. I'll update you as soon as they reply.

Update March 12, 2002

I lost!

Keeping things still on somewhat of the light side, next is Toilet Paper, "The Issue".

Toilet Paper, The Issue?

December 6 2000

Here in FCI Phoenix, inmates do not ask or beg for toilet paper, nor is it just given them. It is "issued"!

Every month an "issue" notice is posted in the unit and it says the following:

"Memorandum to General Population

From: T. Simmons, Laundry Plant Manager

Subject: Toilet Paper Issue

Be advised that the following is the rotation for toilet paper issue for the month. The toilet paper will be an issue of four rolls. You must pick up your issue on your designated day.

You must have your I.D. card to receive your issue. The time for issue is 5:45 am to 7:15 am each morning."

Yes, that was the actual Memorandum bad English and all from Ms. Simmons. Did you happen to notice how many times she used her favorite word "issue"? Only seven!

One last thought on Ms. Simmons. "Rumor" has it that she was "asked" to leave the B.O.P.'s employment. Why? Well again it's only "rumor", but it had something to do with all the "gifts" of B.O.P. clothing (tee shirts, socks, work boots, etc.) that her family had received! This might be a stretch but maybe she even took a few cases of "issue" home?

Back now to the issue of toilet paper. Ms. Simmons four rolls per month for each inmate is not enough for a prisoner's needs! If you challenge my statement feel free to make the Toilet Paper Home Test. Try this:

First, remove the wrapper for a roll of toilet paper but do not trash the wrapper because it is a very important and needed part of your test.

Second, flatten out the wrapper and write the day's date on it using only a blue or black pen. The test must be exact so I suggest you check the calendar to be sure you have the right date. To double check, call the phone number that gives out the right time and date.

Third, and last of all, you'll need a sledgehammer and a three or four inch spike. So, with everything you need now assembled for the test, it's off to the bathroom!

You'll need a witness/helper so call out and see who is the first to join you in the toilet. The test will work best if you have a family member helping you. After all, do you want a perfect stranger in your john? No, I didn't think so.

Look around the bathroom for a suitable spot to nail the toilet paper's wrapper. Yes, my friend you are going to nail the wrapper, dated said facing out so that all will see it and know you are concerned about T.P. being wasted.

Do not spike the wrapper to the back of the door! No, that's not a good spot because with the toilet door open no one will see the wrapper. You do want visitors to notice it and see that it is "dated".

Don't you want them to know that you, "can feel the pain", of the trees that were "murdered" just so you could wipe your chubby backside!

Yes by George! Nail the T.P. wrapper directly over the toilet paper holder and kill two birds with one roll of paper.

Number one, it will most definitely be a conversation piece! How many people do you know who have a toilet paper wrapper spiked to their john's wall?

Number "two", pardon that toilet pun, anyone using your bathroom will have something to read while they do their business.

The last part of the "test" is the hardest, date calculation, and charting the actual T.P. used. A college degree in Computer Science is helpful, but your B.O.P. G.E.D. will have to do.

You should now have a blue or black pen, a logbook of sorts, a calculator, and a wrapped roll of toilet paper ready. All items must be in a highly visible spot in your bathroom.

Only one thing remains before you are up and running, "a town meeting" in your family room. Everyone in your household must be there! If anyone calls and says they will be getting home late, you still must wait for them. But, it's okay to curse them for making you wait.

At 6:00 PM you call the "meeting" to order by banging a beer bottle (Bud Lite?) on the coffee table. May I suggest the following script?

"We are going to monitor closely toilet paper usage in our house. There are far too many trees being destroyed just so we can blow our noses or wipe our backsides! This shameful waste must and will stop at once!"

Next issue these orders to all. "The person using the last sheet on a roll of toilet paper, before placing a new roll in the holder, will enter into the logbook the time and date. Be very exact with all entries, I may want at a later date to compare figures."

In closing, may I suggest that you have a printed cover made up for your logbook. Here are a few titles that you might want to consider. Our Toilet Paper Log, A Family Project, Saving A Tree, or even maybe, because Everyone Here Cares.

My personal favorite is, Economize Use Both Sides!

Yes, you have raised your spoiled "Red", diaper, and doper children correctly and they respond with loud shouts. "Way to go Dad, we just can't wait to get started!"

Do you believe that any family that shows their brats how to chart toilet paper usage is DYSFUNCTIONAL? Also, not God fearing, and I'll bet they grow up to become "Liberals" and vote a straight Democratic ticket!

A few weeks later

After your "test" results were in, you now agree, that one roll of T.P. per person/inmate per week is not enough! But, you cried foul when you found out about your thirteen-year-old daughter Maud who was stuffing her 30 AAA bra with toilet paper!

Next is "Urine Analysis" or as we call it in here, U.A.

URINE ANALYSIS

December 17, 2000

I was in my cell reading the Quran and waiting for the daily four o'clock lock—in, which is done to "count" us bad guys. I personally think it's just one more thing the B.O.P. does to show an inmate who the boss is.

The 4:00 PM <u>Standing</u> <u>Count</u> is a seventy (70) year old B.O.P. tradition and I have written about that in other parts of this book. But, if you forgot, here's a quick recap. Everyday at 4:00 PM inmates are locked in their cells and about twenty minutes later <u>two</u> officers slowly walk the unit and count the standing inmates.

This author has a question about the 4:00 PM "count". What do the officers do between the time they lock us in and the <u>twenty</u> minutes later when they "count" us? There has been gossip about romantic "quickies" going on!

Oh, did I forget to mention that the guard staff here in FCI Phoenix is coed? Maybe the rumors about "romances" during the <u>twenty-minutes</u> are true?

As I write this book it is very difficult to just stay on the chapter's subject matter. Everything just seems to flow and blend together. Please forgive me if at times I give you <u>too</u> <u>many</u> details.

Back to the U.A. At 4:30 PM officer <u>Newson</u> unlocked the cell and said. "Tucci, they called for you to report to U.A." I asked my cellmate <u>Chris</u>. What the hell is an U.A.?" The week before he had been called to U.A., so he explained the finer points to me.

The B.O.P. says. "Anyone picked to report his been selected at random by computer." Yeah sure! Consider the following "facts".

Last night the <u>FCI</u> <u>Phoenix</u> inmate population count was <u>1,404</u>. So what are the chances of <u>two</u> inmates from the same cell being called almost back-to-back? Wouldn't you say <u>slim</u> to <u>none</u>? Do you think I am being paranoid? Okay, let's run the figures.

There are four housing units here; Yuma, Navajo, Pima and Mojave. Each unit sends <u>four</u> inmates at a time to U.A. and that adds up to only <u>112</u> in a full week.

So if <u>Chris</u> went last week and I subtract that 112 from the total population here it comes to <u>1,292</u>. So what are the odds that I would be called from the <u>same</u> cell one week later? Yes, you're right, <u>1, 292</u> to <u>one</u>!

I left the cell and was joined by three other U.A. candidates in the unit's foyer. We waited there for a few minutes for the U.A. officer who then march us towards the Visiting Room. Along the way twelve other inmates joined us from the other three units.

At 4:45 PM we entered the Visiting Room, which I thought a strange place to report for a U.A. A, <u>S.O.C.</u> (Senior Officer Corrections) and Lieutenant <u>Murano</u> were there to administer the "tests".

It seems I had been branded a troublemaker weeks earlier so I was the first inmate <u>Murano</u> spoke to. "Hey old man, can you give me a specimen real fast and get the hell out of my face?" My quick and one word answer was. "No!"

The <u>S.O.C.</u> then asked who was ready and took those inmates away to watch them pee into a lab bottle. As a Muslim I <u>cannot</u> expose my genitalia for public viewing or an officer to gawk at.

At some point I asked Lieutenant <u>Murano</u>. "Why isn't U.A. done by the medical staff? Don't you know that you <u>are</u> handling a hazardous medical waste? The last time I was in <u>Federal</u> prison only the medical department did these tests."

<u>Murano</u> was now paying attention so I added. "Five years from now if you come down with AIDS or Hepatitis remember these tests! Guess what the <u>B.O.P.</u> will say? They'll insist that you acquired the sickness in your private life and they'll probably blame your alternate lifestyle!"

My remarks <u>had</u> hit home with the Lieutenant, so I zeroed in for the kill! "At your next Union meeting I would bring all that up and tell the Union you don't want to do tests that endanger your family's health."

<u>Both</u> officers were thinking. "What if Tucci is right?" Please keep in mind that most officer' I.Q.'s <u>don't</u> even match their weights, or even come close! Anyone can easily become a <u>B.O.P.</u> officer even <u>without</u> a High School Diploma. But, they <u>must</u> obtain a G.E.D. within one year of their hire date.

I suggested to the officers that if they were to buy me a can of soda from the vending machine I <u>might</u> be able to pee. I will <u>not</u> say if they did or didn't!

It was getting close to "<u>pee or flee</u>" time so I took my best and last shot at ruining these mental midgets day.

"Lieutenant I noticed that when you take an inmate to pee you stand right there and watch. Well, no matter how careful a man pees a few drops always bounce off the toilet onto the floor. I also saw your officer walk over to the inmate to retrieve the specimen bottle, and saw him stepping right in the pee on the floor!

By this time <u>Murano</u> was getting a little testy so I figured I better cut to the chase! Here are my closing words to those two semi-normal officers.

"I bet when you get home you don't take your shoes off at the door! Well, if you have carpets you have just deposited the <u>pee disease</u>!"

And next came my "grand finish". What do most of these good old boys love the most? That's easy to answer, their kids' and their dogs, but not <u>always</u> in that order.

I asked. "Hey, do you guys have dogs?" Two, yes answers! "Well when your dog runs across the germs you put into the carpet, jumps up and licks your face, think of whose pee might be on his tongue!"

It was now 6:20 PM and I was the only one who had <u>not</u> filled a bottle, and the deadline was only <u>twenty</u> minutes away! If I didn't pee I would be written-up as a U.A. refusal!

The <u>S.O.C.</u> asked. "Tucci I thought old people have to use the toilet a lot, why can't you pee?"

I explained to him that a Muslim man does <u>not</u> pee standing, and that I would need to sit to pee and would also have to close the toilet's door. He relayed the message to his lieutenant who yelled back. "Just let him piss so we can get the hell out of here tonight!"

Next is "Gorilla Warfare", which was the turning point of my prison life, and what started me on this book!

In the chapter is also the <u>first</u> of my soon to be <u>many</u> battles with the B.O.P.

Gorilla Warfare, Mine!

November 24, 2000

The Quran says, "Great triumphs are born out of great troubles." I certainly do agree with that statement, but every man has a breaking point!

Today I received my first official B.O.P. "shot" (Incident Report) here in FCI Phoenix and from this day forth I would no longer be Mr. Nice Guy! What happened is an example of how far the intelligent guard staff will go to bring a ray of sunshine into the inmate's otherwise dull life.

After my twelve (12) cents per hour high paying job at the Food dis-Service was over, I headed back to the unit and my quite cell. It is winter here in Phoenix with early morning temperatures in the thirty's. Last week we were "issued" our winter coats, which were made in the B.O.P.'s prison industry called UNICOR.

Every coat has four numbers stamped on the lower part of the back, my numbers were 4-1-0-3. Those numbers, with my name, are on file in Ms. Simmon's Laundry Room computer. Do you remember her from the T.P. chapter?

The B.O.P. has two good reasons for the "numbered" coats. First, if the beer drinking guards are chasing you they do not need to catch you! They'll just jot down the coat's "license plate" on your back and deal with you later.

Second, the numbers are also there so that another inmate will not borrow or steal your coat, but there's a big laugh! I'll explain that. There are 1,426 inmates here in my little corner of the B.O.P.'s Disneyland.

Every time the loudspeakers call out an activity maybe 1,000 inmates are on the move, going to the mess hall, Sick Call, Pill Call, Work Call, School Call, Recreation Call, or Church Call.

With that many prisoners on the move it becomes virtually impossible to check the small inch high numbers on a coat. So, if anyone borrows/steals your coat you have a slim to none chance of getting it back. Inmates reading this who have had an "issued" item stolen know exactly what I mean.

Never the less, my 4-1-0-3 coat was "lost" and never found. That's why when I received my replacement coat I thought it would be good ideas to some way "mark" it. My last name starts with a "T", so in small letters I printed "Mr. T." above the coat's numbers.

However, officer P. Timmins didn't like that idea! He confiscated the "marked" coat and wrote me an Incident Report for "defacing Government property". Don't these people have a real life?

I did not get a replacement coat for the second coat until eleven days later! I don't want to sound like a crybaby but I am 62 years old and take blood thinners, which make me feel cold most of the time.

Some readers who have a family member or friend in prison who is a Senior Citizen will be a little more responsive to my plight. But, the "Hard Liners" will no doubt say. "Isn't that what prisons are for, the punishment!"

Well be that as it may be, it is now 5:30AM and I am on the way to my job at the Food dis-Service. Outside it is 37 degrees and I still don't have a coat! Could it possibly get worst? Yes, it sure could. It's raining hard out there today!

That's it! After being cold and getting <u>wet</u> a few days in a row, I decided to react the only way an old man can, "Gorilla Warfare, Mine!" You will be shocked at how many problems this 62 years old Muslim caused the mighty Bureau of Prisons!

But before I entered into battle everything had to be well planned, and always so as not to expose my cellmate (a non-Muslim) or any other inmate to punishment from the B.O.P.!

Yes, you can hurt the B.O.P. by causing them to spend their money! Most of the staff here in FCI Phoenix don't care or believe that, in their mental midget minds it's not their money. But their "mind set" is not at all logical. May I confuse them with the facts?

Doesn't most of the staff here pay Federal Income Tax? Don't the taxes they pay go to run this facility and all the other B.O.P. prisons? So, in fact isn't it really their money?

The B.O.P. and officer Timmins did draw "First Blood" but now the old Muslim will start on a 41 month "Jihad".

Author's note:

The word "Jihad" is derived from "Jhud" which means: To strive hard, fearing none except Allah. There are many types of Jihad. Against the B.O.P. mine would be a, "Jihad Arbabi Adh-Dhum wal Bida wal-Mumkarst". That translates as, "Jihad against the unjust, the innovators and the sinners."

Remember, I work in the Food dis-Service and I can do many costly and covert acts! Pay close attention Warden Ellis all of the following were done while you sat in your office picking your red nose!

First, were the plastic forks and spoons that are used in the mess hall. These are not the cheap throw away kind and they are washed and used over and over again. But, not if I toss them into the garbage pail! At every meal I trashed three forks and three spoons. Oh, you're laughing at me now, but wait until we do the math!

The utensils cost .30 cents each, and six tossed out at each meal, times the three meals each day comes to $5.40 per day. Carrying out the figures it comes to $37.80 per week, $151.20 a month, and at the end of my sentence it will be $6,194.20! Not bad for just tossing a few forks and spoons?

Guess what? I also started the Muslims on trashing their utensils; by convincing them we needed new ones. It's safe to say that the B.O.P. spent at least $10,000.00 to replace the plastic ware the Muslims and I trashed.

Second and third were done while working at the Food dis-Service as a table wiper. Inmates who have finished eating often leave food items on the table for next guy who sits there.

I use to recycle the leftover sugar pockets, hot cereal packages, jelly packets, napkins, syrup packets, boxes of milk, etc. But now anything left on the tables I tossed into the garbage pails! Add at least $100.00 a day to the "Jihad" total.

Next were the salt and peppershakers. Here in FCI Phoenix, these are of the throw-away type, and that's just what I did! Even the full ones! Although salt is cheap black pepper is not, so rack up another maybe $50.00 per day for the shakers.

Oh, I almost forgot there is a "fourth". Every now and then the kitchen cop would put a large trash barrel in front of the dish room's window. The barrel was there to throw "paper" from the meal, potato chip bags, ice cream wrappers, Jell-O containers, etc. I do not doubt that Allah sent the barrel! Why?

Because FCI Phoenix serves their meals on heavy plastic dishes which are not of the throw away type. So, every time the trash barrel was in place my dish, cups and even the tray they were on "accidentally" fell into the barrel! That cost the B.O.P. still more money for replacements, score about $3,000.00 more for the old Muslim!

The estimate total for my actions and that of the other Muslims done at the mess hall comes to $27,194.20! But, I am not even close to the end of my "jihad".

Was there anything else I could do on the job to "Gorilla" them? Yes, not to show up for work at all! In the Forward of this book I wrote. "That those already doing time can get things done using the system to their advantage."

The medical staff here at FCI Phoenix is half Public Health Service (P.H.S.) and half outside contracted help who "bid" on providing services for this facility. By the quality of the services provided I am positive the lowest bidder won!

Most of the P.H.S.'s employees here are young and without much experience in their chosen professions. But they do, as ex-President Clinton says. "Feel your pain." As far as the contracted doctors, nurses and technicians go, that's what the all should do, go!

Let's get back to my "Gorilla" action. To not show up for F/S I first had to report to Sick Call, which starts at 6:30 AM. As always, I left the unit at 5:30 AM for F/S., ate my breakfast slowly and watch the wall clock.

At 6:00AM the dining room opened for the 1,400 or so hungry inmates and as I did each day, I stepped outside. My efforts as a table wiper are not needed at this time because upon opening the doors there are no dirty tables.

At 6:30 AM, I was at the Health Services building, which is on the other side of the compound. But the doors weren't unlocked until 6:40 AM for the 6:30 AM Sick Call.

I have been here for a few months now but I have never seen the Sick Call start on time! If you work for the B.O.P. it is better to be late on the job than early. After all, the inmates have nowhere to go and all day to get there.

Once I stood outside in a pouring rainstorm for ten minutes waiting to get in for Sick Call. How do the B.O.P. and the medical department run a Sick Call?

Well let's pretend it's a Monday morning and you are reporting to Sick Call at 6:30 AM, but as usual the doors aren't unlocked until 6:40 AM! Upon entering you must "sign in" with your name, prison number, and housing unit.

Using the last two numbers of the first five numbers on your I.D. card (each B.O.P. card has eight numbers) you'll stand in one line for 0 to 49 and for 50 to 99 the other line.

Monday is the worst of all days for Sick Call because there is none held on Saturday or Sunday.

Monday's are always packed with transit inmates that show up daily here at FCI Phoenix. All of them are housed in the Yuma Unit and they number about 120. Because their property was boxed and forward to their "next" facility they must stand in a long line for such items as aspirin, band-aids, eye drops, cough syrup, and laxatives. These items are free at Sick Call but it is easier to buy them at the Commissary than stand in line for an hour at 6:30 AM.

As my plan rolls along I see the nurse and tell her. "I think I am coming down with the Flu. This morning I threw up and I had a bad case of the runs. Also, my eyes and nose are running and I ached all over."

After my short speech she stuck a cold thermometer in my mouth, looked up my nose, in my ears, and took my blood pressure. Then she said. "Yeah Pops it looks like you have the start of the Flu.

I asked her. "I work in the F/S should I be going back to work?" She said. "No, because you have the start of the Flu, I'll write you out a lay-in for five days."

With five days off I returned to my unit with my "Jihad" plans for it. Next are two of my all time favorites, the TV's and the microwaves. Yes, there are microwaves in the housing units but not because the B.O.P. wants to be nice to the prisoners.

The microwaves are there as an inducement for the inmates to buy the Commissary's over-priced microweavable food items. But in every prison there is always one ethnic group that will try to monopolize the micros. In this unit there are 128 inmates and two microwaves, and most of the time only one microwave due to on-going repairs.

Here's a question for you. Is it fair for the same group of inmates to "take over" the microwave every morning, seven days a week, from 6:00 AM to 7:00 AM?

What was your answer? My answer was "no" and I backed it up with more "Gorilla" and here's what I did. FCI Phoenix's Commissary sells soda in cans, but maybe not after Warden Ellis reads the next few paragraphs.

With no video cameras in the housing units here I didn't get caught on candid camera as I destroyed my first of four (4) microwaves. My plan is simple and very quick. "Place a can of soda in the microwave, turn the setting to high and run!"

The resulting blast killed two birds with the one can! First, because there was only one microwave working the selfish 6:00 AM to 7:00 AM inmates didn't dare tie up the remaining microwave with their cooking! Second, and what it was all really about, add the cost of a new microwave to the "Jihad" totals times four (4)!

My next sabotage in the unit was the TV'$\underline{s}$. Yes, TV's! Again a simple plan but very effective as I shorted out three (3) of the unit's TV's. Here the Commissary sells a "Cup of Soup", you know a Styrofoam cup that you add water to.

Here's how it was done. Take the wrapper off the cup; punch a hole in the bottom with a pen, fill with water and place on top of the TV set. Soon the water will run out of the cup and down into the TV's workings. Boom! One less TV! Add that to my "Jihad" totals times three (3).

At this point I think it is safe to say that my personal "Jihad" has cost the B.O.P. close to $50,000.00 I had to pay $19.76 for my "defaced" coat. Who do you think won?

The last chapter in this part of the book is, "Hobo Goes Home!" It's about my closest friend John Berry while I was still in FCI Phoenix.

"Hobo Goes Home!"

Author's note"

This is the last writing in Part Two and it does end on a slightly happier theme. Yes, Mr. John Berry B.O.P. # 83302-011 was going home to San Francisco after fourteen (14) years in various Federal facilities. John has been a close friend and a warehouse of knowledge and information as I wrote this book.

May 16, 2001

During the morning it was pouring rain as I walked my friend John to FCI Phoenix's front gate and his long-awaited freedom. Do you believe in signs from the All Mighty? Was the rain a good sign or a bad sign?

At the gate I handed him a stamped envelope with my home address and asked him. "Hobo please use it so that I know what's up with you?" He nodded "yes" and walked away to his freedom and a distant unknown future.

Hobo's trip turned out to be a sad story in itself due to staff stupidity of Mr. Hall and a loud mouthed and lying inmate Bill Hasenauer, B.O.P. # 44595-008. I'll explain about that later in this chapter but first a little background on Hobo and I.

Over the past year "Hobo", as John's friends and I call him, were constantly together. We are close in age, he is sixty-one and I am sixty-two, and some of our prison friends say we even look alike. We had wanted to have our photo taken together but just never got around to it.

Hobo and I first met here in FCI Phoenix when we were both assigned to work AM F/S (morning Food dis-Service) shift. He was introduced to me by the kitchen cop Mr. Dubsky, yes, that's his real name. Dubsky walked Hobo over to me and said. "Hey, Mr. Tucci have you met Mr. Berry? Hey, that sounds like a law firm, Tucci and Berry."

After sitting and talking to Hobo for a short time he informed me. "I've been in this joint before and that cop Dubsky is anti-Semitic and a Jew hater!"

John Berry is of the Jewish faith and was wearing a white yarmulke and I was wearing my black Muslim kufie. Hence, inmates started calling us salt and pepper.

Hobo's prison story is not your average tale of convict woes, it seems that problems fly at him like bees to honey. The following are just two of Hobo's "problems" that I personally witnessed.

Oh how too well I remember our second day together at the F/S. There is a B.O.P. rule, which says. "All Food Service inmates will report to work wearing steel-toed boots/shoes." The B.O.P. was afraid that if we dropped a piece of toast on our foot, we might break a toe and sue them?

Their "rule" became Hobo's first problem here in FCI Phoenix, because of his feet. Please don't laugh but Hobo's shoe size is 10 ½ 5E! Did you notice the 5E? Oh it gets even worst, he also needed a "boxed toe style" shoe/boot.

Mr. Jacobs the Assistant F/S Director spotted Hobo wearing a beat up pair of old sneakers. Jacobs "ordered" him. "Mr. Berry get over to the clothing supply and come back here wearing work boots? Now comes the problem!

Before Hobo arrived here in FCI Phoenix he was imprisoned at FCI Fort Dix in New Jersey. While there he had two pairs of work boots ordered and made especially for him at a cost of $200.00 a pair.

In August 2000 he was shipped here without his $200.00 a pair boots. In fact he arrived here wearing the size 11 ½ torn sneakers that caught Jacob's eye. Yes, the costs of the left behind boots were only $400.00 of the taxpayers' money!

The staff was following B.O.P. policy, which says. "Inmates being transferred to another facility shall turn-in all issued clothing items." The exceptions being only Commissary purchased clothing such as sweat pants, gym shorts, sneakers, etc.

My friend tried in vain to persuade the R&D officers at FCI Fort Dix to let him take at least one pair of the $200.00 boots with him. He pleaded to them that his "size" and "toe style" were a special order and that there would be no boots for him when he got to FCI Phoenix. Time proved Hobo right!

Somewhere during the great boot debate FCI Fort Dix's Clothing Manager came into the mayhem on Hobo's side. She informed the transit officers that. "Mr. Berry's boots were indeed specially ordered for him. If you take his boots away how many in-coming guys will need a size 10 ½ 5E. More than likely they'll stay on my shelf forever."

The lady officer rally tried to help my friend but. "The rules are the rules!" Even dumb or other wise? So if any inmate reading this needs a size 10 ½ 5E, box style toe, boots, contact FCI Fort Dix. Or get yourself transferred there!

Can you guess where this "boot thing" with Jacobs and Hobo is headed? The stage was now set for the coming confrontation. Hobo was to report to F.S. the next day wearing work boots or else!

After finishing our shift Hobo and I went directly over to see Ms. Simmons the Laundry/Clothing Supervisor. He politely asked her. "Do you have a size 10 ½ 5E, box toe boot?" Her snooty reply was. "No, but try these size 11's on."

Needless to say the boots didn't come close to fitting, Hobo told her so, thanked her, and we left wondering about tomorrow.

The next morning at 5:30 AM we reported back to F/S with Hobo of course wearing his sneakers. Officer Dubsky approached us and said. "Mr. Berry where are your work boots today?" My friend's answer, looking at me for back up, was. "They didn't have my size! Right, Frank?"

Dubsky wasn't happy with Hobo's answer and returned quickly with his boss Mr. Jacobs. The line in the sand was now drawn!

Jacobs came right to the point. Mr. Berry you will report here tomorrow wearing work boots or I'll write an Incident Report!" Hobo went on the defense by telling him that Ms. Simmons didn't have his size and that at FCI Fort Dix his boots were a special order.

"Mr. Berry if you don't come in here tomorrow wearing boots don't start working, and I will write you up!" Jacobs had the last words.

Later Hobo and I talked about what he should or could do. "Maybe you should ask for a size 12 wide? At least try them on." I suggested. He answered. "No good Frank buddy they will not be a box toe style. My toes are very long and will scrape against the sides and bleed!"

The next morning, "bootless" Hobo and I headed for the F/S and what later would become a close friendship that lasts even today, Tucci and Berry!

Jacobs true to his word was waiting just inside the dining room's door. He took Hobo aside so I really didn't hear their conversation. But, when they were finished talking Hobo hurried over to where I was eating.

He had a stunned and pained look on his bearded face as he said. "Frank, they're probably going to toss me in Seg!" He was right! In came two officers who marched Hobo over to the Clothing Issue, with Mr. Jacobs bringing up the rear.

Once there Jacobs asked Ms. Simmons to issue Hobo work boots, which of course didn't fit! Hobo later told me that Jacobs give him a direct order. "Put on those boots and report back to F/S!" He didn't do either.

Hobo was handcuffed behind his back and paraded across the compound to the SHU a.k.a. "the hole" for ten (10) days! The charge was "Refusing A Direct Order". A few months later I would also become a guest in the SHU.

Here's a question for you readers? Is sending a sixty-one year old man to "the hole" for ten days just or needed punishment, for refusing to wear boots that cut into his toes? Maybe next the Feds will just line us up and shoot us if our bed is not made by 7:30 AM?

Just to explain to you how stupid, mean spirited and self-serving for Jacobs the whole boot thing was, ten days later Hobo was back at F/S wearing his sneakers!

All that was in August of 2000. But, when they released Hobo in May of 2001 they still had not ordered his 10 ½ 5E boots!

After the "boot problem" Hobo joined me in my Gorilla (Jihad) Warfare and you have already read "Gorilla Warfare, Mine!" Yes, a Jew and a Muslim fighting our common nemesis the B.O.P.!

There is a very old Arabic saying that I like to quote. "The enemy of my enemy becomes my friend." Sorry, B.O.P!

Hobo was however more into causing the prison "problems on paper". Things such as lawsuits, writs, Request to Staff, and the B.O.P.'s lack of kosher food.

The best example of Hobo's problems on paper was the "Toilet Bowl Issue". Here's the background on that.

There are over sixty-(60) inmates on the F/S AM shift and I swear to you the following is the truth. We have only one (1) toilet and one (1) hand sink for our use. That's correct, sixty-(60) inmates and only one toilet and one sink!

Because of the only one toilet many of us urinate into the slop sinks inside the mop closets. I can remember getting caught peeing in those closets twice by Dubsky! He asked. "Tucci what the hell are you doing pissing in the sink?" Dubsky never did write me up, probably because he knew I would file a complaint about the only one toilet.

I didn't, but Hobo did! Here's what he did, and his actions got him a second, this time fifteen-day stay in the SHU Hotel.

One morning Hobo came into the F.S with sixty-(60) typed out "Inmate Request To Staff" forms. The text of which complained about the lack of toilets and sinks. "Tucci I had to do this before someone gets written up for using the sinks to piss in!" Hobo explained to me.

Here's where we separated the men from the boys! I passed out some of the forms and one of my Muslim brothers the rest. Every Muslim and all the Black inmates signed the forms as did Hobo and I. So, out of sixty workers we had forty-five (45) signatures.

Hobo did his research on the matter by checking B.O.P. policy as to how many toilets should be in place for sixty-(60) inmate workers.

The "big mouths", "cry babies", and "tough guys" didn't sign our forms. They were more worried about their huge twelve (12) cents per hour pay than their personal hygiene! One of those groups, I think it was the "cry babies", informed Mr. Jacobs. "Berry is making us sign complaints." That was a lie!

Once the F/S Director heard of it Hobo was on his way to Segregation again and I was given a verbal warning. Hobo was charged with "Insighting Others to Riot", yes, riot!

Outside of these prison walls the act that Hobo tried is called a "Right To Partition". This "right" is granted to all Americans, except B.O.P. inmates! Ask my wife Remy and she'll tell you that your "rights" in prison are only what the B.O.P. lets you have! She knows this first hand from the weekly changes in the visitation "rules".

You have read of only two times that Hobo was sent to "the hole", but during his fourteen years n prison he has made the trip thirty-six (36) times!

He has lost 756 "good time" days and I am checking to see if that is a B.O.P. record.

After Hobo's second release from the SHU he and I "Gorillaed" the B.O.P. until his release on May 16, 2001. After he left I "Gorillaed" them and "Gorillaed" them until Warden Ellis shipped me out of FCI Phoenix.

I have saved my thoughts on Billy Hasenauer B.O.P. #44595-008 for the last paragraph of this chapter because I wanted you readers to know about the fakes, phonies, and frauds like Hasenauer.

Hobo was told by this low-life. "Hey there's no need for you to take the bus all the way to San Francisco. I still have thousands of frequent flyer miles on my card. I'll call my wife and arrange to have a ticket left for you at the Air Alaska counter."

Doesn't that sound too good to be true? Well it wasn't! A few days after Hobo left he used the stamped envelope I gave him.

He wrote to my wife. "Tell Frank that Hasenauer is a lying bastard! There was no ticket left for me and Air Alaska doesn't even fly to San Francisco!"

I hope you are reading this Mr. Hasenauer, shame on you!

Next is Part Three, The End! Chapter 1 tells of Arriving At USP Atwater!"

PART THREE

The End

CHAPTER 1

"Arriving At USP Atwater!"

This chapter starts the last part of my Federal incarceration, which was served at the U.S. Penitentiary in Atwater, California. So let's begin.

June 19, 2002 FCI Sheridan, Oregon.

Ten days earlier I was given ninety-five (95) days in Disciplinary Segregation by the DHO. In my mind I was sure all of those ninety-five days would be spent right there in Sheridan's SHU. But—I was wrong!

This chapter does have a happy ending or as my wife Remy says, "God works in mysterious ways!"

At 1:00 AM the light came on in my luxury suite #308. Lieutenant O'pry and four guards entered with a fanfare.

My first reply, which must have sounded funny because my dentures were not in my mouth, was. "What's up? Is this a social call or did you guys just come in to beat me?"

"Mr. Tucci you're moving on down the road." Said Lieutenant O'pry. "Okay, I give up! What does that mean? I asked.

"That means you get-up, get dressed, and shut-up asshole!" Officer Duncan, a big powerfully built Black man sing songed.

Well this old man (me) never does anything I am told unless I feel like it.

"Hey, Duncan I bet being Black and putting chains and cuffs on White people makes your day. Guess what? I ain't getting up. Just in case you morons forgot I am now on day twelve (12) of a hunger strike. I am not feeling strong enough to stand-up?"

Lieutenant O'pry cut in. Mr. Tucci we have a wheelchair here to help you to the bus and you don't need to dress. First, we'll take you to R&D for travel clothes and then the bus."

After putting my false teeth in my mouth I asked. "Lieutenant where am I going?" He didn't answer! The guards and the lieutenant both knew where they were taking me but they like to play "mind games" with inmates.

I didn't panic; my wife would be on her computer in a few hours. The B.O.P.'s Inmate Locator Line would tell her where I had been moved to. Thanks B.O.P. for that one good thing, however not everyone's family has a computer.

Helped into the wheelchair I was hurriedly pushed over to Receiving and Discharge (R&D), wearing only my boxer shorts and a tee shirt.

"Stand-up and strip!" The R&D officer ordered. As always, I used my standard reply. "I can't stand without my cane you jerk!"

O'pry hearing my loud reply stepped forward and told the two closest guards. "Help him up we're running late here, there's a bus ready to go waiting on us."

The lieutenant came closer and helped me off with my shorts and tee shirt, to which he said. "I don't even do this for my own kids!" He then helped me put on a tee shirt, boxers, pants, and a pullover shirt.

I sat back down in the wheelchair and asked him. "Lieutenant O'pry do I got socks and shoes?" He answered. "You sure do Mr. Tucci, what size shoes?" With the clothing issue done I was speed pushed to the bus.

Two officers lifted me from the wheelchair and we followed O'pry on to the prison's new bus.

I asked the lieutenant if I could be seated across from the bus's toilet because I could not walk. Not only was I very weak from the hunger strike but also Duncan had put heavy leg irons on me.

O'pry pointed to the inmate that was seated next to the toilet. "You, next to the toilet, up! Come to the front of the bus and sit there!" He pointed to the seat I was sitting in.

With O'pry walking in front of me and an officer behind me, they gently got me to the rear of the bus. Now I was next to the water jug and toilet and would not have to go far for either. Now we were ready to leave.

I starting asking some of the inmates (there were forty of us) if they knew we were going. A "brother" said. "Pops we all be going to the Atwater Penitentiary in California." Well, so much for the B.O.P.'s security!

The trip would last about fourteen (14) hours and we would be going south for 638 miles. I thank my wife for that information.

The bus made only three stops. Once to gas-up and twice to feed us. Our "sack" lunches were passed out by an inmate who had no handcuffs or leg irons on. More than likely he was a snitch.

I did not eat anything from that first sack of shit, but ate two small sugar cookies from the second bag of garbage. The crap that they feed you on the bus is always the same. It makes no difference if you're in New York, Florida, Texas, or Oregon.

Somewhere within the B.O.P., there must be a Director of Bus Meals. His only function is to make sure that all 102 Federal Prisons put the same meal in the same size bag on all transfer buses.

The trip would take me from the damp 60 degrees weather of Oregon into 90 degrees of California sunshine and heat. It would work wonders for my arthritic knee joints and swollen hands.

The bus turned off the freeway, Route 99, and in a few more minutes there it was— USP Atwater! High walls, fences, razor wire, and gun towers. Damn if it didn't look intimidating!

This was the first trip to Atwater for all of the bus's officers. They didn't know where the bus was to be unloaded and drove us to the wrong gate.

However, Lieutenant O'pry got off the bus and asked directions from the guard post. You see—real men do ask directions!

The fact that I was in a USP started to sink in! Next the bus was driven to a side part of the prison. One by one each officer (there were four) left the bus to place their weapons in the lock boxes near the gate. With that done we were driven to the unloading area.

The receiving area had twenty-foot high cement walls and was narrow with just enough rooms for one bus.

Each inmate left the bus as his or her names were called, I was last. "Tucci, can you walk?" Asked the lieutenant. "No, I don't think so, I am feeling weak and very dizzy from this heat (it was about ninety degrees) I said."

Two guards carried me off the bus and leaned me up against the courtyard's cement wall. I cannot stand at all and slid down to the ground.

O'pry ran to my side. "Tucci hang in there I'll get you a wheelchair!" One of the Atwater staff was also at my side, and O'pry asked him about getting a wheelchair.

Atwater replied. "We don't do wheelchairs here. If the old bastard's that sick he'll soon be shipped out of here."

Hearing that shocked me! Are these people crazy? Here I am a sixty-three year old man, sitting on the ground unable to walk, and they don't do wheelchairs!

But they had no choice. I couldn't and wouldn't even try to walk. Again I was carried by the two Sheridan officers, this time to the prison's R&D area. Inside I was put into a large cell by myself.

After what seemed like a very long time a guard came into the cell and asked. "What's wrong with you, old man?"

"I have been on a hunger strike and the heat here just took its toll on me. I just need to rest a little." He left without saying anything else.

Captain Morehead was the next visitor and he asked. "You're Tucci, aren't you? Captain Smith (from Sheridan) E-mailed me that you are on a hunger strike. If that's correct, why would you want to do that?"

Weakly, I said. "Yes, I am on a hunger strike and I did it to get moved out of Sheridan. I guess it worked because I am here."

The captain's next question was. "Mr. Tucci are you going to be on a hunger strike here?" My smart-ass reply was. "Do I have to be?" Morehead ended our conversation with. "Eat here and I'll see you in a few days.

"Okay, I'll start eating some soft foods like mashed potatoes, jello and oatmeal." He then left and much later, after all 39 inmates who were on the bus with me were processed, they came for me.

"Hey buddy on your feet let's go!" Thinking to myself—my mind said. Well, Frank it looks like you'll have to break-in a new bunch of guards!

I smiled at him and said very politely. "I am sorry but I can't walk without my cane."

He answered with a question. "Well where is your cane old man?" I explained that I had my cane on the bus but they took it when I entered R&D. He left and returned with my cane.

"Now can you please get-up and try to come out here so that I can get you processed and into a cell?" I told him I was weak but would try to walk.

"Take your time, we have all the time in the world. You're the last one so no need to hurry." He assured me.

The following routine is done the same way, in the same order, at the same area (R&D) in all the Federal system.

Step One.

I was ordered to "strip-out" of my Sheridan travel clothes. Then told to bend, spread my ass, and lift up my balls. A new "request", of which I never had done before was next.

A good name for the SHU officer would be Billy Bob, because of his good old boy accent! Ah, my life just keeps getting better and better!

Billy Bob said. "Open your mouth, are those dentures? Well sir, they'll have to come out to be checked." Pleadingly, I said. "If I take them out I can't put them back in without denture adhesive."

"I don't give a shit they're coming out of your mouth one way or the other. Do you understand me old man!"

He now noticed the hearing aid in my left ear. "Take that there out of your ear and hand it to me."

Whenever you talk about being embarrassed, think of what happened to me next. Put this in your mind's eye.

I am standing naked, holding dentures in my right hand and my cane with my left hand. How do I take my hearing aid out? Maybe Billy Bob will figure it out and tell me to put my teeth back in my mouth first?

No, Billy Bob wasn't that intelligent. So without asking the stupid bastard I put my teeth back in (without denture adhesive) biting down hard to keep them in place.

Then I removed my hearing aid and handed it to him. After a quick check Billy Bob returned it.

Step Two.

The clothing issue. My next officer was Slim, he asked. "What size boxers, tee shirt, and jumpsuit?" Unlike Sheridan's SHU I was given socks and shoes.

Yes, the old man (me) was in an orange jumpsuit again and that meant I was headed for "the hole". Did you expect anything different? Didn't I still have about eighty (80) days left from the DHO to serve?

Step Three.

Fingerprints, a photo for my Atwater USP I.D. card, and last, forms to fill-out. The same fuc-ing B.O.P. forms that I filled-out in eight (8) other B.O.P. facilities!

I don't know how it happened but the El Viejo (old one) in me came alive! I'll have some fun with the B.O.P. at their expense. So—when Slim handed me the forms to fill-in I nicely said. "I am sorry but I can't see to read those forms, my bifocals are with my property."

Slim was lost for words as he asked. "What did you say?" Now it's fun time for Tucci. I said again. "I can't read the forms without my eyeglasses which are with my property."

"Never mind the damn forms right how let's get your finger prints and I.D. photo." I bet you thought he was going to make out the forms for me?

With that done it was the medical department's turn. Most of the B.O.P.'s ad hoc medical staff are foreigners. Rumor has it that soon they (the B.O.P.) will soon start hiring medical staff that actually speaks English.

The doctor (he was Hungarian) went over my list of medications and asked if I had taken all of my meds for the day. I left with five bottles of pills, which was hard to carry with no pockets in my jumpsuit.

Last stop—(door number 3) was the prison's shrink (psychiatrist). My "interview" would last exactly four (4) minutes by the clock on the wall. In that time he evaluated me and addressed all my concerns? Using the four minutes as a cost basis, he would make $5000 a day in private practice!

With the processing done Billy Bob said the magic words. "Cuff-up Tucci!" Next stop Segregation cell #129!

It's okay I said to myself. I can take anything life deals me. Nothing get's Tucci down! The bastard B.O.P. can send me anywhere, and I'll still make my own place!

The dawn came up; it was a Thursday but no Captain Morehead? I ended my hunger strike and started eating with that morning's meal. Because of my Muslim faith I had to send back a few "pork meals" in the days that followed.

That day passed with no visitors to my cell? Unlike Sheridan where each day the Warden, Assistant Warden, Captain, Unit Manager, Case Manager, Counselor, Doctor, or the Psychiatrist would come in just to irritate me. In a USP no one cares!

One good thing was going around in my head. Remy, by now has tracked me via the B.O.P.'s Inmate Locator Line and knows where I am!

I wanted to write her but I had no postage stamps. Had my money from Sheridan's Commissary fund been transferred here? If so, I could buy postage stamp the next Commissary day for the SHU.

Friday came, again no Captain Morehead. What did he mean when he said. "I'll talk to you in a few days Mr. Tucci."

Calm down Frank, only eighty (80) days or so and you'll be out of the SHU, until the next time.!

Bad timing really just seems to follow me. I was able to stop a Counselor in the hall and got some good news and also the bad.

Good news was, yes my money had been transferred here from Sheridan. Bad news, the Commissary was closed for inventory for the week.

Saturday and Sunday passed slowly. The B.O.P. comes to a complete standstill on those two days. It is a safe bet that about seventy percent of the staff have those days off. So—I knew the Captain would not be in.

Monday, June 24, 2002.

The day started early as breakfast was served before 6:00AM. At 7:30 bang, bang, on the cells' door. "Tucci cuff-up!" Those three words tend to piss me off! Is it any wonder that my reply was. "What the f—k for?"

"The Captain wants to see you!" Do your thing Frank, the El Viejo said in my head. So—I said. "Officer I need my cane to walk to the Captain's office." His reply is just what you can expect in a U.S.P. "There ain't no cane out here in the hallway."

Being a little more forceful I answered him. "My cane is in your office, they took it away after I walked into the cell!"

Again the guard's reply is just what you would expect here. "I don't know nothing about no fucking cane!" After he said that the battle line was drawn.

"Are you going to cuff-up?" Well here I go again, new friends to be made in a new facility. "Okay, I am not cuffing-up until you find my cane! I just sit here until the Captain comes down and then I'll tell him you refused to get my cane!"

Without saying anything else he hurried away. I thought for sure I had just gotten my first Incident Report here, a Code 312 Insolence Towards Staff.

But I was wrong! The same guy returned with the cane and said the magic words. "Now will you cuff-up Tucci?"

In front of Captain of Morehead I spoke right up. "I would have been here sooner but the officer wouldn't get my cane and I refused to cuff-up."

Why did I speak-up like that to Captain Morehead? There were two things I wanted him and Atwater to know right from the start.

First that I wasn't going to take any abuse while I was there! Second, that this old man (me) doesn't beg or kiss ass!

Morehead moved closer to his desk, put both hands on it and said. "Mr. Tucci are you ready to go back on the compound?" What did I hear him say? I thought to myself—is he crazy? Doesn't he know about the DHO's time hanging over my head?

"Well, I'm still a little weak from being on a hunger strike. Maybe a few more days of food and rest in the SHU would be a good idea." I said calmly.

"Good idea, I'll see you on Thursday and if you're up to it you'll be sent to a housing unit then." He ended with that and motioned for the guard to take me back to the cell.

On the way back to the cell I asked the officer. "Did you ever heard of anyone asking for a few more days in "the hole" like I just did?"

He smiled widely and said. "No, you're one crazy old man." I was sure he would not write that Incident Report on me now. The smile on his face told me that.

Back in the cell, I heard. "Yo, you old man, Cell #129!" The voice was coming thru the A/C vent in the next cell. Standing on top of the toilet seat I yelled back.

"Yeah what's up?"

The reply back was "As-SA-L AA-MU-A'LAY-KUM!" It was the Muslim greeting of "peace be upon you." I answered back. "WA A LAY-KUM-AS-SA-LAAM!" Which meant, "and peace be with you."

Again he spoke. "I heard you tell the cop that you're a Muslim. I also heard you asking the counselor for stamps. I'll send two over when the next meal comes."

"Thanks but I won't be able to pay you back this week because the commissary is closed." His answer back was very uplifting. "Don't worry about paying me brother, I am also a Muslim!"

True to my Muslim friend's word, when the noon meal was brought the guard handed me an envelope with my food tray.

Written on the envelope was. "Here's two stamps if you need more let me know." It was signed, Steven.

As always, no matter how bad things seemed, I was provided with "His" help!

Later I started writing to Remy, my first letter in a week. That same night I was surprised by mail from her! Remember, she knew where I was via the B.O.P.'s website.

Tuesday and Wednesday June 25th and June 26th dragged by. And now it was Thursday the 27th, would Captain Morehead remember about me? I really didn't expect anything good to become of our conversation but—one can always hope.

Breakfast came. No trip to the captain's office. Lunch, and again no trip to the office? Oh, well, he probably looked closer at my file.

Then at 1:00PM. "Tucci I'll pull you out soon, the Captain wanted me to see you today? Said a lieutenant whose name I didn't get.

An hour later I was cuffed-up and taken to see the lieutenant. Why not Captain Morehead, I wondered?

The lieutenant spoke loudly almost yelling, maybe he saw that I was wearing a hearing aid? "Captain Morehead wanted me to check with you about going out on the yard. Are you ready to leave?"

Yes, Remy, there is a God! Not trying to sound anxious I said. "Yes lieutenant I am ready to go."

Next came a little bad news. "I don't' know if I can get you out of here today, if not, tomorrow for sure."

Okay, Frank, it's only one more day in Paradise. Adding Sheridan's and now Atwater's SHU time together, I had been in Segregation only a mere twenty (20) days. My ninety-eight (98) days in Phoenix's SHU flashed back in my mind.

So—I stopped my worrying and laid down to rest. It seemed like only five minutes later. Bang, bang, bang, on the cell door! "Tucci get your shit together you're leaving."

In reading other chapters of this book you may have noticed that the staff always refer to an inmate's property as shit. That has been the case in every facility I have been in, all nine (9).

Somewhere within a B.O.P. training manual it has to be written. "When informing an inmate he is being moved from the cell or institution the following must   be strictly adhered to:

1.   Bang or kick the cell door to get the inmate's attention.
2.   Speak loudly, especially if it's between the hours of 1 and 5 AM.
3.   Order the inmate to gather-up their belongings. The word "shit" must be included in your Order.
4.   I.E., pack your shit you're leaving, or roll-up your shit you're on the bus out of here.

Trust me, you'll find out! During one of my many moves I thought I would confuse the moron guard who told me. "Tucci pack your shit you're on the bus out!"

I looked him straight in the eye and said. "Hey jerk, I don't have any shit to pack!" He replied. "Okay, then cuff-up and we'll leave!" You see, they do have some rocket scientists working in the Federal prison system.

Back now to USP Atwater and the present situation.

As I left the cell I kept waiting for "the other shoe to fall". Something had to be wrong here? Didn't the DHO give me ninety-five (95) days in Seg? Didn't I still have at least eight (80) days left on that?

Just go with the flow Frank, it's their mistake. If they throw you back in "the hole" at least you have been out for a few days!

The Hispanic lieutenant had arranged a wheelchair for me and instructed his officer. "Wheel Mr. Tucci over to the laundry (for my Atwater clothing) and then take him to Unit 3-A. The wheelchair comes back here, do not leave it at the unit."

Atwater's laundry was a different experience for this old man. The prison had just opened in January of 2002 and everything issued to me was brand new.

U.S.P. Atwater a tough place? Not so far!

It was a long wheelchair ride from a where the laundry was, to Unit 3-A. The officer, not speaking one word, pushed me cross the sunny compound to the extreme end of the facility.

As we got closer to the building the first thing that caught my eye was a video camera above the door. It seemed to say—"Welcome to USP Atwater."

The next thing that told me I was really in a USP was the metal detector inside the Unit's door. I had heard the many stories about shankings (stabbings) and murders in a "pen" so the detector didn't seem out of place.

"Okay Tucci out of the chair, now report to the Unit officer and he'll assign you a cell."

Wow, a state of the art, brand new USP, I thought as I took it all in.

I reported to the "good old boy" who was the unit officer. He told me. "Just you go right ahead and put all your stuff in cell number 108-1. You'll have it all to yourself because it has been empty."

Did I hear him right? He didn't say. "Put your shit in cell number 108-L." Well, he's young and probably a fairly new officer. But, in a short time he'll learn that the official B.O.P. word for an inmate's property is "shit?"

Another surprise, the cell had only two beds! In FCI Sheridan. I had been in a three-man cell. Thanks Kretzchmar B.O.P. # 0663-046!

Inside the cell everything was new and clean. The was well lit by two separate fluorescent light fixtures, one over the sink and the other near the desk.

The lockers, desk, chair, mattress and bed frames were made in Unicor the B.O.P.'s profitable prison industry.

Then looking closer at the bed I notices there were no sheets, blankets, or a pillow. Those items were not issued to me at the laundry? What's going on? More of my punishment?

Again I found the unit officer. "Hey boss I have no bedding or a pillow." Once in a while I call them boss, it strokes their ego and they'll listen to me.

He answered. "Mr. Tucci I'll get all that for you after this movement (recreation time) is over."

I like this guy's style I thought to myself. He called me Mr. Tucci and didn't use any profanity. He is actually doing his job and helping an inmate (me). But, like I said before, he's new and young yet.

Now, I have almost everything to make my home away from home livable. What's missing you ask? My personal property from Sheridan, which would not show-up for two mere weeks.

Here's how you and your property get separated and finally reunited. When you are tossed in "the hole", as I always am, the unit officer will pack-out your personal property, which does not include any B.O.P. issued items.

Then your property is taken over to the SHU in a day or two. Once it is there the Special Housing Unit's Property Officer will un-pack it and inventory everything.

After about a week in Seg you will be allowed certain items out of your property. Things like postage stamps, your shower shoes, and a few hygiene items. No pens, writing paper or envelopes, you must beg these from the guards! Remember—this old man never begged so don't you!

Here's the B.O.P.'s biggest f—k up-if you are transferred while in Segregation, your property does not go with you to your new facility. Many days later it will be shipped via UPS. Doesn't that seem like a lot of wasted money to you?

The bus I was put on had plenty of room, the B.O.P.'s buses are just like the Greyhound buses and they have a huge storage area underneath.

If the B.O.P. had sent my property on the bus, that would have been a small comfort to me. However, they are not about doing anything good for an inmate.

It is only a little over six hundred (600) miles from Sheridan to Atwater but it would take twelve (12) long days for my things to get here.

What did I need so badly you may be asking? Two things. First, my Muslim Prayer Cap and second, my telephone numbers book. Although I was now in a Unit and had use of the phone, I couldn't remember Remy's cell phone or direct line at her job numbers! I guess that due to old age (am 63)?

Quit your bitching Frank, at least you are out of the SHU! Yes, but for how long this time?

Anyway, being in a high security USP is a step-up for the present from the medium security of FCI Sheridan. Thanks again Kretzxchmar, B.O.P. #0663-046.

In the next chapter I will get into the details of everyday life in this U.S.P.

Doesn't Every Cloud Have A Silver Lining?

CHAPTER 2

A Day Inside USP Atwater!

April 10, 2003

USP Atwater opened last year and became the B.O.P.'s 102nd facility. The cell that I was assigned to (108-A) was empty and I suspect never housed a convict/guest. When I arrived in June 2002 the inmate population was only 680. Click on to the B.O.P.'s website today and you'll find a figure between 1, 500 and 1,600!

Yes, the taxpayers are getting their "bang for the buck", with two prisoners in every 8-foot by 14 foot cell here. But mark my words that will change, soon there will be three inmates stuffed into a two man cell. Do you remember my stay at USP Atlanta in Part Two?

I have a still vivid recall of sleeping on the filthy floor and being the third man in a two-man cell! Who knows what diseases I might have picked up from the filthy floor or dirty torn mattress?

Did I have a right to expect any better? Or to be treated any differently? An USP Atlanta guard summed it up best when she said. "Old man you're just one more convicted felon in this here Federal prison!"

Next I'll share with you "A Day Inside USP Atwater."

5:30 AM—everyday.

Click, click, bang! The cell door of 108-A is unlocked and so starts my next USP Atwater day.

Jilil, my Muslim cellie and I, along with two or three other "brothers" head for the empty TV room. Our Sallat ul-Fajr (the dawn Prayer) will take less than five minutes. But if any non-Muslim entered the room he would have a serious problem.

6:45 AM—Sick Call or Breakfast?

Why not do both? Because on Monday, Tuesday, Thursday, and Friday, the slick B.O.P. schedules the Sick Call to run at the same time as the breakfast food line. Here in USP Atwater an inmate who is ill or needs medical attention has these three choices.

1. He can report directly to Sick Call and by the time he is seen the breakfast line will be over!

2. Or he can go straight to Breakfast and when he is done there the Sick Call will be shut down!

3. Lastly, he can jut remain in his bunk, maybe too ill for Breakfast or Sick Call!

Maybe the Medical Department here should franchise their proven method of quick weight loss? Perhaps even buy-out "Weight Watchers"? The B.O.P. could rename it "Choose and/or Lose". There is much more about the B.O.P.'s so-called "health care" coming up in Chapter 4. I hope the facts don't confuse you?

After attending Sick Call or after you have finished eating breakfast, it's back to the housing unit to be locked in again. I have a question? Why do so many inmates run to the mess hall, slam down a meal in record time, and then rush back to the unit to be locked in all that quicker?

8:00 AM—Work Call!

Inmates lucky enough to have a prison "job" get to leave the building for a few short hours each day. In USP Atwater the problem is too many prisoners and not enough "meaningful" work. It's the same thing in all of the other B.O.P.'s penitentiaries.

I may be an old man and not very smart, but can the public answer this question for me? If the "crime rate is at an all time low." Says the F.B.I., then why has the Federal Bureau of Prisons ordered twenty (20) new facilities to be built within the next ten (10) years?

When there is no war doesn't the Government cut down on the military? Therefore, if there is "less" crime shouldn't America need fewer prisons?

In Unit 3-A there are 128 inmates but only 46 have a prison job! The big four here are the Food Service, Laundry, Facility Maintenance, or Unit Orderly.

I am one of the unit's six orderlies, so I do not get to leave the building at Work Call. I must remain "in custody" and labor at my assigned duties. What duties old man? These are my duties, please my dear wife don't laugh at them!

1.   Clean out the lint screens from the unit's three clothes dryers;
2.   Stack toilet paper neatly in the storage area, making sure it is six rolls wide, by four rolls deep, and no more than three rolls high;
3.   Pick up the debris left on the common area tables from the night before and get the trash ready for "Trash Call".

That's the long and the short of my taxing "job" inside USP Atwater. Hopefully these new learned skills will land me a $100,000.00 a year position upon my release? 8:30AM—Trash Call.

The P.A. system loudly announces. "Trash Call, put your trash outside the unit door for pick-up!" A short time later an officer driving a golf cart and towing three empty bins will arrive. That's, Trash Call!
11:00 AM—Lunch Call!

Have you noticed that all functions in USP Atwater are a "Call"? Inmates who did not leave for Work Call have been locked in the unit since 6:30 AM, but now the B.O.P. will allow us to leave for the afternoon meal/punishment. The food here is so bad that it just has to be a part of our punishment.

The reason that I am going to the mess hall is not for the food, but for "meet and greet". What the hell is "meet and greet?"

There is a B.O.P. policy statement that says. "Members of the Administrative and Unit Staffs shall be at the noon meal and be available to address inmate concerns."

That sure does sound helpful but here's the way it really works! Yes, the "suits" are waiting in the dining room with fake smiles painted on their faces, but do these people actually solve any of the inmates' problems? Hell no! In most cases the inmate is instructed to: "See me back at the unit on that."

In Chapter 3, "The Incident Report(s)" and "The Incident Report(s) Part 2", I explain how, "see me back at the unit on that", is really a joke! It's just the old "chuck and jive" with the B.O.P.'s new twist.

Here's a simple question for the so-called "powers that be" out there in B.O.P. land. If Mr. Armendariz says. "Tucci, see me back at the unit on that." How can I see him?

Doesn't Mr. Armendariz stays locked inside his large, comfortable, and guard secured office totally inaccessible to a mere mortal such as I? Getting in to see President Bush would be easier!

Because I cannot gain entrance into the Holy Sanctuary, a.k.a. the Unit Office, I must again wheelchair down to the dining room. Maybe with Allah's help this time I might be able to speak to one of these "rejects" (staff) from the civilian work force?

When/if I locate Ms. Scott (the Case Manager), Mr. Allen (the Officer/Counselor), or Mr. Armendariz (the Unit Manager), they are a.k.a. "The Three stooges", chances are I'll be told:

"Yes, Mr. Tucci, but see me back at the unit I don't have the necessary paper work for that here." Chuck and jive? Or maybe it was what Muhammad Ali used to do? Do you remember his "rope-a-dope?"

In summing up contact or lack thereof, with the unit staff, you have to pay tribute to their wonderful B.O.P. training. I am sure that Larry, Curly, and Moo learned the following:

"When confronted directly by the inmates promise him anything! But when you get back to the safety of your locked office forget what you just promised. After two or three more tries the inmate will get the idea and will cease annoying you with his trivial problem(s)."

11:30 AM—Recreation Call.

What kinds of things are available for recreation at USP Atwater? Well the outdoor rec has a basketball court, a soccer field, and a softball diamond, but gloves, bats and softballs are not plentiful.

The same is true with soccer balls. If in the course of soccer game the ball gets kicked over the rec yard's fence the game is over. There is no second ball to continue to play with!

Atwater is a U.S. Penitentiary so there are no horseshoe pits, bocci ball courts, or weight piles. However, when/if you get shipped off to an FCI they'll have all of those things and more.

Indoor recreation has all of the usual board games and "a" ping-pong table. Yes, one table for 1,500 inmates! Should I reserve the table for you now? Maybe by the time you get here you'll be next?

During rec time the Education Department is also functioning. Again, one more choice for the inmate, recreation or education? What education? Don't get your hopes up too high—there is nothing being taught here that will help you after prison.

The only class the B.O.P. runs here is the G.E.D. Course! Unlike the last time (1980) when I was in Federal prison, there are <u>no</u> college courses, computer classes of job skills being offered to the inmate.

Could it be that the Bureau of Prisons is now thinking: "Why waste time and money on education or rehabilitation, most of the inmates will end up back in prison anyway."

1:30 PM—Recreation Recall.

Hi ho, hi ho, it's back to the unit I go! We are now locked in again, until the supper meal, which comes between 4 and 5:00 PM. But, I did get almost two hour of needed sunshine.

1:45 PM—Trash Call!

The B.O.P. is very sanitarily minded; remember there was an earlier Trash Call at 8:30 AM? Just how much trash could there be only five hours later? Hey—don't laugh but there is still one more Trash Call to come later tonight.

3:30 PM—Stand-Up Count

For reading other chapters in this book you already know the 4:00 PM Stand-Up Count. But here in USP Atwater, it is done at 3:30 PM. Why? I don't have the faintest clue nor does any of the staff.

3:50 PM—Mail Call!

The highlight of my day! In Federal prison Mail Call is only on the five weekdays, even though in the "outside" world the U.S. Post Office works and delivers mail six days a week. The mailroom hacks Murdock and Smith do not.

With twelve Federal holidays coming on a Monday, Mail Call will be only four days those weeks. So, for one fourth of the year mail delivery in USP Atwater is a four-day thing. No wonder that Ace Murdock doesn't want to give up his mailroom position!

There is more about Murdock and the semi-normal mailroom crew coming up in Chapter 3's "Main In Prison".

4:15 PM—Supper Call

You'll quickly find out that nine out of ten suppers here is literally "nothing" to write about. By the time the last meal of the day rolls round many of our Counselors and most of "the suits" have already left the facility.

No doubt they are rushing home to work on their inebriation, but they'll be back semi-sober tomorrow! I bet you thought most B.O.P. employees worked from 9 to 5? Forget that, this is USP Atwater! Yes, that's still one more chapter, which is entitled. "The Staffs' Work Ethics?"

I eat, I wheelchair back to the unit, and I am locked in again. In Federal prison your every day will be de'ja vu!

6:15 PM—Pill Call!

The pill pusher will bring his bag of "nightly sweet dreams" to our unit. There are pill lines with all three-meal calls, held down at the medical window. But this is a special pill line, "Happy Hour!" Almost all of what he is passing out are restricted medication, or in plain words, drugs.

It's easy to tell which inmates were "junkies" on the street, just watch the 6:15 PM—Pill Call! The B.O.P. is not trying to cure these "junkies", if they did so the inmate would not be back here in approximately sixteen (16) months!

6:30 PM—Tuesday, Thursday, and Sunday.

Those are the days and the time that I call my beloved wife Remy. "Wala'y sapayan, mahal ko."

7:00 PM—Night Recreation Call.

I am always the first one out the door as I wheelchair myself down to the chapel. On Wednesdays we Muslims have our "Learning About Islam" classes. Thursday nights it's our Arabic Language Classes.

The rest of the week at this time I work on this book and study the Quran.

9:00 PM—Recreation Recall!

It's back to the unit for the last time this day. Only one (1) hour remains until us bad guys are locked back in our cells for the night.

10:00 PM—Lock Down!

Well that's my day! Today, tomorrow, and everyday until the U.S. Government has their pound of flesh from me! Maayong gabii! That's Bisaya for "good night."

CHAPTER 3

Staff Selling Drugs Inside USP Atwater?

August 2003

The <u>Federal</u> Bureau of Prisons runs 102 facilities and you can bet the farm that in each one of them you'll find a "bad apple" <u>staff</u> member selling drugs to us inmates. That may be a shocking statement to believe, but it is true!

I hope that this short chapter will act as a wake-up call for the general public and the many honest <u>B.O.P.</u> Wardens, Administrators, and Correctional Officers.

Here in <u>USP Atwater</u> the "powers that be" should know, or at least suspect, who their drug dealing officers are. But why do these "powers", and Warden Schultz tend to look the other way at the problem? In my opinion they are just as guilty as the <u>staff</u> that are bringing the drugs in here!

I am sure that Atwater's Administration keeps informing the Central Office in Washington, D.C. "There are no staff members bringing drugs into <u>USP Atwater</u> for inmates." Oh really? We inmates know differently!

Atwater is a <u>U.S. Penitentiary</u>, which means both my <u>out-going</u> and <u>in-coming</u> mail is read. Simply put, this chapter was read twice or more by a lummox staff member. First when it went out written in my shaky longhand, and second, when it came back as typed manuscript from my wife Remy.

The importance of all that will become self-explanatory as you read the chapter.

While vacationing at <u>FCI Phoenix</u> I wrote an article to the <u>Arizona Republic</u> newspaper about the <u>staff</u> selling drugs and liquor to inmates. My short article explained the <u>how, when,</u> and <u>where,</u> as well as <u>naming</u> the four officers involved.

The newspaper didn't print the story but my goal was accomplished. A friendly officer told me later that the mailroom staff read the article and raced it over to <u>Warden Ellis's</u> office.

Let's play the Devil's advocate for a minute. If you were <u>Warden Ellis</u> and an inmate's out-going mail to a newspaper named four officers dealing drugs in your facility what would you do? Guess what Warden Ellis did? Nothing!

Common sense dictated that someone should have spoken to me and questioned why I named <u>four</u> officers as drug sellers. Surely the Special Investigations Administrator <u>Mr. Barton</u> should have had many questions to ask me? Or maybe <u>Barton</u> turned the matter over to the Chief of Security, <u>Captain Miller?</u> I really don't know if the matter ever went beyond the <u>Warden Ellis's</u> office.

However, for the record. "I never spoke to, no was questioned by a staff member, about my article during the sixteen months I was in FCI Phoenix.

Was it just a coincidence shortly there after when I was put on a prison bus and shipped from Phoenix to FCI Sheridan in Oregon 1000 miles away? I don't believe in coincidences! Do you?

After only a few months at FCI Sheridan it was "de ja vu" all over again and a hurried bus ride to my present home here in USP Atwater, California.

As a Sunni Muslim my ties to the Black population in here are very strong. Because of that I was able to find out who the staff drug dealers were in all ten (10) of the B.O.P. prisons I have guested in.

But at some point I ended up in a Catch 22. A few of the "brothers" were very upset with me for writing about the low-life, money hungry, drug-selling officers. I was told. "If you bring down the Man where are we going to get our shit from?" To put it bluntly, there were threats made to me by the non-Muslim "brothers".

There is no need for me to worry as I have many Muslim brothers here to protect me, as they do so to this day!

In the nine other prisons where I was with drug-selling officers, it was much easier to: "Get Tucci on a bus the hell out of here!" Instead of solving the "dirty" staff problem.

Yes, all of the ten (10) B.O.P. facilities I have been in had staff members selling drugs to inmates! The only difference between them is the price they can get for their "poison". The rule of thumb is the higher the security level of the prison the higher the price for drugs or contraband.

Eighty (80) percent of the drugs that enter this high security U.S. Penitentiary are brought in by staff members! There is no way physically an inmate can get drugs in here without staff help. Stop and think about that!

In most cases the worst punishment a confronted or exposed officer receives is a "very tactful transfer" to a different B.O.P. site. But once there the transferred drug-selling officer will soon have a new market and new inmate customers for his wares.

That must have been the case with officer (name on request), who was selling Mexican Black Tar (dope) back in 2001 when I was at FCI Phoenix. He turned up here in USP Atwater about six months ago.

Oh let me guess what you might be thinking, maybe the following? "The officer was a drug addict and only sold drugs in the prison to pay for his habit. He turned himself in for treatment and now he is trying to start over at U.S.P. Atwater."

If you could have seen his face turn pale the first time I passed him in the hall here you would forget what you might have thought. He said. "Tucci it would be a good idea if you didn't tell anyone you know me from Phoenix, they might transfer you again."

The question is. If he was "clean" and not bringing in drugs here why would the Administration transfer me? The answer is. He is again selling drugs in a Federal prison, your tax dollars at work! And here are a few or more questions that need answers and F.B.I. action.

Questions:
1. How do these low-life, drug dealing staff members get their poison into a USP?
2. Where does the staff/drug dealers buy their drugs for resale in <u>USP Atwater</u>?
3. Are there any guidelines in place to prevent the staff from reporting to work with a backpack or lunch cooler filled with contraband?
4. Are staff members ever randomly searched when they report for their "watch"?
5. How much money can a crooked officer make?

Damn <u>good</u> questions, but you may not like the bad answers. A stupid "Liberal" suggested that officers may suffer from the "Stockholm Syndrome", and relate to the drug needs of their prisoners.

Answers:
1. There are several ways the <u>staff</u> can assist or bring drugs into a <u>USP</u> for a profitable sale.
   (a) The easiest and most common way is to hide the dope on their person when they go into work.
   (b) They also can hide their drugs in backpacks, lunch coolers, or in between the pages of a hard cover book.
   (c) Through the Visiting Room which takes a lot of pre-planning but works well in a high level facility.

   Here in <u>USP Atwater</u> when inmates report to the Visiting Room they are "stripped" and redressed in jumpsuits provided there. After their visits they are stripped of their jumpsuits and returned their uniforms.

   If an inmate is well "connected" and "his" officer is on Visiting Room duty the following will happen. A visitor, yes a visitor will hand over the drugs to the officer who will get the merchandise to the visitor's inmate <u>after</u> the visit.

   It's a good idea to have a visitor who does not use drugs make the visit. That way the "sniffer machine" will <u>not</u> pick up the smell of drugs on your visitor. Rubber gloves should also be used in handling the drugs and a good hand washing is in order.

   A <u>woman</u> visitor has a built-in hiding place, I am sure you know what I mean. Drugs can also be hidden inside a child's diaper, which will be "changed" and the drugs removed inside the Visiting Room. Then passed to the waiting officer.

   This is the least risky way from the officer's point of view to make big money.
1. It is no secret that the percentage of Correctional Officers involved in substance abuse is much higher than that in the general public. So—they buy drugs from their own dealers for resale in here. Example: A $20.00 bag of "crack" on the street sells for between $200.00 and $300.00 in <u>USP</u> <u>Atwater</u>. And the bastard doesn't even pay Income Tax on it!

2. No! There are no guidelines in place to keep staff from bringing drugs into USP Atwater. Their backpacks and lunch bags are not searched upon entering the facility to work.

3. No! Staff members are never randomly searched. Thanks to their Labor Unions!

4. The sky's the limit on how much dirty money an enterprising officer can make. It depends on two things, his greed and how many chances he wants to take.

In closing, an age old question comes to my mind. "Who is watching those who are watching me?"

CHAPTER 4

"The Incident Report (s)!"

This chapter was written by my wife and this book's co-author Remy P. Tucci; from the Incident Report(s) our telephone conversations, and information she accessed off the B.O.P.'s website. I hope you enjoy her chapter.

September 27, 2002.

Well, my old man (he's t63) has been kicked to the curb again, this time Frank has lost his telephone privileges for fifteen (15) days. Why? He was testing the intelligence of the mailroom staff and Paul Murdock. Guess what? They all flunked!

In a few more paragraphs you can read the Incident Report "shot" Murdock the mailroom's resident overweight jackass wrote. Yes, he is the same person who has been ripping and rejecting my husband's incoming mail for weeks.

Mr. Murdock is the answer to the question of "how dumb is dumb." Do you remember the movie "Dumb and Dumber?" Well Murdock could play both parts at the same time! His I.Q. numbers don't match his weight not even close. Sorry, Mr. Murdock, the truth always hurts.

What follows is his report exactly as he wrote it:

"While conducting assigned duties in the USP Atwater mail room on 09-27-2002 I removed a letter from the Legal Mail Box addressed to Attorney R.P. Allen, _____Phoenix, AZ 85021. The return address section of the envelope lists Frank Tucci, Inmate Number 03836-014 as the sender. Further investigation of this matter revealed that the address placed on the envelope is the same as his legal residence listed in the sentry database. A check of this inmate Telephone Number Request revealed Remy P. Allen listed as his wife residing at the above address."

Now here is how the B.O.P. went about extracting their "pound of flesh" from my husband.

First, Ace Murdock typed out the "shot" using one finger at a time and his pocket dictionary for words with more than four letters in them. Then he slithered over to the shift lieutenant's office and probably said something like this: "Boy oh boy, today is my lucky day, I just wrote that old bastard Tucci a shot!"

Now the lieutenant must within 24 hours "serve" Frank with that work of fiction, which existed only in the semi-intelligent mind of Mr. Murdock.

When ever he is called to report to the lieutenant's office my Frank never goes. B.O.P. policy says. "An inmate need not be present to receive an Incident Report."

But if an inmate doesn't run right over to the office he will get on the lieutenant's Shit List, just like my Frank always is.

You will piss off the lieutenant if he or she has to get off their ass and bring you the "shot". Their pride will be hurt. But—isn't that why the lieutenants get paid the big bucks?

Frank was new to USP Atwater so this time he did report to their office. The lieutenant that day was a Ms. Williams. She is always good-natured, fair minded, and a "sister."

She read Frank the two-minute claim to fame of Murdock the Magnificent, and with that "shot" Frank was baptized into his new surroundings.

October 1, 2002

The next few steps in the B.O.P.'s Kangaroo Court get even more comical. You will now be convinced of "how dumb is dumb!"

A UDC (Unit Disciplinary Committee) must hang the guilty inmate within 72 hours of the "shot" being served. Notice that I wrote guilty inmate. B.O.P. mentality is "anyone who get's a "shot" must be guilty."

So—at the appointed hour Frank was led into the Holy Sanctuary known as the Unit Office, with a guard, of course.

His UDC would be Mr. Mayberry, the Officer/Counselor and Ms. Orozco, the Unit Manager and resident dwarf. Yes, she really is a dwarf in size.

The dictionary defines dwarf—"A small creature appearing in a fairy tale." If not for Orozco's gender she could be one of Snow White's dwarfs. Which one? Why Dopey of course!

Counselor Mayberry is well mannered and a soft speaking "brother" but Ms. Orozco is the other side of a two-headed coin. She is a spiteful and bitch midget, and from a distance of twenty fee un-identifiable as to which sex she is.

Needless to say, nothing an accused inmate can do will change the mind set of the UDC, which is "An inmate is guilty until proven innocent."

You have already read Murdock's "shot" now here is what Frank said to the UDC.

"My wife has written Power of Attorney for me. I did not write Attorney At Law on the envelope nor did I write Legal Mail. I wrote Attorney and Special Mail.

"Remy's Power of Attorney states, and I quote directly. "I hereby appoint as my attorney in fact to act in my capacity etc., etc."

Frank lost? Even though he has won on that same issue in two other B.O.P. facilities. He even showed the UDC the paperwork from the two prior expunged "shots!" But—in winning twice, he was still the loser. Here's why. The Team knew they were wrong but didn't care and by the time an Appeal could be acted on the punishment would have been served. These people are just plain dumb, and mean!

After the UDC took our telephone privileges for fifteen (15) days Frank did write an Appeal to Warden Schultz. A week went by without a word from the Warden.

But—after his fifteen-day restriction was over, the Warden's office wrote. "Your Incident Report is expunged and your telephone privileges restored. "Gee thanks B.O.P.

Did my dear husband win? In my eyes he is like the MUJAHDEEN and has two things on his side: Allah and me!

Author's note:

After Murdock wrote the "shot" that you have just read about, I added an update to "Mail In Prison," which is next.

You'll see how Murdock further answers this question. "How dumb is dumb?"

Mail In Prison

Update: USP Atwater, California
September 9, 2002

I am considered a Geriatric (age 63) and have Gout and advanced Rheumatoid Arthritis in both hands. Needless to say, my handwriting is at most times <u>not too clear.</u>

To help with this problem, my wife Remy has been putting re-usable address labels on all her mail to me. She tapes them to the envelopes, and I just peel them off and re-stick them on my outgoing letters to her.

<u>Some of the sixth graders who are employed in the Mail Room</u> have noticed Remy's labels on my outgoing mail. So, can you guess what these mature Federal employees have done to earn their $17 to $22 per hour?

Yes! You're correct! They have taken the time to remove each label, peel the back off, re-stick, and re-tape them directly to the envelopes! So now I cannot re-use the labels on letters to my wife. <u>Your</u> tax dollars at their finest hour!

Because this book <u>is</u> Non Fiction I will get the names of the officers involved from September 1, 2002 to whenever. This can be done thru <u>Captain Morehead's</u> office or via a F.O.I Act request.

Update, September 20, 2002.

Two of the mental midgets who have been attacking my mail with a vengeance have been identified. How? They were stupid enough to sign their handy work.

Inmate Systems Officers <u>R. Corley</u> and <u>P. Murdock</u>, both mailed my wife Remy a B.O.P. form #328. It said the following:

"You enclosed with your correspondence stamps or stamped items that can not be given to the inmate."

Maybe <u>Corley</u> and <u>Murdock's</u> deeds are directed against me because I am a Muslim? I really don't care if they are or are not.

The question is, how much did it cost the taxpayers to mail back Remy's address labels? Let us take a closer look at that question.

<u>First</u>, the offending labels were removed from Remy's envelope by the two lummoxes <u>Corley</u> and <u>Murdock.</u>

<u>Second</u>, a form #328 was typed out by these two mailroom children. Four (4) copies are needed; one to the addressee (Remy) one to the inmate (me), a copy for the Mail Room's file, and the last copy goes into the Central File.

<u>Third</u>, the remaining contents of Remy's letter now have to be put into a new, clear B.O.P. envelope, sealed, and re-addressed to me here in Unit 3-A.

Now here is the projected cost of <u>Corley</u> and <u>Murdock's</u> vindictive folly. Correctional Officers are paid a starting wage of $17.00 per hour and I'll use that amount in my calculations.

The way Government workers perform I am sure it took <u>Corley</u> and <u>Murdock</u> at least ten (10) minutes each from start to finish of the "third" step.

By dividing <u>60</u> minutes into their <u>$17.00</u> per hour I get .28 cents per minute. Then multiplying the .28 cents by the 10 minutes they used, the labor cost come to only $2.80. Next add the postage to Remy (37 cents) and the total is now $3.17!

But, remember on this particular day there were two form #328's so the cost to return eight (8) labels was $6.34! Nice going <u>Corley</u> and <u>Murdock.</u>

The bottom line is that everyday, five days a week, up until I am released in fifteen months, Remy will mail in at least two letters per day.

Their cost to re-mail "labels" will be $6.34 per day, $31.70 per week, $126.80 per month. The fifteen-month total will be $1,902.00! A high price to pay for the B.O.P., just to teach a 63-year old man with Gout and Arthritis a lesson.

<u>Update. September 24, 2002</u>

There is one more character to be added to the saga of the mailroom. A <u>Ms.</u> <u>Patricia Quiroz</u>, there that shows you that I am not a sexist. She does not labor in the mailroom but is some sort of an ad hoc supervisor there.

I approached <u>Ms. Quiroz</u> in the chow hall at the noon meal, which is when the staff makes themselves available to us mere mortals.

"Excuse me, <u>Ms. Quiroz</u>, I have this problem with _____." She cut me off in mid-sentence and said dryly. "I know who you are and what your problem is. There are <u>no</u> exceptions to our rules, not even for you Mr. Tucci!"

How did Ms. <u>Quiroz</u> know my name? I don't remember anyone formally introducing us? Hey, if she wants to treat me like shit, or a geriatric serial killer, all signals are off!

"Are you aware <u>Ms. Quiroz</u> that the last two facilities I was at lost on the issue when I appealed to the Regional Office?" I was in her face with my statement.

The little bitch countered with. "Well that doesn't mean anything to me!" I am sorry to say this but <u>Ms. Quiroz</u> has the personality of a barn door and a face to match. To say that she is physically unattractive is a polite statement on my behalf.

<u>Ms. Quiroz</u> figured she had allowed me enough time in her royal presence and dismissed me with a wave of her hand. "Things could get a lot worst with your mail."

I <u>thought</u> to myself. Okay you stupid bitch we go to war now! That same day I fired the first shot with an Inmate Request to <u>Ms. Quiroz</u> as follows:

"Why is my out-going mail being delayed, is it because I am a Muslim? Or is it because of your implied threat about things "could get worse" regarding my mail due to the problems I have with the Mail Room?"

A few days later, October 1, 2002 I sent her a second Inmate Request to Staff. "Is my incoming mail being withheld because I am a Muslim? Or is it part of your recent threat to make "things worst with your mail.?"

I really don't expect Ms. Bitch to answer either request, which <u>is good</u> because I can then take my complaint to the next level.

The text that follows was written on October 15, 2001 while I was in FCI, Phoenix. However, <u>they</u> never messed-up my labels there!

Mail received during your incarceration can be a blessing or a curse. But like everything in prison it is controlled, inspected, and separated.

It is divided into three categories: <u>legal mail</u>, <u>regular mail</u> and <u>institutional mail</u>. I will explain each and give you a few examples of those.

The unit secretary or one of the counselors handles the <u>legal mail</u>. At 3:00 PM Monday through Friday a list is posted of those inmates who have legal mail. It has to be opened in your presence and logged for the record.

However, legal mail is a problem for the staff and complaints occur almost every-day. I had gotten two legal mailings here at FCI, Phoenix and each had been opened and handled out with the regular mail.

Because it is privileged mail, your attorney's office will stamp both sides of the envelope "Legal Mail—to be opened in the Presence of the Addressee".

But the sixth graders who work in the mailroom cannot see the large print on both sides of the envelopes as they open it for inspection.

Sometimes legal mail can be a big smile to my face. I received a notice from a past landlord demanding back rent or, "we shall start legal proceedings against you". Too bad, the Federal Government already beat you guys to "legal proceedings".

Nine out of ten times if your name is posted for legal mail, it is <u>bad</u> news. Here are just two of my friends "bad news". I could do a whole book on those that's how much bad news there is in here!

Ed—his wife mailed him divorce papers after five years and two children. He has been here three years and has about seven more to do. Do you think the <u>Bureau of Prisons</u> will allow him to attend the proceedings in his home state of Maine? Ed's crime was selling drugs.

Tony—received notice that his <u>big rig</u> (eighteen wheel truck) had been repos-sessed and would be sold at auction, "to recover our losses, you have a right to attend said auction and bid to recover your vehicle". Good luck with that trip Tony!

He is pissed-off because he has <u>been down</u> (locked up) eight months and hid the rig before his arrest. He says only one person knew where. "My bitch girlfriend"! Tony's crime was hijacking.

Our regular mail is the high point of each day for some inmates and the low for others. I am blessed with a steady flow of letters from my wife, Remy.

Between her letters and cards she makes time to type the manuscript for <u>"our"</u> book. But that's not all she does. She makes copies of <u>BOP (Bureau of Prison)</u> memos and notices, types and mails out letters, make phone calls, does research and mails in items off the Internet. Without her there would be <u>no book</u>.

Mail calls is the worst part of the day for inmates that are forgotten by their wives, children, families and even the few friends they had outside the walls. It hurts my heart to see them run over to mail call and drag slowly away empty-handed.

Some inmates just to be "called" mail out the inserts in magazines for subscriptions with "bill me" checked. This works for three or four issues before they are cut-off.

Please remember mail <u>is</u> very important to all of us who are incarcerated. Just one letter a month would change many unhappy faces.

Last is the <u>institutional mail</u>, which is our answers to Inmates Requests to Staff.

Nothing changes in prison. No one wants to do anything except pick-up their large paycheck. That, my readers is a whole chapter in itself, staff's pay!

Author's note:

The book's editor insisted when I used the name of a staff member that they be given a copy of that chapter. So—on:

October 10, 2002

This chapter was sent to officers <u>Murdock</u> and <u>Corley</u> with the following "disclaimer."

"I have used your name, copy enclosed, in a short chapter of my book. You may make corrections or issue a statement in rebuttal, which will be printed <u>without</u> editing by the publisher.

However, please be advised my deadline for material is _____. Do you wish to reply?"

<u>Murdock</u> replied! <u>Corley</u> had much more sense.

Mail In Prison—An Update

Author's note"

My lovely wife and this book's co-author, Remy P. Tucci, wrote this chapter. Things have been semi-quite between the Mail Room and my husband Frank. Neither <u>Ace Murdock</u> nor <u>R. Corley</u> has written Frank any new "shots". But now there is a new member at <u>Murdock's</u> hide a way, <u>Mr. R. Smith</u>.

In keeping with the <u>B.O.P.'s</u> continuing policy of musical chairs, <u>Mr. Allen</u>, formally of the Mail Room, is now Frank's <u>Counselor</u> in Unit 3A. Does <u>Allen</u> have any training in the position of Counselor? Or maybe he has a degree in Sociology? The answer to both questions is of course <u>no!</u>

<u>Allen</u> will no doubt receive <u>some</u> O.J.T. (On Job Training) but in the mean time he'll learn by his mistakes at the expense of my husband and the other 3A inmates?

<u>Corley</u> has stopped aiding and abetting <u>Ace Murdock's</u> ongoing mail destroying vendetta against Frank. However the new crewmember <u>Smith</u> has taken up the slack with vigorous enjoyment!

I wouldn't at all be surprised if <u>Murdock</u> instructed <u>Smith</u>—"You'll take care of Tucci's mail, he sure does get a lot of shit mailed in!" <u>Murdock</u> probably also "suggested" how Frank's mail should be handled.

"Make sure you really check them <u>large</u> envelopes from his old lady very carefully. She sometimes hides postage stamps under the flaps, so <u>rip</u> off the flaps on <u>both</u> sides of the envelopes. She also tapes them address labels to the backs of the pages."

I would like to explain why covert deeds like those are necessary. Yes, I do sometimes put postage stamps in strange places on the large envelopes. But I wouldn't have to do that if my Frank's incoming U.S. Postal Money Orders were put on "the books" promptly, so that he <u>could</u> buy stamps at the Commissary!

Whenever I have mailed Frank and one of his "brothers" a money order on the <u>same</u> day, in the <u>same</u> mail box, guess what? His "brother" received my money order almost a full week before Frank's was posted to his account! Thanks <u>Murdock!</u>

<u>Mr. Smith</u> has taken over the job of mailing me the <u>BP 328 Form</u>, which is their Mail Rejection Notice. So he mails back, "4 adhesive address labels", remember every

"4 adhesive address labels", cost the <u>B.O.P.</u> and the taxpayers <u>$3.17</u> (labor and postage added together) to return!

One of Smith's BP 328's said. "There are several prior notices of this violation." As Frank always says in my language (Bisaya) in regards to the B.O.P., "wala'y kaso!", which means, "no big deal"!

April 28, 2003

Murdock and the Mail Room clowns have found still one more childish reaction against our mail.

August 28, 2003

Frank and I have attacked the Mail Room again! This time they thought they were getting smarter, but not even in their dreams! Frank sent home an <u>Inmate Request To Staff</u>, which I typed out and returned Certified Mail to <u>Warden Schultz</u>. Here's what it said.

"The Mail Room is singling me out for punishment. No one else in this USP has the zip codes blacked out on their incoming mail. 3A has been written over both my wife's zip code and mine. They do this so that I cannot remove and re-use the labels. But, they do it to mail from anyone who writes me and I cannot read those zip codes. Could you please put a stop to this childish action?"

May 5, 2003

The Warden's response is printed next.

"Your concerns have been brought to the attention of the mail room staff, and they have been asked to be more cautious when affixing unit assignments."

Paul M. Schultz

Warden, 5-8-03

So aside from ripping off the end flaps from both sides of my large envelopes, tearing some of our book's manuscripts in half and putting eight or ten staples in the envelopes to hold them together, all is well from <u>Murdock, Corley</u> and <u>Smith!</u>

But the joke is on the Mail Room. Why? Because no matter how many labels they "color" on Frank <u>still</u> gets labels to use on his mail back to me!

The population of <u>USP Atwater</u> is <u>1,471</u>. If they spend so much <u>time</u> and <u>tax dollars</u> singling out my husband's mail, can the three Mail Room losers check every one else's incoming mail?

Thank you my dear wife, I couldn't have written what you said any better! At least I can't get a "shot" for what <u>you</u> wrote!

The Incident Report(s)! Part 2

Author's note:

By: Remy P. Tucci

My husband started writing this book in June of 2000. Since that time until now (January 2003) we have mailed or given "disclaimers" to over thirty (30) of the B.O.P.'s staff. Mr. Paul Murdock was the first and only officer to write my husband Incident Reports in retaliation.

Anger doesn't come close to describing the way Frank felt about losing our telephone privileges over Murdock's first "shot". So—Frank quickly took out and updated "Mail In Prison" which he had written while at FCI Phoenix.

On the telephone, yes he still found a way to call me, he sadly said. "Remy people on the outside should be told about this terror called Federal prison. I have got to finish our book."

Murdock's second "shot" to Frank was a Code #312—Insolence Towards A Staff Member. Here is the entire report:
October 8, 2002

"On the above date and time while conducting duties in the USP Atwater Mail Room, I became aware of an inmate request to staff that was sent to Corley and Murdock, R&D. This Request to staff was sent From "Tucci", register number 03836-014. This request to staff states, "I have used your names, copy enclosed in a short chapter of my book" excerpt. The chapter of this Book was stapled to the request to staff. In this "Book excerpt I/M Tucci makes slanderous statements in reference to Inmate Systems Officers R. Corley and P. Murdock. One such statement I/M Tucci directs towards staff reads as follows, "Two of the mental midgets who have been attacking my mail with a vengeance have been identified. How? They were stupid enough to sign their handy work. Inmate Systems Officers R. Corley and P. Murdock, both mailed my wife Remy a B.O.P. form #328."

The lummox Murdock admits that Frank sent him a copy of the chapter and I quote the following: "The Chapter of this book was stapled to the request to staff. "But Murdock did not state Frank also included this disclaimer:

"I have used your names, copy enclosed, in a short chapter of my book. You may make correction or issue a statement in rebuttal, which will be printed without editing by my publisher. Do you wish to reply?" Conveniently Murdock wrote only the first sentence of the disclaimer in his "shot".

It is my belief that Frank asking Murdock if he wished to reply—is like asking a roaster to lay eggs!

The question is simple. Was Frank guilty of Insolence for writing that Murdock and Corley were "mental midgets" in the chapter Mail In Prison?

It is not the same as if my husband just walked up to these two fine officers and said. "Hey you two guys are mental midgets!"

Our book already has a U.S. Copyright (January 2001) and will soon be published in both English and Spanish. In America the First Amendment protects an author's manuscript. But not if he is in a Federal prison?

Murdock was offered a chance to write a rebuttal but he did not reply. If he is still offended by Frank's remarks there is regress thru the U.S. Courts.

Murdock's "shots" are a form of censorship and an outright abuse of his authority as a Federal Correctional Officer. Frank does have an Appeal in to the B.O.P.'s National Office in Washington, D.C., and we hope for the best.

De' Ja' Vu all over again! But—this time when ordered to the lieutenant's office Frank didn't go. The officer "served" the Incident Report under the cell door as Frank slept!

Early in the morning Frank sent this Inmate Request to Ace Murdock:

"Thank you for the second "shot"! It will also be printed in my book "Terror In America". I have written much more about you and I need to be accurate. So, I have asked my outside resources to do a complete personal background check on you. Your motor vehicle driving record, employment history, earnings for the last 10 years under Social Security, educational level, credit file etc., Also, because you offered no rebuttal, the chapter will be printed as is. Have a wonderful day! Cheer yourself up, maybe rip-up some of my mail?

Tucci

Convict/Author

Can you guess what the big lummox Murdock did within minutes of receiving that request? You're right! He wrote another Incident Report, his third against my husband.

More than likely the big-bellied jackass drooled all over himself with excitement as he typed it out. This was a serious charge, a Code #203, Threatening Another with Bodily Harm Or any Other Offense.

If found guilty it would mean thirty days in a Segregation cell. But that doesn't scare Frank, as the old saying goes. "He's been there done that."

That night when going into the dining room, Frank was approached by Lieutenant White and told. "Mr. Tucci would you please see me when you're done eating?"

There was no doubt in Frank's mind as to why the lieutenant wanted to see him. He was positive that Ace Murdock had struck again. Doesn't this guy have a real life? Is he going to make a career out of just writing Frank up?

Nevertheless, there are some descent and intelligent employees within the vast screwed-up B.O.P. system. Lieutenant White is in that category of people.

Frank was trapped and couldn't sneak out, the lieutenant was waiting in the dining room's hallway. So after an expensive and specially catered meal of rice and beans, Frank went out to face his next predicament.

"What's up?" Frank asked and White replied. "I have an Incident Report to serve on you. But—I am recommending that it be expunged."

Frank couldn't believe what he was hearing! Going on the lieutenant added. "I told Mr. Murdock that everything in your request was more or less a matter of public record and that as a B.O.P. employee he should expect scrutiny from time to time."

He couldn't thank the lieutenant enough and told him that his faith in a small part of the system had been restored. Frank left the office and hurried to phone me.

I know that you are remembering that our telephone privileges were suspended. But, my guy found a way to still call me almost daily. He explains how in his chapter "The Telephones".

We have now what the men call a "pissing contest" between Frank and Murdock.

So—Frank wrote still another Inmate Request to the jackass Murdock. Here's what it said:

Thank you for the 3rd "shot", it will be printed along with your other two (2) in my book "Terror In America" subtitled "A Muslim Surviving the Federal Prison System." Nothing changes, you can write as many "shots" as you choose too—but my book goes on sale the week of _____2003. The chapter on Mail In Prison will be printed just as the copy you have is. As always, have a wonderful day."
"Tucci"

Murdock replied the same day and Frank received the following:

"Inmate request to staff forms are for Inmates to state their—question or concern, and the solution they are requesting. If you have no question or concern, do not send staff members an Inmate Request to Staff. Incident Reports are written for violation of Institutional rules."
"P. Murdock, ISO"

Because the two "shots" were written only one day apart both were turned over to the UDC at the same time. I don't want to be repetitive but you'll see how the UDC showed the same old B.O.P. mentality of, "anyone who get's a shot must be found guilty."

After another Royal summons Frank was again led into the Holy Sanctuary of the UDC's office.

That day Counselor Mayberry would not be a part of the UDC and Ms. Orozco (the resident dwarf) would switch over from Chairman to Committee Member. Mr. De Vere who is a, I couldn't care less type of employee, would act as Chairman for Frank's next misadventure.

Is it Warden Schultz who has the staff playing musical chairs? Is that to insure fairness towards inmates? Yeah, sure! Moving the counselors around is like going to your mother-in-law after an argument with your wife. Good luck with that!

"Mr. Tucci on the Code #312—Insolence Towards A Staff Member, our finding is that you committed that prohibited act." Said Mr. De Vere sarcastically as the dwarf nodded in agreement.

Frank up to the point had not said a word but after that statement he exploded with. "Hey, don't I get to say anything?"

De Vere, looking bored, or maybe his underwear was too tight, replied. "Oh yes, Mr. Tucci but make it brief." I know my husband and he can never be brief.

"There is no basis for the charge of Insolence. The alleged Insolence was not verbal, but printed manuscript. B.O.P. 5350.27 allows me to write my book without penalization and the First Amendment protects my manuscript.

"That's enough Mr. Tucci you are quite finished!" Snapped De Vere.

"The Committee imposes a thirty day loss of your phone privileges. Let's move along—next is the Code #203—Threatening Another With Bodily Harm Or Any Other Offense."

De Vere stared at Frank and then looked down the paperwork on the desk. It was almost like he didn't want to read what was on the papers in front of him. "Mr. Tucci the Code #203 is expunged, don't say one word!" He ended with, abruptly.

But Frank did speak-up! Do I get a copy of today's findings?" Ms. Orozco put her two cents into the pot and said. "Ms. Bishop (unit secretary) will make copies for you."

Maybe my husband was born under an unlucky star, the copy machine was down that day. So—no copy of the serious expunged Code #203 "shot".

The next day Ms. Bishop did bring him a copy of the Code #312—Insolence, but not of the Code #203, which was expunged.

On Lieutenant White's recommendation the Committee was forced to expunge the charge of Threatening. Do you think that De Vere and Orozco are going to admit that and provide Frank with a copy to show other inmates?
October 17, 2002

For six days my husband kept asking for a copy of the "expunged shot" but he was getting nowhere! Again, he took pen in hand and wrote an Inmate Request to Mr. Kapusta the Associate Warden.

"This is in response to your Inmate Request to Staff dated October 17, 2002 in which you ask for a copies of your Unit Disciplinary Committee (UDC) findings. Specifically, you indicate not receiving copies of the Incident reports because the unit's copy machine was broken.

However, the underlying issue in your complaint is that your UDC did not provide you with a copy of Incident Report No. 1026957 because the report was expunged. On October 11, 2002 the UDC found you did not commit a violation of code 203. Threatening Another with Bodily Harm Or Any Other Offense. Therefore, in accordance with the Program Statement on Inmate Discipline, "The UDC shall expunge the inmate's file of the Incident Report if the charge is dropped.

The UDC cannot provide a copy of the second Incident Report because a record copy does not exist. Let me know if you have any further difficulties in this matter".

G.T. Kapusta, A.W.
Recapping:

Frank was written-up three times within a two-week period by the lummox Murdock.

"Shot" number one was expunged after Frank served a fifteen-day telephone loss. Delayed justice?

"Shot" number two resulted in another telephone restriction of thirty-days. However, we have an Appeal in to the National B.O.P. office in Washington, D.C. and I'll update this chapter when it is resolved.

"Shot" number three was expunged outright, no problem there.

Adding up the score, it's Frank two Murdock and B.O.P. one!

CHAPTER 5

Health Care of Geriatric Federal Prisoners?

Author's note.

Health care within the B.O.P. at best could be described as fair, sometimes worst. That care becomes even more suspect if you are age 63 and a geriatric as I am here at USP Atwater.

"Even if you are sentenced to prison for the rest of your life, you don't deserve to die by not being treated for an illness. No inmate should die from a disease that is curable."

December 6, 2002

Are older Federal prisoners, those ages 60 or more, being provided with all their life sustaining medical needs? The answer to that is short and sad. No—we are not!

If a geriatric is given a five or ten year sentence by the Court, the B.O.P. can quickly turn that into a death sentence.

What are the chances of a 63 year old sentenced to ten years living through that in a USP? The answer is only thirty percent, or in other words, seven out of ten old-timers don't survive! Not good odds are they?

The "Care" of Federal prisoners is currently in the news with the Afghans being held at Camp X-Ray in Cuba. It is a foregone conclusion that those who took up arms against this country will receive better medical care than I do here at USP

Atwater. I hope the facts don't confuse you.

Fact

The IRC (International Red Cross) is inspecting Camp X-Ray almost daily and they are allowed interviews with the Afghans and other Muslims imprisoned there.

Can you, or anyone you know, ever remember the IRC being allowed into a Federal prison? Has the IRC ever checked on my living conditions? Or my lack of medical care?

Fact

Congressmen and Senators have voiced their concerns if the Muslim prisoners at X-Ray are getting the best of health and medical care.

But—have these same politicians ever investigated the death of one Federal inmate? I strongly doubt it!

Fact

Some of us in Federal prison did serve in our country's military and many have visible reminders. Veterans with missing arms, legs, hands or feet are a common sight in any Federal facility.

But—because these men and women who lost limbs for their country are hidden from public view, there is no rush to provide them with a prosthesis. Shame on the B.O.P. and it's "bean counters".

Fact

Some of my geriatric medical problems are life threatening and others are just painful. The most serious is my heart problem. In 1999 before entering prison I had an Angioplasty and was informed, "That a bypass would be needed in two or three years."

But the Federal Bureau of Prisons is not rushing to provide me with bypass surgery because of the large expense. They are hoping I can make it until 2004 when I am released. Then I will be on Medicare and no longer would the funds have to come from the B.O.P.'s pockets.

Fact

California, February 2002

U.S. District Court Judge Thelton Henderson ruled that the State of California must make a vast improvements in the lax health care of it's 157,000 inmates. California's prison population equals the total in all of the B.O.P.'s facilities added together. Thus this becomes an important Ruling. But—it saddens me to know that Judge Henderson's Ruling does not affect the Federal prisoners within the State of California.

The B.O.P. will continue to provide substandard health care by ill-trained staff, thus inflicting cruel and unusual punishment in their violation of inmates' Constitutional Rights.

Here is a closer look at parts of the Complaint in the California suit, which was won by the Prison Law Office, a non-profit advocate group.

1.   California authorities did not hire enough medical staff.
2.   They delayed treatment and medical tests.
3.   They did not adequately screen in-coming inmates for medical problems.
4.   They lacked proper procedures for dealing with illnesses such as AIDS, diabetes, and heart problems.
5.   They failed to provide Registered Nurses in emergency rooms on a 24-hour basis.

But the Judge's ordered changes for the California Prison System will still go unchanged here in the Federal Corrections Institution at Atwater, California! The facts are clear, that medical care in a Federal Prison is for the most part intolerable. Is asking to have a reasonable chance of getting treatment that meets the minimum acceptable standards too much?

Please go back and reread item number (5). Here in USP Atwater after 10:00 PM there are no medical officers on duly for all seven days of the week.

Why? Maybe because the P.H. dis-S. (Public Health dis-Service) does such a good job that no inmate ever becomes sick after 10:00 PM?

The health care here is inferior in quality to what the California Prison System had before the Judge's order. Those inmates are lucky as changes are headed their way.

But—what about me and all the other Federal prisoners?

Here's the sixty-four thousand dollars question! How could a U.S. District Court Judge (Henderson) issue a Ruling against the State of California's Prison System but yet the same substandard health care still exists in all Federal Prisons?

Once again I want to remind you that this book is non-fiction. The next few paragraphs are found in the Inmate's Handbook for USP Atwater.

Health Service

"It is the policy of the Bureau of Prisons to provide all care and medical treatment during incarceration which is necessary and needed to maintain the health status of the individual."

Author's note.

B.O.P. "policy" sounds good but let's take a closer look at their statement. The key word to look at is "necessary". The American Heritage Dictionary defines the word "necessary" as absolutely essential or indispensable.

However, the P.H. dis-S's understanding of the word "necessary" reminds me of Bill Clinton asking to have the word "is" defined! Do you remember that bit of history?

But the word "necessary" remains the key word for all the health care not provided in a Federal prison. What a "street doctor", an attorney, or a Federal Judge (Henderson) may think the word "necessary" means differs from the B.O.P.'s opinion of the same word!

That is the Federal prison health care problem in a nutshell! Opinion!

Let's go back to the Inmate Handbook for more kicks and giggles. As you read on you'll see why I almost put this chapter in the "Humor in Prison" section of this book.

Sick Call Procedures:

"Routine Sick Call is held Monday, Tuesday, Thursday and Friday. Inmates desiring to be seen in the clinic on a routine Sick Call visit must first report to the Outpatient Clinic on Sick Call days between 6:00 AM to 6:25 AM."

Author's note.

The word "procedures", according to my trusted dictionary means—"a series of steps to an end". But—I know of few inmates who have had a series of steps to an end of their serious medical problems, while in prison.

Everyone has heard the old cliché, "like putting a Band-Aid on a cancer spot". That saying probably was started by someone observing the P.H. dis-S. treating inmates.

"Routine Sick Call is held Monday, Tuesday, Thursday and Friday."

Author's note.

Yes, Sick Call is only four (4) days a week and with all the Federal holidays on a Monday, sometimes only three (3) days a week. Here in USP Atwater the P.H. dis-S can even get out of having a sick call day in the event of "fog". I'll explain.

Because Sick Calls are from 6:00 AM to 6:25 AM, that's right only twenty five (25) minutes, sometimes there is a morning "fog". So the guard staff increases their alertness and part of that alertness is the stopping of all unnecessary inmate movements.

There will be no indoor or outdoor recreation, education classes, prison work details and no Sick Call! Big deal you say, so there is no Sick Call on a "fog" day, after all they must maintain institutional security.

But here is what can happen, starting on Saturday, February 16, 2002.

Saturday and Sunday are non-sick call days. Monday the eighteenth was a legal holiday so no Sick Call. Tuesday was declared a "fog" day by the overnight shift lieutenant, no Sick Call. The next day, Wednesday is a permanently scheduled non-Sick Call day.

The results—five (5) days in a row without Sick Call. That's Federal prison and P.H. dis-S health care! Yes, Sick Call for the entire week was a grand total of fifty (50) minutes. The "outside" H.M.O.'s could learn something from these people!

Now let's get back to the Inmate Handbook.

"The inmate must make his own sick/dental appointment at the Sick Call window located in the hospital. Be aware that the provider signing up Sick Call, depending on the number of inmates requesting appointments may need to prioritize the requests and limit the number of appointments scheduled on a given day."

Author's note.

I know just what you are thinking about the first sentence. "What's wrong with having to go to the hospital to sign-up for Sick Call?"

Here's what's wrong! First, because sick call is held from 6:00 AM to 6:25 AM, not even a full half hour, this tired and ill old man (me) must try to wake up at 5:30 AM to get ready. The guard staff will not provide a "wake up call" Federal prisons are not the Holiday Inn!

Second, the hospital is about a quarter of a mile from the unit I am housed in. So, in the rain, or extremely cold weather, I must wheel (I was wheelchair bound when I wrote this chapter) myself uphill to Sick Call in the darkness of the morning.

Third, my unit door is not always opened at 6:00 AM on the dot. The guard opens the door only when it is time for us to head uphill to the chow hall. If my unit is last on the eating list that day, the door may not be unlocked until 6:15 or 6:20 AM. That only leaves me five (5) minutes to a quarter of a mile, uphill, in bad weather, in my wheelchair.

More than once I arrived at sick call to find the door locked and had to return to my unit until the next Sick Call day.

"Be aware that the provider signing up Sick Call, depending on the number of inmates requesting appointments, may need to prioritize the requests and the number of appointments scheduled on a given day."

Author's note.

What does that sentence mean? In reality it means that even if I do get there (Sick Call) in time, there may too many inmates ahead of me and I may not be seen that day.

I am sorry readers but I must get on a soapbox for the rest of this chapter.

America is no doubt the richest country in the world and people do come from all over the globe for medical treatment here. Our prison system is supposedly the most humane, although we have more inmates jailed than any other of the so-called "civilized" nations.

But those two words, medical treatment and humane, come to a complete stop once you become a Federal prisoner.

If those key words were adhered to be the B.O.P. or the P.H. dis-S., why the hell isn't humane medical treatment available to all prisoners in the Sick Call line? Why then does Sick Call have to stop at a set number of inmates?

Should prisoner number twenty-five in line be treated and inmate number twenty-six be turned away? Please note that inmate twenty-six is also ill and needed to be at Sick Call. He would not have gotten up at 5:30 AM if that weren't so.

But with Sick Call being only from 6:00 AM to 6:25, four days a week, how many inmates can they treat? Hey, one time the person scheduled to run Sick Call didn't unlock the door until 6:10 AM. Guess what? He still stopped seeing inmates at 6:25 AM.

For the B.O.P. and the P.H. dis-S, all "ending times" are chiseled in stone. It's the beginning times that are flexible! Are you getting the idea that I am an angry old man? You bet I am!

What the hell does the ad hoc medical staff do after "working" their twenty-five minutes Sick Call line? Maybe—drink coffee and chat with the person in the next easy chair? But—I could be wrong.

If the P.H. dis-S, had their way Sick Call would only be for passing out Band Aids and Aspirin to the prison's "youths". It certainly does cost a lot of money to provide proper health care for 63 years old Geriatric like me. There again is a key word, proper.

At the start of this chapter the key word in the California lawsuit was "necessary". Do not the words proper and necessary have almost the same meaning?

If P.H. dis-S. personnel are professionals why do they function like players in a "pick-up" basketball game? These professionals haven't a clue as to what proper or necessary health care is, even though they are instructed to provide it to inmates.

To understand just how bad today's P.H. dis-S's medical department are, you must look back to the 1980's. As the old saying goes, "been there done that".

Lewisburg U.S.P. (United States Penitentiary) 1980.

There were no P.H. dis-S., employees working in the B.O.P. system at the time. If they were there, I would have noticed them walking around in their make-believe Navy uniforms.

In 1980 the B.O.P. employed only real medical professionals. Yes, real doctors, nurses, P.A.'s, lab technicians, dentists, even real pharmacists. What does he mean by real? Try these words for starters. Qualified, licensed, degreed, competent, and working as a medical professional before being employed by the B.O.P. or P.H. dis-S. Today's M.D.'s are most suspects to me. It is safe to say that fair shares of them are alcoholics and/or drug addicted.

How can I make such a statement? Can I prove any of it? You can bet the farm on what I tell you next.

My prison is an environment where more than sixty percent of the inmates have been sentenced for drug offenses. If they (the drudgers) can't tell a user who can?

If you ever decide to write a book learn to walk around with your eyes and ears open 24-7!

In FCI Phoenix, 2001.

Is P.A. Duff (real name) a "coke" had? Several of the "brothers" on many occasions said. "Pops the doc is flying today." I asked what they meant and got this answer. "Well he's on some kind of shit, just look at his nose and them eyes."

Doctor Ray (real name) is no doubt an alcoholic and I based this on myself smelling booze on his breath as he treated me. I should know because Jim Beam Bourbon and I were never far apart on the street.

His (Ray's) crime was rumored to be Medicare and Medicaid fraud. But—because he was a doctor and had money the Court in lieu of incarceration sentenced him to Community Service in the prison.

Yes, your doctor or your P.A., or other health care provider may be a convicted felon as you are. The big difference is they can go home at the end of the workday. Only in America!

At FCI Sheridan 2002.

It's not only the doctors or P.A.'s in the B.O.P. that are suspect. Let us look at the others hired as ad hoc medical staff.

Nurses and especially pharmacists are included in the Court's list of Prison Community Service felons. This a non-fiction book and my facts can be proven.

Some of the non-felon medical staff may have lost their professional licenses. But—have no fear, the B.O.P. and the P.H. dis-S to the rescue!

Did you know that a doctor doesn't have to be a licensed physician of the State in which the Federal facility they work in is? Yes, it's true the Federal prison is Federal land, which is exempt from State law, wonderful!

March 2002

On page 11 of Sheridan's Inmate Handbook there is a list of inmate medical "rights". It was "Right" number four (4) that caught my eye and it would become my thorn in their ass! Yes, always use their own rules against them.

Number four says, "Right—you have the right to know the name and professional status of your health care providers." I wonder who wrote that "right" into the Handbook? They were probably taken out and shot or hung, or both—for supplying me with a means to screw them with!

So, on 4 March 2002, I wrote an Inmate Request to Mr. Saltzberg the ad hoc Medical Director here as follows:

"Please provide me with your professional status. Be advised that a copy of this request has been mailed to U.S. Judge Peter C. Dorsey." His (Staltzberg's) reply was quick and a one (1) word answer. "Noted." What the hell kind of an answer is "Noted" suppose to mean?

This old man admits that I am not very smart but did Saltzberg's one (1) word, "noted", answer my question? No, I didn't think so.

And, finally, a notice I think should be posted in all P.H. dis-S. offices as follows:

"It has come to management's attention that workers dying on the job are failing to fall down. This practice must stop, as it becomes impossible to distinguish between death and the natural movement of the staff. Any employee found dead in an upright position would be dropped from the payroll."

I rest my case!

CHAPTER 6

USP Atwater's Dental Care?

September 12, 2002

Since arriving here in June I have not caused a problem, nor did I wish to write an adverse chapter on USP Atwater. But not to write about the events of the last few days, would be a form of surrender to the B.O.P. by me!

On Saturday, September 7, 2002, my upper denture cracked, almost in half, while I was at breakfast. Damn, there is no emergency or even regular dental sick call until Monday AM. So for the rest of that day and all day Sunday I ate no solid food.

In fact I only drink liquids, coffee, tea, and chicken broth, hoping I could nurse my cracked denture along until Monday without it getting worst.

Monday, September 9, 2002

At 6:00AM I started the long walk to the Hospital Services Unit for dental "sick call."

Of course you remember that this is a non-fiction book but please also remember where I am, in a Federal prison.

The P.A. (Physician's Assistant) or as most inmates call him, the Perfect—Asshole, told me I could not see the dentist before the 24th of the month. Fifteen (15) days to wait with a badly cracked denture? Are these people crazy?

Once again U.S. tax dollars in their finest hour. Consider this. If the denture brakes completely in half they will have to make a new one and also replace my lower denture so that the "bite" matches up.

Isn't that sort of like driving your car without putting oil in the engine block, and then having to replace the whole motor?

I was damn pissed-off with the thought of waiting fifteen more days just to see the dentist. And then how long after that before my denture would actually be fixed?

Captain Morehead had put me back into population after only a few days in USP Atwater's SHU (Segregation). Therefore I would keep my word and not cause a scene or problem with the idiot P.A.

I hurried back to the housing unit and called my wife, even though it was only 6:35 AM. "Hello Remy, help!" I asked her to please fax USP Atwater's Warden, Mr. J. T. O'Brien. Here's here exact text of the fax.

"Dear Warden O'Brien:

I am writing for my husband, Francis M. Tucci's health care. He is a geriatric and needs help in fixing his dentures bad crack—it needs attention ASAP. He was told to wait for two (2) weeks—it would be too late.

I implore you to please help him. He needs his dentures repaired fast.

Thank you very much for your help.

Sincerely,

Remy P. Tucci-Allen

Encl.:

Power of Attorney

Please note her enclosure, a Power of Attorney form. In a few more paragraphs I'll explain its significance to you.

Later that same day I called to see if she was able to find-out the warden's private fax number? Yes, she did! Remy never ceases to amaze this old man.

Also that night I wrote a Bureau of Prisons Form #8 (B.P.8) to the unit manager and here is that short note.

Informal Resolution

2.   Nature of complaint: My badly cracked denture. This is considered an emergency at all other B.O.P. facilities. If denture cracks completely in half I will not be able to eat.

3.   Inmate's efforts to resolve problem: I went to sick call and was told the dentist could not see me before 9/24/02, or in fifteen (15) days.

4.   Advice to inmate regarding complaint: "Received at Health Services on 9/10/02 your request for dental sick call in regards to your denture has been scheduled. R. Willis, HSA 9/10/01."

Well guess what? Mr. Willis's answer was not an answer! Why? Because he said "Your request for dental sick call has been scheduled." Didn't I know that already, for the 24th of the month? In the language of the B.O.P. he basically said. "Flip you!"

My day ended with nothing to look forward to but the 24th of the month and the possible repair of my denture then?

Remy was called on again. "They have not scheduled me for an emergency dental appointment, please send Warden O'Brien's office a second fax." I told her.

Here's some more stupidity from the B.O.P. (Bureau of Prisons) and the P.H. dis-S. (Public Health dis-Service).

Wednesday, September 11, 2002

I was on the list to report to the Hospital Unit at 1:00 PM. Was my denture even looked at? Wrong answer! Read on and you'll see why so many inmates end-up in "the hole", for causing a disturbance.

After waiting well over an hour the Health Service Administrator himself, Mr. R. Willis, came out and lead me to his small office.

"Why am I here? Where's the dentist?" I asked him. "You're here to sign a release so that we can answer a letter from your wife." He flatly replied.

Here's where Remy's Power of Attorney comes in. So I yelled at him. "I don't have to sign anything, my wife has a written Power of Attorney and a copy was with her fax to Warden O'Brien!"

In all fairness to Mr. Willis I don't think he knew it was a fax Remy had sent, or that she had included her Power of Attorney with it.

It was almost time to tell this Government bureaucrat to go fry himself but first I asked. "When do I get to see the dentist?"

The stupid answer that bastard (Willis) gave me was B.O.P. textbook. He answered with a phony smile. "Sometime soon."

So, for the third day in a row I was on the telephone! "Remy these morons are not doing a damn thing about my denture. Fax the Warden again and this time send a copy to the Regional Medical Director's office in Dublin, California."

I am sure that Mr. Willis and most of the medical staff think, "You're a locked-up convict what the hell do you expect from me?"

Adding to my problem is the fact that the Unit Manager, Case Manager and Counselor are not accessible. Their offices, although in the building, are behind locked doors 24—7. Here, there is no "open house hours", as in other B.O.P. facilities.

But I got lucky. Ms. Scott was running thru the unit on her way to hiding in her office. I called out to her. "Ms. Scott may I please have a B.P.9 (my next form in the B.O.P.'s paper trail) because the answer I got on my 8 was not acceptable to me."

She was all smiles, but I guess that was just for "kicks and giggles" as she said. "Yes, Mr. Tucci, I'll make sure to log out one and give it to you before I leave today."

Guess what? I bet by now you have figured out the B.O.P.'s staff thinking. It's a big part of the fifteen (15) minutes of advanced training they get!

Here it is in a nutshell. "Promise the damn inmate anything he asks you in person but once locked in your secure office flip him!" That's just what Ms. Scott did to me. She left for the day without getting me the politely requested form.

But Ms. Scott played with the wrong old man (me)! The only thing these mental midgets understand is paperwork! So I wrote the following B.P.8 form to Ms. Scott's boss.

Informal Resolution

2.   Nature of Complaint: Ms. Scott has not provided me with a B.P.9
       Requested on 11 September 2002.

3.   Inmate's efforts to resolve problem: Oral request to Ms. Scott at 5:30
       Wednesday, September 11, 2002 for a B.P. 9 form.

Just to make sure these people knew they were dealing with a Tucci, I also sent an Inmate Request to Staff, to Ms. Scott's boss's boss! Mr. Kapusta the Assistant Warden.

"On 9/11/02 at 5:30 PM I asked Ms. Scott for a B.P.9 form because my B.P.8 request was not resolved. Ms. Scott left for the day without providing me the form. Would you/your office please help me to get a B.P. 9?"

The next day, Thursday, September 12, 2002, all the shit hit the fan! First, I was scheduled to see the dentist at one PM. Second, Ms. Scott knocked on my cell door and handed on a B.P.9 form. She commented. "You're not the only inmate on my case list Mr. Tucci!"

Remy's third fax to Warden O'Brien's office had gotten me in to see the royal dentist and my request to A.W. Kapusta had produced the B.P.9. All praise be to Allah!

At the royal dentist I was told. "Mr. Tucci I'll send your denture out but it will be four or five weeks before it get's back. Do you want me to send it out or not?"

Quickly and loudly I shouted back. "Are you crazy? Ever where else in the B.O.P. my denture would be fixed in a day or two days at the most! Twice already at FCI Sheridan my dentures were repaired in the same day!"

The asshole dentist, who had no nametag on, gave me a look as if to say. "Who gives a rat's ass, you're just a stupid old convict."

In my head I thought. "Oh my friend, you just pissed-off your worst nightmare! A rich old man and his minority wife. Have a nice day while you still can!"

Leaving the dental office I yelled over my shoulder. "Four or five weeks is way out of line! I'll have my wife fax the Warden, Regional Medical Director, and the National Office back in D.C. Oh, I'll start eating again when my denture get's back!"

That ended my day at the dentist and that's the way things stand as I write this on Friday the 13th of September 2002.

Author's note

I will update this chapter ASAP when my denture and I are reunited. As they say in my wife's language—"Ang kang Remy bana isug nga tigulang!"

October 4, 2002 Update

Praise be to Allah! My denture and I are about to be reunited, after the B.O.P. held it ransom for twenty-two (22) days.

"Tucci medical says they have your denture so report there with the afternoon recreation yard move." Said Ms. Popularchick, the unit officer.

Two questions came quickly to my old mind. Was my denture repaired? Or would I be told a new one needed to be made? If that were the case, I would then be weeks without teeth! Calm down Frank, wait and see what's what. I said to myself.

As I headed out the door my favorite song started in my head. "Do you think an ant can move a rubber tree plant? Everyone knows he can't but—he has high hopes", etc., etc.

As soon as I arrived the dentist, now identified as Commander George of the P.H. dis-S. (Public Health dis Service) came for me. The prior time I waited two (2) hours to see his lordship!

Doctor George offered me a chair and produced my denture almost like pulling a rabbit out of a hat. He then added a finishing touch (lining) and shoved the denture into my mouth. He stepped back and smiled.

Maybe I should have thanked him for taking only three weeks instead of four or five? But was he responsible for the "rush service"? Or was it my wife Remy's faxes to the Warden, Regional Medical Director, etc.? Salamat (Bisaya for thank you) Remy!

Now I can eat solid food again, until my denture brakes from their half-assed repair job. Don't worry you can bet I'll write an update on it!

Update: December 12, 2002

Tag-ana kono (guess what)? Just eight (8) weeks after Remy and I won the battle for a speedy and haphazard repair of my upper denture, it has broken again! That doesn't speak well for the B.O.P.'s so called "dental work" but you already knew that!

Mr. Willis, USP Atwater's HSA Health Services Administrator/Asshole) probably would answer something like this. "But Mr. Tucci your denture was cheaply made and it is a miracle the repair lasted for those eight weeks."

Wrong answer Mr. Willis! Give me a break! My "cheaply made" dentures cost $3,000.00 and are made with porcelain teeth, not the plastic the B.O.P. uses when they manufacture inmate dentures.

Never the less, the paper trail begins again, or is it still? First, I wrote the "required" Inmate Request to Staff Member for Doctor George on December 13, 2002, as follows:

"My denture broke again! Can you please see me ASAP? If I go to Sick Call they'll have me come back on Tuesday or Wednesday to see the P.A. After which he'll have me see you in two or three weeks. Help please."

A week later, that's ASAP here in Federal prison, Doctor George answered. Here is his six (6)-word replies:

"Will scledule you for the clinic.

D. George, DDS, VS PHS

Chief Dental Officer

12-16-02"

The good doctor spelled "schedule" wrong but that's okay because he is a dentist and not an English teacher.

January 7, 2003

Three weeks have now passed and I have definitely not been seen ASAP. I sure hope Doctor George had a nice Christmas and New Year's Day? So, I wrote a Re-Request to the doctor saying:

"I have not heard from you since we spoke about rplacing my badly cracked denture on 12-20-02. Please advise as to when you will start working on a new denture?"

Of course the dentist answered, but a week later and with bad news! Are outside H.M.O.'s this bad?

"You were placed on the list to have new dentures made on 12-20-02. There are approximately 41 people on the list ahead of you. We can not say exactly when we will call you to start making the dentures."

March 10, 2003

Three months have quickly passed and Doctor George still has not called me in. I have given-up trying to eat with my now useless dentures in my mouth. But at 11:30 AM today the dentist sent me for! All praise to Allah!

The doctor handed me a 3x5 inch index card with his plan of treatment listing the steps to a new upper and lower dentures.

Excuse me, time out B.O.P., but wasn't this old man right? Remember when I said if my denture got worst it would have to be replaced? And also the lower denture because the "bite" wouldn't line up? Once again your tax dollars wasted! If repaired timely would a new upper and lower denture have been needed?

Be that as it may be, here's Doctor George's written plan:

"1.   Preliminary impressions

2. Final impression
3. Measure jaw relations
4. Try teeth in while set in wax
5. Deliver dentures

Allow at least 4 weeks in between each appointment for mailing to and back from Lompoc Lab."

It is now May 12, 2003 and I do not have my "new" dentures yet but Doctor George and the B.O.P. lab in Lompoc is no doubt working on them. The problem is my release date is September 5, 2003 only four (4) months from now!

A closing question for Doctor George, the B.O.P., and the taxpayers. If I am released before my dentures are finished will the Federal prison mail them to me? Or will they just keep the dentures on the shelf at USP Atwater to remember Tucci by?

Update: June 29, 2003

Maybe it's Allah's will for me not to leave USP Atwater with B.O.P. dentures? It has now been a long sixty-two days since my last trip to Doctor George's chair. Why would Allah want that? I sure don't know, and I am definitely confused!

You have read the doctor's plan for my denture replacement, which says. "Allow at least 4 weeks in between each appointment for mail to and back from Lompoc Lab."

Could it be that the B.O.P. is using "new" math on their calendars? I could be wrong, but isn't 62 days longer than 4 weeks? Yes, once again I needed my dear wife's help from "the outside".

So on June 14, 2003, Remy mailed via certified mail Doctor George the following:

It has now been fifty-two (52) days since my last visit? Please circle one of the following:

(a)   You have no intention of finishing my dentures
(b)   Mr. Willis ordered you not to make my dentures
(c)   The dentures are "in the mail"
(d)   None of the above

Please provide none of the above answer in "(e)".

Ten days later (June 24, 2003) they scheduled me for the dental clinic. But, due to Mr. Willis repossessing my wheelchair, well that's another story, I could not get to the clinic!

My back spasms, leg edema, gout, and arthritic knee joints keep me from walking the long distance to the Medical Unit. Without use of a wheelchair there will be no new dentures! That's the way things stand now with "possibly" only 68 days to my release date.

Even if the mental midget Willis does return my wheelchair there is still one slight problem. There are still three steps left to complete of Doctor George's treatments before my dentures are finished!

Let's do the calculations on the doctor's remaining work. Taking the three steps left, times the 4 weeks to and from the lab for each step, we get 12 weeks or approximately 90 days. But maybe I am only 68 days from going home?

Even if I should remain here until my maximum release date of 1-13-04 nothing will change. No wheelchair to get to Doctor George's office, no dentures!

When Remy and I are on tour with this book I will put on display my dentures, which is now in three pieces! Yes, Mr. Willis you won the "pissing contest" by not allowing me a wheelchair to get my new dentures. But the public outside of USP Atwater will know what kind of a cold hearted and non-compassionate officer you are!

Update: September 1, 2003

Guess what? I will not be leaving for home and my dear wife Remy on September 5, 2003! But, I am sure that Willis and the "so called" dentist, Mr. George, will still continue to scheme so that I do not leave USP Atwater with B.O.P. dentures. Thanks guys!

There are 134 days left until my new release date on Tuesday, January 13, 2004. More than enough time to "finish and provide" this old man with new false teeth, but the "pissing contest" continues!

To get their B.O.P. semi-normal, cheaply made, mis-match colored and ill-fitting dentures, I must walk the long distance over to the Hospital Unit. I cannot do so without having great physical pain. Is my asking His Highness Willis for a wheelchair too much? His Highness thinks so.

Doesn't time go by fast when you are having fun? It seems like only yesterday but this dental nightmare goes way back to December 12, 2002. On that day Boy George's prior lousy repair job resulted in my denture breaking again. It is now nine (9) long months later and I am still gumming my food! Thanks to Willis and George, doesn't that sound like the name of an Undertaking firm? Willis and George!

I am looking forward to our book tour and Remy is working on a "display box" for the denture Prince Willis and Boy George refused to replace.

Is it Allah's will for me not to have B.O.P. false teeth? It must be. And so be it!

CHAPTER 7

More—"Odds and Ends!"

The "Odds and Ends" in this chapter are very different in nature from those of Part Two. All of the following occurred here at the U.S. Penitentiary in Atwater, California, versus any of the other nine (9) facilities the B.O.P. bounced me in and out of.

1. Race Segregation in Federal Prison.
2. Lock Down!
3. The Habitual Criminal?
4. Inmate Interviews.

Next are four serious prison topics, and I have described them in graphic details to you as best I can remember them!

Race Segregation In Prison.

June 4, 2002

Nothing is more a part of prison life than is Race Segregation. It is a major problem and as serious as it gets! Especially where I am now, a high security U.S. Penitentiary in Atwater, California.

Daily in America's prison systems there are hundreds of senseless beatings, rapes, or murders. But does the public care about what really goes on inside my prison's high walls?

Most of the books you read written on "prison life" are by authors who are not now in a Penitentiary or who have never been imprisoned! What the hell does a "Best Selling Author" know about living in a Federal Penitentiary?

Do those authors know about the every day degrading the B.O.P subjects me to? Or the gang rape of a young inmate by four "brothers"? Or the murder of a correctional officer? Or the killing of a fellow inmate? Or all the day in and day out brutality that I see inside these walls?

"Mr. Best Seller" will tend to over imagine or maybe even tone down the level of the violence that truly exists and displays itself to me daily. As a convict/author I did not imagine the violence, nor will I tone down the truth! How could I when the sub title of this book is, "A Muslim Surviving The Federal Prison System"?

A Federal Penitentiary is not a playground, it is a place where hate, Racism, and anger thrive and develop vigorously into violent results. The chances of being raped, beaten, or even killed can happen to anyone of us in here! The prison rule of thumb is that the higher the security level of the facility you are in, the greater your chances of being harmed become.

To explain why is simple. Most convicts in high security prison are serving out long sentences; many have little or no hope of leaving prison except in a coffin!

I strongly believe that Race Segregation contributes a part of, or it may be the root cause, for most of the violence in here. So, let's back up and start with your first contact with Race Segregation in the Federal Prison System.

What, when, or where do you think that first happened to you? I know you will agree with me as you remember the B.O.P.'s bus ride. You did notice that the officers ushered all the Black inmates on the bus first? But, weren't they then seated in the rear of the bus?

It has been about fifty years since the Civil Rights Act was passed; however some things will never change. "Put them Blacks in the back of this here bus."

Depending on what part of this country you are imprisoned in the inmate population by Race percentages will vary. Here in USP Atwater, California, the Hispanics are the majority, followed by the Whites, with the Blacks and Native Americans (chiefs) about even.

Now if you are on the East Coast, as I was for a while in Rhode Island, the Blacks are the majority followed by the Whites, with the Hispanics being the minority.

There is no place in America where Race Segregation is more visible than within its vast and profitable prison systems. You could be doing time in a County Jail, State Prison, or Federal Penitentiary, it doesn't matter, Race Segregation will be there!

Even the B.O.P. officers that are assigned to look after your safety and well being are a byproduct of Race Segregation. They eat with, talk to, and "hang" mostly with their own Race. That can also be broken down further by gender!

The Bureau of Prisons claims that they "do not segregate" but please don't believe their Public Relations spin! Next is a good example of the B.O.P.'s double speak.

All cells here in USP Atwater house two inmates, although that may change in the near future. B.O.P. policy states. "If you assigned to a cell and refuse the cell you will be subject to disciplinary action." Yes, most of the B.O.P.'s written policies have the threatening words "disciplinary action" in them.

Their statement looks good in print but do you know what the B.O.P. is really saying? No Segregation? Wrong answer! Nothing could be further from the truth!

The way their "statement" is written implies that an inmate was assigned to an empty cell and refused it. Maybe he didn't like the wallpaper? Here's the truth. A White inmate was assigned to a cell that already had a Black inmate living in it; or you could even run that vice versa.

No the inmate cannot refuse the cell, but he can ask to be moved to a different cell! If for some reason the "move" cannot be done there and then it will be ASAP. So, does the B.O.P. Segregate?

Yes, if they allow the inmate to change cells. No, if you choose to stay in the cell with an inmate of a different Race. Race Segregation? Here's a little humor for you. I am White but I am a Muslim, so no White inmate wanted to be celled with "a terrorist"! So I remained alone in the cell until a Muslim "brother" moved in.

Trust me, the best rule to follow in a USP is. "Stay with your own Race!" I don't say that as a Racist, but as a realist! There is only one exception to the color and Race rule, if you happen to be a Muslim.

Islam is "suppose to be" color blind but the key words are, "suppose to be". To this very day (May 17, 2003) they are Muslim "brothers" who do not accept me as a Muslim because I am White. But, that's between them and Allah!

In USP Atwater you'll notice that on the long walks over to the mess hall, that the Blacks are with Blacks and the Whites are with Whites. That's just the way it is and always will be in any USP.

I personally am not saying that you should not walk with a friend of a different Race. But, consider this. The radicals in your Race and your friend's group will both have their eyes on you two! The officers will also pay close attention to you and your friend as they try to figure out what you are "plotting".

Remember; in the B.O.P.'s "mind set", a Black and a White inmate do not walk together unless they are "conspiring" to do something! Hey, I do it, walk that is, and not conspire, all the time with my Muslim "brothers".

Inside USP Atwater's dining room the Race Segregation continues and is easy to spot. "Everyday you can draw line where each Race will sit. My first day here I made the mistake of sitting in the "White" section until one of my Muslim "brothers" said. "Sulaiman, we just don't sit here the brothers use the other room." Sulaiman is my Muslim first name.

The housing unit's common TV area and the TV rooms are also a Race Segregation problem. There are seven (7) TV sets in this unit, so the Blacks, Whites, Hispanics, Native Americans and Asians should all be able to have at least one group TV?

But that's not the way things work out with the TV's because the gangs and one or two clicks control the TV's. I gave up trying to watch TV a long time ago and my little radio is my comforter and contact to the outside world.

There have been many split lips and broken noses over TV arguments of who is going to watch what and when. Here's an example of TV "control".

The Hispanics, who are the majority in this unit, always have one TV tuned to the Spanish channel in Fresno. But if there is a Hispanic country playing a televised soccer match they will "take over" a second TV.

How do they do that? They will tape a note to their intended second TV saying "Soccer—Mexico vs. Peru 4 PM!" The rest of the Hispanics will be watching Spanish Movies on "their" other TV.

Isn't Federal prison grand? American Democracy in action, even for Illegal as the majority rules!

The largest and gravest area of concern in regards to Race Segregation is this USP's recreation yard. It is there that most of the beating and fatal stabbings occur. USP Atwater was built with the idea of "controlling" it's inmates "on the yard". What they have done towards that impossible to reach goal?

Four things. First, there are video cameras 24-7 everywhere in the yard. Second, the large recreation yard was divided into three separate yards. Yard #1 has a softball field, Yard #2 a basketball court, and yard #3 a soccer field. Can you already see the Race Segregation plan?

Third, all three yards are fenced off from each other and once you are locked in one yard you can not travel to another one. Fourth, and last. There is a high gun "tower" in the yard #2 with a fence around it so that inmates can't get close to it and out of view of the tower officer.

Shall we look at the B.O.P.'s "master plan" that helps Race Segregation in here? Question number one. What are the three largest groups of Races in this USP? The answer(s) is of course the Hispanics, Whites, and the Blacks.

Question number two. Which one of the three groups will go to play soccer? Yes, you're correct, the Hispanics.

Question number three. Which one of the two remaining groups do you think will head for the basketball courts? You're right again, the Blacks.

Which of course means the softball field is left for the Whites. Is the B.O.P. slick or what? Again ask yourself, does the B.O.P. Segregate? I rest my case!

A quick and short review of what has been covered so far. The three (3) places to stay with your own Race are, the unit TV areas, the dining room, and the rec yard.

Next just a few of the underlying Race Segregation factors here in USP Atwater.

Every prisoner in a USP is required to work unless you are medically excused. "Failure to accept an assigned work detail will result in disciplinary action." That means a written Incident Report and maybe even some time in "the hole".

Here in USP Atwater there are few Black department managers, this causes problems because Black inmates have to work for "the man". So if a Black inmate gets a "shot" for any type of misbehavior, his "boss" becomes a Racist! It's the Old Race Card played again and again. After all didn't it work for Rodney King and O.J.?

The Black and Hispanic officers are another factor, because they do have daily contact with all of us. Time and time again I have seen these minority officers let a White inmate slide on some infraction that they would strongly enforce on their own Race!

Yes these B.O.P. minority officers are in Catch 22! If they are seen being too lenient with those of their own Race the non-minority guards will accuse them of favoritism. But, if they are too hard on their own Race the inmates say the officers are "working for the man".

I am sure that by this time you fully understand what I am trying to relate to you concerning the Race Segregation in this USP.

The United States holds its head high above all other nations of the world in regards to "prisoner's rights". But they do not apply many of those "rights" in their own jails and prisons.

Lock Down!

Author's note:

The following is a composite of three separate lock downs, and the only events in Part Three that did not occur at USP Atwater. They are included in this part of the book because of the violence and spontaneity that are normally found in a U.S. Penitentiary. Hopefully the information in them will prepare you not only for being locked up, but also a Lock Down!

Those of you with little or no knowledge of the B.O.P's system may be asking. "What the hell is a Lock Down?"

Simply put, a Lock Down is a hammer the B.O.P. uses when they have not acted fast enough to prevent a small problem from becoming a big catastrophe!

Looking ahead. Lock Down #1 tells of being in a three (3) man cell 24-7 for eight days and my sixty second birthday.

Lock Down #2 explains how my dear wife Remy coped with the problem and what to expect if your loved one is caught in this display of B.O.P. craziness.

Lock Down #4 goes deeper into the details of who, when, where, and why. There is also a surprise response from Warden Pentesso at its end.

The B.O.P's battle plan for implementing a Lock Down can be summed up in just two words. Restrain and Deny!

1. Restrain all inmates to their cells 24-7
2. Deny use of the telephones
3. Deny use of the showers
4. Deny the inmate "hot" food
5. Deny visiting
6. Deny non-emergency medical care

Those "six" of course are just for starters; the guards' staff will invent more ways to punish us as the L.D. continues from day to day.

First up is Lock Down #1, which lasted from September 16, 2000 until September 25, 2000, and the reason for it.

Yesterday an inmate was badly beaten in the recreation yard by a number of prisoners. I must distinguish between prisoners and guards because they both beat on inmates. But in this case it was inmate on inmate.

Depending on which story you choose to believe, there were between ten and fifteen inmates doing the beating. What cause the beating to happen? Well that too is the subject of two or three different stories to pick from.

September 16, 2000

Earlier tonight one of the "brothers" asked me. "Sulaiman are you going out to the rec? It would be a good idea to stay inside the weight cage and away from the baseball field."

There was a rumor of a possible "getting on" between two of the Mexican gangs so I took Abdul's remark as a hint for my safety. He was right!

After ten minutes of my senior citizen type "work out", I just happened to look over at the baseball field. Many inmates there were headed towards the recreation building, which runs along side the weight cage where I was!

Reaching the building about thirty inmates proceeded to sit down forming a semi-circle, waiting as anticipating a fight to start.

What happened to cause the gathering of the circle? The day before one of the "Border Brothers" gang recognized a member of the "Paisanos" as being at one time a police officer back in Mexico.

The circle was supposed to be a "one on one" fight between the ex-cop and a family member of some one the cop had sent to prison in Mexico. Guess what? Prison is not a good place for an ex-cop to be, Mexican or otherwise!

I noticed that there were many more officers in the yard that night than usual. My guess is that a snitch, yes there are plenty in here, had informed the Warden about the world-be-fight.

Six or eight officers ran over to the gathering and one told the Hispanic inmates to. "Get up and o about your fu-king other business!" Not one of the amigos stood up or made any attempt to leave the area.

Soon the pissed off shift lieutenant was there in the middle of the circle collecting the I.D. cards from the seated inmates. A few seconds later the P.A. system ordered. "Recall, recall, all inmates return to your housing units, now!"

I was forced to leave before I could see the results of the I.D. taking. But the next morning I found out two things. First, the Paisano/ex-cop had been stabbed inside the Yuma Unit and second, the cop was in critical condition at an "outside hospital."

As a result of the Border Brothers violence the Yuma Unit was locked down. The facility's other units were not locked down and the next morning it was back to our "normal" prison routine.

Yuma remained locked down until the next day's morning meal. But, that same day at 6:30 PM the same two gangs were at it again out in the rec yard!

This time I was in my cell reading John Walsh's "Tears of Rage". There was no "Recall" announced over the prison's P.A. system but instead the panic alarm was sounded and the unit's intercom said. "Lock Down, return to your cell!"

All of FCI Phoenix was now in Lock Down status, which lasted for eight days! The L.D. now becomes a sort of "survival test" for the inmates in their small cells, 24-7, for the next eight days. Why is it a "survival test?" Here are a few possible scenarios that answer that question.

First, the food during a L.D. is brought to the cell and handed in through the "slot" in the door. What do you think will happen if one or both of your cellies decide they want your food?

The answer is simple; they'll just take it! Remember, you are locked in, whom can you complain to? Is a "mystery meat" and cheese sandwich worth a black eye?

Second, maybe the 300-pound lummox in the middle bunk wants your bottom bed? Hopefully the inmate on the top bunk will not want the middle bunk you just moved to? But if he does, you will now be making the six-foot climb to the top!

Third, maybe Tiny or Bubba think you are cute? They have been down too long and even your ass looks good to them! Oh, I know what you are thinking. "Hey man, I ain't no homosexual, I don't play that game!"

The stories you hear about a straight guy ending up, as someone's "prison girl" is true! How can that happen? Well for openers a bar of soap in a sock is just as good as a blackjack. Hopefully, you will not be beaten senseless and wake up with your pants down around your ankles, and then know just what I am writing about!

As a Muslim I never encountered any threat of that type of filthiness, because in most cases I was celled with other Muslims. All praise to Allah!

Those are only three examples of what may be a "survival test" for you during a Lock Down. At the end of the eight days there were many requests from the inmates to have their cells changed.

Oh I forgot to mention that September 22nd was my 62nd birthday. For some unknown reason I kept a log of what we were fed for every meal every day.

On my birthday the following was brought to the cell at 8:00 AM: One 4-ounce cup of apple juice and two "out dated" fruit bars, possible rejects the Commissary could not sell? Then at 11:00 AM came the noon and supper meals together: One slice of cheese, two slices of some kind of sandwich meat, a hot dog roll to place the items in, and a packet of generic Kool Aid.

There was also a plate of "hot" food, rice, corn, and meat! We ate the hot food first and saved the rest for later in the day.

Yes, some B.O.P. rocket scientist figured that the staff could save time by serving us two meals at once. But, they did not figure out how to save one dime of the officers' overtime!

I have a question for the B.O.P.? When the unit is not in Lock Down status, and when inmates have free run of the unit, there are only two officers assigned to us. But, now with all inmates locked in their cells, there are four guards assigned to the unit.

Is that what is meant by "maintaining security?" With the whole facility locked down what are the officers assigned to the recreation yard doing? How about the indoor recreation officers? Let's not forget the "teachers" in the GED and other educational classes, what are they doing?

Here are more of the above. How about the officers who run the B.O.P.'s prison industry here (UNICOR), what are they doing? What about the Health Service and it's contracted help? The list goes on and on and there are many others I don't even know about!

Well I hope you get the idea, but if you take the B.O.P.'s side its called "maintaining security." Welcome to FCI Phoenix! Happy birthday Frank!
December 9, 2000

Damn! Here we go again! Lock Down #2. The unit had just left for supper meal when a few minutes later six or eight officers came running into the building. Their leader was yelling. "Lock Down everybody get in your fu-king cell!"

Unquestionably B.O.P. advanced training puts an emphasis on the use of the "F" word. That has to be so because every fifth or sixth word out of an officer's mouth is the "F" word!

Back now to L.D. #2. Normally I do not leave the unit for the supper meal and there are two reasons why. First, is the long line that always awaits me before I am served? Second, is the lack of empty tables to sit down and eat at?

Oh shit they're coming this way to lock me in!

I hope my wife Remy does not panic when I don't get to make our customarily 6:30 PM call, which I do every night. She has already been through an eight day L.D. with me. Yes, you can put your money on her to call FCI Phoenix and ask if we are in Lock Down status.

Many of us in prison have forgotten that our loved ones outside are in ways also doing our sentences. Yes, they worry about us when they cannot visit, or even get a phone call from us due to these frequent L.D.'s.

Remy has told me of the things that run around in her head when we lose contact. She thinks: "Is he alright? He does have a heart problem; maybe he is in the hospital? Or maybe he just couldn't find a phone to use?"

Sometimes when she calls this FCI she gets no answers from the snooty staff members about anything!

Remy and I have a "telephone code." Every morning after I know she has left the apartment I call. Our answering machine's red light will be flashing when she gets back—my home coming to her. Our Caller I.D. box will let her know what time I called and that I am okay as of that morning!

Chris, my cellie is not in the cell he left with the rest of the unit to go eat. Something is funny! My cell door has not been locked? In all the confusion they missed my cell that is all the way in the back corner of the unit?

Looking out the cell door I could see the officers moving in all directions. In front of the office there were five or six large trash bags with inmates belongings in them. That meant they had "packed out" (Moved to Segregation) those inmates.

It's past time to call Remy! It is now 7:00 PM and we are still locked down, so no telephone call!

Two guards are coming towards my cell, which is good because I have just taken two Nitroglycerin pills!

Levin asks. "Tucci are you alright you look kind of pale?" Then they head down the cellblock locking everyone in but me. You can bet they are hoping I don't have another heart attack and die on them. That would mean a pile of paperwork!

Two inmates have died in their cells here in the last six months from heart attacks. FCI Phoenix does not have "panic buttons" in the cells as most of the newer prisons do.

It is now 8:00 PM and everyone has been unlocked so I headed to the phone to call Remy. Well, I was right! She did call here to check if we were locked down and also to inquire about my well being.

Now what? The officers are locking everyone in again? I only had time to say, "I love you and good bye!"

By 8:20 PM the whole unit is locked down again except me? Because of my serious heart problem? Chris never did return from super because the unit was locked down from the inside.

All the inmates from the unit were herded into the rec yard from about 5:30 PM until 8:30 PM, when they were allowed to return to the unit.

Chris the day before had said. "Something is about to happen!" He also mentioned that a few days of L.D. would be good. He added. "It would be nice to have a few days of peace and quiet."

At 8:40 PM Chris returned and the officers now lock our cell. They may have reasoned that having someone to watch me in case of a heart attack the cell could now be locked.

The usual routine is to be locked in for a "count" at 9:00 PM, and then after the "count" let back out until 11:30 PM. But that night we were not let out until 6:00 AM the next morning.

This time Warden Pontesso was good to us by only locking us down for half a day. Oh, I forgot, only my unit, Navajo, was locked down!

What was the reason for only Navajo's Lock Down? The usual thing for FCI Phoenix, a "slice and dice!" I saw the cut-up inmate when they took him out of the unit. He was a bloody mess!

Charlie was badly cut-up by the homemade knife of the prison, the razor/toothbrush. Oh so easy to make, but yet so very effective! Do you have any idea of how many different kinds of weapons can be made from everyday items we have here in prison?

To make a razor/toothbrush knife, as the name suggests, you need a toothbrush and a plastic throw away razor. Both are provided free by the B.O.P. Here's how to make one.

Starting with the razor part first, smash the plastic holding the blade and be careful not to bend the blade as you remove it. Next remove the bristles from the toothbrush. Now attach the blade to the toothbrush. The best way to do that is with epozy glue. Inmates who work in Unicor, the B.O.P.'s prison industry or on the facility's maintenance crew can provide you with the glue.

But, after you have manufactured your "knife" hide it well. If found in your cell even remotely near your possessions you'll be headed to "the hole!" It is a B.O.P. Code 104 Prohibited Act, "Possession of a Weapon" and in the highest category for prison sanctions.

December 12, 2000

I was called at my F/S job and ordered to the Lieutenant's office. This would be my second trip to the office, the first was back in November when I received my first "Incident Report."

Once again an old Texas saying came to mind. "Never be early to a hanging unless it isn't yours." So, like I always do, I took my time getting there and arrived late!

There were five other inmates from the unit waiting outside the office and I asked one. "What's up guys?" But no one had an answer or a clue, until the first inmate came out of the Lieutenant's office.

It was a fact-finding inquiry about the "slice and dice" the past Sunday in our unit. The inquiry was not being done by the Lieutenant but instead by Mr. Barton a moron. He is the Special Investigator here at FCI Phoenix.

In less than two (2) minutes my interview was over! My answers to his questions were very simple. "No, no, no, no and no, and I wouldn't tell you anything even if I knew something!"

I am glad that's over, now back to F/S and working on my book. Well that brings us to Lock Down #4, hopefully you will never be shipped to FCI Phoenix!

January 5, 2001

The B.O.P. on its website (bop.gov/inmate html) rates FCI Phoenix, Arizona as a medium security institution, but the guard staff chooses to imagine it as a high level U.S. Penitentiary in disguise.

A rotten smell was in the prison's air and the ill winds of despair have again blown my way. Once again rumor and my gut feeling proved right.

Last night when I called Remy I told her. "Don't be surprised if we have another Lock Down very soon!"

You have already read about Lock Down #1 and Lock Down #2 so I will not rehash those two events. But by the way things are going here in FCI Phoenix I could write a whole book on just lock downs!

I will try to write this chapter with a different outlook and also provide you with some new information and facts.

So here we go. Why did Lock Down #4 happen? In this particular case a serious situation left an inmate near death. His throat was cut and he had lost a lot of blood before he could be moved to the "outside" hospital.

Correctional officers are taught some basic First Aid, but I strongly doubt they were prepared for the gushing throat wound they were witnessing! Yes, the officers did panic and stood there almost frozen.

Maybe they were thinking. "It's not my job let's wait for the medical people!" Or even, "With all that blood flowing, if I touch him I could get AIDS!"

My prior time in Federal prison (1980) there was no such thing as AIDS, but there still wasn't a guard willing to help a stabbed inmate!

Back now to the current Lock Down situation. You already know that the staff and officers enjoy our lock downs. Do you remember from L.D. #1 and L.D.#2 what they are doing while we are locked in 24-7? Nothing! Officer Newson said it best. "Less work and more overtime money when you guys are locked."

January 6, 2001

It is 8:00 AM and breakfast has just been tossed at us, if you can call one stale fruit bar and a carton of milk a breakfast?

The fruit bar's label says. "Best of sold by 8-2000." Because today is 1-2001, that means the bar should have been sold five months ago "on the street." I did much better with the carton of milk; it was only three days passed its date for use.

Yes my dear Remy I remember where I am. In a Federal prison and everything here is a part of my punishment!

January 8, 2001

Today will be a busy day as the guard staff, both male and female, monitors our showers. The B.O.P. rules say. "A shower is to be offered to inmates after three continuous days of a lock down."

You will be allowed only five minutes and at the end of your time the officer will bang on the shower door with some dumb remark like. "Okay asshole let's go, a lot of other jerks need to shower!"

But—if it is officer Hoffman, who is a homosexual, and he likes the look of your genitalia, you can shower for hours!

Also today, because we are locked down and missed the unit's monthly toilet paper issue Newson delivered my four rolls. It bet you can't call up Fry's and have them run over to your house with just four rolls of toilet paper!

The rest of this chapter turns a serious note on what FCI Phoenix is doing wrong and in fact causes these lock downs.

Seventy percent of all problems and troubles in here come from the Yuma Unit but yet all the other housing units are punished for Yuma's wrong doings!

Example: If two inmates from the Yuma Unit beat on each other in the rec yard, or even in their own building, all the units get locked down! Why is that? I am glad you are thinking that question.

The Medical Department's doctors and psychology staff are continually treating inmates for Paranoia. May I suggest they start interviewing the Warden, his staff, and the guards!

On what do I base my observation? Let's go back to the example of the two fighting inmates from the Yuma Unit. Here is the way this guard staff must think. "Although both inmates involved in the fight are from the same unit, one of them may have friends in another unit who may be planning a pay back."

So what does FCI Phoenix do? You guessed it, they lock the whole facility down!

The fault in their thinking, or lack thereof, is two-fold. First, both of the "fighters" will be relocated to different institutions. Second, if both inmates are no longer here, who would a "payback" be directed at?

Locking down the whole facility time after time can only be one of two things, either it is stupidity or just plain meanness? You call it!

In fairness to Warden Pontesso (Warden Ellis arrived on 6/01/01) many of his problems are caused by the B.O.P. Either from the regional office in Dublin, California or the national headquarters in Washington, D.C.

The main problem the Warden has is the steady flow of holdovers (inmates in transit) and the Immigration Nationalization Service detainees that arrive almost daily.

Should the I.N.S. be housing prisoners in FCI Phoenix? Almost all of the undocumented (Mr. Clinton's word for illegal) aliens have committed no crime except jumping the border from Mexico into Arizona.

A few years ago these illegal aliens were just sent back to Mexico but today they are imprisoned. Maybe for their cheap labor? Without a high school diploma or a G.E.D. they are paid only $5.25 a month. That is written B.O.P. policy.

Isn't that ironic? The U.S. government says the illegal Mexicans cannot work in this country but in Federal Prison they are forced to work! Is that illegal?

FCI Phoenix is rated as a medium security facility. Punishment for the crime of Illegal Entry is only a few months which is to be served at a low or minimum security facility."

A few paragraphs back I mentioned that seventy percent of this FCI's problems are caused by the Yuma Unit. Can you guess whom they housed in that unit? That's right—the holdovers and undocumented aliens.

The law is very clear. If one of the illegal were to become injured or killed, the B.O.P. could be sued for placing him with inmates of a much higher security level.

It can't be Warden Pontesso's choice to have a steady stream of illegal aliens coming and going. Therefore it must be the B.O.P.'s idea.

In my opinion they (the illegals) should not be allowed to mix in with the regular inmate population here.

Most of the Mexicans are young, between the ages of seventeen and twenty-three, and gang members (a later chapter covers Gangs In Prison). Knowing that they are only passing thru, and with only a few months of sentence, they will "steal" anything they can get their hands on.

The joke here is. "If you are missing something, look in the Yuma Jail." And because many of their gang is with them, they will fight at the drop of a hat.

Just two years back all the undocumented aliens were not allowed out of the Yuma unit, hence the nickname Yuma Jail.

At that time the "jail" was self-contained, its inmates were fed in the unit and used an attached fenced-in area for their recreation. Even the medical staff went to the unit to treat prisoners.

Here's some information. Eighty-six inmates arrived here last night. Seventy-two are I.N.S. illegals and fourteen are regular inmates. Eight of the regulars are assigned here (FCI Phoenix) and the other six will be moved with the I.N.S. group in a few days.

How did I, a mere prisoner get that information? Easy, my friend, Tomas works as the Lieutenant's orderly.

I am not harsh towards the Mexicans as most of the inmates here are. Even the Hispanics from other countries, Cuba and Puerto Rico mostly, are somewhat hostile towards the Mexicans.

The Mexicans as a people have strong family ties, are church going, but dirt poor. It's no wonder that they keep trying to enter America. I have a close friend in Flagstaff, Arizona who started crossing the border when he was only twelve. But he was unable to make it across until he was fifteen. Hello Marco!

The Mexican Government must take ninety percent of the blame for so many of its people jumping the border. Mexico has no real economy to speak of, a less than adequate school system, and a poor national medical plan. That Government does little or nothing for the "peasantry" in most of its provinces.

These "peasants" do not get food, medicine, housing, jobs, or even an education from the government. An undocumented alien is better off in a U.S. prison than if he were free in Mexico!

Let's take a closer look at the five factors just mentioned.

1.   Food—Almost none of the Mexicans can boast of having three meals a day every day in their homeland. If you could see the speed at which they consume food you would agree that they come here hungry.

2.   Medicine—This is a sore spot for me because my wife Remy is from a "third world country." I did not write this book sitting on my ass in a cell. My Spanish is good enough that I am able to ask questions of my Hispanic friends. I explained to them that I was writing a "libro" (book). Many of them do not have the childhood shots that we here must get before entering school. Almost none have been to the dentist "just to have teeth cleaned" and no one leaving Mexico comes to Federal prison wearing eyeglasses. They will return to the homeland with a status symbol, B.O.P. eyeglasses.

3.   Housing—Except in the larger cities, which very few of them come from, there is no government housing or government help to buy a home as we have in America. Many of our home's garages are in better shape than the housing they left behind in Mexico. I have been in Mexico many times so don't say that I am exaggerating.

4.   Jobs—There are some jobs in Mexico but few for the un-educated peasants. This is the core of Mexico's problems, without an education a "peasant" is doomed to a life of manual labor, which is a status their government doesn't seem to mind, or try to change. How can Mexico run its government and services without taxes from a "working class?" That's easy to answer! Indirect U.S. aid. For every Mexican who enters here illegally the burden stops on the Mexican government, he is now the U.S.'s problem. Does the country to the north of us have its people jumping the border to get in here? No, of course not, because Canada has all of the factors I mentioned, which Mexico doesn't and probably never will have.

5.   Education—At this FCI every inmate must have a G.E.D. or obtain one while doing their sentence. This includes the Mexicans who are doing time for crimes other than illegal entry. There is a "catch 22", the Mexicans can take the course in Spanish. I believe if the B.O.P. were serious about helping them, it would make classes in English mandatory. Right?

January 11, 2001, 8:45 AM—Thursday

This Lock Down is now over!

I was getting use to all the benefits of a Lock Down. Here's just a few of them:

1.   Not having to get up at 5:00 AM for my F/S position.

2.   The table service—an officer unlocking the cell and putting the bags of cold food on the cell's table.

3.   Mail delivery—the guard sliding letters under the cell door.

4.   Pill Call—not having to leave the cell to stand in a long line at the medical unit. My meds brought right to the cell!

Update—February 9, 2001

Warden Pontesso has seen the light; he now realizes that the Yuma Unit should be isolated. I do wonder where he got that idea? Please go back in this chapter on about the fifteenth page and start re-reading from the third or so paragraph on.

In those paragraphs, I suggested what I thought could be done, about not locking the whole prison down time after time. Do you think the Warden peeked at my manuscript?

Much to his credit Warden Pontesso has taken decisive action. Or was it someone in the Western Regional Office who "ordered" him to? Maybe the B.O.P. in Washington, D.C. "ordered" the Western Region Office to "order" the Warden to take action? Who cares?

Who ordered who doesn't matter, what matters is that life is now better for the inmates designated here. If you don't believe me ask my wife Remy, who has been through four lock downs in the few months that I have been in FCI Phoenix.

There are a few inmates in the Yuma Unit who were designated to this FCI, but because of their short sentences are staying in the unit. I'll explain.

After the last "slice and dice" in the Yuma Unit, only it was locked down. That should have been done the prior four times that unit caused the whole facility to be locked down, better late than never!

The few "regular inmates" housed in the unit are also locked in, even thought they were designated here and working at a prison job, which they have now lost. Those inmates are paying the high price of living in the unit with it's I.N.S. and holdover inmates.

The sad part of it all is that the holdovers and I.N.S. detainees who caused the Lock Down will be moved out of here but the unit will remain locked down.

Question. Why not move the "regular" inmates out of the unit? There is a simple two-word answer, no room. Today's inmate population is 1,326. One month back it was only l,102.

Summing up—the Yuma Unit is locked down but they are allowed the use of the recreation yard for two hours a day, Monday thru Friday. They are not allowed the use of the regular library or law library, isn't that illegal?

Yuma Unit is fed alone and before all other units at these times, 5:15 AM, 10:15 AM, and 3:15 PM. They are marched to the dining room under guard and have only twenty (20) minutes for each meal.

Yuma Unit remains locked down from 3:45 PM unit breakfast at 5:15 AM. The only good part of this mess is that the inmates in FCI Phoenix's other three units sleep better knowing that Yuma is in Lock Down.

Update February 18, 2001

I have now been in FCI Sheridan almost five months. Guess what? Not one Lock Down! Inmates, who have been here much longer, have told me. "A Lock Down last about two or three hours here, at the most one day. Don't worry about it Pop."

There are more inmates here than in Phoenix, why no lock downs? Maybe Warden Hood could send for Phoenix's Warden Ellis, who could be Sheridan's Designated Lock Down Warden. Hey—B.O.P. I think I just created a new job position.

If Warden Ellis can't come here, Warden Hood will just have to learn how to be indifferent, mean-spirited, stupid, and how to create large amounts of Lock Down overtime, to the pleasure of the guard staff. It works for Mr. Ellis!

Next is "The Habitual Criminal" which has many twists I am sure you are not aware of.

The Habitual Criminal?

Author's note:

Here inside U.S. Penitentiary Atwater the Habitual Criminal abounds! He may be easy to spot but very hard to befriend. I know three Habitual Criminals who are doing "Natural Life" sentences, which means no possibility of ever being released, except by their deaths!

There are some Habitual Criminals here who have been totally broken in spirit. But there are others who have turned bitter against "the system" and everyone around them, staff or fellow inmates.

May 27, 2003

This chapter will answer these serious questions:

1. Who does society consider a Habitual Criminal?
2. What crime are most Habitual Criminals involved in?
3. Can an eighteen year old be a Habitual Criminal?
4. Can a sixty-two year old "geriatric" be a Habitual Criminal?
5. Why are most of a prisons' population Habitual Criminals or as the B.O.P. likes to call us, "repeat offenders?"

Pardon my pun, but as an "insider" I'll try to provide you with the answers. What does the word "habitual" mean to you? The Oxford American Dictionary defines it as. "An activity repeated so frequently that it is done without thinking." And my friend Tucker says. "Hey, that sounds like sex with my soon to be ex-wife!"

Question number one. Who does society consider a Habitual Criminal? There use to be a simple answer to that question and it was. "Anyone who keeps getting sent to prison." But the answer isn't simple anymore because of the new age "Liberal" politicians.

The "Liberals" answer is a lot longer and goes something like this. "The young alleged offender had no chance at a productive life because he grew up in the intercity with drugs, crime, and murder all around him!"

The "Liberals" can even make excuses for the crimes the "youth" committed by saying. "With no father in the house the kid had to resort to crime to provide substance for his poor mother, sisters and brothers!"

That is pure bullshit! Ninety percent of the money he made doing crime he spent on himself! You will read about Martin in the next chapter, he made five million dollars dealing in drugs. But, he left his family zero dollars to live on while he is in here for nine more years.

There are many famous people who were raised under worst intercity conditions than Martin but they didn't turn to crime or drugs. Remember, poverty is a fact of life not an excuse to tell the Judge when you get caught!

On the other side of the aisle are the "Conservatives" politicians. These nutty people want to lock-up anyone convicted of a third felony for "Life."

These "Conservatives" are pushing for a national "Three Time Loser Law". Many States already have that Law on their books going back to the early 1940's but it is seldom used or strictly enforced. All praise to Allah!

Here's an example of why the "Loser Law" should not be used blindly in all third felony convictions. It happen here in California, where else?

A "loser" with prior felony convictions robbed a pizza delivery person of $9.00 and the pizza. He was caught "red handed" at the scene, probably the pizza sauce? He was tried as a Habitual Criminal and given a life sentence!

Yes, a life sentence for a $9.00 robbery, and I bet the pizza wasn't even that good? Why didn't his liberal attorney argue that he was hungry and only robbed the pizza person so he could eat that day? So the answer to question #1 is anyone convicted a third felony in California is a Habitual Criminal!

The next question has two answers. What crime are most Habitual Criminals involved in? If you go by the numbers the answer is a no brainer, Drug Related Crimes. But if you go by the percentages the surprise answer is Sex Offenders!

Drug criminals in Federal prison return at the rate of sixty (60) percent, in other words six out of ten will be back in here within eighteen months! That doesn't speak well for the Fed's so called "War on Drugs! "Does it?

Do you want proof that their "War" is just a public relations ploy to keep-up the funding for the DEA? Click on your computer and go to—"Federal Bureau of Prisons Quick Facts". Move to the page with the heading "Federal Prison Population Over Time/Drug Offenders."

First look at the figures for the year 1991.
1.   Total sentenced population 52,176.
2.   Total sentenced drug offenders 29,667.
3.   Percentage of prisoners who are drug offenders 56.9

Next go down the chart to the year 2000. Winning the "War on Drugs?" I don't think so, remember these are B.O.P. facts not mine!
1.   Total sentenced population 112,898.
2.   Total sentenced drug offenders 63,898.
3.   Percentage of prisoners who are drug offenders 56.9

So over the last almost ten (10) years the percentages of Federal drug criminals remain the same at 56.9? The "Conservatives" will be quick to point out that although the percentages are the same these are more drug people in prison today.

Yes, that's true only 29,667 in 1991 with a huge increase to 63,898 in the year 2000. But isn't the percentage the same at 56.9?

I may not be too bright, but if the Government is indeed winning the "War" shouldn't the percentage of people in prison on drug crimes be less? Isn't the DARE program and other Drug Education classes working?

The other part of the answer to question #2 was Sex Offenders. As of today's date (May 30, 2003) there are only 1,559 Sex Offenders in Federal prisons, but even one (1) of these low lives is too many!

The all-knowing and sensitive B.O.P. "protects" these rapists, homosexuals, Child Molesters, and who know what other kinds of perverts here in Federal Prison!

Yes, "protects!" That's a strong statement to make but easy to back up. Go back to the B.O.P.'s Quick Facts (website), look at page three. There is only one heading, "Sex Offenders," it isn't broken down into sub-headings like many of the other crimes listed are.

Examples from page 3.

2. Firearms, Explosives, Arson:

6.　　Extortion, Fraud, Bribery:

7.　　Homicide, Aggravated Assault, and Kidnapping Offenses:

I can quickly think of three kinds of "Sex Offenders", rapists, homosexuals, and Child Molesters. It is the Child Molesters that the B.O.P. protects the most!

In Federal prison these "baby doers" are not allowed in with the regular inmate population and they are kept in P.C. (Protective Custody). Thus they are "protected!"

Even the toughest criminals have a younger brother or sister on the "outside." Can you just imagine what they would do to one of these Child Molesters if the chance presented itself?

The medical world says Child Molesters are sick and need help, not prison. Try telling that to the families of the children they molested!

The Child Molesters repeat and repeat and repeat their crime, getting short sentences like 18 months, 30 months, or maybe a whole four years.

Please also consider this Child Molesters have the highest percentage group wise of repeat offenders! Care to guess at the percentage? Sit down first, because it is eighty (80) percent!

Where's the damn "Three Time Loser Law" when you really should use it? Or is it that these Child Molesters are "sick" bastards and that Law doesn't apply to them, or their crime?

After a third conviction for Child Molesting I believe the Death Penalty should be imposed! My wife and I would like to hear your comments on that issue. Please contact us at her website remy125@msn.com

Moving on to question number three. (Can an eighteen-year-old "youth" be a Habitual Criminal? The answer of course is yes, especially in today's drug craziness with its all too easy money. In the next chapter Martin tells of how he started selling drugs at the age of fourteen.

Many of the "youths" in here are gang members and had been getting arrested since their early teens. In the chapter on "The Gangs" you read how one of these gangers went from shoplifting to cop-killer in just ten short years.

Most of today's Habitual Criminals were yesterday's troubled intercity "youths". Who is there to blame? The answer is you—"the public", the DEA, and the Federal Bureau of Prisons, and I will explain why!

The Sentencing Project is a group that supports alternatives to incarceration and they said. "The Black inmate population is now unprecedented. If the Black male inmates in local jails are added in, the proportion rises to nearly one in seven." Said Marc Mauer, their spokesman.

One reason the number of Black inmates continues to rise is the DEA's laughable so called "War On Drugs." Convictions for drug offenses accounted for a 27 percent increase in Black inmates, compared with 15 percent for Whites and only 7 percent for Hispanics.

States are more likely to lock people up for violent offenses than for drugs, so the Feds (DEA) has taken up the slack. Drug crimes account for the 59 percent increase in Federal prison inmates!

Question? Does that mean without drug offenders in them Federal prisons would be only 41 percent full? There is a specious argument going around that the moment you bust one drug dealer another takes their place. Trust me readers, that is a true statement!

If the DEA ever hopes to win their "War on Drugs" they had better get more serious about fighting it! Their way isn't working because no matter how many prisons and prisoners they have, it hasn't made a small dent in the drugs flowing in the streets of America!

I bet right now you are thinking. "Okay, Mr. Author, what is your answer to the problem?" Oh, I do have an answer but you, the DEA, and a lot of Government people will not like it. Please pay attention Feds you just might learn something?

The number one cash crop in California today (2003) is marijuana, not navel oranges! Since the event of 9/11 the growers and sellers have been having banner years, because they know the Government's resources are stretched thin with the "terrorism."

Columbia and Mexico are exporting drugs and death to American streets. They are killing our citizens just as surely as the terrorists did! Isn't that an act of war? Why then does the U.S. continue aiding countries that are killing our people? Why send them a penny?

Here's the why! Because gang countries like Colombia and Mexico are holding America hostage. They already owe U.S. banks billions of dollars in loans they cannot pay back in the foreseeable future. The U.S. bankers are running scared and the Government bows to their wishes so that their already shaky loans are not put in further jeopardy.

Doesn't that make the bankers drug importers? You bet it does! That's just one old man's view of things, but I hope it gets you thinking about the real drug problem here in America, the Government!

Question number four. Can a sixty-two year old "geriatric" be a Habitual Criminal? Yes and no, but I am sorry to say, that I am the "geriatric" in the question.

The yes part is, if someone was arrested at age 35 for a third felony and given a 30-year sentence. Then after many years in prison you could call him a "geriatric" Habitual Criminal.

The no part is, that if an old timer were a "true" Habitual Criminal he would have been locked up long before he became a "geriatric."

One theory is that if you haven't been arrested and convicted of a third felony by the age of sixty-(60), you are a successful mature bad guy and not a Habitual Criminal!

My last prior conviction was in 1980 over twenty-three (23) years ago! But, my current offense was my third conviction for firearms sales. However, I still do not consider myself or my crime of selling weapons to third world nations a violent act, but the B.O.P. does.

In fact, the CIA sold weapons to countries that I refused to sell to. We all know what a good track record the CIA has, Cuba, Libya, Iraq, etc.

The Government could not sentence me as a Three-Time Loser, because my last prior conviction was more than twenty (20) years back from my current offense! The Sentencing Guidelines allow the Court to go back only ten (10) years for sentencing purposes.

The last question is. Why are most of a prison's population Habitual Criminals, or as the B.O.P. likes to call us, repeat offenders?

If you were here in USP Atwater as a prisoner you would know the answer to that no-brainer question.

Here are some documented facts on why so many Federal prisoners are "repeat offenders."

Sources: Urban Institute—Justice Policy Center and Bureau of Justice Statistics.

1.   A study conducted by BJS found that 66 percent of all released prisoners are likely to be re-arrested and returned to prison within 30 months.
2.   About 50 percent of all inmates released are drug offenders and 25 percent are violent offenders.
3.   The median educational level of released prisoners is only the 11th grade.
4.   About three-quarters of released inmates have a history of substance abuse and many of them also suffer from mental illness.
5.   Studies show in-prison programs help reduce recidivism among released prisoners but there is no vocational training, only G.E.D. for educational advancement, and a non-existing substance abuse program here in USP Atwater.
6.   Only 6 percent of the prison's budget is allowed to support Federal rehabilitative programs—vocational, educational, abuse treatment, but 94 percent is spent on staffing, building prisons, and housing inmates.
7.   Of all released prisoners with substance abuse problems, only 18 percent received treatment while incarcerated.

Can anything be done now to cut down the percentage of returning offenders? Yes of course, but nothing will be done. Things that worked well in the 1980's would work again if brought back in 2003. Those schooling and job programs worked and they would work even better if brought back now!

What's that I said? Explain "will work better" now? Here's my thought, but you be the judge.

Today in 2003 a Federal inmate must serve 85 percent of his sentence in prison, and the courts are giving out extremely longer sentences. Doesn't the fact that inmates are doing more of their sentenced time, and serving longer sentences in the prison, give the B.O.P. more time to educate or train prisoners for jobs on the outside?

Sounds like a no brainer to me! Don't you agree? Then whey can't the "powers to be" see that? Oh, I have that answer for you. Federal prisons have become a big business in the U.S.!

The answer is not more jails and prisons. The answer is education and job training, which need to re-appear quickly in the Federal prison system!

Somewhere along the way the B.O.P. lost sight of the fact that education is a preparatory experience.

Because the inmate is thrust back into the world lacking the basic tools for survival disaster follows!

No wonder he is unemployable!

No wonder he goes on welfare!

No wonder he winds up back in prison, for it is the milieu in which he is the most comfortable!

Are my fellow-inmates Habitual Criminals? Shucks no. They're just very hard to place in the outside work place!

Inmate Interviews is the next chapter with five (5) fellow convicts telling their stories.

Inmate Interviews

Author's note:

Every word in these next interviews is true to the best of my knowledge and belief. Sixty-three (63) percent of inmates in this Federal prison are here for drug crimes! So, I went with the flow and interviewed a "big money" drug dealer first.

There are seven (7) points of information before each guy's story so let's begin.

1.   Name—Martin (Marty to his friends)
2.   Present age—30 years old
3.   Race—White
4.   Age when crime was committed—24 years old
5.   Sentence—15 years
6.   Crime—drug selling
7.   Time in prison current offense—6 years

Questions and Answers

Q—Marty, what was your crime, the one you're in here for?

A—Drugs, Pop, the same as most of the other people in here, Pop. What was yours?

Q—Hey, you already know why I am in here, and besides you are the one being interviewed.

A—Okay, Pop, just a little gallows humor there. I am in this shit hole for selling drugs, lots of drugs!

Q—Be that as it may, what exactly did you do in the drug world?

A—I was a middleman that is I bought drugs from a dealer and resold them to my friends at a profit. Let me tell you Pop that was a sweet set-up because the money I made selling drugs paid for all my drugs.

Q—Marty, in dollars, how much were your daily needs?

A—At the time not that much only two or three hundred dollars a day.

Q—Marty, did you become a serious drug addict?

A—I sure did and by that time my daily habit went to about five hundred bucks a day.

Q—How did you then pay for the dope you needed? I mean did you have a good paying job? Rich parents? Or something going for you?

A—Not the first two old man but you were fucking close on the last one.

Q—Explain, please!

A—Well, Pop what I had was I already was selling drugs, so all I needed to do was sell more to pay for my habit and to have a few dollars left over.

Q—Marty, what I understand your story to be, correct me if I get anything wrong. You were doing drugs and to pay for yours, you starting dealing to your friends only. At some point you became addicted and had to increase your "sales" to support your daily habit?

A—That's it in a rat's ass, Pop.

Q—So what was your drug of choice?

A—Crack!

Q—That's strong stuff isn't it? I heard you can become addicted after one use only, is that true?

A—Yea, its good shit but I personally don't know anyone who got addicted after one use.

Q—Are you, as of today, still addicted to drugs?

A—I think I am but the B.O.P. says no. They have me on some heavy shit in here, all they did was swap one drug for another.

Q—Marty, people hear about how much money there is in selling drugs. What was your take when you were dealing large?

A—Well, I never did add any of it up but I would guess eight hundred to a thousand dollars a day.

Q—A day?

A—Yea, Pop one fucking day.

Q—That's some serious money doing the figures, it comes to about a half million dollars a year. Does that sound right to you?

A—Sure, maybe a little bit more the year before I got busted.

Q—How did the Feds get you?

A—Someone "ratted" me out!

Q—Are you sure it was a rat, not just good police work?

A—Naw, it was a rat, almost all the dealers in here have been ratted out or set up by other dealers. No such thing good cops work. Pop you just hit a nerve with me. Can I tell you how they find all the rats?

Q—Hey, I am not the one in a hurry here, go ahead!

A—Here's the way the shit works. First, the cops arrest a day shit very small dealer. Threaten him with ten (10) years if he doesn't inform on his supplier. So he rolls him and now the police arrest the supplier and squeeze him next. Pop, do you see how they get their arrests? Not good police work, but rather bad rats.

Q—Now that you informed me all about drug rats, my next question is easy. Where did you live at the time of your arrest?

A—LA and Vegas, mostly.

Q—How many years were you selling before you were finked on?

A—Eight or nine, maybe ten.

Q—Wait a second Marty, if you are not thirty years old, been down six years and sold drugs for ten years, were you fourteen or fifteen when you started?

A—Yea, what's the big deal, Pop?

Q—You're not pulling my chain, Marty?

A—No, because I can remember quitting school while I was in Junior high.

Q—I guess you did start with drugs at a young age?

A—I sure did and quitting school was a high point in my life.

Q—Did you save any money for a rainy day or for your family to live on while you're in here?

A—Fuck no! Why? I made it and we spent it.

Q—I guess my next question will light your fire. How come with about a quarter of a million dollars a year, for all those years, you have nothing at this time?

A—What the fuck are you old man the IRS?

Q—No, I was only trying to show the readers how much money there is in drugs.

A—Well for one thing we never ate at a Burger King or Denny's and I didn't drive a shit box Ford car. My bitch and I didn't buy our clothing at WalMart or Sears.

Q—I am having a very hard time trying to understand how five million bucks went in and out your hands with none being saved or invested?

A—Hey, shit, I was young, in my early twenty's and the money was flying in. Who the fuck ever thought I be in prison giving a crazy old man my life story?

Q—So right now you have nine (9) years left on your present sentence, do you have any hope for an early release?

A—None the fuck all! Because right now drugs are the "in" thing, with the Courts.

Q—Marty, do you think you'll ever come back to prison again?

A—Well, I hope the fuck not but what's out there that will pay me five hundred a day? See what I mean, Old Man?

Q—Yes, I agree with you on one thing, drugs are easy money, but the sentences are too long. I'll just stick to selling weapons.

A—Yea Pop I sure is hard to go from having all kinds of money in your pockets to this shit hotel.

1.   Name—Jerry
2.   Present Age—27 years old
3.   Race—White
4.   Age when crime was committed—14 or 15
5.   Sentence—Life with no parole
6.   Crime—Murder of a Federal Agent
7.   Time in prison this offense—12 years

Q—Jerry, how old were you when you committed the murder?

A—Pop, let's get one thing straight from the start—I didn't kill anyone. I was just a stupid kid of fourteen or fifteen at that time.

Q—Whom did they say you killed?

A—A government agent, FBI or ATF I am not sure which.

Q—How was it that at age fourteen you were mixed-up with agents?

A—I wasn't it was my stepfather, let me take that back it was my step, stepfather. My whore mother was married three times before I hit fifteen.

Q—Just to keep things short, what was your step, step daddy's first name?

A—Todd.

Q—So then Todd killed the agent?

A—No, he did not! They killed him first.

Q—Somewhere I took a wrong turn, let me go back just a little. Todd was the reason the agents came to your house?

A—That's correct, it was about 3:00 or 3:30 AM. They came to arrest him and instead of giving up he started shooting.

Q—Then what happened?

A—Well my ma and younger sisters and brothers ran out the back door of the house.

Q—How many brothers and sisters do you have?

A—Two sisters and three brothers. I am the oldest.

Q—Jerry, why didn't you run out of the house like the others?

A—To this day I really don't know why I didn't run. I guessed I didn't use my brain.

Q—So they came to arrest Todd and he just started shooting at them?

A—No! He was a real man; he told the Feds he was sending my ma and the young kids out the back door.

Q—Did the agents know he was armed?

A—Hell, yes! If they didn't they sure were dumb.

Q—Why were they dumb, Jerry?

A—Because he had been arrested for armed robbery and a few bank robberies in this part of the country!

Q—Do you mean Arizona or the Western part of the U.S.?

A—Both! He was a fucking one-man bank-robbing machine!

Q—So the agents knew Todd was armed and dangerous, but did they know you were in the house too?

A—Yea, sure my ma or one of the kids would have told them.

Q—Did the Feds call your name and ask you to come out?

A—Hell, no! That's movie shit you're talking.

Q—What do you mean "movie shit?"

A—Well, they didn't even ask Todd to step out. They just shot the house full of tear gas bombs.

Q—When did the bullets start flying?

A—One of the cops got to close to the opened front door. I think he was getting ready to toss something in when Todd shot him in the leg. He told me to never aim for their body because they wear those vests. You should aim for the legs, or if needed their heads.

Q—But Jerry, if you aim at their heads aren't you trying to kill them?

A—Fuck, yes! What do you think they were trying to do after Todd winged the Nigger?

Q—What kind of weapons are we talking here, I mean the agents?

A—They had everything—shot guns, automatic rifles, pistols—you name it!

Q—What weapons did you and Todd have?

A—Well he had a 357 Magnum with a six inch barrel, a police shot gun (probably a Remington #370) and some six shot rifle. Me, I only had my "22" rifle.

Q—Jerry, I sold guns and sounds to me like you and Todd had a no brainer. Why didn't you guys give it up?

A—Pop, I am glad you asked the question! No one believes me when I told them we did try to surrender. Hey, after all one of their guys was already shot. I was sure they were trying to kill us.

Q—Did Todd try to talk to them a second time?

A—He sure did! He was trying to get them to let me out. They weren't buying.

Q—So after Todd called out to the agents, what happened next, after he told them you were in the house?

A—The bullets started flying in from all sides of the house. My step daddy was hit twice.

Q—Was he seriously hurt, I mean was he dying?

A—Yes, he was bleeding from his mouth and chest!

Q—Did you try to yell at them to stop shooting and help Todd?

A—Oh, God! I yelled and yelled and yelled—I guess they couldn't hear me with all that shooting.

Q—Go on Jerry.

A—Next thing I know I am shot in my left side and my foot.

Q—What did you do after you were shot?

A—I crawled on the floor towards the back door.

Q—Jerry, why the back door?

A—Because nobody was firing from that direction.

Q—So, were you carrying a gun or anything that they might of thought a weapon?

A—No! I was not. All I was trying to do is get the fuck out of there alive.

Q—Did you fire any shots at the officer?

A—No! Never had my rifle even in my hands. When they entered the house my rifle was still in my room!

Q—Did Todd kill the agent?

A—No, not at all.

Q—So, Jerry, how did the Agent got killed?

A—Pop, you and I are friends so what I am going to tell you is God's truth. I did not shoot the agent or even had a gun in my hands that day!

Q—Okay I'll bait, explain to me how the officer was killed?

A—As I told you I was crawling on the floor tying to get out the back door. Somehow an agent got in through the front door, just then someone was also coming in the back door. The agent who came in the back door was shot dead right in front of me by the other agent. That's the God's truth, Pop.

Q—Okay, Jerry, relax, this is what I think you are saying and correct me if I am wrong! You're saying that one agent shot and killed the other agent?

A—Hell, yes old man I didn't kill the fucker his buddy did!

Q—What gun did they say did the killing?

A—The shotgun that Todd had, it was "police issue", he stole it out of a patrol car a few years back. It was the same make and model that the agents were carrying that day.

Q—Then what you are saying here today, is that a Federal Agent is guilty of the crime you have been sentence for?

A—Yes, remember Pop a shot gun leaves no marks on their shells like pistols or rifles. My attorney could not prove their weapons did it and they couldn't prove Todd's gun did. But here I am!

Name—Johnny
Present age—36 years old
Race—Black
Age when crime was committed—24 years old
Sentence—17 years possibility of parole
Crime—Bombing a Federal building and injury to a Federal employee
Time now in prison—12 years

Author's note: Johnny is not your stereotype Black inmate. He is highly educated and not from the "hood". Let's see what he has to tell us today.

Q—Johnny, my first question is what building did you blow-up and why?

A—Well Frank, the question is not that easy to answer and I have to start at the very beginning.

Q—No problem Johnny we have nothing but time, right?

A—Cut me off if I start to get long winded on an answer.

Q—Go on, This Is Your Life (does anyone remember that old TV show)?

A—Back then—

Q—When was then Johnny, what year?

A—1987 or 1988, I really not sure which. Well, anyway I was dating this White woman.

Q—Stop, John!

A—What, did I say something wrong?

Q—Yes, you certainly did. Why did you mention the race of the woman you were dating?

A—I just wanted you to know that I wasn't a "street nigger" like most of the "brothers" (other Black's) in here.

Q—Okay, my wife is Brown should I put her photo on my bio-page so that I can Appeal to the Brown's to buy my book?

A—Sure, why not? Can it hurt?

Q—Now getting back to our interview. The last question was, about you dating the White woman. Damn, now you got me doing the race thing.

A—Well anyway—she and I were an item for about a year. Then I guess someone must of reminded her that I am Black. I really loved that woman but she had made-up her mind to end it.

Q—I guess it didn't end well with the "bomb" and you here.

A—No it did not. She wouldn't answer the phone when I called her at home or work and she worked in a secured Federal office building, I just couldn't walk in off the street and get on the elevator.

Q—Oh, I get it Johnny. You decided to blow the building up just to scare her?

A—No, not even close old man!

Q—Well go on I am all ears!

A—I didn't send the bomb to her workplace!

Q—Back-up Johnny, did I miss something?

A—No but I didn't get to the part about sending the bomb yet.

Q—So tell me about the bomb.

A—She did everything she could to avoid me, even stopped mail delivery at her apartment. Now she started working lot's of overtime so she then had all her mail forwarded to her workplace. That my friend is why we are having this conversation.

Q—By George, I've got it! You made the bomb and mailed it to her apartment and the Post office sent it to the office?

A—Almost right, Frank, I did not use the U.S. Mail, I sent the bomb by UPS. They are the ones who delivered it to her; they forwarded the envelope to her office. Also, it wasn't a very large bomb; everything was in a 9 by 12 inch envelope.

Q—Can you really put enough explosives in a letter "bomb" to kill someone?

A—It depends on the skill of the person making the bomb.

Q—Johnny, what keeps the bomb "stable" while in transit?

A—The way it is put together. Some of us know our shit and others don't. That's why you hear about people's fingers being blown off or eyes put out. Those are just kids trying to make bombs!

Q—Johnny isn't killing someone by bomb considered a cowardly way of doing things? Blacks as a rule don't do "bombs", that's a White man's thing.

A—Hey, are you saying that I as a Black am not smart enough to build a bomb?

Q—Hell no, but try and tell me when the last time you heard of a Black "bombing" someone?

A—So you rather I just rang the door bell and shot her in the head?

Q—Okay, let's do that question over? Is killing someone by letter bomb a cowardly thing to do?

A—No. I consider it a "skill", from singling out the person, to making the bomb and then getting it to them with perfect results.

Q—What results?

A—You almost caught me on that one.

Q—Going back a question or two, explain what you mean by "skill"?

A—Right—let's say I have a bomb planted on some dude's car and—

Q—Hold it hold it, I thought we were talking about a letter bomb here?

A—What ever, it makes no difference, Frank. I can wire anything to blow-up.

Q—Fine, finish up on the car and then let's get back to the reason you are in here!

A—When I wire a car the bomb is activated by a remote control switch, which I have on me.

Q—So what's the big deal?

A—Frank, old buddy, you don't know shit about bombs!

Q—No, am I suppose to?

A—Well, let's say it's a very cold day in Jersey, and the bad guy sends his wife or girlfriend to start their car. If the car was only wired to blow on starting, boom no wife! Now that would be a strong warning, and I wouldn't get a second chance near his next car. But ten (10) minutes later he comes out, gets in his car and I press the switch, end of story.

Q—All right you're Mr. Nice Guy for not making lawn fertilizer of his wife?

A—That's correct.

Q—Well, can we please get back to the "letter bomb"?

Q—Johnny, if UPS didn't forward the envelope you wouldn't be here would you?

A—Yes, that's the long and the short of it.

Q—Johnny I am very curious as to how that caught you?

A—So am I! No—just kidding, it wasn't that hard for them to find me this last time.

Q—What do you mean?

A—Well, I have been arrested five or six times for "bombs" before.

Q—How many times?

A—Five or six.

Q—John you were arrested all those times and you were still loose on society?

A—Yea, ain't life grand?

Q—No John, I don't expect you to admit to anything you're not "Doing Time" for. Where you ever convicted in any of your other "bomb" arrests?

A—No!

Q—You were arrested all those times and charged, but not convicted? How can that be?

A—Maybe I didn't do the crimes.

Q—I, for one do not believe you and I could have my wife get your record off the computer.

A—It will show that I am an effective criminal because I have all those arrests, but only this one conviction.

Q—Remind me not to play poker with you!

A—I sure will.

Q—We're almost done Johnny. Please tell me about who got hurt with the envelope and how they found you.

A—Well, first of all she never got the bomb. The UPS driver took it to the building's mailroom, which was in the basement. In all Federal Buildings the incoming mail and packages are x-rayed before being delivered.

Q—So then someone else got hurt instead of the woman, correct?

A—Correct.

Q—Were they badly hurt?

A—No, not at all just burns on his arms and chests, no permanent damage. The bomb, however, did a lot of fire damage to the building. Catching me was too easy for them. The mail clerk had logged into their mail book the envelope. But, I did not have my name or address on the envelope.

Q—How did you get the package to UPS?

A—In the lobby of the apartment where I lived, UPS had a drop off box.

Q—Let me guess. You paid for the delivery with your credit card?

A—No, wise guy, but I bought a money order in a store. However, the driver who picked up my envelope must have wrote down where he picked it up.

Q—The arrest was too easy. They're probably still smiling.

A—Oh you think you figured it out?

Q—I think so.

A—Okay, tell me what you got?

Q—First, they did the obvious and asked your ex-lady friend if she knew of anyone who would send her a bomb. Second, they tracked where the envelope came from. Then some cop figured out that the "bomb" and someone who wanted to hurt the lady were the same address. Third, and last your name popped out on the computer and here we are in sunny California!

A—Damn Frank you should have been a Cop!

Q—Not me, and it pays shit for money.

A—Bombing pays good but it's hard to find work. Most bomb makers do it just for their personal life.

Q—I know Johnny you can't hang out a sign at hour house, "Bombs Made Inquire Within".

A—So true, my friend.

Q—Yeah, let's go eat supper.

Name—Tony
Present Age—27 years old
Race—White
Age when crime was committed—26 years old
Sentence 5 years
Crime—Truck hijacking
Time in prison this offense—10 months

Q—Tony no one will believe your answer, but one short question before we do the interview.

A—Sure, why not.

Q—Where did we meet in here and what was I doing at the time?

A—You're right old man no one will believe me but I met you at the "weight pile", old person you were trying to lift eight pounds.

Q—I wasn't trying to lift eight pounds. I had already done five sets (a "set" is a how many times in a row you lift) of five or in other words, I had lifted the eighty pounds twenty five times!

A—Alright Mr. Atlas can we get with the interview?

Q—Sure thing, what were you busted for Tony?

A—Frank they stacked seven or eight charges on me but it plea-bargained out to Truck Hijacking.

Q—We don't have to finish this in one day. We can stop at anytime if you want to.

A—Naw, I'm cool. I not tripping about the time.

Q—So what exactly did you do to end up in prison?

A—I stole trailers filled with goods and sold most of the loads in Mexico. I didn't steal the tractor part, but only the trailers. It was too damn easy!

Q—Explain how easy it was?

A—All I did was back my "horse" (tractor also called the cab) up to the trailer, hooked up the lines and drive off singing. Easy as sin.

Q—No one ever tried to stop you?

A—Hell no, who was there to stop me?

Q—Well it does seem too easy what's the catch?

A—I think I should explain to you how trailers get from point "A" to point "B".

Q—So, explain?

A—Let's say there is a shipping company in Phoenix, that has orders that need to get to New York City in a hurry. It could be something that will not keep, like produce or frozen foods. Overland by truck is fastest and cheapest way to ship.

Q—Tony is it cheaper than by rail or boat?

A—Hell yes! Most times you'll see what you call piggybacks or even triples (three trailers hooked together).

Q—I know that some states do not allow, "triples" on their highways and that some roads do not let the piggybacks on. What happens in those cases?

Q—Well, the driver will have to put into a trailer depot and drop one or two of the trailers. That's when someone like me off and steals those trailers.

A—Tony is it harder to steal a trailer now than it was a few years ago?

Q—Oh, shit yes. Many of the large tracking companies have that new satellite tracking discs on their rigs. I personally think that there are also "trackers" hidden inside the trailer loads.

Q—So if you see a satellite dish on a tractor, do not try to steal it?

A—No, I didn't say that because I know how to shutdown the dish.

Q—My next question may sound silly to you, but how did you know what was in the trailer's load? Or even if the trailer was in fact empty?

A—Very simple old buddy, did you ever hear of the CB radio?

Q—Of course, I have. So?

A—Remember now when I am out stealing I am also driving a rig. What I did was pull in behind a tractor-trailer and turn on my CB. I'd say some bullshit like; "You got the Iron man at your back door with a load of tires headed north."

Q—Oh, I get it, sort of strike-up a conversation and then ask a few questions about his load.

A—Bingo! You catch on fast for a senior citizen.

Q—Was there any particular kind of cargo you liked to get hold of?

A—Yeah, sure liked them Radio Shack trucks, TV's, VCR's, phones, computers and a whole lot more.

Q—How did you decide what, when and where to steal?

A—Well it never was that hard. I drove for J.B. Hunt at that time and had worked for other large companies over the years, so I knew the ropes sort of. I also owned my own rig as you already know. (Read more about Tony's rig in "Mail In Prison". I got the idea to steal a trailer long before I did one.

Q—What do you mean?

A—Way back, when I was hauling other people's cargo, and would put into a trailer rest area, I would watch the trailers being picked-up and dropped off. That give me the idea of how to steal one. On my day off I drove my own rig to one of those "trailer depots" and watched the comings and goings for a full day.

Q—I can almost see this one coming but please, go on Tony.

A—Well, I did say it was simple. So one day I pulled into a lot and quickly spotted two or three trailers with the company's logo that I was then employed with. In less than ten minutes I was backed-in, hooked-up and on the road towards northern Arizona. Nobody thought anything of a J.B. Hunt tractor leaving the yard pulling a J.B. Hunt trailer.

Q—You're right Tony, that was too easy, go on.

A—I then drove the load over to Scottsdale (Arizona) and dropped the box (trailer) off at my farm. Then I re-hooked up the trailer I left there earlier and started back on my deliveries.

My farm is about a mile to my closest neighbor and they are used to seeing me driving my rig in and out. Frank, are you getting all this?

Q—Yes, but wasn't it very risky doing that in front of so many people and in daylight? Didn't you run into other drivers that knew you?

A—No not all! No one ever asked me who I was, or what I was doing picking-up this trailer or that trailer. As far as other drivers knowing me, no one likes to be a fink.

Q—I think I have a good question for you. How did you explain all the extra miles on the tractor from running over to your place twice?

A—You call that a good question? Come on think, haven't you heard of traffic accidents, road repairs, detours, and my favorite excuse—"I just got lost boss".

Q—Next question, can you remember what was in the first trailer you stole? Also, what did you do with the empty trailer?

A—The very first time was a load of rugs, I remember because there was only two sized in the whole load. There were about three hundred rugs, and after we did our house and some friends houses I still had plenty left. So, I just loaded-up my pick up truck with a dozen at a time and headed for "Flea Marts," I tagged each rug at only fifty dollars every trip was a six hundred dollar deal. What was that other question?

Q—The question was what did you do with the empty trailer?

A—Now don't laugh but I hitched it up to my own tractor, not J.B. Hunt's and left it somewhere in Mexico, it may still be there.

Q—Did you learn anything from your first heist?

A—Lots, you bet I did. First, always know what you are stealing. Second, try to have the load sold before you steal it. Third, always steal only during daylight hours, as the cops won't give you a second look.

Q—I don't want to bust your bubble, but someone must have given you a second look or we wouldn't be having this interview?

A—Oh you mean how they fuck did I get busted?

Q—In a word, yes!

A—Okay, but first I would like to point out that I did not get caught stealing a trailer.

Q—So what has that got to do with being in prison?

A—My pride, I guess. I stole many more boxes than they could even dream of, but they only nailed me for one. The D.O.T. on a routine paperwork check stopped me.

Q—Go ahead and explain what did happen.

A—The Arizona Police and the Arizona D.O.T. were pulling over all the trucks that day. There was no way I could get off the highway. When they got to my rig the paperwork for the tractor and trailer didn't match and here we are having this conversation.

Q—That's almost as dumb as the way I got snagged.

A—Yes, Frank how did you get caught?

Q—Buy my book when it comes out—anything else you want to add Tony?

A—Only this Frank, you and I are alike we both say "crime does pay".

Q—Say good night, Tony!

A—Good Night, Tony!

Name—George
Present Age—20 years old
Race—White/Asian
Age when crime was committed—18 years old
Sentence—51 months
6. Crime—Credit Card Fraud/Identity Theft
Time in prison current offense—1 year
Author's note:
George, who is nicknamed "Boy George" because of his young age, is a new wave criminal. His crime of Identity Theft accounts for only 4.6 percent (7,066 inmates) of the B.O.P.'s total population of 169, 676 as of June 2003. However Identify Theft is currently in today's news and rising fast.

Q—George my first question is why the hell are you in a U.S. Penitentiary for a non-violent crime?

A—That's a good question Frank, my mother and father keep asking anyone that will listen that same question, but here I am at USP Atwater in sunny California.

Q—Did you have a serious prior criminal history before being sentenced for your crime?

A—No way! I didn't even have a fu—king traffic ticket! Maybe the Feds wanted to scare others from doing Identify Theft?

Q—That could be it, the Government does nasty things like that all the time. So "Boy George" tell me about this new thing called I.D. Theft?

A—There's not that much to tell, it's all very simple. You just use someone else's name and credit and they get the bills.

Q—George I just thought of something funny. Isn't that what a non-working wife does? Doesn't she use her husband's name and credit and he gets the bills? Any way, tell me about Credit Card Fraud and then we'll do the Identify Theft last.

A—There are many different ways to use someone else's credit card or to get a new card in the mail. You won't believe how easy it really is.

Q—Do tell us George.

A—Two years ago I was working at a ritzy uptown L.A. hotel. Part of my job was to empty the wastebaskets at the front desk, the cashier's office and the other offices in the hotel. This hotel has a thing about being civic-minded and hires many ex-offenders.

Q—"Boy George", stop for a minute and let me guess what happened. You met some criminal low-life who worked there; he took you under his wing and then he led you down the path into a life of crime?

A—Gee how did you know all that Frank?

Q—I saw the movie? George, all kidding aside, that's why most of the people are in here. They also met the wrong person or persons, or maybe joined a gang. Please go on?

A—So this older guy and I were teamed-up to work the midnight shift as janitors at this hotel. Can I say the hotel's name?

Q—No kid because they might get mad and stop hiring ex-offenders. So?

A—One night Gene and I were emptying the trash into our large barrel on wheels and I stopped, and went to the hotel's kitchen for sodas. When I got back Gene was looking through the trash. He was holding a small pile of copies of credit card charges and I asked him what he was doing but he didn't answer. So I just let the whole matter drop.

Q—Come now "Boy George" what the hell did you think he was up to?

A—Okay I had a good idea but I wasn't really sure at that time.

Q—Didn't you figure out that your buddy Gene was an ex-con?

A—Well he never did tell me that but I pretty well guessed he was.

Q—Oh, really, how did you come to the conclusion "Boy George"?

A—Well for one give-away he had tattoos all over his hands and arms. And he also wore his pants with his ass hanging out just like we see it in here.

Q—Good points my young friend. So when you caught Gene collecting the charge slips that was your final clue that he was an ex-felon? Did you ask him to cut you in on what ever he was up to?

A—Yeah that was the clue and no I didn't ask him to cut me in!

Q—Okay kid calm down. So what did happen that got you sent to the big house? Explain please.

A—Gene wasn't such a bad guy and after working together for a month we became friends of a sort. You know, like I would pick him up and drive him to and from the hotel, and he would buy our lunch.

Q—"Boy George" could we cut to the chase? When and how did you get involved in Gene's scam?

A—The when was quite soon after all the buddy-buddy shit started, and the how was telephone scamming using the charge slips. It worked like charms until I returned to school that fall, which is when I stopped. Frank, think about this—if you wanted something all you had to do was pick up the phone and order it! And it's yours without paying for it! Sweet isn't it?

Q—That's cool all right, but explain how you did that?

A—Every day we looked for the charge slip copies in our trash and we sorted them out keeping only the ones not from California.

Q—Hold it! George how the hell could you guys tell which slips were from out of State?

A—Frank keep your day job because you don't know shit about credit card crime!

Q—Okay my smart-ass friend explain how you could tell by the charge slips if the customer was from out of the State?

A—Simple, hotel policy was for the desk clerk to write the customer's drivers license number on the charge slip as a second form of I.D. So—CA was for California, OR was Oregon, AZ for Arizona, and so on, get it Frank?

A—Yes George I get it. Let's see if I have what you have told me correct so far. Gene turned out to be an ex-felon, you became friends, and he got you into his credit card scam? But why did you guys use only out of State cards?

A—Yeah you got the story right Pops. The reason we used only out of State cards? Guess Frank? Okay, do you give up?

A—Yes kid you got me again, I give up!

A—Now think about this Frank, If a customer used their credit card at the hotel, and they were from out of State, chances are they used their card to get to the hotel.

Q—Okay "Boy George" now I am starting to get the picture. Don't stop, enlighten me.

A—Yeah they used their cards for airline tickets, automobile expenses, restaurants, gift shops, chain stores, or what ever. Which meant their credit card company knew they were away from home and wouldn't think anything was strange when we ran up a few hundred dollars on their card.

Q—Gee I never would have thought of that. But—why didn't you guys use a California person's card in California?

A—Because the credit card company would pick up quickly if we used the California card for things that broke the owner's normal buying habits. They catch shit like that all day long on their computers. Better safe than sorry, right?

Q—So, if someone is on a vacation and away from their home State, the credit card people don't have a clue what the card will be used for next? Am I right George?

A—Bingo! But still keep your day job.

Q—Thank you George. Do you have some tips for the readers on what you have told me so far?

A—Yeah, here's two important things to remember. First, never use a card for a second day, in fact burn it out in jut a few hours. Second, make a list of what you are going to buy. Gene and I used to sit for hours deciding what to scam before we hit the telephone book for the numbers we needed to call.

Q—That's my next question, where did you two-telephone "scam" shop?

A—I'll have to explain how first we set things up before the shopping.

Q—What do you mean by set-up?

A—The first thing we did was check the phonebook for stores that rented postal boxes, only ones that offered a "street address", you know, companies like Mail Boxes Etc.,

Q—Odd you should mention Mail Boxes, Etc., I used them when I was a fugitive from the U.S. Marshal.

A—Yeah, yeah Mr. Tough Guy can we finish this so I can get to my afternoon nap?

Q—By all means, do go on George.

A—L.A. is a big city and there was maybe 50 or 60 places to rent mailboxes from in the telephone book. My part of the scam was to go out and rent the boxes, only getting one at a time, which we kept for no more than a month.

Q—What was your buddy Gene's part?

A—His job was to make the phone calls and do the buying. He was about 40 years old and his voice would sound much more convincing than my 18 year old one.

Q—Going back a few questions, didn't you have to show some kind of I.D. to rent the boxes?

A—Frank, Frank, in L.A. there is no problem in getting fake I.D.'s. I had a great source for Drivers Licenses, Social Security Cards, Student I.D.'s, and even Alien Green Cards.

Q—Okay you guys have credit card numbers and a rented box, what comes next?

A—Hi-ho, hi-ho, it's off to buy we go!

Q—That's cool, but explain exactly how you and Gene did that?

A—Gene just picked up the phone and called the places that had what we wanted to scam. Mostly he called places the had a mail order catalog like Sear's, J.C. Penny, or like the catalogs you get in your mail. Those greedy people only ask the caller three questions. First, what is the exact name on the card? Second, what date does the card expire? And third, how do you want the package shipped, UPS or U.S. Postal Service? Never have anything sent to you by UPS!

Q—Why not UPS "Boy George"?

A—Because they'll pull up in their little brown truck and send someone in to get a signature for the package. There's a part of a paper trail you don't need. On the other hand, the U.S. Post Office will leave a package without needing a signature.

Q—Good points to remember my friend. So—all I need to do is rent a box using a phony I.D., get some poor smuck's credit card number, and I am in business!

A—That's the long and the short of it. You see how easy it really is?

Q—That's easy all right but can you get stuff from stores without using the mails?

A—Yes, but you are somewhat limited to stores that have a catalog sales department. Again that would be Sear's or Penny's. Gene made the calls and I went to the stores for the pick-up. Because the goods were already charged over the phone I was never asked for I.D. Maybe that's changed now?

Q—George I think you have covered the credit card numbers scam well. Now how about sharing your Identity Theft skill with us?

A—Gosh old man do you want all my trade secrets in one day? Okay here goes. I got into Identity Theft completely by accident while I was working my second summer at the same hotel. Gene was still working there but he wasn't involved in it and I never told him what I was doing.

Q—By accident? Please explain that one?

A—Yeah by accident! One night Gene and I were cleaning up in the Human Resources Office. Next to the door were three large plastic tubs with a note taped to them that said. "Please dump the papers and return the tubs. Thank you." Never mind, I'll tell you. They were filled with two years of old employment applications!

Q—George I think I know what comes next but I could be wrong. Please continue.

A—Yes, everything I needed to apply for dozens of bogus credit cards was on those discarded applications. How stupid can that hotel be? Especially since they hire so many ex-cons?

Q—So next you tried your solo hand at Identity Theft and life became good?

A—Yep, old man it sure did!

Q—George, could you give us a run down of how you got going?

A—Well, just like with the telephone scam I needed to rent a box to have a street address, so it was back to Mail Boxes Etc. Then I went around to gas stations and picked up their credit card applications. Gasoline cards are the easiest to get and in a few weeks I had Exxon, Shell, and Getty in my pocket.

Q—George I hate to bust your bubble, but what if the person's name you were using already had a card from the gasoline company that you were applying to?

A—That's almost a no brainier. On the Employment Application there is a section that asks. "Please list credit that you have now established." I checked that section before applying for the gasoline cards. Besides today most people just use their ATM card to buy gas.

Q—You know what "Boy George" you are right about the ATM card for gasoline. What other cards are among the easiest to obtain?

A—Chain stores like WalMart, K-Mart, and OfficeMax.

Q—How did you make out when applying for major credit cards like Visa, MasterCard, or American Express?

A—Those weren't hard to get but I had to scam a little harder.

Q—Explain please?

A—I would check the Employment form, if someone has any of the "big three" cards you can bet they will have listed it in the credit established section. Let's say they wrote down Visa and MasterCard, and then I would apply for the American Express card. If they listed Visa, I would apply for MasterCard and American Express.

Q—So you would apply for only the credit card companies they didn't put on their applications?

A—Correct! And there is a new helper for people who want to try Identity Theft. It's on the computer; you can get a free credit report on yourself. Here's what I did many times. I went to the Public Library and used their computer to request a "free credit report", providing the information from an Employment Application.

Q—Wow George that's scary! You used the information, which of course was correct, from the applications to get a complete list of a person's credit?

A—Yeah, and then I applied for more credit using the good credit he had for references.

Q—I am going to sum-up what you have told me about Identity Theft and then you can add anything else you wish to say.

A—Go for it!

Q—So, you found the discarded forms in the trash, rented a box with a street address, and started applying for cards in various names. You backed that all up, by getting credit checks on these people mailed to your box, which you requested off a website service?

—Ditto to all of the above!

CHAPTER **8**

The Light At The End Of The Tunnel!

Author's note:

In every letter home to Remy I now include this sentence. "Matan'aw na nako ang hayag sa langob!" That's in her Bisaya language for. "I can see the light at the end of the tunnel!"

This should have been the easiest and happiest chapter in the book to write, but it was not to be!

Ninety percent of my problems, frustrations, mental anguish, headaches, upset stomachs, and diarrhea are caused by the "Three Stooges", a.k.a. the 3A-Unit Team.

I am now within 91 days of my release! But the "Team" didn't tell me that my wife Remy did. I am starting to get ahead in the chapter so I'll stop here and let you read another of Remy's writings.

Author's note:

By Remy P. Tucci

It seems like the closer Frank gets to his release date the more problems the "Three Stooges", as Frank calls them, cause us. I'll try to control my anger, but you know the old saying. "There is no scorn like a woman's scorn!"

May 21, 2003

I just got off the phone with my husband and he was in a state of hostility, almost Jihad. His "want-a-be" Case Manager Ms. Scott had caused it by her latest and continuing stupidity.

Moo (Ms. Scott) earlier in the day handed Frank his latest B.O.P. Progress Report, which had a serious error on line number six.

"6. Offense/Violator: Homicide—Felon In Possession of a Firearm."

Frank is not in Federal prison for a "Homicide", nor has he ever been arrested for, or charged for a Homicide! All his Progress Reports for the last 36 months never showed a "Homicide"? How could Moo explain it away as "just a typing error"?

Our troubles with the Unit Stiffs, a.k.a. the "Three Stooges", started back in December 22, 2003. Frank had arrived in USP Atwater that June.

At his first USP Atwater "Program Review", not to be confused with a "Progress Report" which is a different review, Frank was informed.

"Mr. Tucci you will be released within the jurisdiction of the Court where you were sentenced to serve your probation."

Frank never holds his tongue and spoke his mind loudly. "Are you two morons crazy? You're sending me back to Connecticut for my three years of probation? My wife and home are in Phoenix?"

His remarks terminated the meeting and two guards were called to return Frank back to his cell.

Inside USP Atwater, Unit 3A, an inmate can not ask questions nor challenge the less than intelligent decisions of the "Three Stooges". Their mind set is no doubt the following.

"How dare a mare inmate tell me he doesn't accept what I say as the unquestionable truth? Doesn't the bastard know I have power over him everyday that he is here?"

Frank needed my help because he couldn't get anything done from the inside, so I started on the outside. The very first issue we needed to resolve was the transfer of his U.S. Probation. Frank was arrested for his crime in 1997 in Connecticut, jumped bail, and was rearrested here in Phoenix in June of 2000, and returned to Connecticut for trial.

In January 2003 I wrote to the Chief U.S. Probation Officer in Connecticut asking for help in getting my husband's case transferred. Soon after on February 18, 2003, I received a positive reply back.

Dear Mrs. Tucci-Allen:

Thank you for your recent letter to Chief U.S. Probation Officer Maria McBride concerning your husband. Mrs. McBride has asked me to respond to your inquiry.

Please be advised that I have contacted your husband's case manager at USP Atwater and will follow-up with a letter, advising of your husband's request that his supervision be transferred to Arizona. In light of the fact your husband's new release date is September 5, 2003, there is ample time for the Bureau of Prisons to initiate a transfer of supervision.

I have the utmost confidence that the necessary arrangements will be made in a timely manner. Should you require any additional assistance, please do not hesitate to contact me.

Sincerely yours,

Maria Rodrigues McBride
Chief U.S. Probation Officer

(Signed) Michael E. Sheehan
Supervising U.S. Probation Officer"

Hopefully that problem is solved. As I read her letter over a second time it then hit me! "In light of the fact your husband's new release date is September 5, 2003, there is ample time for the Bureau of Prisons to initiate a transfer of supervision."

What? Frank's new release date is September 5, 2003! The B.O.P. website that I always pull up shows his release as 1-13-2004? It is now already February and if Mrs. McBride's date is correct Frank will be home in only seven (7) more months!

Assuming her date is correct why haven't any of the "Three Stooges" told my husband? I have learned one important thing from Frank! Never, never shoot off your mouth without facts to prove your arguments, so I turned on our home computer.

Yes, everything I needed to help him was right there on the B.O.P.'s outstanding website! There were two Program Statements that had just what I was searching for:

PS #7310.04—Community Corrections Center (CCC)
Utilization and Transfer Procedure.

PS # 5325.06—Release Preparation Program (RPP).

There are many "directives" in those Program Statements that were overlooked, ignored, or simply just not done by the "Stooges". Why? How come? Well in Curley's case that's easy to answer, his vast lack of job knowledge.

Mr. Allen (Curley) is a likeable, light colored "Brother", but with no prior training or educational qualifications for a Counselor's position. A job, which he no doubt got due to diversification. If you were to ask him what a Program Statement was his answer would probably be. "Isn't that a listing of what's on TV?"

Larry is a different case all together! Unit Manager Mr. Armendariz (Larry) is a midget tyrant Mexican who fancies himself as a total dictator. It is rumored that he turned down the role of "Mini Me" in the Austin Powers movies just to stay here at USP Atwater. Frank says all the inmates are sorry he "kept his day job!"

Lastly there is Moo who is the token female with the "Stooges". Ms. Scott (Moo), or any woman who works in a men's Federal prison is considered by Muslims to be of low character and ill repute.

I have known power hungry women like Moo and the thought of having complete control over 128 male inmates no doubt gives her a "high" she could never find at a non-prison job.

Muslims believe that any woman who works in a men's prison must be also one of the following: A man hater, a lesbian, or from a very dysfunctional family. I'll write more about the "Three Stooges" later in my chapter.

But first let's take a look at the B.O.P.'s Program Statement #7310.04. Please turn to Page 7, number 8.

"Release Plan

Staff shall begin release planning at an inmate's first team meeting, normally the initial classification, and shall continue throughout the inmate's confinement."

Sounds helpful, but Frank arrived at USP Atwater in June of 2002 and it is now already June 2003. At no time have Larry, Curley, or Moo ever spoken to my husband about "release planning" nor have them ever asked him about his release plans! Frank is now just 90 days from release!

A second look at the Program Statement, again number eight (8) at part "6". It says.

"b. Preliminary decisions regarding eligibility for CC Programs are to be made well in advance of the last year of confinement."

Isn't 3 months less than a year? But yet Frank has not been told if he is eligible for a CC (Halfway house).

In part "CC," the Program Statement repeats itself somewhat as it says:

"C. A final and specific release preparation plan, including a decision as to CCC referral, is normally established at a team meeting no later than 11 to 13 months before an inmate's projected release date."

Once again I ask the B.O.P. and the "Three Stooges" isn't 3 months less than 11 to 13 months? Why haven't these mental midgets told my Frank he is going to a halfway house?

Yes, he is going! The "Team" didn't tell Frank, I did! How did an inmate's wife find out what the "Stooges" weren't telling my husband? I am not really sure, but I know God had a hand in it!

I told Frank about the letter I sent back to Connecticut and he asked. "Remy, please try to get the address of the B.O.P.'s halfway house in Phoenix. But, if it is not suitable for a Muslim I'll just stay in here until my time is up!"

He also asked. "Palihug daw pagsulat ug husto nga sentensya. (Please make me a proper sentence). Frank wanted two sentences in Bisaya, my native tongue, written in my next letter to him.

Frank is learning my language and now writes all his letters to me in Bisaya, which causes the B.O.P. fits! Here are the two sentences he asked for:

1.   Mosulod ba kaha ako sa halfway house?
     Should I go to the halfway house?
2.   Mosabut ka kaha kong dili ako mosugot?
     Would you understand if I didn't go?

When he asked those sentences I knew he was hinting for me to be strong if he didn't leave on September 5, 2003. I hung up the telephone almost in tears.

On May 6, 2003, I was able to contact the B.O.P.'s CCM Office in Phoenix and I asked for the address of the halfway house here. The person who answers the phone must have assumed my husband was told he was going there, and asked me.

"Inmate's name and register number?" His reply made my day! "Yes, your husband has been assigned to the Phoenix halfway house and he will be sent here on September 5, 2003."

I was filled with excitement waiting for Frank's next telephone call to give him my good news! That was on May 7, 2003, less than 4 months from his release to the halfway house and still those "Three Stooges" haven't told him a damn thing!

Maybe a second letter to the U.S. Probation Office in Connecticut would help? So on June 2, 2003 I typed out the following:

June 2, 2003

                    Michael E. Sheehan
Supervising U.S. Probation Officer
U.S. District Court Probation Department
Connecticut Financial Center
157 Church Street, 22nd Floor
New Haven, CT 06510

Re: Francis M. Tucci—Reg. No. 03836-0l4

Dear Micheal E. Sheehan:
In your letter to me dated February 18, 2003, you said. "Should you require my additional assistance, please do not hesitate to contact me." This is the reason for my letter today. Please refer to attached photocopy of said letter.

My husband, Francis M. Tucci, reg. # 03836-0l4 is about 100 days from release. But his Case Manager nor the Unit Manager has not given Frank a release date.

I have contacted the BOP's Phoenix CCM Office and was informed that Frank is in their computer for release on September 5, 2003.

The Unit team has told him nothing nor is helping Frank to get clothing sent in, his driver's license, etc. Can you help us please?

Also, Frank sent a copy of his 5/21/03 Progress Report and item no. 6 listed him as Violator Offense: Homicide—Felon In Possession of a Firearm which I believe is in error! Is the offense categorized as Homicide? Would this prevent him for the halfway house program? If this were an error, would his record be corrected?

Thank you for your assistance and have a good day.

Sincerely yours,

Remy P. Tucci-Allen

Encl:
Photocopy of your 1/18/03 correspondence
Photocopy of 5/20/03 Progress Report
As of today, June 22, 2003, we have not received a reply, but I am sure the help "is in the mail!" It is now only 3 months until my husband's release.

June 16, 2003

All praise to Allah! The Unit bulletin board said. "The following inmate will have a review of June 19, 2003 at 10:00 AM."

Tucci #03836-014

Etc.

Etc.

Etc.

I'll stop writing here and wait the three days until June 19th. Hopefully, Frank's telephone call that night will be good news. Agad-agad (let's wait and see)!

June 18, 2003

Tomorrow is our day! For over three years Frank and I have not known the exact date the B.O.P. had planned for his triumphal return to society. But come tomorrow all of our concerns, questions, and remaining unknowns are supposed, key word "supposed", to be answered.

Tomorrow at 10:00AM two of the "Three Stooges" will host the last "screwing of old man Tucci," at Frank's Team Review. I am positive the two lacking in brains B.O.P. Counselors will not enjoy the meeting. After all, these jackasses now have to give Frank the good news of when he is leaving.

Tomorrow with laughable fake smiles on their stupid faces Mr. Armendariz (Larry) and Ms. Scott (Moo) will inform Frank of their Godlike decisions?

But that's tomorrow, right now it's time to read Frank's letter of the day, eat, sleep, and wait for tomorrow.

June 20, 2003

It is now tomorrow. Only four hours until Frank's Review! Sometime after 6:30 AM he will telephone to "signal" that he is okay at the start of his USP Atwater day. Do you remember how that works?

Frank calls after I leave the apartment. When I arrive home the answering machine's flashing red light, and our Caller I.D. greet me, letting me know that he is okay and thinking of me.

Darn, today I am far too nervous and uneasy to go off to work! Frank will be surprised when I answer the phone! Our answering machine is set to pick up after five rings.

Ring! Ring! Ring! I ran for the telephone and answered on the third ring. "Hello!" I said. Frank replied. "Maayo'ng buntag (good morning). Why are you home dear wife? Are you sick?"

"Mahal (dear) I was just too upset to go to work today and I didn't sleep well last night thinking about your Team." We talked for a few more minutes then said goodbye, Frank promised to call the minute he gets out of the office.

10:45 AM

Ring! Ring! The call I was waiting for? Yes, but once again the "Stooges" had rained on our parade! Frank sadly said. "Remy, the officer (Mr. Enos) just told me that Armendariz has rescheduled me for tomorrow at 8:00 AM.

So, as they say in my language. "Lain na usab nga adlaw ugma!" Which means, "Tomorrow is another day!" Frank's officer friend Mr. Preston has a sentence that best sums it up for both of us.

"Tucci the B.O.P. has had you on one hell of a ride!" We thank you for that line Mr. Preston.

June 20, 2003

Quickly it's tomorrow again. I just remembered an old saying from my country. "Yesterday's tomorrow is today!" Think about that.

8:10 AM

Ring! I jumped for the telephone on the first ring. My expected joy turned to sadness within seconds! My hard was racing as I asked Frank. "Honey, are they releasing you on September 5th?"

Sadly Frank answered. "Remy the idiots didn't give me a date! I asked Moo to correct the mistake she made by putting a Homicide on my last Progress Report, and she got snotty about it. Next I asked Larry when I was leaving."

"Nothing has been approved yet for you Mr. Tucci." That's what Armendariz told Frank. What? Did I hear Frank correctly? We already have a release date from Chief Probation Officer Mrs. McBride and the B.O.P.'s Phoenix CCM Office has his release there as September 5, 2003!

Frank couldn't do anything more from inside USP Atwater it was now up to me! That's were we stand today only 77 days from the release date that we already have.

I will update this chapter as our battle continues and the events unfold.

Update: July 20, 2003

A whole month has quickly passed without Frank being ordered to remake a pilgrimage to their "sacred place", a.k.a. the Unit Office. We now realize that one way or the other the "Stooges" will try to keep him locked up until his maximum release date of January 13, 2004. If that's Allah's will so be it!

Moo's malicious error of listing a "Homicide" on her paperwork to the Halfway House Office in Phoenix no doubt played a part in Frank not leaving USP Atwater on September 5, 2003.

So, because one good deed always deserves another, we have firmly decided to file a civil law suit against Ms. Scott (Moo) when Frank is finally released.

Our attorney said. "The suit will be for violating your husband's Civil Rights, because Frank was not sent to a Halfway House due to Ms. Scott's error of putting a Homicide on his record."

Yes, Ms. Scott (Moo) there's more! You can also be sued for Libel as your remarks were in a written statement.

Isn't it ironic that Frank and I have a 300-page book and no one is suing us for Libel? But, Ms. Scott typed out only 7 pages of a Progress Report and we are suing her.

I sincerely hope Moo's husband is an understanding person. She'll need it!

The Unit mis-Manager!

Author's note:
By: Remy P. Tucci

June 12, 2003

I wasn't planning to write a whole chapter on the mental midget Mexican, who is also midget sized physically, who calls himself a Unit Manager. But Mr. Armendariz, a.k.a. Larry of the "Three Stooges", pissed Frank off today!

For the last two weeks Frank have been trying to file a "Religious Discrimination" complaint against Lieutenant Bourn, who just like Larry is anti-Islamic.

Just what happens in Federal prison to a Muslim who tries to right a wrong or seek legal regress? He can expect a lack of sensitivity, stubbornness, stupidity, and the prevalent "buck passing!" Where the hell are the "Liberals" when you really need them?

May 12, 2003, Frank sent the following Inmate Request to Captain Moorhead.

To: Mr. Joseph Moorhead, Captain   Date: 05-12-03
From: Frank M. Tucci   Register No.: 03836-014
Work Assignment: Orderly   Unit: 3-A

I am formally filing charges of "Religious Discrimination" against Lt. Bourn. He has insulted Islam and personally refused to allow me to remove my "Religious Meals" from the dining room. A Memo dated 4-23-03 is in effect that allows me to do so. But, quoting Lt. Bourn directly, "Until the Captain tells me I'll keep taking every meal away from you." I will pursue this matter further unless a written apology from Mr. Bourn is done within ten (10) working days.

Uncharacteristically for Mr. Moorhead he didn't answer Frank's request. Maybe because it was of a "Religious" nature? Remember now, President Bush said. "We respect and value the friendship of the Muslims here in America." Really, but Mr. President you forgot to tell that to the people who run the B.O.P! Are there different values for Muslims in Federal prisons?

Because the Captain didn't answer, the next step was to file a B.P. 8 form with Larry. So on May 15, 2003 here's what Frank wrote:

Inmate's comments:

1.   Complaint: My charge of "Religious Discrimination" against Lt. Bourn has not been answered as filed on 5-12-03. A copy is with this form.
2.   Efforts you have made to informally resolve: Inmate Request to Captain Moorhead on 5/12/03.
3.   Names of staff you contacted: Captain Moorhead

The mental midget Mexican's reply was B.O.P. training at its best, and once again proved he wasn't hired for his intellect. Here's his answer:

Correctional Counselor's Comments:

1.   Efforts made to informally resolve and staff contacted: You will need to submit BP8 that have been issued from the Unit Counselor (Allen) or other Unite Team, not Mayberry.

I'll explain his comment. Frank used a "form" that was signed and given to him by a Counselor, who no longer works for the B.O.P. Yes, Mr. Mayberry went on to a new job outside the B.O.P., and no doubt bettered himself.

Mr. Armendariz (Larry) refused to accept his B.P.8's because neither he nor the other two "Stooges" had given it to him.

In Federal prison there is extreme control over any "Form" that an inmate could write a request or complaint on. A good example of "Form" control, and the battle to obtain one, was in the "Dental" chapter.

Yes, the "Three Stooges" will delay as long as they possibly can, before giving you a B.P.8, B.P.9, B.P.10, or B.P.11 Forms. Their strategy is simple and surely B.O.P. written policy, which probably says. "Promise the inmate the requested form(s) and then forget to send or give them to the troublesome inmate."

As I wrote in the very first paragraph of the chapter Mr. Armendariz had now really pissed Frank off! On May 27, 2003 he wrote this Inmate Request to Larry with copies to Warden Schultz and the B.O.P. Religious Coordinator at 320 First Street, NW, Washington, DC 29534.

You are working exactly where you belong. You are a by-product of the B.O.P.'s "mind set", and the reason, if the shoe fits wear it, the public is fed-up with Affirmative Action! Instead of answering my issue of "Religious Discrimination" against Lt. Bourn on the merits of the complaint, you deny it because it is "on the wrong form". I have mailed your answer and the "wrong form" to the central office. Let's see what they say about your denying a Muslim his rights.

As of today, June 16, 2003 we are awaiting a reply from Washington. Hopefully there will be a positive answer and I will Update this chapter, when and if I receive a response.

Now back to Larry. I wonder what the B.O.P.'s qualifications for the position of Unit Manger are? They can't be all that hard, after all Mr. Armendariz did get hired! I rest my case! Next is a true example of how the B.O.P. hires.

When Frank was doing his internship in FCI Phoenix there was a young and pretty woman working as the unit's secretary. One day she suddenly disappeared! But she soon reappeared as a Case Manager over in the next Unit (Yuma).

I bet I know what you are thinking? Maybe "Pretty Woman" was over-qualified for the secretary's job? Trust me, she wasn't! Her best qualifications were her tight blouse and short skirt.

Or maybe she was just waiting for a Case Manager's position to open up? You're wrong again. I'll explain. At the time when Pretty was working as the Unit's secretary, Frank's Unit was without a Case Manager for many weeks.

So then why would the B.O.P. place her in another Unit, when the one she was working in was without a Case Manager? I know the answer! Pretty was not qualified for a Case Manager's job and all the inmates in the Unit knew that! That's why she was moved to the Yuma housing unit when no one knew of her dumbness!

The Yuma Unit acts as the "in take" building there. Every prisoner who enters FCI Phoenix goes there first and later he will be assigned to one of the other three housing units.

Because Yuma is the "in take" unit very little if any "Case Managing" takes place in there. Also important to note is the fact that Yuma's Counselors and Case Managers are not easily accessible to the inmates.

Wasn't that an ideal setting to place an un-qualified Case Manager in? But only a few months later the ad hoc Case Manager was gone from FCI Phoenix. Maybe even the B.O.P.? Did her lack of qualifications catch up with her? Or did she run out of short skirts?

Well, be that as it may be, back to Larry. The inmates there in USP Atwater have nicknamed him "the Mexican dictator." But, we refer to him as "super Mex."

Everyday I hear stories of how Larry screwed this or that up for an inmate. He replaced Ms. Ozoco, who needed replacing, as the Unit Manger only a few months ago but already he has the unit upside down!

It's a toss-up between an uneducated chimpanzee and Mr. Armendariz as to who has the lower I.Q. As much as we like animals Larry gets to win this one. But it was close.

The sad part about all this is that Larry can get away with being stupid. First, because he is a B.O.P. employee. Second, because he is a minority "hire", Hispanic, bilingual, and a Veteran. Taxpayers, are you getting the best bang for your buck with Mr. Armendariz? I don't think so!

Ms. Scott, The Unit Stoogette

Author's note:

By: Remy P. Tucci

It is now June 24, 2003 and only 73 days from our hoped for release date. But because of Moo's (Ms. Scott) stupidity, or more likely spitefulness, with a touch of mean spiritless, my husband may not leave USP Atwater on September 5, 2003.

Moo these next few pages are just for you! Don't you think the inmates in the five other housing units have a right to know how you screwed up Unit 3A, and my husband's life? Just in case Warden Schultz moves you to a different unit!

At the beginning of this chapter I explained how Moo "accidentally" typed in the word "Homicide" on line 6 of Frank's last Progress Report. She then forwarded her erroneous and anti-Muslim paperwork to the CCM (Halfway House) office in Phoenix. There is no doubt that her intent was to prejudice them against approving Frank a stay here.

As a rule Halfway Houses do not accept inmates with a record of violence. So Ms. Moo added the ultimate violence to my husband's record, "Homicide". Thanks for nothing, Ms. Moo!

With now only 73 days left until September 5, I still don't know if Frank is coming home or not. If he doesn't then his next release date will be Tuesday, January 13, 2004. Maybe that's Allah's will? Agad-agad (let's wait and see)?

On June 26, 2003 I typed the following Inmate Request and sent it certified Mail to Moo in regards to "correcting" line 6.

"5/20/03 Progress Report is in error. Please see Item 6, circled and highlighted (attached). Please make the necessary correction. Thank you."

No matter how many bad things I can say or write about Larry (Mr. Armendariz) at least he is working in his own environment, a man in a men's prison. But Ms. Moo is puzzlement!

It is my firm belief that a woman who works in a men's prison can only be one of two things: A man-hater or a lesbian!

Frank has often complained to me about female officers being present during strip searches. What kind of a woman would enjoy watching men spreading their rear-ends or lifting up their genitals? Yes, only a man hater or a lesbian!

Moo was just a common B.O.P. Officer, until she schemed and manipulated to get the Case Manager job. Now she is above doing strip searches! Instead as Moo now walks around the unit she gets to see men's bare behinds n in the open shower area, inmates sitting on the exposed toilets in their cells, or catch guys masturbating in their beds. Some promotion you got there, Ms. Scott!

It probably wouldn't be so bad for Frank and the inmates in 3A if Moo had some kind of a clue as to what the heck she was supposed to be doing there.

As always the B.O.P. is the cause of the problem. Why? Because the B.O.P. continually promotes people who are totally unqualified, putting them into positions that require intelligence which they do not have.

That's what happened when Moo became a Case Manager and Curly (Mr. Allen) went up the ladder from Mail Room Clerk to Unit Counselor. Isn't that like taking someone at Sear's who is selling TV sets and making him their chief auto mechanic?

Maybe the next employment ad the B.O.P. runs should say:

"Are you in need of a GED? Do you have low self-esteem? Are you grossly overweight? Do you smoke at least two packs of cigarettes daily? Do you have trouble holding a steady job? Bad Credit? No Credit? Slow Credit? The Federal Bureau of Prisons can help? Apply at any B.O.P. facility or on line at www.bigmoneysoon.com"

Stop laughing, Captain Moorhead once told Frank. "We don't hire people for their intellectual abilities." Now there's an honest man!

Now back to the tale of Ms. Moo. I think a little background would be helpful to you readers.

Ms. Scott is White and married to a Black man, who also works at USP Atwater. Frank, as a Muslim expected better treatment from Moo because of the fact that she is married to a "brother". However things turned out to be the direct opposite!

Frank found out that Moo was lacking in the brain department at their first "Meeting". She told him. "Mr. Tucci you need to have your Social Security card sent here so that we can put it in our files."

"Why's that?" He asked her. She replied. "The B.O.P. needs your card so that we can document that you are a U.S.citizen, for the purpose of release money. We do not give gate money to illegals."

May I ask you readers—would anyone in their right mind put their Social Security card in the U.S. Mail? So, on July l8, 2002, I mailed Moo a photocopy of Frank's SS card with this short note. "Enclosed is a copy of Frank M. Tucci's Social Security card." Problem solved.

In the "Dental" chapter Frank wrote about his next misadventure with the bottled redhead. Remember that mess? Here's a quick replay for you.

Frank's denture broke; he went to medical and was told it would be fifteen days before he could see the dentist. He asked Moo for a B.P.8 form to complain about the 15-day wait. She promised the form but Frank ended up writing to Mr. Kapusta the Assistant Warden to get her to give him one.

The woman (Moo) has done nothing to help Frank and I. Even the date for his last "Team Meeting" she kept as a State Secret! Frank's prior Progress Report listed 6-03-03 as, "date for next review". On June 12, 2003, I sent an Inmate Request to Ms. Moo on Frank's behalf asking. "When is my next Team Review?"

Her written reply to my husband was. "July 19, 2003, at 10:00 AM." Well I guess the 19th is close enough to the 3rd for Government work.

Hopefully my husband will leave USP Atwater this September, if not I am sure there will be more updates to add on about Ms. Scott a.k.a. Moo.

I hope you got my message about her. If Allah sends your loved one to USP Atwater you'll already know about the brassy redhead.

Author's note:

By Frank

Thank you my dear wife. Your writing may get you the first Incident Report written on a non-prisoner.

CHAPTER 9

Home! At Last!

Authors note:

July 11, 2003, Remy and I still do not know if I will be released from USP Atwater on September 5, 2003, or January 13, 2004? We well update this chapter as more information become available to us.

"Home—a place where one lives, to go or return home." The dictionary's wording is short, too short for such an important day in a convict's life! But, in many cases that definition does not apply to releasing Federal prisoners.

True, the B.O.P. at some point will release me, but that doesn't necessarily mean I will get "to go or return home." Or even that I will arrive at "a place where one lives."

The bastards who are the "powers to be", with the complicity of the "Three Stooges", are famous for relocating inmates thousands of miles away from their families or loved ones. Please go back to Chapter 7 and read again how the Stoogette tried to ship me back to Connecticut! Hopefully that will not happen but there is always that sad possibility.

Does the B.O.P. along with Larry, Curley, and Moo somehow arrive at a sexual gratification when they inflict mental pain on us lesser mortal inmates! I am sure they do! Especially Ms. Moo!

I saw the following sign neatly framed and posted in Mr. Hall's office back at FCI Phoenix. "Inmate beatings will continue until moral improves!" Only a sick minded son of a bitch would display something like that in a prison office!

The big question has to be; who's moral is suppose to improve? The inmate's or Mr. Hall's?

I am a Sunni Muslim and will never turn my other cheek! If you do so it only allows your enemies to slap you on the other cheek. The Quran says. "Revenge is not Revenge when it rights a wrong." Do you agree?

Do I have 55 days left or 182 days? Pero, wala'y kaso (but, no big deal). It's your call oh mighty Bureau of Prisons.

Update: August 6, 2003

Frank's Tuesday 6:30 AM telephone call has brought darkness to "The Light At The End Of The Tunnel!" Our "Light" is now in the past and becomes only a faint memory of a hoped-for soon-to-be togetherness.

Why? Because the U.S. Probation Officer in Arizona mailed the following information to Moo (Ms. Scott).

"Ms. Suzanne Scott

Re: Tucci, Francis
    Register No. 03836-0l4
    Relocation Request Denied
This relocation request is denied and any future request for reconsideration will not be considered.
    Sincerely,
    Adelina Bustainante
    Senior U.S. Probation Officer"
A copy of Ms. Bustainante's letter was handed to Frank by the third shift officer Mr. Preston.

Moo was probably too scared to come out of her hiding place behind the locked doors of the Unit office to deliver it herself. Nor did the "Team" have Frank ushered in to inform him of the letter.

How many times can a man be kicked to the curb and bounce back? My husband's answer is. "As many times as I have to bounce back! These people are not going to ruin our lives, we'll find a way to beat them as we always have."

The bottom line is, Frank will go back to Connecticut, find a place to live, and then I'll continue to fight them! At the right time we will return to my country.

Salamat tungod sa kalooy sa Diyos ug Allah!

Update: August 28, 2003

Twenty-two (22) days have now passed since we were given the "bad news" that Frank was headed back to Connecticut to serve out his U.S. Probation. Please go back and re-read the fourth paragraph of this chapter, which was written back on July 11, 2003.

At 11:00 AM the day watch officer Mr. Riley told Frank. "Tucci, Mr. Armendariz wants to see you in his office. Maybe you'll get something else to write about for your book?"

A few minutes later Frank was at the sealed off area where a heavy locked metal door leads into the Unit Office. As he entered Larry's (Armendariz's) spacious and well-furnished room he noticed that Moo (Ms. Scott) was also there.

It was she that spoke first. "Mr. Tucci are you aware that your request to have your probation relocated to Arizona has been denied? And so we are sending you back to Connecticut from here."

Frank answered her with his favorite one word reply. "So?" Moo wasn't pleased with his response, maybe she thought he would beg or argue? She quickly asked her next question. "Mr. Tucci do you have a release plan for when you get back to Connecticut?"

I bet Moo didn't like his next answer either, which was. "I sure do! I am 63 years old so I'll sign up for Social Security Disability Payments, Medicare, Medicaid, Food Stamps, Welfare, and Government Housing."

She added. "Well all that is fine but we need some kind of a plan while you are in a Halfway House there." Frank cut-in with. "Excuse me! I am not going to a Halfway House!"

Moo asked. "Is that a refusal Mr. Tucci?" "Ms. Scott, what part of not going didn't you understand?" Frank ended with.

That night he telephoned me and explained. :"Remy the longer I stay here in USP Atwater the better our chances are of getting them to not send me back East."

Once again my husband needed my help from the "outside" and I quickly typed a letter to Ms. Bustamante's supervisor, Ms. Magdaline Jensen, Chief USPO for the District of Arizona, as follows:

To: Magdaline Jensen, Chief USPO
District of Arizona
405 West Congress Street
Tucson, AZ 85701-5022

Date: August 18, 2003
                    Re: Frank M. Tucci—#03836-014
Yes, I was shocked at what Ms. Bustaimante told me when she visited me. But, never the less I told her I didn't care about Frank's past. I informed her repeatedly that I did not consider myself a "potential victim."

She did not inform you of all the facts. Did you know that Frank is ill and 63 years old?

When he was at FCI Phoenix I visited him once or twice each week for the 16 months that he was there. I can not visit him because he is far away at USP Atwater but we both write daily letters and talk on the telephone three or four times a week.

Frank leased the apartment I am not living in and he has given me Power of Attorney (copy enclosed, please note date) and has left his Lexus automobile in my care.

You/your office will not allow him to remain with me here. An injustice has been done to us.

The bottom line is I will just pack up and move to wherever he is sent.

Sincerely,

(Signed) Remy Tucci-Allen
I also sent a copy of the above to Ms. McBride, Chief USPO for the District of Connecticut, and this letter to her:

To: Ms. Maria Rodrigues McBride, Chief USPO
Probation Department
Connecticut Financial Center
157 Church Street, 22nd Floor
New Haven, CT 06510
Date: August 19, 2003
                    Re: Francis M. Tucci—03836-014

Because of my prior letters, faxes, and many telephone calls to Mr. Sheehan, you know that I do not consider Frank a threat to my well being. But, Ms. Jensen based her decision on the report of one of her staff, Ms. Bustaimante, who would not listen to my pleas that I wanted to be with Frank.

What happens now? Can you/your office send him back here to Arizona after his arrival there? He is 63 years old and has many medical problems. The cold weather will shorten his life as well being away from me. Please help us.

Sincerely,

(Signed) Remy Tucci-Allen

cc: Michael E. Sheehan, Supervising U.S.P.O.

Hopefully my God and Frank's Allah will help us as He always has. Yes, it is only l34 days to Frank's release, but to where?

Update: September 12, 2003

By: Remy P. Tucci

One of the things that makes our book unique are the Updates in many of the chapters, which I enjoy writing. It seems as if nothing ever ends! There is always just one more thing to write about, as the B.O.P. and its staff of "losers" try to force their will on Frank and I.

September 2, 2003

A posted Memo read:

"Unit: 3A Team Meeting

Date Posted: 9-02-2003

Meeting Date: 9-12-2003

Meeting Time: 1300 hours

45432-008 PESHLAKI

90475-011 STEPHENS

15717-085 VANDERHAGE

03836-014 TUCCI

66285-065 KELLY

15296-112 SMITH"

Well here we go again! Or is it still? Frank just met with the "Stooges" (a polite word for Morons) a few weeks back. Normally his "Team" sees him every six months?

He checked the 12th on the calendar and found that is was on a Friday, and at 1300 hours he would be at his Muslim Prayer Service. So—Frank wrote an Inmate Request to Ms. Moo as follows:

To: Ms. Scott, Cs. Mgr   Date: Saturday, 9-6-03

From: Tucci   Register No. 03836-0l4

You have scheduled a Team for me on 9-12-03 at 1300 hours. Unfortunately my Muslim Prayer Service is at about the same time. I am sure that neither the B.O.P. nor you wish to interfere with me attending Religious Services. May I suggest earlier in the day? Or after my Muslim Service?

Moo's answer was:

"You will be seen 9-12-03 at 12:45 to accommodate your prayer service."
Signed: S.Scott"

My previous Update tells how my husband not so politely refused Larry and Moo's offer of 120-day staff in a Connecticut Halfway House. Why should that have surprised the "Stooges"? Aren't both Frank's home and I here in Phoenix?

September 13, 2003

Yesterday the same two lacking in brains "Team" members again tried to persuade Frank to leave USP Atwater and make the 3000-mile trip to a Connecticut Halfway House.

Long before Larry or Moo, or even the Bureau of Prisons existed, the U.S. Government had a 200 year history of sending prisoners thousands of miles from their homes and/or families. Let us never forget the plight of the American Indian, or the treatment of Black Slaves in this country! The current B.O.P. mentality is a throwback to those times.

Frank's 5:30 PM call tonight was a great disappointment to me, but there are now only 122 days left before his release date!

He told me. "Mas maayo ang magpabilin usa ako diri ug dugay-dugay aron maasikaso ang angay nga buhaton!" Which translated means. "The longer I stay here the better our chances of getting things done!" He was referring to not having to go back East.

In the meantime I have contacted our U.S. Senator, John McCain by Certified Mail with this short letter:

"My husband, Frank M. Tucci is a constituent of yours also having worked on your campaign in Flagstaff. He is currently an inmate at the USP in Atwater, California.

Our problem is that although he is an Arizona resident (copy of his driver's license enclosed), his Case Manager Ms. Scott has told him he is being sent back to Connecticut.

The time is now short because his release date is 1-13-04 in just four (4) months. His home that I shared with him is here in Phoenix. Please help us!

I thank you in advance for your help and I am anticipating a favorable response."
Sincerely,
(Signed) Remy Tucci-Allen

Frank is an Arizona resident and we are right in asking the "Stooges" and the B.O.P. that he is returned to me here in Phoenix. But sometimes "right" takes a long time to happen. Allah always answers, but not always at the first call!

CHAPTER 10

Our Happy Ending!

January 27, 2004

Two weeks have quickly passed since leaving USP Atwater and my Muslim brothers behind. This very cold morning of only seven degrees finds me living at the YMCA in downtown Hartford, Connecticut. And a fast approaching New England winter storm promises a foot or more snow for tomorrow.

It was the will of Allah that sent me here and His teaching tells us. "You can not have a rainbow without first having the rain!" So—with that thought in mind I remember and write about my last day in Federal Prison.

January 13, 2004

Later today I will pass through Atwater's steel doors, razor wire fences, and electric gates to my freedom. But it will not be as Remy and I have prayed for.

At 5:30AM my cell door (#108 in Unit 3A) was unlocked by the sleepy midnight to eight officer. He switched on the light, smirked at me and said. "Hey, Tucci just in case you forgot you are being released today. But I am sure you knew that." Not wanting to engage in a conversation with the mental midget, I answered with only one word. "So?"

Soon it was 6:10AM and time for the Sunrise Prayer with the four other Muslims in the unit. When our prayer was finished they all walked with me back to the cell. It was not time to divide up my few personal belongings and I had written a list weeks before of who got what.

Prize items such as my battery powered shaver, radio and headphones, coffee mug, microwave bowls, and sweat pants, sweatshirts, sneakers and combination lock were reserved for the brothers in the unit. Other things, like unopened food, tea, soup, cookies, popcorn, peanut butter, and candy would be given to the rest of the Muslim community at the Friday Prayer.

As a Muslim I am not allowed to give goods or charity to a non-Muslim. Many times in USP Atwater "Skin Heads" had threatened me, for not providing them with a book of postage stamps ($7.40), a bag of coffee ($5.25), or other commissary bought items.

Yes, I always mentioned any attempt at extortion to the Muslim brothers/enforcers, whom solved the problem.

The "Skin Heads" are a very small group in this prison and the rest of the Whites here want nothing to do with them. But, on the other hand the Blacks who are not Muslims will always come to the aid of a "brother". Not good odds if you're a "Skin Head"!

An hour later, 8:05AM, the day watch officer also came to my cell and informed me. "R and D (Receiving and Discharge) will be calling for you some time between now and noon time so be ready to go. Also, strip your bunk and put all of your institutional clothing in front of the laundry room door."

No, I did not strip the bed or take clothing anywhere! Because I was celled alone I could leave a mess without causing another inmate a problem. In fact, I taped the following note on the cell door. "Maid, please make up the room ASAP! Thanks! Tucci."

Time was moving slowly and at 11:50AM a brother knocked and entered. "Well, Sulaiman (my Muslim name) the cop said he wants you in his office. I guess this is good bye!"

Still having a wheelchair in my cell, the result of winning a prior court battle with Atwater's Medical Department, I pushed off for the guard's office. Truthfully I really didn't need the wheelchair, it was just a case of showing them that I could get one. Thanks Judge Henderson!

The squat, over weight and stupid looking officer put down his hero sandwich and greeted me with. "Mr. Tucci they just called over for you, are you ready to go?"

A question? If you were in prison for a number of years and some moron asked you on your releasing day. "Are you ready to go?" What would your answer be?

Where does the B.O.P. find these characters? Hopefully KMART will come out of bankruptcy and reopen most of their stores so that the present, B.O.P. staff can get their old jobs back!

I stared at Stupid and after a few seconds answered him. "Was that your attempt at a trick question? Would anyone in their right mind tell you they weren't ready to leave this chamber of horrors?"

"Oh lighten-up Tucci! I was just trying to be polite, personally I don't give a fuck if you never leave here!"

It was almost time for my last jab at Warden Schultz, Doctor Franco, and the "so called" medical director, Mr. Willis. But first it was Stupid's turn and I said. "We have an old saying in Texas only a horse eats where he works!"

Slightly pissed off he put down his king sized sandwich and asked. "What he hell is that suppose to mean?" I do have the kind of personality that gets to some people and it sure was working now. So I explained about the "horse".

"Haven't you seen a horse wearing a feed bag while pulling a wagon or plow? Isn't the horse eating and working at the same time? If your Union doesn't allow you time to eat in the dining room you have a piss poor Union!"

I finished up with. "I'll need one of the Muslims to push my wheelchair over to R&D because my back spasms are real bad today." Stupid didn't answer me and did what any properly trained B.O.P. employee should do, he picked-up the telephone.

"Hello Lieutenant Spencer? This is Officer Stupid in 3A. Inmate Tucci says he needs someone to push his wheelchair over to R and D. Can we let him do that?" Stupid said, "yes" a few more times and then hung up the phone.

"Tucci the lieutenant said it was okay and that if necessary he would push the chair himself just to get you out of here!"

I quickly returned to cell #108 for the last time and tossed my Prayer Rug, Qur'an, and Prayer Caps into a B.O.P. drawstring bag. Then I looked around the unit for one of the other Muslims.

Brother Hayes with his ever-present smile was walking towards me. He must have read my mind as he asked. "Brother Sulaiman do you need a push over to R and D?" Our religion (Islam) gives a special blessing to those who help the elderly, so there was always someone to push me here and there.

On the long trek from Unit 3A to the R&D, Hayes told every Muslim that we met along the way. "Brother Sulaiman is going home now and I am pushing him over to R and D!"

Hayes pushed me along very slowly; it was sort of like the "Green Mile" for me knowing that today was my last day with my Muslim brothers. At the locked R&D door we shook hands and said our good byes. Yes, this author's eyes did became watery, no doubt it was just my allergies acting up?

He left and I kicked the door two or three times hoping to wake up a staff member to come and unlock it. After a few minutes a short female officer opened the door and started to quiz me.

"Are you inmate Tucci?" I replied by nodding my head yes. "What's your Social Security number?" Shorty didn't like my next sarcastic answer. "I don't remember it because I haven't used it in a long time." More questions followed.

"Can you remember your inmate number?" I gave her the same answer I have given a hundred or so officers over the last four years. "I never memorized it because to do so would mean that I have become institutionalized." If Shorty's looks could kill I would be a dead man! Her last question was, "Can you at least tell me your date of birth?"

I answered her and asked. "So did I get that right? Shorty said nothing and pointed me into a cell, and then she slammed and locked the door with a smirk on her face. Isn't it strange that only minutes from my release I should be locked in a cell? But maybe only Muslims get this kind of special treatment? Or was it punishment until the very last second of a Federal sentence?

Twenty-three minutes later (I had a digital watch on) the female turnkey returned and unlocked the cell. "Tucci get your ass out here. What size pants do you wear?" I answered her politely, "40 x 28."

Shorty led me down the hall to the B.O.P.'s poor excuse for a release clothing room. She handed me the right size waist but the length was 36 inches long! "Excuse me officer but these pants are eight inches too long!" I said.

Her answer should make Warden Schultz and the B.O.P. proud. "Hey Tucci this isn't a Wal-Mart, do you want the pants or not?" Then I asked. "Where are the winter boots, hat, coat, and gloves I am supposed to get?"

Shorty made a sour face and smirked. "Hey old man why should you be different than any other convict in here?" I still had one more Ace to play!

Already knowing that I was headed for Connecticut in the middle of its winter many weeks before I wrote the warden a request. Here is his answer:

"This is in response to your correspondence, dated October 14, 2003, in which you request the institution provide you with winter clothing for your release in January to Connecticut.

Investigation of this matter disclosed the following information: Your unit team has indicated that they were not going to approve your request of release gratuity of $500.00 based on your deposits and withdrawals in excess of $1,121.00. However, the institution will provide you with appropriate release clothing for your departure to Connecticut in January.

(Signed) Paul M. Schultz   10-20-03"
Warden   Date

I handed Shorty a copy of the above memo. She read it slowly, moving her lips as she went along. After her second time through it she answered. "I don't know anything about all that shit. We don't have any winter boots, coats, or hats. Remember we are in California!"

When the B.O.P.'s finest was done verbally blasting me there was really no need to carry on the conversation. But never the less I added. "Why don't you call the warden and ask him why he wrote the memo if you don't have any winter clothing here!"

Shorty fired back some more words of wisdom and said. "Tucci if you were me would you call the warden?" Someday I hope to find out the real truth. Did Warden Schultz lie in his memo knowing that USP Atwater had no winter clothing? Or did he inform Ms. Scott and Mr. Armendariz to get the clothing for me and they dropped the ball? Or did Shorty have my clothing there but didn't know about it?

The bottom line is that I left Atwater on 13 January 2004, headed for Connecticut's winter freeze wearing only sneakers, a sweat shirt over a tee shirt, and very light weight summer pants! And only $50.00 gate money for almost a 3,000 miles trip! That's God's truth!

Next came the highlight of the day. Shorty turned me over to another officer who would walk me out to the gate. A "transport officer" waited there who would drive me to the Greyhound station in downtown Merced.

At the gate I was asked again. "Tucci what is your inmate number?" And also. "What is your date of birth? Yes, I answered the same way as I had done for Shorty a few minutes before. The gate slowly opened and I stepped out into freedom!

"Wait here Mr. Tucci and I'll go get the truck." Said the jolly and kind officer, who's name I never did get. The ride to the bus station in downtown Merced took about ten minutes and I had a plan as we entered the building.

The B.O.P. does not hand you an actual ticket but instead a printout for the clerk who will then "cut" your ticket. The Unit Stooges had tried to pull a fast one on me by arranging for a route that would go north and then across the top of the U.S. to Connecticut.

But here's how the Old Muslim again, or is it still, outsmarted the B.O.P.! Many weeks before I had asked Remy to get and mail me a Greyhound Route Map.

At the ticket counter I unfolded the map and asked the clerk. "Could I please be re-routed going south through Phoenix and ending at the same location in Connecticut?" The kindly officer looking at the clothing I was wearing came to my aid.

"What he is trying to do is stay away from the cold weather by going south and across the bottom of the country. Can you do that for him?"

The young female clerk, who likely knew the officer from prior trips to the station smiled at him and said. "Sure no problem!" She then started punching keys on the computer and in less than five minutes the first part of my plan was now a fact." All praise to Allah!

Ten minutes later. "Well Mr. Tucci here comes your bus. I hope everything works out for you and I am definitely going to buy your book!"

Authors note:

If the officer who drove me to the Greyhound is reading this please contact Remy and I. We want to again thank you and send you a rebate for the price of our book.

The bus had only four other passengers on it, and the trip would be about 640 miles or 12 hours with all the stops to be made. At the first stop I hurried off the bus to telephone Remy.

Ring! Ring! I hope she is home? And then. "Hello!" My heart soared and I didn't answer Remy at first because I was still programmed for using the B.O.P.'s prison telephone system. I'll explain it to you as follows: In Federal prison all outgoing calls have a prompt that says. "This call is from a Federal Prison Facility. If you wish to accept this call please press the number five now!"

Yes, I keep waiting to hear the "prompt" even though Remy had already said hello! Again she said. "Hello!" I finally caught on and answered her. "Remy I am on the way to Phoenix, I'll call you when I get there!"

After fourteen hours I was home in Phoenix, the first part of operation Screw the B.O.P. had gone smoothly. But—it was now the 14th and I was due late on Friday the 16th in Connecticut. How could I pull that off?

I called Remy and told her I was in Phoenix. "Honey please stay awake I'll be there as soon as I can get a taxi!" The driver told me the cost of the ride would be $23.00 and I gave him a $2.00 tip. There quickly went one half of my $50.00 gate money!

As the cab turned into our driveway my heart started racing, and here's a little humor for you. I had forgotten where our unit was and walked around for what seemed like a long time looking at numbers on doors!

I had to walk up close to each door so I could see the numbers because my B.O.P. issued eyeglasses were not as sharp as those made by a real optical place like Lens Crafters. Around another corner, more doors to check, but then there it was 179, home!

On the first knock Remy pulled open the door and I said something stupid like. "Lucy I'm home!" This author nor any one else, can write words to describe the feeling of seeing a loved one after years of being apart. Remy and I just held each other for a long time and cried until there were no tears left.

Inside my head I thought. "God if this is only a dream please don't ever wake me up!" But it wasn't a dream and I was awake as reality came closing in. The clock was running, I was due at the U.S. Probation Office in Hartford, Connecticut on January 16, 2004, in only two days!

When our tearful reunion was over I removed my jail clothing. The sweatshirt, tee shirt, pants, boxer shorts, socks, and shoes were put into a bag by Remy and taken outside to the dumpster. Next I headed for a hot bath and tried to wash four (4) years of B.O.P. odor off!

Author's note:

The rest of this final chapter will hopefully anger, annoy, disgust, irritate, provoke, and rattle, the following listed people, all of whom thought they were smarter than I, a mere prison inmate. But, do any of them have a published book?

USP Atwater, California:

Warden, Mr. Schultz

Health Service Director, Mr. Willis

Dentist (?), Mr. George

Doctor (?), Mr. Franco

Unit 3A Manager, Mr. Amendariz

Case Manager, Ms. Scott

U.S. Probation Office, Arizona:

Chief Probation Officer, Ms. Jensen

Probation Officer, *Ms. Bustaimante

*A special note should be made of Ms. Bustaimante. It was she who visited and interviewed Remy. It was also she, who recommended that I be sent back to Connecticut to serve out my probation.

January 14, 2004

After getting a few hours of sleep, and other much needed bedroom activities, it was now time for the next part of operation Screw the B.O.P. This part of our scheme became what Remy and I now affectionately refer to as the Ms. Bustaimante Factor.

Author's note:

Please do not mistake the semi-normal and lovely Ms. Bustaimante for anything other than what she really is. Yes, an under-educated, overweight, and a true product of the Affirmative Action Program, your Federal employee. She even dressed very unprofessional (tee shirt and shorts) the day she dropped in on Remy. A closing thought on Ms. Bustaimante, Remy said. "She looked like a lesbian to me."

While in USP Atwater I discussed my relocation to Connecticut problem with some of the bet legal minds in the country. There are hundreds of attorneys/inmates doing time within the Federal prison system, so why not take advantage of their expertise?

The stumbling block was that Remy and I were not legally married. "Tucci, get married and they will have to let you be with your old lady." Attorney/inmate Fredrick instructed me. With his advice in mind we hurriedly left the apartment to "get married".

Marriage in the State of Arizona is quick and easy; there is no waiting time or blood tests. All praise be to Allah!

However, at the Glendale Municipal Court, after we made out the paperwork and paid the fees, we were told. "Please come back tomorrow at 5:30PM and the Judge will marry you then." After waiting four years to marry my dear Remy what's one more day?

Early the next morning, January 15, 2004, I rented a car and was thankful that Remy was able to renew my driver's license via our home computer. I urge everyone locked-up to have his or her licenses renewed in this manner if at all possible. Who needs the hassle of the Motor Vehicle Department upon their release from prison?

Two very important things had to be done today and the clock was running fast against Remy and I.

First, was a drive over to the Social Security Office in the northern part of Phoenix? Yes, I had become a senior citizen, while in Federal prison and would now file a claim for disability benefits. I didn't want to take a Government hand-out but what chance does a 63-year old felon, with a heart problem, gout, and arthritis in both hands and knee-joints have of getting a job?

Sorry Mo (Ms. Scott) but this old Muslim doesn't need to work as a part of my Probation if I am on Social Security!

Here's a last word on Mo. A month later at the Social Security office in Connecticut an official told me. "Mr. Tucci your Case Manager in prison should have helped you with your claim before you left there!

Second, the other and most important item, was a return trip to the Marriage Bureau. At last our special dream was about to come true, Remy and I would finally be married!

Things went well at the Social Security office and my first check would be issued on 24 February 2004. To celebrate the event I took Remy to lunch telling her. "Honey money is no object, you pick the place! McDonald's Wendy's, or Burger King?" Yes, I was joking with her.

Later (5:30PM) we returned to the Court to be married. There were only two other couples getting the knot tied and as luck would have it we were called last.

Those others had brought flowers, video cameras, and friends. Why Remy and I had not thought to do so I don't know? Maybe because nothing was on our minds except to hurry up and get married?

"Next!" Said the clerk. It was our turn and getting married at age 63, as we both were, can still stir/up one's emotions. In fact, I personally found it damn scary!

Five minutes later Judge Colleen French smiled and said. "I now pronounce you man and wife." The two witnesses, which cost us ten dollars, clapped and wished Remy and I the best.

Okay, if you can put away the tear-soiled handkerchief I'll go on with our true story.

It was now time to leave for Connecticut ASAP! Getting back on the bus was now entirely out of the question because I was due in Hartford tomorrow, January 16, 2004. The next series of events convinced me that Allah is never far from my side.

Please consider the following:

1.   The Greyhound Bus that I had a ticket for, if on time would arrive in Hartford eight o'clock at night.

2. No doubt at that time the U.S. Probation Office would be closed and Mr. Rothi, my assigned P.O., would not be there.

3. The next two days were Saturday and Sunday, which of course meant the office, was closed.

4. But also on that Monday, January 19th, the Probation Department remained closed, because of the Martin Luther King holiday.

5. I could stay with Remy four more days, buy a plane ticket, and still arrive on time in Connecticut!

However, due to bad snowstorm my flight would now land in Connecticut after the Probation Office had closed. While changing planes in New York I quickly got on the phone to Remy. She left the following message for Mr. Rothi. "Frank Tucci will not be able to reach your office on time due to the weather delaying his trip."

If the Bureau of Prisons/Ms. Scott had bought me a plane ticket in the first place, I would have been in Hartford, Connecticut within only eight hours. But they choose to send me instead on a four-day punishment bus trip, which did allow Remy and I to marry! They sure screwed themselves!

Not only could the 3000 miles trip be very punishing to this 63-year old man, it would also be a sizable waste of the taxpayers money. As you read on please don't get angry but do get even by calling or writing your elected officials. Maybe someday the U.S. Congress might do an investigation?

Here are the true and easily verifiable facts. The Greyhound Bus (www.greyhoundbus.com) ticket from Atwater, California to Hartford, Connecticut is $179.00, tax and other charges not included. But if that same ticket is bought a week in advance the cost drops to a low $119.00.

Well there's a no brainer for you! Pay $179.00 instead of only a $119.00? Both the B.O.P. and Mo (Ms. Scott) have known of my 1-13-04-release date for at least a year. So what didn't Mo purchase the advance ticket and save the taxpayers $60.00?

If you do the math the $60.00 off is a savings of 30 percent! Why would anyone pass-up a chance to save 30 percent? The answer to that question is very simple. It wasn't her money Mo was spending, it was the taxpayers!

Did you know that the Federal prison system has 102 facilities at the present time? If each of them released just two inmates per day the monthly B.O.P. total would be 6,120 prisoners returned to society.

The B.O.P.'s website (www.bop.gov) shows an actual monthly figure much higher, at between 7,000 and 9,000 prisoners being released each month. But I'll use the lower number of 6,120 to make my point.

How many more are there like Ms. Scott in the "system" not buying the advance ticket price offered by Greyhound? But why aren't they? They know the exact releasing date of every inmate at least a year ahead of time!

There are three possible answers to that question and I am sure you will not like any of them.

1. The B.O.P.'s Case Managers and Unit Managers are not aware of the advance pricing offered by Greyhound.

2.   The B.O.P.'s Case Managers and Unit Managers are aware of the advance pricing offered by Greyhound but just don't care! After all it's not their money being used!

3.   The B.O.P.'s Case Managers and Unit Managers are getting a hefty "kick back" from the owners of their local Greyhound outlet!

We will soon have answers when some of my Muslim brothers are released and contact me with the "price" of their Greyhound tickets and their destinations.

Now back to the present time and another day here in my winter wonderland, a.k.a. Connecticut.

February 15, 2004

Yesterday I moved out of the YMCA and the City of Hartford, ending up at the Siesta Motel, 2089 Berlin Turnpike in the nearby Town of Newington. Leaving the "Y" for the Siesta is like walking out of a Wal-Mart and into a Nordstrom's.

Normally any move brings out all kinds of problems, but not if you only have one small suitcase to move. Yes, living out of a suitcase sucks! But it was still better than being in a cell in USP Atwater.

March 1, 2004

Our struggle seems hopeless at times. But never the less Remy and I keep trying to convince the "powers that be", that they should transfer my probation back to Arizona.

The U.S. Probation office in Hartford, my P.O., Mr. Otto Rothi and his immediate supervisor Ms. Kim Cerullo are on our side. However the bastards/morons in the Phoenix office refuse to allow my return.

Last week Mr. Rothi spoke to U.S. Judge Peter C. Dorsey on my behalf but without any success. The Judge said. "Have Mr. Tucci surrender his passport to the Court stay out of trouble, and in six months I'll reconsider his request for a transfer of probation."

Trust me, I know these people. In six more months they will find another reason to delay my relocation, it's just they way they are! Something other than just our daily prayers had to be done. We needed to "push the envelope"!

March 15, 2004

In every war there is one battle that becomes the turning point for victory or defeat. Early this morning I went to speak with an attorney who specializes in Civil Rights matters. After consulting with him for over an hour I headed for Mr. Rothi's office with a bounce in my step and new important knowledge in my head.

At long last I had the real facts and now knew my Rights! On the long walk from the lawyers office to the Probation Department I went over in my mind what I would say to Mr. Rothi.

Yes, when you don't know your Rights you tend to go along with what the people in authority tell you. But, if you don't try to find out the truth you are stupid. The Government loves stupid people because that makes their jobs easier.

Many times while in prison you may "right" but be prepared to pay the price for being "right". Although most times while there in USP Atwater I was "right" it didn't matter.

The B.O.P., Warden Schultz, and the two morons Ms. Scott and Mr. Armendariz didn't care about "right". Their anti-Muslim plan became clear when Armendariz yelled at me. "Tucci you are a trouble maker and I don't for one minute believe all this shit about you being a real Muslim!"

To arrive at the Abraham Ribicoff Federal Building is one thing, but to actually get inside is another. Hopefully it will not be your misfortune to reach there just as the U.S. Court is opening for its business day. If that happens you will be in for a long wait to pass through the metal detector line. I waited 25 minutes the last time I was there.

But that wasn't a problem for this old Muslim. Hadn't I been standing in the B.O.P.'s metal detector lines for years while in prison?

Today was my lucky day of sorts, all praise to Allah. There wasn't anyone standing in the detector line? That was the good news. The bad news was I got the V.I.P. treatment.

No, not as a Very Important Person, but instead what I think the Government should call Verify Investigate Persecute! Why me? Could it have been my long white beard? Or was it the Muslim prayer cap on my head? Or was it a training exercise for the Protective Service Officers?

The guard, who seemed to be in charge, asked me. "Do you have a photo I.D.? What floor are you gong to be on? Who are you here to see?"

"Excuse me!" I said. "Why are you asking me for an I.D.? I have never seen you ask anyone else." The lieutenant answer me politely, but loud, maybe he thought because I was old I couldn't hear so well?

"We are able to do so if we feel that someone appears suspect to us." Readers please look at my photo. Do I look "suspect" to you?

After my bout with the guards I got on the elevator in a worst mood than before I entered the building. I would reflect that a few minutes later in Mr. Rothi's office.

Room 735 is the Probation Office, and once inside you pick up the telephone, in front of a heavy glass window, to report in.

"Tucci here to see Mr. Rothi." I said forcefully into the phone. He came out almost immediately and led me back to his office.

The first words out of my mouth were. "I am through playing with you people and have just come from my attorney's office!" That got Mr. Rothi's attention!

Next I got louder and said. "I am going to sue you, your boss, and the U.S. Probation Department, because you will not allow me to visit my wife! My attorney says you can not refuse to let me visit Remy!"

Well that got his attention and he picked up the phone. "Kim (Kim Cerullo) Mr. Tucci is in my office could you please come in here?"

Soon Ms. Cerullo entered the small office and Mr. Rothi relayed my request to her.

"Mr. Tucci says he is going to sue me if I don't let him visit his wife in Arizona." Next Ms. Cerullo answered with what must have been a blessing from Allah.

"He can visit his wife! Mr. Tucci who told you couldn't?" She asked. Mr. Rothi was seating there in a mild case of shock as I quickly answered her question.

"Mr. Rothi told me I could not get approved for a visit to Arizona because the Probation Office there doesn't want me in Arizona ever!"

She added. "We want you to go there, believe me we are on your side. Yes, you can visit, work out the details with Mr. Rothi and I'll call Arizona and let them know you have our permission to go there!"

So after many months, weeks, and days of crying, expectations, and praying, I could now at last return home to Remy! There can be only one answer as to the how/why this was happening. Yes, all praise to Allah again!

My conversation with Mr. Rothi ended as I said. "I would like to have a month's visit with my wife, not just a few days." He countered with. "Well Mr. Tucci we may not be able to allow you to visit for a whole month on your first visit. But, maybe the next time?"

Did I hear him correctly? My next visit could be for a month? Wow! My feet barely touched the floor as I hurried to the pay telephone on the ground floor.

Because of the current "terrorism" problem all the pay phones in this seven-story Federal Building have been removed. The only public phone is on the first floor across from the metal detector.

"Maayo'ng buntag akong asawa, aduna ako'y maayong balita!" Translated that means: "Good morning my wife. I have good news!"

Remy had been sitting by the telephone all day waiting to hear what I had learned at the attorney's office. My news about being able to visit was a complete surprise to her!

I know that she went, as her and I call it, Lucy, Lucy! Although I could not see her face I knew there where tears in her lovely brown eyes. Yes, mine also, just my allergies acting up, yeah sure.

Yes, you could call the latest development (a visit) a huge victory for Remy and I. Never the less we kept waiting for the other shoe to drop.

Anyone who has dealt with the U.S. Justice Department's lies and broken promises knows exactly what "waiting for the other shoe to drop" means.
March 22, 2004

Early this afternoon I received a large envelope with "U.S. Department of Justice, Official Business Only", printed in large letters on it.

Gee thanks Mr. Rothi for letting staff of Siesta Motel know that the guy (me) in Room 113 is involved with the U.S. Justice Department! The Government doesn't make it easy, if you are a convicted felon.

The envelope contained a letter and 16 pages of forms that "must be completed before a visit will be allowed."

The paperwork to made out was a 7 page "Net Worth Statement" and an 8 page "Cash Flow Statement". Both started with the following paragraph:

"Having been convicted in the United States District Court, you are required to prepare and file with the probation officer a statement fully describing your financial resources, including a complete listing of all monthly cash in–flows and out-flows."

Yeah sure I will? Just in case the Government hasn't been able to locate and steal your money they now want you to tell them where it is!

The I.R.S. has already cleaned out two bank accounts of mine and now they (the I.R.S.) have even attached my Social Security checks! But that's as much as they'll get!

Finding the bank accounts and attaching my Social Security checks was easy for them, because they all had my correct Social Security number on them.

Another condition, for allowing the visit was the returning of my U.S. Passport to the Court. Were these people worried about me getting my "rumored" 1.2 million dollars out of a bank and then fleeing the country?

One part of Mr. Rothi's letter was somewhat laughable, he stated. "You will be asked to report to the U.S. Probation Office in Phoenix immediately upon your arrival, and comply with reporting instructions of that office."

Hopefully I'll get to visit with the infamous Ms. Bustamante there at the Phoenix office? I certainly hope so! I wonder if Remy was correct when she told me. "She (Ms. Bustamante) looked like a lesbian to me." Yes, I wanted to get a look at this piece of walking human garbage that had terrorized Remy.

But, in the meantime, many things had to be worked out before I could leave Connecticut. I still had the "return" part of my Continental Airlines ticket from my arrival here in January—but the return date of July 30th now had to be changed to April 23, 2004.

Remy and her computer skills were needed again. To change the return date to April 23, 2004, cost us an additional $100.00. And the new round trip ticket was $289.40. The room at the Siesta costs $880.00 per month, and I used about $100.00 each week for other items like food, transportation, etc. At this pace, 1.2 million dollars won't last forever!

Soon everything was almost in order. Remy had the flights booked, and I was working out the 16 pages of paperwork. Only one problem remained. My U.S. Passport! Judge Dorsey insisted that I turn it in before he would grant my visit.

Maybe the Judge heard the rumors about my 1.2 million? After all, he couldn't take a chance that a sickly 63-year old man (me) would skip out to the Philippines and deny the U.S. Government their pound of flesh!

My closing thoughts on the Court System and Judge Dorsey are these questions. Did the judge in the Michael Jackson case ask Mr. Jackson to surrender his passport? Why was Jackson allowed to leave the country on his "music tour"? Wasn't Michael facing 25 years in jail for child molesting?

Well folks, that's the way our Government does things! Their method of operation is to hammer those who can least fight back the hardest. Yes, like this old man and all the Muslims in prisons.

Looking back to USP Atwater here is a perfect example of the above, one that I'll never forget.

A former CEO of a nationwide "loan company" is serving only an 18-month sentence for ripping off his company and its customers for 40 million dollars.

But, one of my Muslim brothers received a 6-year-term for robbing a bank by handing the teller a note that said. "This is a robbery!" He left the bank with only about $11,000.00. American justice?

April 4, 2004

Tomorrow is the day! I will report to Mr. Rothi's office at 2:30PM, with all the above-mentioned items, and then on April 23, 2004, I'll be on my way home to Arizona and Remy!! All praise to Allah!

Author's note:

You are now at the end of our book and next is really—"Our Happy Ending!" Yes, the "Tucci's have won a very important battle, and the war wages on! I know in my heart and mind, and with Allah's help, Remy and I will soon be reunited forever. Please wipe your eyes and read on.

April 5, 2004

I awoke at 2:30AM this cold morning and could not fall back to sleep. Maybe it had something to do with how important this day would be? So—at 3:15 AM my feet hit the floor and I started with Saddam Hussein might call, "the mother of all days!"

The alarm clock is always set to wake me early, 5:00AM, for the Sunrise Prayer, which today can be said between 4:45 and 6:17 AM. After the Prayer my bouncing stomach would not allow breakfast and a serious and worried feeling came over me. Many questions were running around in my head.

What could go wrong today at the Probation Office and help me from a visit to Arizona? Did I have all sixteen pages of Mr. Rothi's paperwork filled-out correctly? If he tells me I can not visit, how would I possibly call Remy with that bad news?

With all of the above fresh in mind I left the motel and headed for downtown Hartford. Yes, I was terrified with the thought that the Government might screw me one more time!

At 2:30PM I entered the Federal Building, passed through the metal detector, and took the elevator to the seventh floor. "Room 735 U.S. Probation Office". Oh well here goes nothing!

I picked-up the outer office phone and said. "Tucci here to see Mr. Rothi."

"He is with someone and will be with you shortly". Came the reply. I sat down to wait and quickly all kinds of bad scenarios started in my head. "Frank get a hold of yourself!" I thought to myself.

Two other probationers were writing out their Monthly Reports but neither was there for Mr. Rothi. A few minutes later a "brother" entered the office wearing a Burger King uniform. He was not a young man, maybe in his late 40's or early 50's.

He politely asked. "Is any of you here waiting to see Rothi?" I informed him that I was. He then again politely asked. "Does you mind if I cut in front of you? I have a ride waiting downstairs and I need to get to the job on time."

Answering him I said. "I am in no hurry you can go ahead of me. No big deal." Just then his beeper went off and he pulled a cell phone, the new photo phone kind, out of his coat pocket.

Last week I had priced one of those picture cell phones and they go for between $280.00 and $400.00. If the "brother" could buy one on his Burger King paycheck maybe I should get a job there?

Or maybe, just like everyone else, he took the job to show some income and to get the Probation Department off his back? Was he really trying to readjust to society?

I took a closer look at Burger King and gave him what in prison is called the "jailhouse wealth test". Unfortunately he passed! Chances are he is still involved in some kind of criminal activity?

What the hell is the jailhouse wealth test you may be asking? That's easy to explain.

At USP Atwater the inmates who have money will not wear the prison's issued work boots. They will instead purchase at the Commissary a pair, or pairs, of sneakers, which run in price from $35.00 to $110.00. So—the higher the price of the shoe the inmate wore the more "wealth" he had?

The "brother" in the waiting room was wearing black $150.00 to $200.00 M.J.'s! Soon the receptionist opened the double locked door and told him. "Mr. Rothi will see you now."

When Burger King returned, Rothi was with him and he said. "Mr. Tucci here is your Report form please fill it in and I'll be back for you in a few minutes."

Oh how I hate all the paperwork, forms, and reports these people make us do. I am sure it is another part of their punishment!

A short time later Mr. Rothi returned and as I followed him back to his office I kept waiting for "the other shoe to fall". But next came a comedy routine of sorts.

The first words out of his mouth were. "Mr. Tucci did you bring your passport?" My quick answer was. "Am I going to visit Remy or not?" But again he repeated himself. "Did you bring your passport?"

So I repeated myself. "Am I going to visit Remy or not?" We stared at each other for a few seconds, then I stood up and almost yelled in his face. "Do I look stupid to you? Why should I give you my passport if I am not getting the visit?"

Before Mr. Rothi could reply I added. "You want something and I get nothing?" I was now done talking and sat down to wait for the "shoe to fall."

He spoke. "I didn't say you could not visit, but the Judge made it clear that I was to get your passport. If you have it here today you will get your visit."

What? No shoe is dropping? All praise to Allah! Was he telling the truth? I'll test him!

"Mr. Rothi would you please call Remy and tell her that I can visit?" My reasoning was, that if he didn't make the phone call he was lying to me and therefore would have to use force to take my passport from me.

He better not try using force on this 63-year old Muslim, especially if I am angry! And not when I have a solid oak cane for a weapon!

But Mr. Rothi surprised me and picked up his phone and inquired. "What is your wife's phone number?" Normally I give him our 800 number but today I would make the Government pay and gave him our regular home phone number.

He said a few words to Remy and handed me the telephone. I wasn't sure, but knowing my wife, she was more than likely crying.

And that's "Our Happy Ending!" Only fifteen more days and I'll again be with my beloved! Although Remy and I am not reunited for good, this is a start!

The strangest part in all of this is that I must report to Ms. Lori Wantland at the U.S. Probation Department in Phoenix while I am in Arizona. The same person who refuses to let me relocate there! I can't wait to see her!

Chapter 11

Epilogue

In the dictionary you will find that the word Epilogue means, "a short section at the end of a literary or dramatic work, often discussing the future of its characters." However, there is no Epilogue that I can write for my Muslim brothers or any other Federal prisoner released back into society, because they will have no future!

I explained in the chapter "Habitual Criminals", and provided truthful statistics, on how next to nothing is being done inside USP Atwater to educate or rehabilitate prisoners. Did their facts confuse you?

Maybe I should have entitled this chapter "An Eulogy?" The dictionary defines Eulogy as "A praising of one who has died". This may shock you but to put it bluntly, most releasing Federal prisoners have no future and for all intent and purposes they are dead!

The sleeping public can thank their so-called Conservative politicians for creating long mandatory sentencing, which in turn created the no future and dead problem. But the judges and politicians today are not in touch with the real opinions of the public's Joe Six Pack.

In other words, the use of long mandatory sentencing is not working. Crime in America's streets is still up! The prisons are still full and over crowded! The percentage of repeat offenders returning to prisons still keeps going up and up!

Would you like some facts on my statements? The Sentencing Project, which is located in Washington, D.C. has published their most significant findings as follows:

"1.   The public is generally misinformed on crime and criminal justice policy.

2.   Public Opinion is more complex than policymakers assume.

3.   Politicians misjudge public attitudes.

4.   Public opinion shifts in relation to political initiatives.

5.   Public opposition to rehabilitation and prevention is exaggerated.

6.   Public embraces alternative sentencing options when offered."

"Recent studies of public opinion on crime and punishment contain important information concerning sentencing practices. Much of the data contradicts the rationale offered by policymakers to support punitive sentencing policies. Many of these findings are surprisingly decisive, and could encourage policymakers to reevaluate current sentencing policy."

The answer is simple and brief. The taxpaying public wants changes made in their criminal justice system. But, no changes will be made! The "powers to be" want to keep the Bureau of Prisons as the $Cash Cow $ of the American Government!

A $ Cash Cow $ you ask? You bet! Please consider these additional facts, also provided by the Sentencing Project.

New figures released by the Bureau of Justice Statistics indicate that the number of inmates in America's prison and jails has now exceeded two (2) million for the first time. Between midyear 2001 and midyear 2002, the State prison population increased only 0.9, or a little less than one percent. The Federal (B.O.P.) grew by a rate of 5.8 percent!

The B.O.P. system is now the largest in America, growing 3 percent in the first six months of 2002 and accounting for 40 percent of all prisoner growth. Why does the Federal prison population continue to grow at a far more rapid rate than State prisons?

The answer is largely due to the impact of Federal mandatory sentencing policies, and that 57 percent of its inmates are incarcerated for drug related offenses. Unless the U.S. Congress reconsiders these policies, we can anticipate more continued growth!

Also the expansion of the Federal prison population is fueling the grown of the for profit private prison industry, another $Cash Cow $, which houses one in eight Federal inmates.

Public opposition to rehabilitation is highly exaggerated! The reality is that public support for rehabilitation is far greater than political rhetoric would tell you. A study by the National Opinion Survey on Crime and Justice revealed significant support for rehabilitative measures.

"A large percentage of U.S. adults indicated rehabilitation should be the principal goal in sentencing offenders." In that same survey they found. "Nearly two thirds of respondents supported granting prisoners early release through good behavior and participation in work programs."

If the public is in favor of the above why did I do 90 percent of my sentence? My crime was not drug related, or violent in nature. I can only guess that the $ Cash Cow $ continued to need its tits sucked by the thousands of employees of the B.O.P. and the U.S. Court system!

The "Quran" says: "There is more truth in one sword than in ten thousand words."
The End?

0-595-32496-7

www.ingramcontent.com/pod-product-compliance
Lightning Source LLC
Chambersburg PA
CBHW061339280526
45784CB00001B/72